Critical essays on Chaucer's "Troilus and Criseyde" and his major early poems

Edited by C. DAVID BENSON

D0075107

UNIVERSITY OF TORONTO PRESS
Toronto   Buffalo

First published in North America in 1991 by
University of Toronto Press
Toronto and Buffalo

ISBN 0–8020–5006–9 (cloth)
ISBN 0–8020–6937–1 (paper)

Canadian Cataloguing in Publication Data
Main entry under title:
Critical essays on Chaucer's Troilus and Criseyde
    and his major early poems
Includes index.
ISBN 0–8020–5006–9 (bound) ISBN 0–8020–6937–1 (pbk.)
1. Chaucer, Geoffrey, d. 1400 – Criticism and
interpretation. 2. Chaucer, Geoffrey, d. 1400.
Troilus and Cressida. 3. Troilus (Greek mythology)
in literature. 4. Trojan War in literature.
I. Benson, C. David.
PR1924.075   1991   821'.1   C91–094450–4

Printed in Great Britain

Contents

Abbreviations

ELH   *ELH: A Journal of English Literary History*
JEGP   *Journal of English and Germanic Philology*
MLN   *Modern Language Notes*
MLQ   *Modern Language Quarterly*
MLR   *Modern Language Review*
MP   *Modern Philology*
PMLA   *Publications of the Modern Language Association of America*
SP   *Studies in Philology*

Note on the text

Original punctuation and spelling have been retained throughout. Editorial amendments and additions, except for the correction of typographical errors and the re-numbering, where necessary, of Notes, are in square brackets.

Although every effort has been made, it has not proved possible to trace the holders of copyright on all original material reproduced here. The publishers would be pleased to hear from any copyright holders we failed to identify or trace.

Introduction

C. DAVID BENSON

This volume is the first in thirty years to collect representative essays on Chaucer's *Troilus and Criseyde* and his most famous early poems: *The Book of the Duchess, The House of Fame,* and *The Parliament of Fowles.* Since the publication of Richard J. Schoeck and Jerome Taylor's *Chaucer Criticism, Volume II: Troilus and Criseyde and The Minor Poems* (Notre Dame: University of Notre Dame Press, 1961), Chaucer criticism has increased exponentially and choosing among so much excellent work has been difficult. My principles of selection have been quality and influence. I have tried to choose criticism that will give readers a stimulating introduction to the questions that modern Chaucerians have found most important. In the following pages, readers will discover points of sharp debate (on matters of fact, aesthetics and ideology) as well as areas of agreement. No one (including myself) will agree with everything said in this volume, but I hope that each piece will provoke deeper interest in these continually challenging poems. The essays from journals or collections are reprinted in full (with one minor excision) and the extracts from books are only occasionally modified. Considerations of space, as well as the special problems they raise, have made it impossible to include criticism on Chaucer's minor lyric poems or *The Legend of Good Women.*

In the first centuries after its composition *Troilus and Criseyde* was the work by Chaucer most frequently cited by other writers. During the eighteenth century, however, the popularity of the *Canterbury Tales* grew and by the nineteenth century *Troilus* was frequently dismissed as too long and dull. George Lyman Kittredge's lively reading of *Troilus and Criseyde* in *Chaucer and His Poetry* (1915) signals a renewed appreciation for Chaucer's only completed masterpiece and the greatest poem on sexual love in English. Despite the obvious anachronism of terms like "first novel" and "psychological novel," Kittredge's emphasis on the Trojan setting and on characterization have remained central in subsequent criticism.

C. S. Lewis's enormously influential essay on Chaucer's transformation of Boccaccio's *Filostrato* (1932) takes a more scholarly approach to the literary and intellectual context of *Troilus.* In contrast to Kittredge's claims of modernity for the poem, Lewis argues that Chaucer "medievalized" his source, through means of history, rhetoric, doctrine and, especially, the ideals of courtly love, whose history Lewis further explored in *The Allegory of Love*

(1936). Although the very existence of courtly love has been severely questioned, the term has never been successfully replaced. John McCall's later essay (1962) is another example of historical criticism, one that explores the complex relationship between the tragedy of Troy and the tragedy of Troilus with both learning and responsiveness to the literary text.

The 1950s and 1960s were an especially fertile period for literary criticism of *Troilus and Criseyde*. Charles Muscatine, whose *Chaucer and the French Tradition* (1957) remains perhaps the single best introduction to Chaucer's poetry, follows Lewis in discussing *Troilus* as a transformation of Boccaccio's *Filostrato*. In the brief extract reprinted here, Muscatine stresses the patterned contrasts of style and ethos that are found within Chaucer's poem, especially a comic realism that coexists with an equally pervasive courtly idealism. Morton Bloomfield (1957) demonstrates the increasing sophistication of Chaucer criticism during this period in his discussion of the narrator as a deliberate literary construct who is not necessarily the direct voice of the poet as had often been assumed. The narrator has continued to be a major topic of Chaucer criticism (see, for example, the extracts by Donaldson (1958) and Evans (1986)), though no one has surpassed Bloomfield's sensitivity in exploring the tension between the narrator as distant historian (separated from his story by time, space and culture) and his human concern for the joys and tragedy of the characters.

In addition to stylistic studies, this period saw a spirited debate over the meaning and purpose of the poem that still influences discussion today. In the extract reprinted here and in other essays collected in *Speaking of Chaucer* (1970), E. Talbot Donaldson (1958) presents *Troilus* as a subtle work of art that elegiacally celebrates human values while also recognizing their transitoriness. Sympathetic to the principal characters, especially the alluring but enigmatic Criseyde, Donaldson emphasizes the elusiveness of the poem and its openness to multiple interpretations. In contrast to Donaldson's humanistic approach, D. W. Robertson, Jr. (in a reading first published in 1952 but reprinted here in its 1962 form) declares that *Troilus* is a medieval moral tragedy based on the principles of Boethius's *Consolation of Philosophy*. The apparent praise of the love affair and sympathy for the characters is thus deeply ironic, and the illicit passion of Troilus and Criseyde a false heaven that creates a hell on earth. Elizabeth Salter's reading of *Troilus* (1966) is as extreme, powerfully argued and personally engaged as Robertson's, though her conclusions could not be more different. Starting with Lewis's emphasis on the poem as a love story, Salter argues that *Troilus* is not a unified and consistent whole, and certainly not orthodox, but a work during whose composition Chaucer came to question the Christian suspicion of human sexual love.

Three recent essays reconsider from various perspectives Chaucer's Troy and the nature of the central love affair. The special fascination that Criseyde has always evoked in readers is developed by Mark Lambert (1979), who argues that the heroine is the Chaucerian character most like the poet himself. His "Criseydan reading" of the first half of the poem celebrates Chaucer's

Troy as an attractive locale of friendship in which romantic love becomes domesticated and unthreatening. Marxist and feminist perspectives lead David Aers (1979) to a darker reading of the poem, one that analyses the political forces beneath the courtly facade of Troy that force Calchas's daughter to act as she does. Aers notes the amelioration that mutual love can produce in *Troilus*, but it is Jill Mann (1980), with her different analysis of power in the poem, who fully defends the love affair as a mature and complex relationship appealing to modern and medieval readers alike. Murray Evans (1986) discusses the narrator and that other site of critical dispute – the conclusion of *Troilus*. Following Donaldson's "The Ending of *Troilus*" (in *Speaking of Chaucer*) but also with the aid of contemporary literary theory, Evans stresses the internal tensions at the close of the poem and the demands this puts on individual readers to discover the meaning of *Troilus*.

The essays reprinted here on Chaucer's three major early poems, beginning with a masterful survey by Wolfgang Clemen (1963), respect the individual achievements of these poems while viewing them in the context of Chaucer's entire career. John Livingston Lowes (1934) discusses the associative process and individual genius by which Chaucer transformed the traditions of the French dream vision in *The Book of the Duchess*. Lisa Kiser (1983), who agrees with Lowes that the poem is characteristic of Chaucer's mature work, emphasizes the role of the narrator, dreaming and the serious play of poetry.

Sheila Delany (1972) shows how Chaucer's scepticism about the truth of dreams and poetry in *The House of Fame* creates a new and more problematic relationship between poet and audience. Piero Boitani (1983) also argues that *The House of Fame* wrestles with the relationship of poetry, language and reality. Boitani shows that the choices Chaucer makes in the poem, which reveal his deep knowledge of contemporary culture, point to the kind of literature he will later produce.

In a brief extract from his elegant book on Chaucer (1960), Bertrand Bronson suggests that for all the comic nimbleness of *The Parliament of Fowls* the ostensible love vision is deepened with political, moral and spiritual themes. John Fyler (1979) argues that the deliberate antithesis and inconclusiveness of so many elements of the *Parliament* makes it "in many respects the thematic epitome of his poetry".

1 | Troilus

G. L. KITTREDGE

Originally published as the beginning of Chapter 4 in George
Lyman Kittredge, *Chaucer and His Poetry* (Cambridge, Mass.:
Harvard University Press, 1915, pp. 108–21). Reprinted by
permission of Harvard University Press. The original pagination is
recorded within square brackets. The endnotes originally appeared
as footnotes and are here renumbered. In the rest of Chapter 4,
Kittredge discusses the three principal characters in detail.

Chaucer is known to everybody as the prince of story-tellers, as incompar-
ably the greatest of our narrative poets. Indeed, if we disregard the epic,
which stands in a class by itself, I do not see why we should hesitate to call
him the greatest of all narrative poets whatsoever, making no reservation
of era or of language. His fame began in his own lifetime, and was not
confined, even then, to the limits of his native country. It has constantly
increased, both in area and in brilliancy, and was never so widespread or
so splendid as at the present day. Besides, he is a popular poet, and this
popularity – more significant than mere reputation – has grown steadily with
the gradual extension of the reading habit to all sorts and conditions of men.

To most readers, however, Chaucer means only the *Canterbury Tales*; and
even so, it is with but half-a-dozen of the pilgrims that they are intimately
acquainted. This is manifest destiny, which it would be ridiculous to deplore:
"What wol nat be, mot nede be left." Nor should we lament what Sir
Thomas Browne calls [109] "the iniquity of oblivion"; for oblivion has
treated Chaucer generously. She has exempted enough of the poet's achievement to bring him popularity, which the conditions of his own time could
neither afford nor promise, and she has spared besides, for such of us as care
to read it, that masterpiece of psychological fiction

> In which ye may the double sorwes here,
> Of Troylus, in loving of Criseyde,
> And how that she forsook him er she deyde.

[I. 54–56]

The Troilus is not merely, as William Rossetti styles it, the most beautiful
long narrative poem in the English language: it is the first novel, in the
modern sense, that ever was written in the world, and one of the best.

Authorship is a strange art: it is nearest akin to magic, which deals with the incalculable. Chaucer sat down to compose a romance, as many a poet had done before him. The subject was to be love; the ethical and social system was to be that of chivalry; the source was the matter of Troy; the material was Italian and French and Latin. His readers were to be the knights and ladies of the court, to whom the fame of the hero as a lover and a warrior was already familiar. Psychology it was to contain, or what passed for psychology in the mediæval love-poets, the analysis of emotion in terms of Chrétien de Troyes and the *Roman de la Rose*. Yet the work was not, in [110] Chaucer's intention, to be a romance precisely. He conceived it as what scholars then called a "tragedy," – though with a somewhat peculiar modification of the standard term. Tragedies described the malice of Fortune when she casts down men of high estate and brings them to a miserable end. This was to be a tragedy of love, and the fall of the hero was to be from happy union with his lady to the woe and ruin of her unfaithfulness. And so Chaucer took his pen in hand, and drew his quire of paper to him, and wrote a prologue.

The magician has marked out his circle, and pronounced his spells, and summoned his spirits. He knows their names, and the formulas that will evoke them, and the task that he shall require them to perform. And lo! they come, and there are strange demons among them, and when the vision is finished and the enchanter lays down his wand, he finds on his desk – a romance, to be sure, which his pen has written; a tragedy, in the sense in which he knew the word; a love-tragedy, with a background of the matter of Troy, and thousands of lines from Boccaccio, with bits of Benoit and Guido delle Colonne, and a sonnet of Petrarch's, and a section out of Boethius, and a closing prayer to the Christian God. Everything is as he had planned it. But, when he reads it over, he finds that he has produced a [111] new thing. Nothing like it was ever in the world before.

The Troilus is a long poem, extending to more than eight thousand verses, but the plot is so simple that it may be set forth in a dozen sentences.

Troilus, Priam's son, and second in valor to Hector only, is a scoffer at love and lovers. On a high holiday, as he strolls idly about the temple of Pallas, heart-free and glorying in his freedom, his eye falls upon Cressida, daughter of Calchas. Her father has fled to the Greeks, to escape the doom of Troy; but Cressida remains in the city. She is a widow, young, rich, and of surpassing beauty. Troilus falls madly in love, but fears to reveal his passion. Pandarus, Cressida's uncle and Troilus' friend, coaxes the secret from him, and helps him with all his might. Cressida yields, after long wooing, and the lovers see naught but happiness before them.

One day, however, during an exchange of prisoners, Calchas persuades the Greeks to offer Antenor for Cressida, whom he fears to leave in the city of destruction. To resist is impossible. The lovers are parted; but Cressida promises to return in ten days, feeling sure that she can cajole her aged father. Her woman's wiles are fruitless: she must remain in the Grecian camp, where Diomede pays court to her assiduously. [112] He wins her at length, though not without her bitter grief at the thought of her unfaithfulness. Troilus is slain by Achilles.

This is the barest outline, but it suffices to show the simplicity of the story. The interest lies in the details, which are told with much particularity, and in the characterization, which is complex and subtle in a high degree. Readers who look for rapid movement and quick succession of incident, are puzzled and thwarted by the deliberation, the leisureliness, of the Troilus. The conversations are too long for them; they find the soliloquies languid; the analysis of sentiment and emotion and passion fails to keep their minds awake. But the Troilus is not a tale for a spare hour: it is an elaborate psychological novel, instinct with humor, and pathos, and passion, and human nature. Condensation would spoil it. Once yield to its charm, and you wish that it might go on forever.

Fate dominates in the Troilus. The suspense consists not in waiting for the unexpected, but in looking forward with a kind of terror for the moment of predicted doom. The catastrophe is announced at the outset: we are to hear of "the double sorrow of Troilus in loving Cressida, and how she forsook him at the last." Neither Troilus nor Cressida suspects what is to come; but we know all about it from the beginning. [113] There is no escape for anybody. We are looking on at a tragedy that we are powerless to check or to avert.

Chaucer himself conveys the impression of telling the tale under a kind of duress. Not, of course, that there is any literal compulsion. It is rather that he is entangled, somehow, in the subject, and that, since he has begun, he is in duty bound to finish his task.

> Sin I have begonne,
> Myn auctor shal I folwen, if I conne.[1]

There is no weariness, as in some of the tales in the Legend of Good Women. His interest in the matter is intense, and it never falters. But he feels the burden of the ruin that is to come. At times he even seems to struggle against the fate which has allotted him so sad a duty. He would change the tale if he could, but he must tell the truth, though it is almost more than he can bear. He would actually impugn the evidence if that were possible: –

> For how Criseyde Troilus forsook –
> Or, at the leest, how that she was unkynde –
> Moot hennesforth be mater of my book,
> As writen folk thurgh which it is in minde.
> Allas that they shulde evere cause fynde
> To speke hire harm! and if they on hire lye,
> Ywis hemself sholde han the vilenye.[2]

[114] So mightily is he stirred by Cressida's grief that he would extenuate her guilt, or even excuse it altogether, for sheer pity. She has been punished enough; and, after all, she was only a weak woman, "tendre-herted, slyding of corage."

> Ne me ne list this sely womman chyde
> Ferther than the story wol devyse.
> Hir name, allas! is publisshed so wyde,
> That for hir gilt it oughte y-now suffyse.
> And if I mighte excuse hir any wyse, –
> For she so sory was for hir untrouthe, –
> I-wis, *I wolde excuse hir yet for routhe.*[3]

This extraordinary outburst works powerfully upon our feelings. The case is hopeless. There is no excuse but destiny, and destiny, though irresistible, cannot be pleaded even in extenuation. Such is the law, and Chaucer bows to its everlasting antinomy, which, like Œdipus before him, he does not pretend to reconcile.

Everywhere in the poem we find this idea of a compelling destiny. It was Troilus' fate to love;[4] he rode by Cressida's palace on "his happy day," –

> For which men say, may nought disturbed be
> That shal betyden of necessite.[5]

"Swich is love," so Cressida moralizes, "and eek myn aventure."[6] The oak topples over when it [115] receives "the falling stroke."[7] Troilus apostrophizes the Parcæ, who settled his life for him before he was born: –

> "O fatal sustren, which, er any clooth
> Me shapen was, my destine me sponne!"[8]

"Pleasure comes and goes in love," says Pandarus, "as the chances fall in the dice."[9] It was Fortune that cast Troilus down, "and on her wheel she set up Diomede," [IV. 11] but Fortune is only the "executrix of weirds," and the influences of the stars govern us mortals as the herdsman drives his cattle: –

> But O Fortune, executrice of wierdes,
> O influences of thise hevenes hye!
> Soth is that, under God, ye ben our hierdes,
> Though to us bestes been the causes wrye."[10]

Most significant of all is the long meditation of Troilus on foreknowledge and freedom of the will in the Fourth Book.[11] This is from Boethius, and Chaucer has been as much blamed for inserting it as Shakspere for making Hector quote Aristotle. Doubtless the passage is inartistic and maladjusted; but it is certainly not, as some have called it, a digression. On the contrary, it is, in substance, as pertinent and opportune as any of Hamlet's soliloquies. The situa[116]tion is well-imagined. Cressida is to be sent to the Grecian camp. Parliament has so decided, and resistance would be vain. Troilus, in despair, seeks the solitude of a temple, and prays to almighty and omniscient Jove either to help him or to let him die. Destiny, he feels, has overtaken him, for there seems to be no likelihood that Cressida, if once she joins her father, will ever return to Troy. What can he do but pray? Perhaps Jove will work a miracle to save him. And as he meditates, in perplexity and distress, his mind travels the weary maze of fate and free will, and finds no issue, unless in the god's omnipotence.

All this, no doubt, is un-Trojan; but that is a futile objection. We have already accepted Troilus as a mediæval knight and a mediæval lover, and we cannot take umbrage at his praying like a man of the middle ages, or arguing with himself in the mediæval manner. In details, to be sure, the passage is open to criticism, and it is undoubtedly too long; but in substance it is dramatically appropriate, and it is highly significant as a piece of exposition. For Troilus finds no comfort in his meditation. Whatever clerks may say, the upshot of the matter is that "all that comth, comth by necessitee." Whatever is foreknown, must come to pass, and cannot be avoided.

[117]   "And thus the bifalling
        Of things that ben wist biforn the tyde,
        They mowe nat been eschewed on no syde."

                                                [IV. 1076–78]

The fate which darkens the loves of Troilus and Cressida is strangely intensified (in our apprehension of it) by the impending doom of Troy. This is no mere rhetorical analogue – no trick of symbolism. Their drama is an integral part of the great Trojan tragedy. They are caught in the wheels of that resistless mechanism which the gods have set in motion for the ruin of the Trojan race. This is a vital, determining fact in their history, as Chaucer understands it, and he leaves us in no doubt as to its intense significance. Calchas, we are told at the outset, deserted Priam because Apollo had revealed the doom of Troy: –

        For wel wiste he, by sort, that Troye sholde,
        Destroyed ben, ye, wolde whose nolde.

                                                [I. 76–77]

And again and again we are reminded, as the tale proceeds, of the inevitable outcome of the ten years' war. Troilus is smitten with love when he sees Cressida in the temple. It is the great festival of Palladion, a relic, Chaucer calls it, in Christian phrase, in which the Trojans put their trust above everything. They were celebrating "Palladion's feast," for they would not intermit their devout observances, although [118] the Greeks had shut them in, "and their cite biseged al aboute." When Pandarus finds his friend plunged in a lover's grief, despairing of ever winning the least favor from the lady he has seen in the temple, the gibe that he casts at him, – for the nonce, To anger him and arouse him from his stupor – is an accusation of cowardice: – "Fear, perhaps, has prompted you to pray and repent, as at the approach of death."

        "God save hem that biseged our toun;
          And so can leye our iolitee in presse,
          And bringe our lusty folk to hevinesse!"

                                                [II. 558–60]

When Pandarus first reveals to Cressida the secret of Troilus' love, he approaches the subject carefully, so as not to startle her. "I could tell you something," he cries, "that would make you lay aside your mourning." "Now, uncle dear," she answers, "tell it us, for love of God! Is the siege over, then? I am frightened to death of these Greeks."

> "As ever thryve I," quod this Pandarus,
> "Yet coude I telle a thing to do yow pleye!"
> "Now, uncle dere," quod she, "telle it us
> For Goddes love! Is than thassege aweye?
> I am of Grekes so ferd that I deye!"[12]

Cressida felt the first thrill in her heart when she saw Troilus riding through the street on his re[119]turn from battle – his helm hewn to pieces, his shield pierced with Grecian arrows and cut and broken with the blows of swords and maces, – and the people were all shouting in triumph as he passed.

Always and everywhere we are oppressed by the coming doom of the city. This it is that prompts Calchas to beg the Greeks to give up their prisoner Antenor in exchange for Cressida. They need not hesitate, he argues; one Trojan captive more or less is nothing to them, – the whole city will soon be theirs. The time is near at hand.

> "That fyr and flaumbe on al the toun shal sprede,
> And thus shal Troye turne in asshen dede."[13]

And, when Hector opposes the exchange, the Trojan people, in a riotous parliament, shout out their unanimous vote in its favor, and carry the day. Hector was right, though he did not know it for he was acting, not from policy or superior foresight, but from an honorable scruple: Cressida was not a prisoner, he contended; and Trojans did not use to sell women. And the people were fatally wrong. The "cloud of error" hid their best interests from their discernment; for it was the treason of Antenor that brought about the final catastrophe. It is, then, [120] the impendent doom of Troy that parts the lovers; and from this time forward, there is no separating their fate from the fate of the town.

When Cressida joins Calchas in the Grecian camp, she means to return in a few days. She has no doubt whatever that she can trick her father, and she has won Troilus over to her scheme. But she soon discovers that she has matched her woman's wit, not against her dotard father merely, but against the doom of Troy. No pretexts avail, not because Calchas suspects her plot, but because he knows that the city is destined to destruction. Nor does she dare to steal away by night, lest she fall into the hands of the savage soldiery. And finally, when Diomede wooes her, and gets a hearing, though little favor at first, his most powerful argument is the certain and speedy fate of Troy. He does not know that Cressida loves Troilus, – she tells him that she is heart-whole, but for her memory of her dead husband, – yet he cannot believe that so fair a lady has left no lover behind her, and he has seen her ever in sorrow. "Do not," he urges her, "spill a quarter of a tear for any

Trojan; for, truly, it is not worth while. The folk of Troy are all in prison, as you may see for yourself, and not one of them shall come out alive for all the gold betwixen sun and sea!" [V. 879–86]

Thus, from first to last, the loves of Troilus [121] and Cressida are bound up with the inexorable doom that hangs over the city. The fate of Troy is their fate. Their story begins in the temple of the Palladium; it is Calchas' foreknowledge and the people's infatuation that tear them asunder; it is the peril of the town that thwarts woman's wit, until Diomede subdues the inconstant heart. The tragedy of character grows out of the tragedy of situation.

Notes

 1 ii. 48–49; cf. i. 265–266, v. 1765–1769.
 2 iv. 15–21.
 3 v. 1093–1099.
 4 i. 520.
 5 ii. 622–623.
 6 ii. 742.
 7 ii. 1383.
 8 iii. 733–734.
 9 iv. 1098–1099.
10 iii. 617–620.
11 iv. 958 ff.
12 ii. 120–124.
13 iv. 118–119.

2 | What Chaucer really did to *Il Filostrato*

C. S. LEWIS

Originally published in *Essays and Studies* 17 (1932):56–75.
Reprinted by permission of the English Association. The original
pagination is recorded within square brackets. The endnotes
originally appeared as footnotes and are here renumbered.

A great deal of attention has deservedly been given to the relation between the *Book of Troilus* and its original, *Il Filostrato*, and Rossetti's collation placed a knowledge of the subject within the reach even of undergraduate inquirers. It is, of course, entirely right and proper that the greater part of this attention has been devoted to such points as specially illustrate the individual genius of Chaucer as a dramatist and a psychologist. But such studies, without any disgrace to themselves, often leave singularly undefined the historical position and affinities of a book; and if pursued intemperately they may leave us with a preposterous picture of the author as that abstraction, a *pure* individual, bound to no time nor place, or even obeying in the fourteenth century the aesthetics of the twentieth. It is possible that a good deal of misunderstanding still exists, even among instructed people, as to the real significance of the liberties that Chaucer took with his source. M. Legouis, in his study of Chaucer to which we all owe so much, remarks that Chaucer's additions 'implied a wider and more varied conception' than those of Boccaccio; and again 'Chaucer's aim was not like Boccaccio's to paint sentimentality alone, but to reflect life' [Emile Legouis, *Geoffrey Chaucer*, trans. L. Lailavoix (London: Dent, 1913), p. 134]. I do not wish to contradict either statement, but I am convinced that both are capable of conveying a false impression. What follows may be regarded as a cautionary gloss on M. Legouis's text. I shall endeavour to show that the process which *Il Filostrato* underwent at Chaucer's hands was first and foremost a process of *medievalization*. One aspect of this process has received some attention from scholars,[1] but its importance appears to me to be still insufficiently stressed. In what follows I shall, therefore, restate this aspect in my own terms while endeavouring to replace it in its context.

[57] Chaucer had never heard of a renaissance; and I think it would be difficult to translate either into the English or the Latin of his day our distinction between sentimental or conventional art on the one hand, and art

which paints "Life" – whatever this means – on the other. When first a manuscript beginning with the words *Alcun di giove sogliono il favore* came into his hands, he was, no doubt, aware of a difference between its contents and those of certain English and French manuscripts which he had read before. That some of the differences did not please him is apparent from his treatment. We may be sure, however, that he noticed and approved the new use of stanzas, instead of octosyllabic couplets, for narrative. He certainly thought the story a good story; he may even have thought it a story better told than any that he had yet read. But there was also, for Chaucer, a special reason why he should choose this story for his own retelling; and that reason largely determined the alterations that he made.

He was not yet the Chaucer of the *Canterbury Tales*: he was the *grant translateur* of the *Roman de la Rose*, the author of the *Book of the Duchesse*, and probably of 'many a song and many a lecherous lay'.[2] In other words he was the great living interpreter in English of *l'amour courtois*. Even in 1390, when Gower produced the first version of his *Confessio Amantis*, such faithful interpretation of the love tradition was still regarded as the typical and essential function of Chaucer: he is Venus' 'disciple' and 'poete', with whose 'ditees and songes glade ... the lond fulfild is overal'. And Gower still has hopes that Chaucer's existing treatments of *Frauendienst* are only the preludes to some great 'testament' which will 'sette an ende of alle his werk'.[3] These expectations were, of course, disappointed; and it is possibly to that disappointment, rather than to a hypothetical quarrel (for which only the most ridiculous grounds have been assigned), that we should attribute Gower's removal of this passage from the second text of the *Confessio Amantis*. It had become apparent that Chaucer was following a different [58] line of development, and the reference made to him by Venus had ceased to be appropriate.

It was, then, as a poet of courtly love that Chaucer approached *Il Filostrato*. There is no sign as yet that he wished to desert the courtly tradition; on the contrary, there is ample evidence that he still regarded himself as its exponent. But the narrative bent of his genius was already urging him, not to desert this tradition, but to pass from its doctrinal treatment (as in the *Romance of the Rose*) to its narrative treatment. Having preached it, and sung it, he would now exemplify it: he would show the code put into action in the course of a story – without prejudice (as we shall see) to a good deal of doctrine and pointing of the amorous moral by the way. The thing represents a curious return upon itself of literary history. If Chaucer had lived earlier he would, we may be sure, have found just the model that he desired in Chrestien de Troyes. But by Chaucer's time certain elements, which Chrestien had held together in unity, had come apart and taken an independent life. Chrestien had combined, magnificently, the interest of the story, and the interest of erotic doctrine and psychology. His successors had been unable or unwilling to achieve this union. Perhaps, indeed, the two things had to separate in order that each might grow to maturity; and in many of Chrestien's psychological passages one sees the embryonic allegory struggling to be born.[4] Whatever the reason may be, such a separation took place. The story sets up on its own in the prose romances – the "French book" of Malory: the doctrine and psychology set up on their own in the *Romance of the Rose*. In this situation if a poet arose who accepted the doctrines and also had a narrative genius, then *a priori* such a poet might be expected to combine again the two elements – now fully grown – which, in their rudimentary form, had lain together in Chrestien. But this is exactly the sort of poet that Chaucer was; and this (as we shall see) is what Chaucer did. The *Book of Troilus* shows, in fact, the [59] very peculiar literary phenomenon of Chaucer groping back, unknowingly, through the very slightly medieval work of Boccaccio, to the genuinely medieval formula of Chrestien. We may be thankful that Chaucer did not live in the high noon of Chrestien's celebrity; for, if he had, we should probably have lost much of the originality of Troilus. He would have had less motive for altering Chrestien than for altering Boccaccio, and probably would have altered him less.

Approaching *Il Filostrato* from this angle, Chaucer, we may be sure, while feeling the charm of its narrative power, would have found himself, at many passages, uttering the Middle English equivalent of 'This will never do!' In such places he did not hesitate, as he might have said, to *amenden* and to *reducen* what was *amis* in his author. The majority of his modifications are corrections of errors which Boccaccio had committed against the code of courtly love; and modifications of this kind have not been entirely neglected by criticism. It has not, however, been sufficiently observed that these are only part and parcel of a general process of medievalization. They are, indeed, the most instructive part of that process, and even in the present discussion must claim the chief place; but in order to restore them to their proper setting it will be convenient to make a division of the different capacities in which Chaucer approached his original. These will, of course, be found to overlap in the concrete; but that is no reason for not plucking them ideally apart in the interests of clarity.

I. Chaucer approached his work as an 'Historial' poet contributing to the story of Troy. I do not mean that he necessarily believed his tale to be wholly or partly a record of fact, but his attitude towards it in this respect is different from Boccaccio's. Boccaccio, we may surmise, wrote for an audience who were beginning to look at poetry in our own way. For them *Il Filostrato* was mainly, though not entirely, 'a new poem by Boccaccio'. Chaucer wrote for an audience who still looked at poetry in the medieval fashion – a fashion for which the real literary units were 'matters', 'stories', and the like, rather than individual authors. For them the [60] *Book of Troilus* was partly, though of course only partly, 'a new bit of the Troy story', or even 'a new bit of the matter of Rome'. Hence Chaucer expects them to be interested not only in the personal drama between his little group of characters but in that whole world of story which makes this drama's context: like children looking at a landscape picture and wanting to know what happens to the road after it disappears into the frame. For the same reason they will want to know his authorities. Passages in which Chaucer has departed from his original to meet this demand will easily occur to the memory. Thus, in i. 141 et seq., he excuses himself for not telling us more about the military history of the Trojan war, and adds what is almost a footnote to tell his audience where they can find that missing part of the story – 'in Omer, or in Dares, or in Dyte'. Boccaccio had merely sketched in, in the preceding stanza, a general picture of war sufficient to provide the background for his own story – much as a dramatist might put *Alarums within* in a stage direction: he has in view an audience fully conscious that all this is mere necessary 'setting' or hypothesis. Thus again, in iv. 120 et seq., Chaucer inserts into the speech of *Calkas* an account of the quarrel between *Phebus* and *Neptunus* and *Lameadoun*. This is not dramatically necessary. All that was needed for *Calkas's* argument has already been given in lines 111 and 112 (cf. *Filostrato*, IV. xi). The Greek leaders did not need to be told about Laomedon; but Chaucer is not thinking of the Greek leaders; he is thinking of his audience who will gladly learn, or be reminded, of that part of the cycle. At lines 204 et seq. he inserts a note on the later history of *Antenor* for the same reason. In the fifth book he inserts unnecessarily lines 1464–1510 from the story of Thebes. The spirit in which this is done is aptly expressed in his own words:

> And so descendeth down from gestes olde
> To Diomede.
>
> (v. 1511, 1512)

The whole 'matter of Rome' is still a unity, with a structure and life of its own. That part of it which the poem in hand [61] is treating, which is, so to speak, in focus, must be seen fading gradually away into its 'historial' surroundings. The method is the antithesis of that which produces the 'framed' story of a modern writer: it is a method which romance largely took over from the epic.

II. Chaucer approached his work as a pupil of the rhetoricians and a firm believer in the good, old, and now neglected maxim of Dante: *omnis qui versificatur suos versus exornare debet in quantum potest.* This side of Chaucer's poetry has been illustrated by Mr. Manly[5] so well that most readers will not now be in danger of neglecting it. A detailed application of this new study to the *Book of Troilus* would here detain us too long, but a cursory glance shows that Chaucer found his original too short and proceeded in many places to 'amplify' it. He began by abandoning the device – that of invoking his lady instead of the Muses – whereby Boccaccio had given a lyrical instead of a rhetorical turn to the invocation, and substituted an address to *Thesiphone* (*Filostrato*, I. i–v, cf. *Troilus*, i. 1–14). He added at the beginning of his second book an invocation of *Cleo* and an apology of the usual medieval type, for the defects of his work (ii. 15–21). Almost immediately afterwards he inserted a *descriptio* of the month of a May (an innovation which concerned him as poet of courtly love no less than as rhetorician) which is extremely beautiful and appropriate, but which follows, none the less, conventional lines. The season is fixed by astronomical references, and *Proigne* and *Tereus* appear just where we should expect them (ii. 50–6, 64–70). In the third book the scene of the morning parting between the two lovers affords a complicated example of Chaucer's medievalization. In his original (III. xlii) Chaucer read

> Ma poich' e galli presso al giorno udiro
> Cantar per l'aurora che surgea.

He proceeded to amplify this, first by the device of *Circuitio* or *Circumlocutio*; *galli*, with the aid of Alanus de Insulis, became 'the cok, comune astrologer'. Not content with this, [62] he then repeated the sense of that whole phrase by the device *Expolitio*, of which the formula is *Mutiplice forma Dissimuletur idem: varius sis et tamen idem*,[6] and the theme "Dawn came" is varied with *Lucifer* and *Fortuna Minor*, till it fills a whole stanza (iii. 1415–21). In the next stanza of Boccaccio he found a short speech by *Griseida*, expressing her sorrow at the parting which dawn necessitated: but this was not enough for him. As poet of love he wanted his *alba*; as rhetorician he wanted his *apostropha*. He therefore inserted sixteen lines of address to Night (1427–42), during which he secured the additional advantage, from the medieval point of view, of 'som doctryne' (1429–32). In lines 1452–70 he inserted antiphonally Troilus's *alba*, for which the only basis in Boccaccio was the line *Il giorno che venia maledicendo* (III. xliv). The passage is an object lesson for those who tend to identify the traditional with the dull. Its matter goes back to the ancient sources of medieval love poetry, notably to Ovid, *Amores*, i. 13, and it has been handled often before, and better handled, by the Provençals. Yet it is responsible for one of the most vivid and beautiful expressions that Chaucer ever used.

> Accursed be thy coming into Troye
> For every bore hath oon of thy bright eyen.

A detailed study of the *Book of Troilus* would reveal this 'rhetoricization', if I may coin an ugly word, as the common quality of many of Chaucer's additions. As examples of *Apostropha* alone I may mention, before leaving this part of the subject, iii. 301 et seq. (*O tonge*), 617 et seq. (*But o Fortune*), 715 et seq. (*O Venus*), and 813 et seq. where Chaucer is following Boethius.

III. Chaucer approached his work as a poet of *doctryne* and sentence. This is a side of his literary character which twentieth-century fashions encourage us to overlook, but, of course, no honest historian can deny it. His contemporaries and immediate successors did not. His own creatures, the pilgrims, regarded *mirthe* and *doctryne*,[7] or, as it is elsewhere [63] expressed, *sentence* and *solas*,[8] as the two alternative, and equally welcome, excellences of a story. In the same spirit Hoccleve praises Chaucer as the *mirour of fructuous entendement* and the universal *fadir in science*[9] – a passage, by the by, to be recommended to those who are astonished that the fifteenth century should imitate those elements of Chaucer's genius which it enjoyed instead of those which we enjoy. In respect of *doctryne*, then, Chaucer found his original deficient, and *amended* it. The example which will leap to every one's mind is the Boethian discussion on free will (iv. 946–1078). To Boccaccio, I suspect, this would have seemed as much an excrescence as it does to the modern reader; to the unjaded appetites of Chaucer's audience mere thickness in a wad of manuscript was a merit. If the author was so 'courteous beyond covenant' as to give you an extra bit of *doctryne* (or of story), who would be so churlish as to refuse it on the pedantic ground of irrelevance? But this passage is only one of many in which Chaucer departs from his original for the sake of giving his readers interesting general knowledge or philosophical doctrine. In iii. 1387 et seq., finding Boccaccio's attack upon *gli avari* a little bare and unsupported, he throws out, as a species of buttress, the *exempla* of *Myda* and *Crassus.*[10] In the same book he has to deal with the second assignation of Troilus and Cressida. Boccaccio gave him three stanzas of dialogue (*Filostrato*, III. lxvi–lxviii), but Chaucer rejected them and preferred – in curious anticipation of Falstaff's thesis about pitch – to assure his readers, on the authority of *thise clerkes wyse* (iii. 1691) that *felicitee* is felicitous, though *Troilus* and *Criseyde* enjoyed something better than *felicitee*. In the same stanza he also intends, I think, an allusion to the *sententia* that occurs elsewhere in the Franklin's Tale.[11] In iv. 197–203, immediately before his *historial* insertion about Antenor, he introduces a *sentence* from Juvenal, partly [64] for its own sake, partly in order that the story of Antenor may thus acquire an exemplary, as well as a *historial* value. In iv. 323–8 he inserts a passage on the great *locus communis* of Fortune and her wheel.

In the light of this sententious bias, Chaucer's treatment of Pandarus should be reconsidered, and it is here that a somewhat subtle exercise of the historical imagination becomes necessary. On the one hand, he would be a dull reader, and the victim rather than the pupil of history, who would take all the doctrinal passages in Chaucer seriously: that the speeches of Chauntecleer and Pertelote and of the Wyf of Bath not only *are* funny by reason of their sententiousness and learning, but are intended to be funny, and funny by that reason, is indisputable. On the other hand, to assume that sententiousness became funny for Chaucer's readers as easily as it becomes funny for us, is to misunderstand the fourteenth century: such an assumption will lead us to the preposterous view that *Melibee* (or even the Parson's Tale) is a comic work – a view not much mended by Mr. Mackail's suggestion that there are some jokes *too* funny to excite laughter and that *Melibee* is one of these. A clear recognition that our own age is quite abnormally sensitive to the funny side of sententiousness, to possible hypocrisy, and to dulness, is absolutely necessary for any one who wishes to understand the past. We must face the fact that Chaucer's audience could listen with gravity and interest to edifying matter which would set a modern audience sleeping or sniggering. The application of this to Pandarus is a delicate business. Every reader must interpret Pandarus for himself, and I can only put forward my own interpretation very tentatively. I believe that Pandarus is meant to be a comic character, but not, by many degrees, so broadly comic as he appears to some modern readers. There is, for me, no doubt that Chaucer intended us to smile when he made Troilus exclaim

What knowe I of the queene Niobe?
Lat be thyne olde ensaumples, I thee preye.

(I. 759)

But I question if he intended just that sort of smile which we actually give him. For me the fun lies in the fact that [65] poor Troilus says what I have been wishing to say for some time. For Chaucer's hearers the point was a little different. The suddenness of the gap thus revealed between Troilus's state of mind and Pandarus's words cast a faintly ludicrous air on what had gone before: it made the theorizing and the *exempla* a little funny in retrospect. But it is quite probable that they had not been funny till then: the discourse on contraries (i. 631–44), the *exemplum* of Paris and Oenone, leading up to the theme 'Physician heal thyself' (652–72), the doctrine of the Mean applied to secrecy in love (687–93), the *sentences* from Solomon (695) and elsewhere (708), are all of them the sort of thing that can be found in admittedly serious passages,[12] and it may well be that Chaucer 'had it both ways'. His readers were to be, first of all, edified by the doctrine for its own sake, and then (slightly) amused by the contrast between this edification and Troilus's obstinate attitude of the plain man. If this view be accepted it will have the consequence that Chaucer intended an effect of more subtility than that which we ordinarily receive. We get the broadly comic effect – a loquacious and unscrupulous old uncle talks solemn platitude at interminable length. For Chaucer, a *textuel* man talked excellent doctrine which we enjoy and by which we are edified: but at the same time we see that this 'has its funny side'. Ours is the crude joke of laughing at admitted rubbish: Chaucer's the much more lasting joke of laughing at 'the funny side' of that which, even while we laugh, we admire. To the present writer this reading of Pandarus does not appear doubtful; but it depends to some extent, on a mere 'impression' about the quality of the Middle Ages, an impression hard to correct, if it is an error, and hard to teach, if it is a truth. For this reason I do not insist on my interpretation. If, however, it is accepted, many of the speeches of Pandarus which are commonly regarded as having a purely dramatic significance will have to be classed among the examples of Chaucer's doctrinal or sententious insertions.[13]

[66] IV. Finally, Chaucer approached his work as the poet of courtly love. He not only modified his story so as to make it a more accurate representation in action of the orthodox erotic code, but he also went out of his way to emphasize its didactic element. Andreas Capellanus had given instructions to lovers; Guillaume de Lorris had given instructions veiled and decorated by allegory; Chaucer carries the process a stage further and gives instruction by example in the course of a concrete story. But he does not forget the instructional side of his work. In the following paragraphs I shall sometimes quote parallels to Chaucer's innovations from the earlier love literature, but it must not be thought that I suppose my quotations to represent Chaucer's immediate source.

1. Boccaccio in his induction, after invoking his mistress instead of the Muses, inserts (i. vi) a short request for lovers in general that they will pray for him. The prayer itself is disposed of in a single line

> Per me vi prego ch'amore preghiate.

This is little more than a conceit, abandoned as soon as it is used: a modern poet could almost do the like. Chaucer devotes four stanzas (i. 22–49) to this prayer. If we make an abstract of both passages, Boccaccio will run 'Pray for me to Love', while Chaucer will run 'Remember, all lovers, your old unhappiness, and pray, for the unsuccessful, that they may come to solace; for me, that I may be enabled to tell this story; for those in despair, that they may die; for the fortunate, that they may persevere, and please their ladies in such manner as may advance the glory of Love'. The important point here is not so much that Chaucer expands his original, as that he renders it more liturgical: his prayer, with its careful discriminations in intercession for the various recognized stages of the amorous life, and its final reference *ad Amoris majorem gloriam*, is a collect. Chaucer is emphasizing that parody, or imitation, or rivalry – I know not which to call it – of the Christian religion which was inherent in traditional *Frauendienst*. The thing can be traced back [67] to Ovid's purely ironical worship of Venus and Amor in the *De Arte Amatoria*. The idea of a love religion is taken up and worked out, though still with equal flippancy, in terms of medieval Christianity, by the twelfth-century poet of the *Concilium Romaricimontis*,[14] where Love is given Cardinals (female), the power of visitation, and the power of cursing. Andreas Capellanus carried the process a stage further and gave Love the power of distributing reward and punishment after death. But while his hell of cruel beauties (*Siccitas*), his purgatory of beauties promiscuously kind (*Humiditas*), and his heaven of true lovers (*Amoenitas*)[15] can hardly be other than playful, Andreas deals with the love religion much more seriously than the author of the *Concilium*. The lover's qualification is *morum probitas*: he must be truthful and modest, a good Catholic, clean in his speech, hospitable, and ready to return good for evil. There is nothing in *saeculo bonum* which is not derived from love:[16] it may even be said in virtue of its severe standard of constancy, to be 'a kind of chastity' – *reddit hominem castitatis quasi virtute decoratum.*[17]

In all this we are far removed from the tittering nuns and *clerici* of the *Concilium*. In Chrestien, the scene in which Lancelot kneels and adores the bed of Guinevere (as if before a *corseynt*)[18] is, I think, certainly intended to be read seriously: what mental reservations the poet himself had on the whole business is another question. In Dante the love religion has become wholly and unequivocally serious by fusing with the real religion: the distance between the *Amor deus omnium quotquot sunt amantium* of the *Concilium*, and the *segnore di pauroso aspetto* of the *Vita Nuova*,[19] is the measure of the tradition's real flexibility and universality. It is this quasi-religious element in the content, and this liturgical element in the diction, which Chaucer found lacking

[68] in his original at the very opening of the book, and which he supplied. The line

> That Love hem bringe in hevene to solas

is particularly instructive.

2. In the Temple scene (Chaucer, i. 155–315. *Filostrato*, i. xix–xxxii) Chaucer found a stanza which it was very necessary to *reducen*. It was Boccaccio's twenty-third, in which Troilus, after indulging in his 'cooling card for lovers', mentions that he has himself been singed with that fire, and even hints that he has had his successes; but the pleasures were not worth the pains. The whole passage is a typical example of that Latin spirit which in all ages (except perhaps our own) has made Englishmen a little uncomfortable; the hero must be a lady-killer from the very beginning, or the audience will think him a milksop and a booby. To have abashed, however temporarily, these strutting Latinisms, is not least among the virtues of medieval *Frauendienst*: and for Chaucer as its poet, this stanza was emphatically one of those that 'would never do'. He drops it quietly out of its place, and thus brings the course of his story nearer to that of the *Romance of the Rose*. The parallelism is so far intact. Troilus, an unattached young member of the courtly world, wandering idly about the Temple, is smitten with Love. In the same way the Dreamer having been admitted by Ydelnesse into the garden goes 'Pleying along ful merily'[20] until he looks in the fatal well. If he had already met Love outside the garden the whole allegory would have to be reconstructed.

3. A few lines lower Chaucer found in his original the words

> il quale amor trafisse
> Più ch'alcun altro, pria del tempio uscisse.

> (I. xxv)

Amor trafisse in Boccaccio is hardly more than a literary variant for 'he fell in love': the allegory has shrunk into a metaphor and even that metaphor is almost unconscious and fossilized. Over such a passage one can imagine Chaucer [69] exclaiming, *tantamne rem tam negligenter?* He at once goes back through the metaphor to the allegory that begot it, and gives us his own thirtieth stanza (I. 204–10) on the god of Love in anger bending his bow. The image is very ancient and goes back at least as far as Apollonius Rhodius.[21] Ovid was probably the intermediary who conveyed it to the Middle Ages. Chrestien uses it, with particular emphasis on Love as the avenger of contempt.[22] But Chaucer need not have gone further to find it than to the *Romance of the Rose*:[23] with which, here again, he brings his story into line.

4. But even this was not enough. Boccaccio's *Amor trafisse* had occurred in a stanza where the author apostrophizes the *Cecità delle mondane menti*, and reflects on the familiar contrast between human expectations and the actual course of events. But this general contrast seemed weak to the poet of courtly love: what he wanted was the explicit erotic *moral*, based on the special contrast between the ὕβρις of the young scoffer and the complete

surrender which the offended deity soon afterwards extracted from him. This conception, again, owes much to Ovid; but between Ovid and the Middle Ages comes the later practice of the ancient Epithalamium during the decline of antiquity and the Dark Ages: to which, as I hope to show elsewhere, the system of courtly love as a whole is heavily indebted. Thus in the fifth century Sidonius Apollinarus in an Epithalamium, makes the bridegroom just such another as Troilus: a proud scoffer humbled by Love. Amor brings to Venus the triumphant news

> Nova gaudia porto
> Felicis praedae, genetrix. Calet ille *superbus*
> Ruricius.[24]

Venus replies

> gaudemus nate, *rebellem*
> Quod vincis.

In a much stranger poem, by the Bishop Ennodius, it is not the ὕβρις of a single youth, but of the world, that has stung [70] the deities of love into retributive action. Cupid and Venus are introduced deploring the present state of Europe

> Frigida consumens multorum possidet artus
> Virginitas.[25]

and Venus meets the situation by a threat that she'll 'larn 'em':

> Discant populi tunc crescere divam
> Cum neglecta iacet.[26]

They conclude by attacking one Maximus and thus bringing about the marriage which the poem was written to celebrate. Venantius Fortunatus, in his Epithalamium for Brunchild reproduces, together with Ennodius's spring morning, Ennodius's boastful Cupid, and makes the god, after an exhibition of his archery, announce to his mother, *mihi vincitur alter Achilles.*[27] In Chrestien the rôle of tamed rebel is transferred to the woman. In *Cligès* Soredamors confesses that Love has humbled her pride by force, and doubts whether such extorted service will find favour.[28] In strict obedience to this tradition Chaucer inserts his lines 214–31, emphasizing the dangers of ὕβρις against Love and the certainty of its ultimate failure; and we may be thankful that he did, since it gives us the lively and touching simile of *proude Bayard.* Then, mindful of his instructional purpose, he adds four stanzas more (239–66), in which he directly exhorts his readers to avoid the error of Troilus, and that for two reasons: firstly, because Love *cannot* be resisted (this is the policeman's argument – we may as well 'come quiet'); and secondly because Love is a thing 'so vertuous in kinde'. The second argument, of course, follows traditional lines, and recalls Andreas's theory of Love as the source of all secular virtue.

5. In lines 330–50 Chaucer again returns to Troilus's scoffing – a scoffing this time assumed as a disguise. I do not wish to press the possibility that Chaucer in this passage is attempting, in virtue of his instructional purpose, to stress [71] the lover's virtue of secrecy more than he found it stressed in his original; for Boccaccio, probably for different reasons, does not leave that side of the subject untouched. But it is interesting to note a difference in the content between this scoffing and that of Boccaccio (*Filostrato* I. xxi, xxii). Boccaccio's is based on contempt for women, fickle as wind, and heartless. Chaucer's is based on the hardships of love's *lay* or religion: hardships arising from the uncertainty of the most orthodox *observances*, which may lead to various kinds of harm and may be taken amiss by the lady. Boccaccio dethrones the deity: Chaucer complains of the severity of the cult. It is the difference between an atheist and a man who humorously insists that he 'is not of religioun'.

6. In the first dialogue between Troilus and Pandarus the difference between Chaucer and his original can best be shown by an abstract. Boccaccio (II. vi–xxviii) would run roughly as follows:

T. Well, if you must know, I am in love. But don't ask me with whom (vi–viii).
P. Why did you not tell me long ago? I could have helped you (ix).
T. What use would *you* be? Your own suit never succeeded (ix).
P. A man can often guide others better than himself (x).
T. I can't tell you, because it is a relation of yours (xv).
P. A fig for relations! Who is it? (xvi).
T. (after a pause) Griseida.
P. Splendid! Love has fixed your heart in a good place. She is an admirable person. The only trouble is that she is rather *pie* (*onesta*): but I'll soon see to that (xxiii). Every woman is amorous at heart: they are only anxious to save their reputations (xxvii). I'll do all I can for you (xxviii).

Chaucer (I. 603–1008) would be more like this:

T. Well, if you must know, I am in love. But don't ask me with whom (603–16).
P. Why did you not tell me long ago? I could have helped you (617–20).
T. What use would *you* be? Your own suit never succeeded (621–3).
[72] P. A man can often guide others better than himself, as we see from the analogy of the whetstone. Remember the doctrine of contraries, and what Oenone said. As regards secrecy, remember that all virtue is a mean between two extremes (624–700).
T. Do leave me alone (760).
P. If you die, how will she interpret it? Many lovers have served

for twenty years without a single kiss. But should they despair? No, they should think it a guerdon even to serve (761–819).

T.   (much moved by this argument, 820–6) What shall I do? Fortune is my foe (827–40).

P.   Her wheel is always turning. Tell me who your mistress is. If it were my sister, you should have her (841–61).

T.   (after a pause) – My sweet foe is Criseyde (870–5).

P.   Splendid: Love has fixed your heart in a good place. This ought to gladden you, firstly, because to love such a lady is nothing but good: secondly, because if she has all these virtues, she must have Pity too. You are very fortunate that Love has treated you so well, considering your previous scorn of him. You must repent at once (874–935).

T.   (kneeling) Mea Culpa! (936–8).

P.   Good. All will now come right. Govern yourself properly: you know that a divided heart can have no grace. I have reasons for being hopeful. No man or woman was ever born who was not apt for love, either natural or celestial: and celestial love is not fitted to Criseyde's years. I will do all I can for you. Love converted you of his goodness. Now that you are converted, you will be as conspicuous among his saints as you formerly were among the sinners against him (939–1008).

In this passage it is safe to say that every single alteration by Chaucer is an alteration in the direction of medievalism. The Whetstone, Oenone, Fortune, and the like we have already discussed: the significance of the remaining innovations may now be briefly indicated. In Boccaccio the reason for Troilus's hesitation in giving the name is Criseida's relationship to Pandaro: and like a flash comes back Pandaro's startling answer. In Chaucer his hesitation is due to the courtly [73] lover's certainty that 'she nil to noon suich wrecche as I be wonne' (778) and that 'full harde it wer to helpen in this cas' (836). Pandaro's original

> Se quella ch'ami fosse mia sorella
> A mio potere avrai tuo piacer d'ella

(xvi)

is reproduced in the English, but by removing the words that provoked it in the Italian (E tua parenta, xv) Chaucer makes it merely a general protestation of boundless friendship in love, instead of a cynical defiance of scruples already raised (Chaucer 861). Boccaccio had delighted to bring the purities of family life and the profligacy of his young man about town into collision, and to show the triumph of the latter. Chaucer keeps all the time within the charmed circle of *Frauendienst* and allows no conflict but that of the lover's hopes and fears. Again, Boccaccio's Pandaro has no argument to use against

Troilo's silence, but the argument 'I may help you'. Chaucer's Pandarus, on finding that this argument fails, proceeds to expound the code. The fear of dishonour in the lady's eyes, the duty of humble but not despairing service in the face of all discouragement, and the acceptance of this service as its own reward, form the substance of six stanzas in the English text (lines 768–819): at least, if we accept four lines very characteristically devoted to 'Ticius' and what 'bokes telle' of him. Even more remarkable is the difference between the behaviour of the two Pandars after the lady's name has been disclosed. Boccaccio's, cynical as ever, encourages Troilo by the reflection that female virtue is not really a serious obstacle: Chaucer's makes the virtue of the lady itself the ground for hope – arguing scholastically that the *genus* of virtue implies that *species* thereof which is *Pitee* (897–900). In what follows, Pandarus, while continuing to advise, becomes an adviser of a slightly different sort. He instructs Troilus not so much on his relationship to the Lady as on his relationship to Love. He endeavours to awaken in Troilus a devout sense of his previous sins against that deity (904–30) and is not satisfied without confession (931–8), briefly enumerates the command[74]ments (953–9), and warns his penitent of the dangers of a divided heart.

In establishing such a case as mine, the author who transfers relentlessly to his article all the passages listed in his private notes can expect nothing but weariness from the reader. If I am criticized, I am prepared to produce for my contention many more evidential passages of the same kind. I am prepared to show how many of the beauties introduced by Chaucer, such as the song of Antigone or the riding past of Troilus, are introduced to explain and mitigate and delay the surrender of the heroine, who showed in Boccaccio a facility condemned by the courtly code.[29] I am prepared to show how Chaucer never forgets his erotically didactic purpose; and how, anticipating criticism as a teacher of love, he guards himself by reminding us that

> For to winne love in sondry ages
> In sondry londes, sondry ben usages.[30]

(ii. 27)

But the reader whose stomach is limited would be tired, and he who is interested may safely be left to follow the clue for himself. Only one point, and that a point of principle, remains to be treated in full. Do I, or do I not, lie open to the criticism of Professor Abercrombie's 'Liberty of Interpreting'?[31]

The Professor *quem honoris causa nomino* urges us not to turn from the known effect which an ancient poem has upon us to speculation about the effect which the poet intended it to have. The application of this criticism which may be directed against me would run as follows: 'If Chaucer's *Troilus* actually produces on us an effect of greater realism and nature and freedom than its original, why should we assume that this effect was accidentally produced in the attempt to conform to an outworn convention?' If the charge is grounded, it is, to my mind, a very grave one. My reply [75] is that such a charge begs the very question which I have most at heart in this

paper, and but for which I should regard my analysis as the aimless burrow-
ings of a thesismonger. I would retort upon my imagined critic with another
question. This poem is more lively and of deeper human appeal than its
original. I grant it. This poem conforms more closely than its original to the
system of courtly love. I claim to prove it. What then is the natural conclusion to draw? Surely, that courtly love itself, in spite of all its shabby origins
and pedantic rules, is at bottom more agreeable to those elements in human,
or at least in European, nature, which last longest, than the cynical Latin
gallantries of Boccaccio? The world of Chrestien, of Guillaume de Lorris,
and of Chaucer, is nearer to the world universal, is less of a closed system,
than the world of Ovid, of Congreve, of Anatole France.

This is doctrine little palatable to the age in which we live: and it carries
with it another doctrine that may seem no less paradoxical – namely, that
certain medieval things are more universal, in that sense more classical, can
claim more confidently a *securus judicat*, than certain things of the Renaissance. To make Herod your villain is more human than to make Tamburlaine
your hero. The politics of Machiavelli are provincial and temporary beside
the doctrine of the *jus gentium*. The love-lore of Andreas, though a narrow
stream, is a stream tending to the universal sea. Its waters move. For real
stagnancy and isolation we must turn to the decorative lakes dug out far
inland at such a mighty cost by Mr. George Moore; to the more popular
corporation swimming-baths of Dr. Marie Stopes; or to the teeming marsh-
lands of the late D. H. Lawrence, whose depth the wisest knows not and on
whose bank the hart gives up his life rather than plunge in:

> þær mæg nihta gehwæm niðwundor seon
> Fyr on flode!

Notes

1 *v*. Dodd, *Courtly Love in Chaucer and Gower*, 1913.
2 *C. T.* [*Canterbury Tales*], I 1086.
3 *Conf. Am.* viii. 2941–58.
4 *v. Lancelot*, 369–81, 2844–61; *Yvain*, 6001 et seq., 2639 et seq.; *Cligès*, 5855 et seq.
5 *Chaucer and the Rhetoricians*, Warton Lecture XVII, 1926.
6 Geoffroi de Vinsauf, *Poetr. Nov*, 220–5.
7 *Canterbury Tales*, B 2125.
8 Ibid., A 798.
9 *Regement*, 1963 et seq.
10 This might equally well have been treated above in our rhetorical section. The
   instructed reader will realize that a final distinction between *doctrinal* and *rhetorical*
   aspects, is not possible in the Middle Ages.
11 *C. T.*, F 762.
12 Cf. *C. T.*, I 140–155.
13 From another point of view Pandarus can be regarded as the *Vekke* of the *R. R.*
   [*Roman de la Rose*] (cf. Thessala in *Cligès*) taken out of allegory into drama and
   changed in sex, so as to 'double' the rôles of *Vekke* and *Frend*.
14 *Zeitschrift für Deutsches Alterthum*, vii, pp. 160 et seq.

15 Andreas Capellanus, *De Arte Honeste Amandi*, ed. Troejel, i. 6 D² (pp. 91–108).
16 Ibid., i. 6 A (p. 28).
17 Ibid., i. 4 (p. 10).
18 *Lancelot*, 4670, 4734 et seq.
19 *Vit. Nuov*. iii.
20 *R. R*. 1329 (English Version).
21 *Argonaut*, iii. 275 et seq.
22 *Cligès*, 460; cf. 770.
23 *R. R*. 1330 et seq.; 1715 et seq.
24 *Sid. Apoll*. Carm. xi. 61.
25 Ennodius Carm. I, iv. 57.
26 Ibid., 84.
27 Venant. Fort. VI, i.
28 *Cligès*, 682, 241.
29 A particularly instructive comparison could be drawn between the Chaucerian Cresseide's determination to yield, yet to seem to yield by force and deception, and Bialacoil's behaviour. *R. R*. 12607–88: especially 12682, 3.
30 Cf. ii. 1023 et seq.
31 *Proceedings of the Brit. Acad*., vol. xvi, Shakespeare Lecture, 1930.

3 | Troilus and Criseyde

CHARLES MUSCATINE

Originally published as the beginning of Chapter 5 in Charles
Muscatine, *Chaucer and the French Tradition: A Study in Style and
Meaning* (Berkeley and Los Angeles: University of California Press,
1957, pp. 124–32). Reprinted by permission of the University of
California Press. The original pagination is recorded within square
brackets. The endnotes originally appeared on p. 262. In the rest of
Chapter 5, Muscatine discusses the principal characters and the
ending of the poem.

Troilus and Criseyde stands as the focal point in Chaucer's artistic career. It
draws together in full development every talent shown in the early poems,
and has, besides, its own new amplitude. Like the *Canterbury Tales*, it
contains a world. The later work excels it only in particularity of reference,
not in control of form or depth of conception. Like many of Chaucer's (and
Shakespeare's) works, it has a direct "source." Chaucer took for it most of the
plot, the content of many whole stanzas, and even words and rimes from
Boccaccio's romance *Il Filostrato*.[1] Textual comparison shows many ways in
which Chaucer enlarged on his model; thus he added two fairly long sequences that are only suggested in the Italian. But the nature of his originality
cannot be fully understood by subtracting, as it were, one poem from the
other. All of the "source" has been changed by a change in the large
conceptions of form and value that dominate the composition, and this in
turn accounts for the addition of the literally "original" parts of the poem.
The nature of the change can be seen in terms both of history and of style;
the two are related, and together they provide a useful index to the meaning
of the *Troilus* itself.

[125] Boccaccio's *Filostrato* has a strongly autobiographical cast. The author
dedicates it to a "nobilissima donna," and says that he expresses through the
story of Troiolo's sorrow his own feelings about his lady's absence from the
city. Since much of Boccaccio's biography for the 1330's is read from between
the lines of his romances, we can be sure of little. But the tone of this
romance lends support to the theory that the lady is Maria d'Aquino, the
voluptuous, illegitimate daughter of King Robert of Naples – she was
Boccaccio's sometime mistress – and that the poem not only records her
absence, but perhaps also forecasts her imminent desertion of the poet.[2] The

narrator is in complete sympathy with his hero. The twenty-five-year-old Boccaccio *in propria persona* is both, and the manners of the poem strongly reflect its origin in the sophisticated, prosperous, and licentious Neapolitan court of the time.

Naples under the Angevins was a particularly cosmopolitan part of Italy; Boccaccio was later to import some of its sophistication into his barbaric paternal city of Florence. He had already written, adapted perhaps directly from the French, much of the *Filocolo*, his ornately "classical" and courtly version of *Floire and Blancheflor*. As a basis for the *Filostrato* he took an incident from one of the earliest romances in French, Benoît de Sainte-Maure's *Roman de Troie*. He added to Benoît's story of Briseida's desertion of her Trojan lover an invented account of their previous affair. Writing two centuries later than Benoît, he is able to draw on his knowledge of later romance and on the lyric tradition of the *stilnovisti* to elaborate his story greatly in the direction of courtly love. Thus his treatment is far more detailed and more elevated than Benoît's. But at the same time he creates what few French romances are, an urban poem. Courtly life in Italy is characteristically a version of city life, and Boccaccio himself was and always remained a *borghese*.[3] His courtliness thus has a sensuality and a sauce of cynicism, a realistic knowingness, that is foreign to the French and even more to the English courtliness of the Middle Ages.

Boccaccio's heroine, for instance, is conceived less ideally than French heroines are. Criseida is rather *known* than invented at all. She is beautiful, but also instinctive and calculating, faithful only in her own fashion; she submits to practical events in a purely creatural way. The ambiguity of her feminine responses to her suitors is designedly transparent.[4] The mystery, the reticence, the *dangier* of the French mode are gone, as is the semireligious awe of the French hero. He is a young but already experienced city type. The narrator, one is made to feel, knows women. In his frankly indulgent attitude toward sex he forecasts the philosophy of the *Decameron*.

[126] Yet Boccaccio's realism and sensualism already approach in the *Filostrato* that remarkably graceful compromise with French refinement which is his typical characteristic. The style and structure of the poem reflect this poise of feeling. It is preponderantly lyrical, and rises easily to emotional intensity. It uses much of the rhetorical figuration of the high style. Yet it can bend easily, and in short space, to a relaxed, moderately realistic description, with no suggestion of disharmony between imaginative elevation and realistic immediacy. It is thus much a Renaissance poem. The first stanza describing Criseida rises and falls in an unembarrassed modulation of style:

> Tra li qua' fu di Calcas la figliuola
> Crisëida, quale era in bruna vesta,
> la qual, quanto la rosa la vïola
> di biltá vince, cotanto era questa
> piú ch'altra donna, bella; ed essa sola
> piú ch'altra facea lieta la gran festa,

stando del tempio assai presso alla porta,
negli atti altiera, piacente ed accorta.

(I, 19)

[Among whom was the daughter of Calcas, Criseida, in dark dress, who, as much as the rose conquers the violet in beauty, so much was she more beautiful than any other lady; and she alone more than any other made glad the great festival, standing very near the door of the temple, in manner stately, gracious, and agreeable.]

The stanzas describing the undressing of Criseida are similarly curved:

Lungo sarebbe a raccontar la festa,
ed impossibile a dire il diletto
che 'nsieme preser pervenuti in questa;
ei si spogliaro ed entraron nel letto,
dove la donna nell'ultima vesta
rimasa giá, con piacevole detto
gli disse: – Spogliomi io? Le nuove spose
son la notte primiera vergognose. –

A cui Troiolo disse: – Anima mia,
io te ne priego, si ch'io t'abbi in braccio
ignuda si come il mio cor disia. –
Ed ella allora: – Ve' ch'io me ne spaccio. –
E la camiscia sua gittata via,
[127]   nelle sue braccia si ricolse avaccio;
e strignendo l'un l'altro con fervore,
d'amor sentiron l'ultimo valore.

(III, 31)

[Long would it be to recount the pleasure and impossible to tell the delight they took together when they had come there; they undressed and got into bed, where the lady, still in her last garment, said to him in a charming way: "Shall I undress myself? The newly wed are timid the first night." To whom Troiolo said: "Soul of me, I pray you do, so that I may have you in my arms naked as my heart desires." And she then: "Look, I am rid of it." And her chemise thrown away, she quickly nestled in his arms; and clasping one another with passion, they felt the uttermost value of love.]

For Boccaccio, love's "ultima valore," which Chaucer translates "grete worthynesse" (III, 1316), has nothing in it so remote and elevated that it cannot dwell with the intimate and closely appreciated detail of sexual play. The playful smile with which the heroine's voluptuousness is regarded does not at all interfere with the high valuing of her.

The whole poem's style is ranged in this manner, between limits that are rarely felt to be far apart.[5] The description is, on the whole, thin; there is no particular effort either to realize a contemporary setting or to fabricate a romantic one.[6] The direct discourse is rich in lyric monologue, but Boccaccio's patent interest in the sentiments of his characters does not impel him far in the opposite direction, toward realistically conceived dialogue. When it comes briefly and naturally into the scenes between Pandaro and Criseida, it has neither the stichomythic formalism of courtly dialogue nor the turbulence of the bourgeois style. The idiom of the narrative, while rich enough in poetic figure – even to epic simile and personification, – has nevertheless been described, in comparison to that of the *Filocolo*, as "simpler and humbler . . . sometimes prosaic."[7]

The narrative itself proceeds in a confident, linear fashion. Troiolo is so much the focus of interest that little space is given to the important interventions of others in his affairs. Pandaro's machinations to arrange the rendezvous with Criseida are told as briefly as possible, and the whole account to her wooing by Diomede occupies only twenty-six stanzas. Considering the elaboration and intrigue characteristic of romance, the poem well merits De Sanctis' description of it as a *novella* under epic appearance.[8]

The Italian city poet in Boccaccio co-exists with the *trouvère* in so friendly a fashion that one is actually surprised that they have found so few differences [128] between them. The former has a smiling wit that turns periodically on his heroine and once or twice on himself. The other is bound heart and soul to his lady, takes himself very seriously and, in almost hopeless knowledge of his betrayal, can still defend her *gentilezza* to the world.[9] Both are Boccaccio, accommodated by a restricted, social idealism that is fairly encompassed in Troiolo's declaration to Criseida:

> "Ma gli atti tuoi altieri e signorili,
> il valore e 'l parlar cavalleresco,
> i tuoi costumi piú ch'altra gentili,
> ed il vezzoso tuo sdegno donnesco,
> per lo quale apparien d'esserti vili
> ogni appetito ed oprar popolesco,
> qual tu mi sei, o donna mia possente,
> con amor mi ti miser nella mente."

(IV, 165)

["... but your stately and elegant manners, your fineness and your courtly speech, your ways more gentle than others', and your pretty, feminine scorn, whereby every vulgar desire and action seemed to you base – such are you to me, O my mighty lady – set you in my mind with love."]

To our less enchanted eyes, indeed, this description seems to apply more to Troiolo than to his mistress. But be that as it may, it is clear that both the light irony and the heavy pathos of the poem are based on a surprisingly narrow conception of good and evil. It is not wide enough to suggest broad reaches of meaning, to sustain either comedy or tragedy. The poem's ostensible moral is its actual one: "Giovane donna è mobile." To the end it is a personal, autobiographical cry, a young man's poem.

The difference between *Il Filostrato* and the *Troilus* follows broadly the differences between the poets and their cultures. Chaucer wrote his poem in an England nagged by an interminable war and beset internally by social, political, and religious turmoil, and in a city with an economy based more on hard-won commerce than on feudal tribute. His whole milieu cannot have approached the leisure, the sophistication, the cultural poise of Boccaccio's Naples of fifty years before. Futhermore, England's culture was still dominated by its French history with a weight that the Italian debt to France did not approach. Italian art had never been so Gothic as English art, and the Italian Trecento, with Giotto, Boccaccio, and Petrarch, was already a "renaissance" century. English politics, religion, art, and social organization were going through a much more protracted [129] and difficult changing; with suppression and regression, England was not to have its own renaissance for another two hundred years. Meanwhile, its problems took shape according to the traditional medieval formulations, growing out of the medieval dualism of culture that I have mentioned before. The contrast between country and city, between courtly and commercial life, between religion and secularism, was becoming actually less sharp. But it is a characteristic of English thinking in this period that practical events are continually cast up against an ever-brightening notion of the receding ideals of the past. We find the same revivalist nostalgia in Wycliffe, in Langland, in Malory, and in Caxton. In each, theory and actuality produce a violent, late Gothic contrast.

Chaucer was temperamentally far better situated than Boccaccio to appreciate the wider meaning of his material. There was no autobiographical impulse behind Chaucer's poem. His stance as a poet had always been one of semidetachment. He was, at forty-six, more capable of both humor and seriousness than Boccaccio was at twenty-five. He had recently translated Boethius' *Consolation of Philosophy*.

The differences between the cultures and the men can be seen at once in the broad characteristics of their poems. There is no telling how Chaucer read *Il Filostrato*, but it is clear that what caught his imagination was neither the simple availability of this new "material" nor the novel, renaissance neatness of it; he had plenty of material at hand, and he made the Italian story less neat. The point of contact is a trait that has already given us a moment's pause: the curiously easy amalgamation in the *Filostrato* of critical wit and naïve devotion, of animal sensualism and romantic idealism. With an English consciousness nourished on the French literary tradition, on medieval Christianity, and on Boethius, Chaucer may have felt that what he was to produce was *in* the Italian poem rather than in the structure of his own vision. But it appears more likely that he gauged to the minutest fraction the age of its nameless narrator, the breadth of his concerns, the depth of his philosophy. He saw, as Boccaccio himself may not have seen, what antithetical values had somehow diminished and coalesced in that youthful, urban, pagan, immoral poem. Then he recast it, perhaps consciously and correctively, objectifying its point of view, setting into bold relief the moral issues it barely suggested, making its private, present pathos something *storial*, a comedy and tragedy of universal and timeless dimensions. Thus Chaucer's poem is neither simple in structure nor homogeneous in style. Rather than being linear in design, it is composed of patterned contrasts, encompassing a great diversity of moods and tones, often abruptly juxtaposed.[10] Its characters, rather than being "all of a piece" (in Legouis's phrase),[11] are complex [130] to the point of bafflement. Its plot is complicated with intricate and difficult maneuvering. Supporting this medieval structure is a very broad range of style, embracing in precisely controlled coördination the two major styles of the French tradition.

C. S. Lewis is the first critic to have grasped the historical significance of what Chaucer did to *Il Filostrato*. His theory of the medievalization of it anticipates (if it did not actually suggest to me) fully half of the view presented here. Chaucer, he shows us, amplified the Italian poem after the manner of the medieval rhetoricians, added much doctrine and *sentence*, and, most importantly, purified its rendering and elaborated its teaching of courtly love. "The majority of his modifications are corrections of errors which Boccaccio had committed against the code ..."[12] Elsewhere Lewis shows how closely the opening movement of the *Troilus* parallels in narrative form the movement of Guillaume de Lorris' allegory, and he invites us to "regard it as a new *Launcelot* – a return to the formula of Chrétien but a return which utilizes all that had been done between Chrétien's day and Chaucer's."[13] This "all" is the fine psychological analysis of Guillaume de Lorris, which, Lewis suggests, frees allegory from itself and makes possible the narrative treatment of a love story.

Standing on Lewis' shoulders, we can hope to see a little more. His view is immensely valuable as a corrective to the typical post-Victorian one, which reads the poem only for its "modern" psychological realism. But at the same time he undervalues the medieval realism that jostles courtly convention all through the period and all through the *Troilus*. Although Lewis rightly finds Jean de Meun's Duenna (Vekke) and Ami (Frend) behind Chaucer's Pandarus, he does not take into serious account the achievement of the bourgeois tradition between Chrétien and Chaucer. Medieval love poetry, he writes:

> protects itself against the laughter of the vulgar – that is, of all of us in certain moods – by allowing laughter and cynicism their place *inside* the poem; as some politicians hold that the only way to make a revolutionary safe is to give him a seat in Parliament. The Duck and Goose have their seats in Chaucer's *Parlement* for the same reason; and for the same reason we have satire on women in Andreas, we have the shameless Vekke in the *Rose*, we have Pandarus in the *Book of Troilus* ... the comic figures in a medieval love poem are a cautionary concession – a libation made to the god of lewd laughter precisely because he is not the god whom we are chiefly serving – a sop to Silenus and Priapus lest they should trouble our lofty hymns to Cupid. When this has been understood (and not till then) we [131] may, indeed, safely admit that Chaucer had sympathy with the Goose and the Duck. So had every knight and dame among his listeners.[14]

The general observation contained here is wise and sensitive, and deserves a fair representation. But its particular application to Chaucer, and also to Jean de Meun, is questionable. We have seen that there had been in Chrétien himself an impulse to illuminate courtly romance from the direction of comic realism. In *Flamenca* the love poetry had been pushed to its limits as such by a similar spirit. But this realism in medieval love poetry can justly be called temporary vagrancy, "a sop to Silenus," only until the late thirteenth century, until Jean de Meun. Thereafter we must be prepared to reckon with it seriously, on an equal basis, for Jean's poem shows that it has become an equally serious factor in the culture itself. Chaucer was "a court poet of the age of Froissart," but not so much a spokesman for a class as Froissart, whose sympathies are exclusively courtly as only those of a certain kind of bourgeois can be. For Chaucer, with his bourgeois parentage, his Controllership of Customs on wools, skins, and hides, and of the Petty Custom on wines, his commercial-courtly milieu, his temperament, there is no question of minor concessions to popular attitudes, or of merely concessionary realism.

But my argument – that Chaucer medievalized *Il Filostrato* in two directions, not one – finds its major justification in the poem, in what Chaucer does with the French tradition itself. The whole meaning of the poem depends as fully on the style and ethos represented by Jean de Meun as on the values of Chrétien and Guillaume de Lorris. This is to say that its courtliness is not that of the twelfth century, merely raised in technical sophistication; it is a fourteenth-century courtliness, seen in a *context* of deepened naturalism. Jean had shown with what effectiveness naturalism could be appended to romance for the purpose of rounding out the possible views of love, and Chaucer follows Jean's lead, but not directly. He sees, as Jean does, the elements of presumption, of naïveté and of impracticality in courtly idealism, and he admires the wholesome sanity of ordinary life. But, unlike Jean, he also prizes courtly idealism for its very real virtues, for its recognition of nobility, of beauty, and of spirit, and he detects in the incessantly practical pursuits of common life the shadow of futility cast over any human activity in which these higher concerns are neglected. His view, more than Jean's, is continuously complex. It is this very round, very comprehensive view of the values of human experience that is implicit in Chaucer's treatment of the story of Troilus and Criseyde.

[132] Beyond this lies another level of perspective. Chaucer is a spiritual pupil of Boethius. He sees in turn the whole sphere of human experience against eternity. He sees the imperfection inherent in any mode of life – be it practical or idealistic – wherein the end itself is *earthly* joy, and hence wherein the prize may at any moment be washed away by the same tides that brought it in.

These two levels of perspective are intimately related, and this relationship gives the poem a philosophical depth which sets it far above conventional medieval moralizing. To dwell at length on the attractiveness of earthly love and then to repudiate all in a palinode is neither philosophical nor artistic.

But to present secular idealism as a beautiful but flawed thing, and to present practical wisdom as an admirable but incomplete thing, to present them, indeed, as antithetical and incongruous to each other, is by implication to present a third view, higher and more complete than either. This philosophical third view hovers over every important sequence in the *Troilus*, and is made explicit in the epilogue.

The stylistic structure of the *Troilus* is coextensive with its meaning. Two equally admirable, equally incomplete attitudes toward life are presented in the poem, and the value of each of these attitudes is communicated in the style specifically developed by tradition for its most effective realization. The negative element, the weakness inherent in each attitude, is presented through the reflection of the one on the other. On a stylistic level, by juxtaposition of scenes and passages alternatingly conventional and naturalistic, with all the attitudinal implications that go with those styles, Chaucer creates a pervasive, literary, structural irony which is at the same time profoundly expressive of the irony of his view of life.

Notes

1 There have been many comparisons of the two poems. Among the most important are: Karl Young, *The Origin and Development of the Story of Troilus and Criseyde*, Chaucer Society (London, 1908), with elaborate analysis of the sources of the *Filostrato* and of other sources of the *Troilus*; Hubertis M. Cummings, *The Indebtedness of Chaucer's Works to the Italian Works of Boccaccio*, Univ. of Cincinnati Studies, Ser. II, Vol. X (Cincinnati, 1915), pp. 50–122; Mario Praz, "Chaucer and the Great Italian Writers of the Trecento," *Monthly Criterion*, VI (1927), 24–34, 153–156; N. E. Griffin, intro. to *The Filostrato of Giovanni Boccaccio*, ed. and trans. Griffin and A. B. Myrick (Philadelphia, 1929), pp. 95–107; C. S. Lewis, "What Chaucer Really Did to Il Filostrato," *Essays and Studies by Members of the English Association*, XVII (1932), 56–75; Karl Young, "Chaucer's 'Troilus and Criseyde' as Romance," *PMLA*, LIII (1938), 40–56; Thomas A. Kirby, *Chaucer's "Troilus": A Study in Courtly Love*, Louisiana State Univ. Stud., XXXIX (University, La., 1940), pp. 121–284; Sanford B. Meech, "Figurative Contrasts in Chaucer's *Troilus and Criseyde*," *English Institute Essays*, 1950 (New York, 1951), pp. 57–88. On Chaucer's use of a French translation see R. A. Pratt, "Chaucer and Le Roman de Troyle et de Criseida," *SP*, LIII (1956), 509–539.

2 Henri Hauvette, *Boccace* (Paris, 1914), pp. 87–88; Vincenzo Pernicone, "Il 'Filostrato' di Giovanni Boccaccio," *Studi di Filologia Italiana*, II (1929), 77–86.

3 This is put more strongly by Francesco De Sanctis, *History of Italian Literature*, trans. Joan Redfern, I (London, 1930), 311: "... it is a page from the secret history of the Neapolitan court, a portrait of that bourgeois, mediocre life, halfway between the rough ingenuity of the people and the ideal feudal or chivalric life." Cf. Pernicone, "Il 'Filostrato,'" pp. 126–127.

4 *Il Filostrato*, ed. V. Pernicone, in *Scrittori d'Italia*, CLXV (Bari, 1937), Pt. II, st. 124–127; VI, 31.

5 There are occasional passages in which a particular mundanity or colloquialism might seem to the modern reader jarring in its context. See, e.g., II, 135; III, 68; V, 20; VI, 7; VII, 101. Usually the context shows that these are not felt to be jarring by Boccaccio.

6 For relatively intimate details of the physical setting, and of realistic look or "business," see II, 120; III, 26, 28; IV, 22, 77, 100, 114; V, 51; VI, 23.

7 Carlo Grabher, *Boccaccio* (Turin, Unione Tipografico, 1945), p. 69.

8 *History*, p. 312.

9 *Filostrato* VII, 93–99.

10 When I first set forth this general view of the importance of the ironic contrasts in the poem ("The Form of Speech in Chaucer," diss. Yale, 1948), it had already been partly anticipated by John Speirs, "Chaucer: (I) 'Troilus and Criseyde,'" *Scrutiny*, XI (1942–43), 84–108 (repeated in his *Chaucer the Maker* [London, 1951], see esp. pp. 51–52, 73–79); it has since been strikingly affirmed by Meech, "Figurative Contrasts," pp. 58–63.

11 Emile Legouis, *Geoffrey Chaucer*, trans. L. Lailavoix (London, Dent, 1913), p. 133.

12 "What Chaucer Really Did," p. 59. Lewis' thesis is amplified by Young, "'Troilus' as Romance."

13 *Allegory of Love* [Oxford, 1936], pp. 177–182.

14 *Allegory of Love*, pp. 172–173.

4 Distance and predestination in *Troilus and Criseyde*

MORTON W. BLOOMFIELD

Originally published in *PMLA* 72 (1957):14–26. Reprinted by permission of the Modern Language Association of America. The original pagination is recorded within square brackets. The endnotes originally appeared as footnotes. Part of note 4 has been omitted.

For we are but of yesterday. – Job viii. 9

In *Troilus and Criseyde* Chaucer as commentator occupies an unusual role. It is indeed common for authors to enter their own works in many ways. Writers as diverse as Homer, Virgil, Dante, Cervantes, Fielding, Thackeray, and George Eliot all do so. Sometimes, as with Fielding, the author may keep a distance between himself and his story; sometimes, as with Dante, he may penetrate into his story as a major or the major character; and sometimes, as with Homer, he may both enter and withdraw at will. When Homer directly addresses one of his characters, he is deliberately breaking down, for artistic reasons, the aloofness to which he generally holds.

Chaucer also frequently appears in his own works, usually as one of his dramatis personae, and participates in the action.[1] Although he is not always an important or major character, his actions or dreams within the work frequently provide the occasion for, or give a supposed rationale to, his literary creations. Chaucer the character's decision to go on a pilgrimage to Canterbury provides the ostensible justification for the *Canterbury Tales*. His dreams as a character, following a great medieval literary convention, give rise to the *Parlement of Foules* and the *Hous of Fame*.

In *Troilus and Criseyde* Chaucer plays his artistic role with a striking difference. Here he conceives of himself as the narrator of a history, of a true event as the Middle Ages conceived it, which happened in the past; and as historian he meticulously maintains a distance between himself and the events in the story. His aloofness is similar to and yet different from Fielding's in *Tom Jones* or Thackeray's in *Vanity Fair*. In these works the authors look upon their puppets from their omniscient, ironical, humorous, and at times melancholy point of view and make comments on them or their predicaments, using them as excuses for brief essays or paragraphs on different subjects. In *Troilus* Chaucer does not look upon his characters as his creations. His assumed role is primarily descriptive and expository. Though we are continually reminded of the presence of Chaucer the historian, narrator, and commentator, at [15] the same time we are never allowed to forget that he is separate from the events he is recording.

Troilus is not a dream vision nor is it a contemporary event. It is the past made extremely vivid by the extensive use of dialogue, but still the past. Chaucer cannot change the elements of his story. As God cannot violate His own rationality, Chaucer cannot violate his data. Bound by his self-imposed task of historian, he both implies and says directly that he cannot do other than report his tale.

If we assume that Chaucer is a painstaking artist – and it is impossible not to – it is clear that the nature of the role he assumes has an extremely important meaning in the economy and plan of the poem. Why, we must ask, does Chaucer as character-narrator continually remind us of his aloofness from and impotence in the face of the events he is narrating? An historian takes for granted what Chaucer does not take for granted. A Gibbon does not tell us constantly that the events of the decline and fall of the Roman Empire are beyond his control. That is an assumption that anyone reading a true history makes at the outset. Chaucer introduces just this assumption into the body of his work, continually reminding us of what seems, in the context of a supposed history, most obvious. What is normally outside the historical work, a presupposition of it, is in the history of Troilus and Criseyde brought into the poem and made much of. This unusual creative act calls for examination.

We must also wonder at the quantitative bulk of Chaucer's comments on the story. Frequently, even in the midst of the action of the inner story, we are reminded of the presence of the narrator – sometimes, it is true, by only a word or two. We cannot dismiss these numerous comments merely as remarks necessary to establish rapport with the audience under conditions of oral delivery. The few remarks of this nature are easy to pick out. If we compare the simple comments made by the narrator in, say, *Havelock the Dane* or any other medieval romance with those made by the *Troilus* narrator, I think the difference is plain.

Although many stanzas belong completely to the commentator *in propria persona* and others pertain to the events of the tale, so many are partly one or the other, or merely suggest the presence of a narrator, that a mathematical table which could reveal the actual percentage of commentator stanzas or lines would be misleading and inaccurate.[2] Anyone [16] who has read the poem must be aware of the presence of the commentator most of the time; one is rarely allowed to forget it for long. And even more impressive than the number of comments are the times and nature of the author's intervention. At all the great moments he is there directing us, speaking in his own person close to us and far from the events of the tragedy which he is presenting to us within the bounds of historical fact.

This sense of distance between Chaucer as character and his story is conveyed to us in what may be designated as temporal, spatial, aesthetic, and religious ways, each reinforcing the other and overlapping. For the sake of clarity, however, we may examine each in turn as a separate kind of aloofness.

The aspect of temporal distance is the one most constantly emphasized throughout the poem. Chaucer again and again tells us that the events he is recording are historical and past. He lets us know that customs have changed since the time when Pandarus, Troilus, and Criseyde lived. The characters are pagans who go to temples to worship strange gods and are caught up in one of the great cataclysms of history. Their ways of living are different from ours. Their love-making varies from the modern style. They lived a long time ago, and Chaucer, to tell their story, is forced to rely on the historians. In order to understand their actions, we must make an effort in comprehension. Yet, says Chaucer, diversity of custom is natural. At times, it is true, Chaucer is very anachronistic, but he still succeeds in giving his readers (or listeners) a feeling for the pastness of his characters and their sad story and for what we today call cultural relativity.[3]

Throughout, Chaucer tries to give us a sense of the great sweep of time which moves down to the present and into the future and back beyond Troy, deepening our sense of the temporal dimension. He tells us that speech and customs change within a thousand years (II. 22 ff.) and that this work he is writing is also subject to linguistic variability (v. 1793 ff.). Kingdoms and power pass away too; the *translatio regni* (or *imperii*) is inexorable – "regnes shal be flitted/Fro folk in folk" (v. 1544–45). The characters themselves reach even farther backward in time. Criseyde and her ladies read of another siege, the fall of Thebes, which took place long before the siege of Troy (II. 81 ff.). Cassandra, in [17] her interpretation of Troilus' dream (v. 1450–1519), goes into ancient history to explain Diomede's lineage. We are all part of time's kingdom, and we are never allowed to forget it.

Yet, as I have already mentioned, Chaucer vividly reconstructs, especially in his use of dialogue, the day-by-day living of his chief characters. This precision of detail and liveliness of conversation only serve to weight the contrast between himself in the present and his story in the past, to make the present even more evanescent in the sweep of inexorable change. It is the other side of the coin. These inner events are in the past and in a sense dead, but when they occurred they were just as vivid as the events that are happening now. The strong reality and, in a sense, nearness of the past makes meaningful its disappearance and emphasizes paradoxically its distance. If there are no strong unique facts, there is nothing to lament. We cannot escape into the web of myth and cycle; the uniqueness of the past is the guarantee of its own transience. This is the true historical view and this is Chaucer's view. For him, however, even unique events have meaning, but only in the framework of a world view which can put history into its proper place.

Not frequently used, yet most important when it is, is the sense of spatial distance which Chaucer arouses in his readers. The events of the poem take place in faraway Asia Minor. Chaucer creates a sense of spatial distance by giving us a shifting sense of nearness and farness. At times we seem to be seeing the Trojan events as if from a great distance and at others we seem to be set down among the characters. This sense of varying distance is most subtly illustrated in the fifth book when Chaucer, after creating a most vivid sense of intimacy and closeness in describing the wooing of Criseyde by Diomede, suddenly moves to objectivity and distance in introducing the portraits of the two lovers and his heroine (799 ff.) – a device taken from Dares. With the approach of the hour of betrayal, as we become emotionally wrought up and closely involved, Chaucer the narrator brings us sharply back to his all-seeing eye and to a distance. The same technique may also be seen elsewhere in the poem. This continual inversion of the telescope increases our sense of space and gives us a kind of literary equivalent to the perspective of depth in painting.

Chaucer, in his insistence on cultural relativity, not only emphasizes chronological but also geographic variability. "Ek for to wynnen love in sondry ages,/In sondry londes, sondry been usages" (II. 27–28). Above all we get this sense of spatial distance in the final ascent of Troilus to the ogdoad, the eighth sphere,[4] where in a sense he joins [18] Chaucer in looking down on this "litel spot of erthe" and can even contemplate his own death with equanimity.

The sense of aesthetic distance[5] is evoked by the continual distinction Chaucer makes between the story and the commentator, between the framework and the inner events. Although his basic "facts" are given, Chaucer never lets the reader doubt for long that he is the narrator and interpreter of the story. Once, at least, he adopts a humorous attitude towards his dilemma. He insists that he is giving his readers Troilus' song of love (I. 400 ff.), "Naught only the sentence" as reported by Lollius but "save oure tonges difference" "every word right thus." This attitude is, however, rare. But it is not unusual for Chaucer to insist upon his bondage to the facts. Yet he strains against the snare of true events in which he is caught. Indeed Chaucer tries again and again, especially where the betrayal of Criseyde is involved, to fight against the truth of the events he is "recording." He never hides his partiality for that "hevennysh perfit creature" (I. 104), and in this attitude as in others he notifies us of the narrow latitude which is allowed him. As he approaches the actual betrayal, he slows down; and with evident reluctance, as his reiterated, "the storie telleth us" (v. 1037), "I fynde ek in the stories elleswhere" (v. 1044), "men seyn – I not" (v. 1050) show, he struggles against the predestined climax. The piling up of these phrases here emphasizes the struggle of the artist–narrator against the brutality of the facts to which he cannot give a good turn. As a faithful historian, he cannot evade the rigidity of decisive events – the given. Criseyde's re[19]ception of Diomede cannot be glossed over.[6] All this makes us more aware of Chaucer the narrator than ordinarily and increases our sense of aesthetic distance between the reporter and what is reported, between the frame and what is framed.

Finally we may call certain aspects of Chaucerian distance religious. Troilus, Pandarus, and Criseyde are pagans who lived "while men loved the lawe of kinde" (*Book of the Duchess*, l. 56) – under natural law. The great barrier of God's revelation at Sinai and in Christ separates Chaucer and us from them. Chaucer portrays them consciously as pagans, for he never puts Christian sentiments into their mouths.[7] He may violate our historic sense by making the lovers act according to the medieval courtly love code, but not by making them worship Christ. They are reasonable pagans who can attain to the truths of natural law – to the concept of a God, a creator, and to the rational moral law but never to the truths of revealed Christian religion. Chaucer is very clear on this point and in the great peroration to the poem he expressly says

> Lo here, of payens corsed olde rites,
> Lo here, what alle hire goddes may availle;
> Lo here, thise wrecched worldes appetites;
> Lo here, the fyn and guerdoun for travaille
> Of Jove, Appollo, of Mars, of swich rascaille!

> (v. 1849–53)

In general, until the end of the poem, Chaucer, as we shall see, plays down his own Christianity for good reason. He even, at times and in consonance with the epic tradition which came down to him, calls upon the pagan Muses and Furies, but he does not avoid the Christian point of view when he feels it necessary to be expressed. Although the religious barrier is not emphasized until the conclusion, we are left in no doubt [20] throughout as to its separating Chaucer from his characters. This sense of religious distance becomes at the end a vital part of the author's interpretation of his story.

A close study of Chaucer's proems written as prefaces to the first four books bears out the analysis offered here. In these Chaucer speaks out, and from his emphases and invocations we may gain some clues as to his intentions. At the beginning of the first proem, we are told of the subject of the work and of its unhappy fatal end. Chaucer does not allow us to remain in suspense at all. He exercises his role as historical commentator immediately at the outset. Tesiphone, one of the Furies, is invoked as an aid. She is a sorrowing Fury, as Dante had taught Chaucer to view her. She is responsible for the torment of humans, but she weeps for her actions. She is also in a sense the invoker himself who puts himself in his poem in a similar role. Chaucer is also a sorrowing tormenter who is retelling a true tale, the predestined end of which he cannot alter. Though ultimately he is to conquer it through religion, Chaucer the commentator is throughout most of the poem a victim of the historical determinism of his own poem. Although it is set down in the introduction to the poem, we may not understand the full meaning of Chaucer's entanglement and the escape provided by Christianity until we reach its end. There the Christian solution to the dilemma of the first proem is again presented but deepened by our knowledge of Troilus' fate and by a greater emphasis. Then, we shall have followed through the sad story under Chaucer the commentator's guidance and the answer is plain. In the proem, on the first reading, however, the problem and the solution cannot be clear in spite of Chaucer's open words. We too must discover the answer.

On the other hand, in the first prologue, he does tell us, so that we may understand, that he the conductor and recorder of his story is like Troilus after the betrayal, unhappy in love. In the *Book of the Duchess*, the dreamer's unhappiness in love is assuaged within the dream and inner story by the grief of the man in black, whose loss of his beloved foreshadows what would have happened to the dreamer's love in one form or another, for all earthly love is transitory. Death is worse than unhappiness in love. Chaucer the *Troilus* narrator who dares not pray to love "for myn unliklynesse" is also going to learn in his tale that the love of the Eternal is the only true love. Actually Chaucer, because he conceives of himself as historian, has already learned before he begins. Hence, it is not quite accurate to say as above that he is going to learn, for he already knows. The reader, however, unless he is extraordinarily acute, remains in ignorance until he finishes the whole work. He discovers in the course of the experience of the history what Chaucer already knows and has really told him in the beginning, for Chaucer concludes his first proem by calling on all lovers both successful and un[21]successful to join him in prayer for Troilus. It is, he says, only in heaven, in the *patria* of medieval theology, that we can find lasting happiness. Troilus will find a pagan equivalent for this in his pagan heaven at the end. One cannot, however, quite believe Chaucer here until one reads the poem and finds that he is deadly serious when he prays that God "graunte" unhappy lovers "soone owt of this world to pace" (I. 41). It is the love of God which is the answer to the love of woman and of all earthly things.

In other words, Chaucer in his introduction to the poem indicates his bondage to historical fact, his own grief at his position, the problem of the unhappiness in this world which he, like Troilus and all unhappy lovers, must face, and the only true solution for all the lovers of this world.

The second proem appeals to Clio, the Muse of history, and alludes to the diversity of human custom and language. The sense of history and cultural relativity manifested here emphasizes the distance in time which temporal barriers impose. "For every wight which that to Rome went/Halt not o path, or alwey o manere" (II. 36–37).

The opening of Book III calls upon Venus, goddess of love, and, although it makes other points as well, underlines again the pagan quality of the history. Venus in her symbolic, astrological, and divine role conquers the whole world and binds its dissonances and discords together. It is she who understands the mysteries of love and who explains the apparent irrationality of love. The proem closes with a brief reference to Calliope, Muse of epic poetry, as Chaucer wishes to be worthy, as an artist, of his great theme of love.

Finally, in the last proem, we have an appeal to Fortune the great presiding deity of the sublunar world. Here as always she suggests instability and transience. Chaucer then alludes to the binding power of his sources. He closes his prologue with an invocation to all the Furies and to Mars with overtones suggesting his unhappy role as commentator and the paganness of the story he is unfolding.

These proems cannot be completely explained in terms of my interpretation, for they are also, especially the third and fourth, appropriate artistically to the theme of the books they serve to introduce and the various stages of the narrative. In general they emphasize the tragic end of the tale, the unwilling Fury-like role Chaucer has to play, the historical bonds which shackle him, the pity of it all, the aloofness and distance between the Chaucer of the poem and the history itself he is telling, and the one possible solution to the unhappiness of the world. Nor are these sentiments confined to the prefaces. They occur again and again throughout the body of the poem.[8] Chaucer takes pains to create [22] himself as a character in his poem and also to dissociate this character continually from his story.

The attitude of Chaucer the character throughout makes it possible for us to understand the crucial importance of the concept of predestination in the poem. In the past there has been much debate in Chaucerian criticism over the question of predestination in *Troilus*. We know that Chaucer was profoundly interested in this question and that it was a preoccupation of his age. It seems to me that, if we regard the framework of the poem – the role that Chaucer sets himself as commentator – as a meaningful part of the poem and if we consider the various references to fate and destiny in the text, we can only come to the conclusion that the Chaucerian sense of distance and aloofness is the artistic correlative to the concept of predestination. *Troilus and Criseyde* is a medieval tragedy of predestination because the reader is continually forced by the commentator to look upon the story from the point of view of its end and from a distance. The crux of the problem of predestination is knowledge. So long as the future is not known to the participants in action, they can act as if they were free. But once a position of distance from the action is taken, then all can be seen as inevitable. And it is just this position which Chaucer the commentator takes and forces upon us from the very beginning. As John of Salisbury writes, "however, when you have entered a place, it is impossible that you have not entered it; when a thing has been done it is impossible that it be classed with things not done; and there is no recalling to non-existence a thing of the past."[9] All this presupposes knowledge which is impossible *in media re*. It is just this knowledge that Chaucer the commentator-historian gives us as he reconstructs the past. Hence we are forced into an awareness of the inevitability of the tragedy and get our future and our present at the same time, as it were.

Bound by the distance of time and space, of art and religion, Chaucer sits above his creation and foresees, even as God foresees, the doom of his own creatures: God, the *Deus artifex* who is in medieval philosophy the supreme artist and whose masterpiece is the created world.[10] But Chaucer is like God only insofar as he can know the outcome, not as creator. Analogically, because he is dealing with history, and, we must remember, to the medieval

Englishman his own history, he can parallel somewhat his Maker. He is not the creator of the events and personages he is presenting to us; hence he cannot change the results. On the other [23] hand God is the creator of His creatures; but He is bound by His own rationality and His foreknowledge. The sense of distance that Chaucer enforces on us accentuates the parallel with God and His providential predestination. We cannot leap the barriers which life imposes on us, but in the companionship of an historian we can imitate God *in parvo.* As God with His complete knowledge of future contingents sees the world laid out before Him all in the twinkling of an eye, so, in the case of history, with a guide, we share in small measure a similar experience. The guide is with us all the way, pointing to the end and to the pity of it. We must take our history from his point of view.

It is, of course, as hazardous to attribute opinions to Chaucer as it is to Shakespeare. Yet I suspect both were predestinarians – insofar as Christianity allows one to be. It is curious that all the great speeches on freedom of the will in Shakespeare's plays are put into the mouths of his villains – Edmund in *Lear,* Iago in *Othello,* and Cassius in *Julius Caesar.* This is not the place to discuss the relation of Chaucer to fourteenth-century thinking or to predestination, but I think he stands with Bishop Bradwardine who, when Chaucer was still very young, thundered against the libertarians and voluntarists because they depreciated God at the expense of His creatures and elevated man almost to the level of his Creator. Even the title of his masterpiece *De causa Dei* reveals clearly his bias. God's ways are not our ways and His grace must not be denied. His power (i.e., manifest in predestination) must be defended. Chaucer is probably with him and others on this issue and in the quarrel over future contingents which became the chief issue[11] – a reduction of the problem to logic and epistemology as befitted a century fascinated by logic and its problems. Regardless of Chaucer's personal opinion, however, I think I have shown that one of the main sources of the inner tensions of *Troilus* is this sense of necessity of an historian who knows the outcome in conflict with his sympathies as an artist and man, a conflict which gives rise to a futile struggle until the final leap which elevates the issue into a new and satisfactory context. This conflict causes the pity, the grief, the tears – and in a sense the ridiculousness and even the humor of it all.

Yet, throughout, the maturity of Chaucer's attitude is especially noteworthy. Predestination which envelops natural man implicates us all. Only from a Christian point of view can we be superior to Troilus and Criseyde and that is not due to any merit of our own, but to grace. As natural men and women we too are subject to our destiny whatever it may be. Chaucer links himself (and us) with his far-off characters, thereby strengthening the human bond over the centuries and increasing the [24] objectivity and irony of his vision. We are made to feel that this is reality, that we are looking at it as it is and even from our distance participate in it.

There is no escape from the past if one chooses to reconstruct artistically, as Chaucer does, the past from the vantage ground of the present. Chaucer's creation of himself in *Troilus* as historian-narrator and his emphasis on the distance between him and his characters repeat, in the wider frame of the present and in the panorama of complete knowledge, the helplessness and turmoil of the lovers in the inner story. The fact that Chaucer regards his story as true history does not, of course, make his point of view predestinarian; in that case all historians would be committed to a philosophy of predestination. The point is that the author creates a character – himself – to guide us through his historical narrative, to emphasize the pitiful end throughout, to keep a deliberate distance suggested and stated in various ways between him and us and the characters of the inner story. He makes his chief character awake to the fact of predestination towards the end of the story and at the conclusion has this character join, as it were, us and Chaucer the character – in space instead of time – in seeing his own story through the perspective of distance. It is all this which gives us the clue. The outer frame is not merely a perspective of omniscience but also of impotence and is in fact another level of the story. It serves as the realm of Mount Ida in the *Iliad* – a wider cadre which enables us to put the humans involved into their proper place.

Every age has its polarities and dichotomies, some more basic than others. To believing medieval man, the fundamental division is between the created and the uncreated. God as the uncreated Creator is the unchanging norm against which all His creatures must be set and the norm which gives the created world its true objectivity. The true Christian was bound to keep the universe in perspective: it was only one of the poles of this fundamental polarity. The city of God gives meaning to the city of the world.

The impasse of the characters can only be solved on this other level and in this wider cadre. Actually for Troilus and Criseyde there is no final but merely a temporary solution – the consolation of philosophy – from which only the betrayed lover can benefit. Troilus begins to approach his narrator's viewpoint as he struggles against his fate beginning in the fourth book. The political events have taken a turn against him, and he tries to extricate himself and his beloved. But he is trapped and, what is even worse, long before Criseyde leaves he becomes aware of his mistake in consenting to let her go. In spite of her optimistic chatter, he predicts almost exactly what will happen when she joins her father. And he tells her so (IV. 1450 ff.). Yet like one fascinated by his own [25] doom he lets her go. He struggles but, in spite of his premonitions, seems unable to do anything about it.

It has long been recognized that Troilus' speech in favor of predestination (IV. 958 ff.) is an important element in the poem.[12] It certainly indicates that Troilus believes in predestination, and I think in the light of what we have been saying here represents a stage in Troilus' approach to Chaucer. When, in the pagan temple, he finally becomes aware of destiny,[13] he is making an attempt to look at his own fate as Chaucer the commentator all along has been looking at it. The outer and inner stories are beginning to join each other. This movement of narrator and character towards each other in the last two books culminates in the ascent through the spheres at the end where Troilus gets as close to Chaucer (and us) as is possible in observing events in their proper perspective – *sub specie aeternitatis*. As Boethius writes in the *Consolation of Philosophy*

> Huc [Nunc] omnes pariter uenite capti
> Quos fallax ligat improbis catenis
> Terrenas habitans libido mentes
> Haec erit uobis requies laborum,
> Hic portus placida manens quiete,
> Hoc patens unum miseris asylum.

(III, metrum x)

Or as Chaucer himself translates these lines

> Cometh alle to gidre now, ye that ben
> ykaught and ybounde with wikkide cheynes
> by the desceyvable delyt of erthly
> thynges enhabitynge in your thought! Her
> schal ben the reste of your labours, her is
> the havene stable in pesible quiete; this
> allone is the open refut to wreches.

From this vantage point all falls into its place and proper proportion. [26] Troilus now has Chaucer's sense of distance and joins with his author in finding what peace can be found in a pagan heaven.

Just before this soul journey, Chaucer has even consigned his very poem to time and put it in its place along with all terrestrial things (v. 1793 ff.) in the kingdom of mutability and change. As Chaucer can slough off his earthly attachments and prides, even the very poem in which he is aware of their transitory nature, Troilus his hero can also do so.

Thus towards the end, in the last two books, we see the hero beginning to imitate his narrator and the narrator, his hero, and the distance set up between the two begins to lessen and almost disappear. A dialectic of distance and closeness which has been from the beginning more than implicit in the poem between God, Chaucer the commentator-narrator, and the characters – notably Troilus – of the inner story, becomes sharply poised, with the triangle shrinking as the three approach each other.[14] A final shift of depth and distance, however, takes place at the end. The poem does not come to a close with Troilus joining Chaucer. A further last leap is to establish again, even as at the beginning, a new distance. Beyond the consolation of philosophy, the only consolation open to Troilus is the consolation of Christianity. In the last stanzas, Chaucer the narrator escapes from Troilus to where the pagan cannot follow him; he escapes into the contemplation of the mysteries of the Passion and of the Trinity, the supreme paradox of all truth, which is the only possible way for a believing Christian to face the facts of his story. The artist and the historian who have been struggling in the breast of Chaucer can finally be reconciled. Here free will and predestination, human dignity and human pettiness, joy and sorrow, in short all human and terrestrial contradictions, are reconciled in the pattern of all reconciliation: the God who becomes man and whose trinity is unity and whose unity is trinity. Here the author-historian can finally find his peace at another distance and leave behind forever the unhappy and importunate Troilus, the unbearable grief of Criseyde's betrayal, the perplexities of time and space, and the tyranny of history and predestination.

Notes

1 On this point in connection with the *Canterbury Tales* see Donaldson's stimulating "Chaucer the Pilgrim," *PMLA*, LXIX (1954), 928–936. I am indebted to Professor Donaldson for several suggestions made orally to me which I have woven into this article – notably the root idea of n. 14 below.

2 For what they are worth, I give the following statistics on the first book. All Chaucer quotations are from the edn. of F. N. Robinson, Boston, 1933. The following passages seem to me to belong wholly or partially to the narrator as commentator: ll. 1–56 (proem), 57–63, 100, 133, 141–147, 159, 211–217, 232–266, 377–378, 393–399, 450–451 (a direct rapport remark), 492–497, 737–749 (doubtful), 1086–92. Excluding ll. 737–749, we find that 141 lines out of 1092 may be said to be comments by the author as commentator. Roughly 12% of the lines of the first book (one line in 8⅓ lines) belong to the commentator. Even allowing for subjective impressions, 10% would certainly be fair. This is a remarkably high percentage I should say. The proem I shall analyze below. The other remarks bear on his sources, moralize, establish a mood of acceptance, indicate distance and pastness and refer to fate and destiny. For overt references to fate and providence in the poem, see the list in Eugene E. Slaughter, "Love and Grace in Chaucer's *Troilus*," *Essays in Honor of Walter Clyde Curry* (Nashville, 1955), p. 63, n. 8.

3 See Morton W. Bloomfield, "Chaucer's Sense of History," *JEGP*, LI (1952), 301–313.

4 Although irrelevant to the point I am making about the sense of distance in the journey to or through the spheres, there is some question as to the reading and meaning here (v. 1809). I follow Robinson and Root [ed. *The Book of Troilus and Criseyde* (Princeton: Princeton University Press 1926)] who take the reading "eighth" rather than "seventh" as in most manuscripts.[. . .]

5 Needless to say I am not using this phrase in the sense given it by Edward Bullough in his " 'Psychical Distance' as a Factor in Art and an Aesthetic Principle," *Brit. Jour. of Psychol.*, v (1913), reprinted in *A Modern Book of Esthetics, An Anthology*, ed. Melvin Rader, rev. ed. (New York, 1952) pp. 401–428. He refers to "distance" between the art object on the one hand and the artist or audience on the other. The distance here referred to is within the poem, between the character-narrator Chaucer and the events.

6 Chaucer sets himself the problem of interpreting Criseyde's action here by his sympathetic portrayal of her character and by his unblinking acceptance of the "facts" of his history. Boccaccio evades it by his pre-eminent interest in Troilus. Henryson gives Troilus an "unhistorical" revenge. Shakespeare has blackened Cressida's character throughout. Christopher Hassall, in his libretto for William Walton's recent opera on the subject, makes Criseyde a victim of a mechanical circumstance and completely blameless. Only Chaucer, by a strict allegiance to the "historical" point of view, poses the almost unbearable dilemma of the betrayal of Troilus by a charming and essentially sympathetic Criseyde.

7 The only exception is to be found in the Robinson text where at III. 1165 we find

the reading in a speech by Criseyde "by that God that bought us both two." I am convinced that the Root reading "wrought" for "bought" is correct. It would be perfectly possible for pagans to use "wrought" but not "bought." If we admit "bought" it would be the only Christian allusion put into the mouths of the Trojan characters and would conflict with the expressedly pagan attitude of these figures. I now take a stronger position on the matter than I allowed myself to express in "Chaucer's Sense of History," *JEGP*, LI (1952), 308, n. 17. Various references to grace, the devil (I. 805), a bishop (II. 104), saints' lives (II. 118) and celestial love (I. 979) need not, from Chaucer's point of view of antiquity, be taken as Christian.

8 See n. 2 above.

9 *Policraticus*, II, 22, ed. C. C. I. Webb (Oxford, 1909), I, 126. The translation is by Joseph B. Pike, *Frivolities of Courtiers* (Minneapolis, 1938), p. 111. Incidentally it should be noted that Calchas' foreknowledge through divination is on a basic level the cause of the tragedy.

10 "We are looking on at a tragedy that we are powerless to check or avert. Chaucer himself conveys the impression of telling the tale under a kind of duress" (G. L. Kittredge, *Chaucer and his Poetry*, Cambridge, 1915, p. 113).

11 On this dispute in the 14th century, see L. Baudry, *La querelle des futurs contingents* (Paris, 1950), and Paul Vignaux, *Justification et prédestination au XIVᵉ siècle* (Paris, 1934).

12 I am aware, of course, that this famous speech was added only in the second or final version of the poem as Root has clearly shown. I do not think that this point is of much relevance to my argument one way or another. Inasmuch as we can probably never know why Chaucer added the passage, one explanation is as good as another. We must take the poem in its final form as our object for analysis. My case, which is admittedly subjective, does not rest on this passage. It may be that Chaucer felt that by adding this speech he was making clearer a point he already had in mind. Or it is possible that it was only on his second revision that he saw the full implications of his argument. Or finally it may have occurred to him that by bringing Troilus closer to his own position before the end, he would deepen the significance of what he wished to say. These explanations for the addition are at least as plausible and possible as any other.

13 The location of this speech is not, I think, without significance. The end of pagan or purely natural religion is blind necessity, and in its "church" this truth can best be seen.

14 Another triangle has its apex in Pandarus who is, of course, the artist of the inner story as Chaucer is of the outer one and as God is of the created world. Pandarus works on his material – Troilus and especially Criseyde – as his "opposite numbers" do with their materials. All are to some extent limited – Pandarus by the characters of his friend and niece and by political events; Chaucer by his knowledge and by history; God by His rationality. All this is another story, however; my interest here is primarily in the triangle with Troilus as apex.

5 Troilus and Criseide

E. TALBOT DONALDSON

Originally published as a commentary in E. T. Donaldson, *Chaucer's Poetry: An Anthology for the Modern Reader* (New York: Ronald, 1958, pp. 965–80). The text here is from the second edition (1975, copyright by Scott, Foresman and Company, pp. 1129–44). Reprinted by permission of Harper Collins, Publishers. The pagination of the second edition is recorded within square brackets.

Chaucer's longest single poem is his greatest artistic achievement and one of the greatest in English literature. It possesses to the highest degree that quality, which characterizes most great poetry, of being always open to reinterpretation, of yielding different meanings to different generations and kinds of readers, who, no matter how they may disagree with one another on even its most important points, nevertheless agree in sharing the profoundly moving experience the poem offers them. Its highly elusive quality, which not only permits but encourages a multiplicity of interpretations, is in no way the result of incompetence on the part of the poet, but something carefully sought after as the best way of expressing a complex vision.

Chaucer is believed to have completed the work about 1385 or 1386, with some fifteen years of productivity remaining to him. Only extraordinary resourcefulness could bring it about that, having accomplished in *Troilus* what might well seem the principal work of his life, he was able to turn to other themes and other attitudes with undiminished energy and enthusiasm for experimentation. Readers occasionally wonder why romantic love – which is both a theme and an attitude – plays so little part in the *Canterbury Tales* that employed the last years of his life: the explanation lies in *Troilus*. Chaucer was apparently aware that he could not surpass his own treatment of this subject. And magnificent as the Canterbury collection is, both in the large conception and in the individual tales, *Troilus'* grandeur remains unsurpassed.

The source of the poem is one of Boccaccio's youthful works, the *Filostrato* (the Love-Stricken, according to Boccaccio's false etymology), a passionate narrative of 5700 lines in stanzaic Italian verse, completed before 1350, probably about 1340. Boccaccio's poem, in the original Italian and in a French translation, furnished Chaucer the essential plot, most of the narrative details – [1130] though Chaucer made a number of important additions – and even with a number of lines readily adapted to translation into English. Yet the qualities of the two poems are entirely different, and Chaucer's is, artistically speaking, by far the more original. In the clear, brilliant light of the Italian work everything seems fully realized, fully understood. One reads with interest, admiration, and excitement: the mind's eye is filled. Yet there is little in the poem that does not meet the eye, and the reader does not tend to re-create what he has seen after he no longer sees it. By contrast, Chaucer's poem is mist-enshrouded: the sun does, indeed, break through at times, but things are difficult to see steadily for more than a short period, reappear in changed shape, become illusory, vanish; as the poem progresses one finds oneself groping more and more in a world where forms are indistinct but have infinite suggestiveness; the mind creates and re-creates; and at the end one has not so much beheld an experience objectively as lived it in the emotions.

As in so many of Chaucer's poems, the guise of the narrator is important to an interpretation of the work. At the outset this seems to be the familiar one of the unloved servant of the God of Love, the man whose inexperience renders him singularly ill-fitted to write a romance, but who will nevertheless perform the pious act of translating – of all things! – an unhappy love story. As in the *Parliament of Fowls*, the value of love within the poem is heightened by the narrator's exclusion from it, his yearning toward it. But this lyrical function of the narrator is in *Troilus* less important than his dual, paradoxical function as a historian whose knowledge of the story is wholly book-derived and as an invisible yet omnipresent participant in the action. It is as a historian that he first presents himself – a rather fussy, nervous scholar who has got hold of some old books, particularly one by Lollius, that tell the story of the Trojan lovers. This he means to translate, although he complains that his sources fail to give as much information as they ought. Nevertheless, they present the essentials: the sorrow Troilus suffered before he won Criseide, and how she forsook him in the end (Bk. I, 55–56). Starting out with such inadequate and unpromising data, the historian proceeds to re-create the story as if he himself were living it without knowing its outcome. His second guise, that of the participant, unlike the guise of the historian, is largely implicit, a matter of the emotional intensity and lack of ob[1131]jectivity with which he approaches the characters. As the poem proceeds, the tension between the two attitudes, the historian dealing with incontrovertible fact, the participant speaking from equally incontrovertible emotional experience, increases until it becomes almost unendurable. By the beginning of Book IV (lines 15–21) the narrator's love for Criseide has become such that when he finds himself forced to face the issue of her perfidy he comes close to denying the truth of his old books. *For how Criseide Troilus forsook*, he begins, forthrightly enough; but reluctance to credit the bare statement causes him to soften it:

> Or at the leeste, how that she was unkinde,
> Moot hennesforth been matere of my book,
> As writen folk thurgh which it is in minde:

> Allas that they sholde evere cause finde
> To speke hire harm – and if they on hire lie,
> Ywis, hemself sholde han the vilainye.

It is a strange historian who becomes so emotionally involved with the personages of his history that he is willing to impugn the reliability of the sources upon which his whole knowledge of those personages presumably depends.

These two divergent attitudes of the narrator come to form an image of the philosophical speculation that permeates much of the poem: is it possible in this world to maintain a single firm idea of the reality of any given human situation or character? This speculation may be best illustrated in its bearing on Criseide, upon whom so much of the emotional force of the poem centers. History records the literal fact that Criseide proved, in the end, unworthy of the love Troilus bore her. This is the flattest, most basic, and least assailable of realities. (At the time Chaucer was writing, Criseide's character may not yet have suffered the deterioration that, by Shakespeare's time, made her a kind of literary model of the unfaithful woman; nevertheless Chaucer's method of handling her is essentially what it would have been if the process had already taken place.) Despite our knowledge of the ending, the narrator's loving presentation of Criseide in the course of the poem makes us feel the powerful attraction that brought about Troilus' love; and we are even persuaded that she was worthy of it. Indeed, *Troilus* gains something of the poignancy of the elegy by the very fact that we are aware of Criseide's eventual perfidy at the same time the [1132] narrator is depicting the profound spell she casts – just as we know that Blanche, in the *Book of the Duchess*, is dead even while the Black Knight describes the charm of her vitality. History tends to pronounce judgment on the final perfidy of Criseide as effectively nullifying her positive worth as a human being; but the historical point of view does not exhaust the reality of Criseide as the heroine of the poem.

It is true that at the end of the poem we are left with two widely different versions of Criseide's reality, versions made mutually exclusive by the conventions of romance. These conventions make it impossible for a heroine worthy of love to prove faithless; and ultimately we must, of course, bow to the fact of her faithlessness. We must remember, however, that it was Chaucer's aim to make the reader suffer vicariously the experience of Troilus. The poet therefore creates in the person of Criseide one of the most alluring of heroines; and more, he persuades us that her downfall does not so much falsify our first judgment of her as compel us to see the tragic nature of reality, in which the best so often becomes the worst.

Criseide's most emphatically displayed characteristic is amiability – that is, lovability: she has almost all the qualities that men might hope to encounter in their first loves. This is perhaps the same as saying that she is above all feminine, suggesting for a young man like Troilus the compelling mystery and challenge of her sex. She is lovely in appearance, demure yet self-possessed, capable of both gaiety and gravity, glamorous in the truest sense of the word. Although she says nothing really witty, she responds to Pandarus' wit in such a way as to seem witty; her constant awareness of implications beneath the surface of the situation suggests, if it does not prove, intelligence. With her uncle and with Troilus she has the curiously endearing charm that arises from her consciousness, humorously and wryly expressed, of her own complicity in the events that befall her. The grace and tenderness with which she finally yields to Troilus (Bk. III, 1210–11) are almost magically appealing.

But Chaucer did something more than present Criseide as the completely agreeable heroine; he also suggested in her a really complex human being, filled with all sorts of latent qualities which are much more than mere enhancements of her magnetism. Chaucer's presentation, indeed, is so full as to invite his readers to find in Criseide the seeds of her eventual falseness; [1133] but Criseide's potentialities as a human being, so brilliantly sketched as partly to justify calling *Troilus* a psychological novel, elude us in the end. Several excellent critics have purported to find in this or that one of her qualities the definitive clue to her betrayal, but others continue to feel that the mainsprings of her action lie hidden. It seems to follow that if the poet were trying to make her motivation psychologically clear, he failed badly. It is, however, certain that this was not his purpose. Instead, he meant to present in Criseide a broad range of the undefined but recognizable potentialities inherent in human nature.

Our longest and seemingly most penetrating view into Criseide's character is afforded by Book II (596 ff), when we are shown her reactions to the news her uncle brings her about Troilus' love. These reactions are filled with apparent clues to her basic character, but when analyzed they lead to the ambiguous conclusions. Criseide is much concerned with Troilus' high estate as a prince of Troy, and this concern might be interpreted as indicative of opportunism; conversely, because her already precarious situation in the city might make it dangerous to refuse him, her concern might be interpreted as fearfulness. If the fact of her concern, regardless of what it springs from, is taken as an indication of an overcalculating nature, then the impression is counterbalanced by her involuntary moment of intoxication when she sees Troilus, in all his martial glory, riding homeward from battle. This incident in turn might suggest an oversensual nature; but the circumspection with which, a little later, she considers the whole affair might well reinforce an impression of her frigidity. Again, her inability to make up her mind might be taken to prove her indecisiveness and ineffectuality; on the other hand, since the problems she is facing are entirely realistic, it might be used to prove her native practicality.

The narrator is of singularly little assistance to the reader who is trying to solve the enigma. On every crucial psychological issue both he and his old books are silent. We do not know, though we may suspect, what Criseide thought when Pandarus told her Troilus was out of town the day she came to dine. We never know to what extent she was influenced by her uncle's

specious, often self-contradictory, arguments. And the narrator's explanations are even worse than his silences. For instance, just after Criseide
experiences the moment of intoxication mentioned above, the narrator
pauses to consider the hypothetical objection [1134] of some envious person
that she was falling in love too fast (Bk. II, 666 ff). With a fine show of
indignation he protests that she did not fall in love immediately: she merely
began to incline toward Troilus, who had to win her with long service. The
effect of this kind of explanation – of which there are a number in the poem –
is complex, not to say chaotic. The reader, who may never have thought that
Criseide is proceeding too fast, is suddenly encouraged to think she is by the
narrator's gratuitous denial. The reader is made, as it were, an involuntary
critic of the action instead of a mere spectator. Moreover, he is made to judge
Criseide according to a norm that the narrator's tone assumes to be well
known but that is in fact undefined and totally unknown, namely, the
decorous rate of speed with which a woman should fall in love. Finally,
having cleared Criseide of a charge which only he has made, the narrator
asserts, in the very next stanza, that it was not her fault but Troilus' destiny
that she should fall in love with him so soon. Analyzed by the intellect alone,
the passage seems to suggest that Criseide did fall in love too quickly. Yet it
precedes the far longer one in which she considers the whole matter so
carefully that some critics have accused her of proceeding too deliberately!

The fact is that we do not read poetry with the intellect alone, and that
when poetry makes two contradictory statements they do not cancel each
other out. Both remain as part of the essential poetic truth, which is not the
same thing at all as logic. There is surely no abstract, logical, ideal course of
action for a woman falling in love, but we can recognize the process as being
truly represented by Criseide. Some parts of her nature are driving her
forward with a speed that is utterly terrifying to the rest of her nature, and a
bewildering variety of motives assert themselves in turn. But however we
analyze these, in the long run we can say with assurance only that they are
human. Any one of them, given a development which the poem resolutely
refuses to permit, might become the reason for her eventual betrayal: mere
timidity, mere opportunism, mere sensuality, mere inefficiency – even mere
femininity. As it stands, however, we are emotionally no more prepared for
the denouement than Troilus, though we have had one important advantage
over him: we have been permitted to see, and have been disturbed by,
suggestions of depths in Criseide that her lover could not have seen. Our
confidence in her is less serene, particularly as a result of the narrator's [1135]
reassurances. It may be that her very elusiveness makes us nervous. If so, that
is as it should be, since the only possible resolution of the two realities
mentioned earlier lies in the unpredictability, the instability, of even the most
lovely of mortal women.

Just as in later literature Criseide was to become the type of a faithless
woman, so her charming, witty, intelligent uncle Pandarus was, by a worse
fate, to become the type of a pimp. In a long conversation in Book III
(238–420) Pandarus and Troilus discuss, among other things, the implications of Pandarus' helping Troilus win Criseide. The conclusion they come

to is less than satisfactory: Pandarus' help is not the act of a procurer because he receives no reward for it. Thereafter the matter is not one of the overt issues of the poem, though in his last speech to Troilus (Bk. V, 1734–36) Pandarus reverts to it almost as if he foresaw the deterioration of his name Pandar to pander. And while not overt, the issue once raised can never be wholly banished from the mind. Parallel to the question the poem raises about Criseide, "Is her reality that of a worthy lover or that of an unfaithful wench?" is the question it raises about Pandarus' assistance of Troilus: "Is this the action of a loyal friend or of a mere pimp?"

History – in this case later literary history – has answered the question to the detriment of Pandarus, but the answer this poem gives is less absolute. The reader is assured by everyone – by Troilus, by Pandarus himself, by the narrator – that what Pandarus does is done wholly because of his devotion to Troilus, and surely the moralist must admit that human action is qualified by the motives of the agent. Yet, just as was the case with Criseide, when we watch his character in action we seem to glimpse potentials – undefined, to be sure – that are not of a piece with the notion of a friend acting with entire altruism. In general he seems, like his niece, a person of great charm: gay, cheerful, witty, mocking and self-mocking, friendly, helpful, practical, intelligent, sympathetic, loyal – one could hardly wish for a better companion or friend. But despite these qualities, one's confidence in him does not remain altogether secure. Perhaps his pleasure in arranging this affair is too great. The brilliant comedy he performs at the lovers' bedside – a touch of the *Miller's Tale* – is perhaps suggestive of some vital flaw in his nature (and the narrator does nothing to improve the situation by failing to send Pandarus off to his own chamber). Even the delightful [1136] scene of Pandarus' visit to Criseide's bedside after Troilus has departed is not without a hint of prurience. In the long run, it may be said of the complexity of Pandarus, as of the complexity of Criseide, that it displays such a rich array of human qualities that we are at a loss in analyzing his ultimate motives and character.

Pandarus bears a relation to the problem of reality – and hence to the philosophical speculation that is carried on in the poem – in another way. He is what would generally be called today a thoroughgoing realist. Paradoxically, this seems to mean that he has no respect for reality at all. For him, things are whatever one makes them. To accomplish a given action, all one has to do is manipulate the situation so as to produce the proper pressures on the actors. It does not matter in the least if these pressures are in reality non-existent; it only matters that the actors should think them real. In putting his philosophy to work, Pandarus becomes the master-spinner of illusions. A persecutor from whom Criseide needs protection is conjured up out of thin air. A dinner party is manipulated with excruciating attention to detail so that Criseide may be introduced to Troilus under the most respectable of circumstances. When Criseide must be induced to receive Troilus in her bedchamber, a rival lover named Horaste, whom Criseide had never smiled upon and Troilus had never felt jealous of, emerges full-blown from Pandarus' fertile mind to produce the necessary pressure. And if Pandarus cannot actually produce rain, his foreknowledge that rain will come serves the magician's purpose of insuring that his dinner guest will stay the night. The love affair itself seems to result largely from the illusions Pandarus creates for the paralyzed Troilus and the passive Criseide. One would not be surprised if he were to dictate Troilus' first letter to Criseide and then to dictate her response, so close does he come to being the author of a living fiction.

Upon the significance of all this illusion-spinning the poem makes no overt comment. It even fails to distinguish clearly between real and illusory pressures exerted on Criseide: for instance, we do not know whether Pandarus' account of his discovering Troilus' love-sicknesses (Bk. II, 505–53) is in the realm of fact or merely a charming invention with which to please Criseide. But in the poem's totality the implications of Pandarus' illusions cannot be avoided, because we know that in the end [1137] Criseide's love of Troilus will prove to be a kind of illusion. Moreover, the dominant role the illusions play in the love affair, whether commented on or not, forces them on our consciousness, and once more we experience a sense of insecurity. This is embodied in the poem by the interchange between the lovers when their love is consummated (Bk. III, 1338–52); both of them, especially Troilus, express uncertainty whether such bliss can in fact be true.

Pandarus continues a realist and a would-be manipulator of realities until the end, when reality defeats him. His first reaction on hearing that Criseide must leave the city is that the love affair is finished. He tries to persuade Troilus to give her up (Bk. IV, 380 ff), to forget about her, and when that practical approach fails, as it is doomed to, he tries another equally practical one, equally doomed to fail: forcefully to prevent her going. When Troilus replies, with his usual integrity, that he cannot constrain Criseide against her will, Pandarus observes that if Criseide consents to leave Troy, Troilus must consider her false (Bk. IV, 610–15). With this speech – which, incidentally, is the most strikingly revealing of several of Pandarus' reflections on Criseide in the last two books – his effective role in the poem is completed. From then on all he can do is act as go-between. His efforts to rearrange reality in order to preserve the love affair are paltry and futile. After Criseide's departure from Troy we see him upholding Troilus' hopes even when he himself recognizes their futility, and while in the earlier books Pandarus' attempts to uphold illusion did not seem offensive, now they seem the work of a half-hearted trickster. It is almost as if the reality he had tortured were having its revenge on him by redefining his actions as those of a mere procurer: for Criseide, after all, becomes little better than a whore. In the end Pandarus – and Pandarus alone – accepts history's version of Criseide: by saying, in his pathetic last speech (Bk. V, 1731–43), that he hates her, he makes clear that for him any other value she may have seemed to possess has been canceled out. He submits to the ultimate reality as Troilus, who can never "unlove" Criseide, refuses to do; yet one has felt that Pandarus' love for his niece was, in its way, as great as Troilus'.

Troilus, the hero of the poem and the most important of its personages, may seem in some respects less interesting than Pandarus or Criseide. If, however, he lacks their human variety, his [1138] *trouthe*, his integrity, makes him in the long run a more fully realized person. This integrity, the quality that he will not surrender even to keep Criseide with him, is the one human value the poem leaves entirely unquestioned: it is because of it that Troilus is granted his ultimate vision. It places him, of course, in sharp contrast with Criseide and her *untrouthe*, and since one of the meanings of *trouthe* is reality, he emerges as more real than she. The sad fact that integrity does him no practical good does not in any way impair its value; indeed, its value seems enhanced by its preventing him, at least on one occasion, from attaining an apparent good. If he had been a different person – a Diomede, for instance – he might well have used force to stop Criseide's exchange. This is what Pandarus advises and what both narrator and reader momentarily find themselves hoping for. But Troilus is acutely aware of both the public and the private implications of such an act. Criseide's exchange had been legally determined by the parliament and duly ratified by King Priam, and to prevent it forcefully would be to substitute anarchy for law: the Trojan war had itself been caused by Paris' rape of Queen Helen, and to seize Criseide would be once again to risk precipitating endless violent countermeasures. Furthermore, according to the medieval conventions of courtly love, the lover was the servant of his mistress – as the word *mistress* still suggests – and for the servant to overrule the mistress was unthinkable. As it frequently does, the courtly convention here merely articulates a real factor in the relationship of civilized men and women. A lover cannot impose his will upon his love, for unless she remains at all times possessed of free will, love itself becomes meaningless and the love affair vitiated. Similarly, to seize her would be inevitably to disclose their love affair and ruin her good name, which, according to the courtly code, he was sworn to protect. In view of these matters, for Troilus to "ravish" Criseide would be for him to violate his own nature, which, as Criseide perceives, is one of moral virtue, grounded upon truth.

But if Troilus is the only unequivocally worthwhile person in the poem, why, one must ask, is he its principal sufferer? Troilus ascribes his misery to the operation of Fortune, or malevolent fate. A heavy atmosphere of fatality does, indeed, hang over the poem, so that even if the reader had not been told the outcome of the love affair he might feel it inevitable that Troilus should [1139] in the end fall, like Troy. Yet with one exception all the specific incidents, although the narrator may invoke for them the causality of the stars, seem equally attributable to the action of one of the three actors in the love tragedy. The exception is the intervention of Criseide's forgotten father Calchas, an intervention that comes from his sure foreknowledge of the city's doom and that is beyond the control of Pandarus or the lovers. Elsewhere causality is ambiguous. For instance, the narrator ascribes to astrological influences entirely remote from Criseide's control the rain which prevented Criseide's leaving her uncle's house. On the other hand, we are aware that the rain had been foreseen by Pandarus, so that what may be deemed fate in its relation to Criseide is at the same time mere machination on the part of Pandarus. Nor are we sure enough of Criseide's state of mind in accepting her uncle's invitation – the narrator has been marvelously ambiguous about that too – clearly to exonerate her from an acquiescence in a foreseen fate so prompt as to make fate's role negligible. But here as elsewhere the impression of fatal influence is not canceled out by the impression of human responsibility: both impressions remain and even unite into a single impression poetically truer than either by itself. Similarly, Troilus' failure to prevent Criseide from leaving Troy, while it is the result of his own free will, might still be ascribed to fate, for in order to have stopped her Troilus would have had to be someone other than Troilus, and this he could not be.

In a more universal and more tragic sense, the impossibility of a human being's becoming anything but what he is is one of the principal points – perhaps the principal point – that the poem makes, and it is toward this point that the poem has been steadily moving. The form, as has been said above, is that of a history, the end of which is known, being lived by personages who do not know their end, and presented at times as if neither narrator nor reader knows it. Preoccupied constantly during the presentation with the charm and delight of humanity as represented by Criseide and Pandarus, we can little more believe that things will turn out as they do than can Troilus. The fact that they turn out as they do almost seems, at times, a violation of our idea of reality; within the poem we are now and again apt to ascribe the ending to a malevolent fate which, in order to bring about what it foresees, contorts and constrains events and persons from their natural course. This is the ultimate conclusion of [1140] which Troilus is capable in his lifetime. His long soliloquy in Book IV (958–1078) on predestination and free will comes in its tortured circularity to nothing more than a statement that what God has foreseen must be – that free will does not exist. This soliloquy, of course, precedes any suspicion on his part of Criseide's infidelity, so that he is not forced to consider the problem of her free will operating evilly. When suspicions have once occurred, he is no longer able to think even as clearly as he does here, but vacillates pathetically between the two conflicting realities, Criseide's apparently true love and Criseide's faithlessness. His still relatively happy ignorance stops him in his soliloquy from going to the extreme of accusing his god of devising a plot that does not fit its characters; but this is an accusation that occasional readers have, with some reason, made against Chaucer the poet, just as Chaucer the narrator comes close to making it against his old books.

But to the profoundly medieval, profoundly Christian Chaucer there could be no other plot because there could be no other characters. According to some medieval thinkers, the whole duty of the historian was to find in recorded history the image of instability: it is in this sense that the *Monk's Tale* presents history, bad as the tale is. The premise underlying such a definition of history is that natural, fallen man is unstable. Chaucer, while surely not bound to any arbitrary point of view, presents in *Troilus and Criseide* a pattern of human instability. Criseide is its chief exponent in terms of human character; Pandarus in terms of human action. Troilus comes, because of his *trouthe*, as near to stability as man may come; but within a world where mutation is the law – and in a world in which the stability of a Christian God does not exist – it does him no good. Given Boethius or Christian doctrine, Troilus might have progressed beyond the point he does in his soliloquy on foreordination. As it is, he concludes where Boethius began in his *Consolation of Philosophy*, before Philosophy had persuaded him that he must not commit himself wholly and exclusively to this unstable world. Troilus' *trouthe* is, as has been said above, a real value; but within the terms set by the poem, it must remain only a moral value, imitating one aspect of God, who is *Trouthe*, but hopelessly limited in other respects. Despite its alternate meaning, reality, it cannot help Troilus perceive ultimate reality, which only God can perceive; conversely, it cannot defend him [1141] against illusion – the illusion of Criseide's stability, of the enduring power of human love. It cannot, in short, enable him to see that of all the conflicting realities the poem presents none is in the end real, since compared to the reality of God no earthly substance has reality.

The poem comes to its tragic conclusion by no such bald statement as the above. We have seen how in the ambiguity of the characterization of Criseide and Pandarus there has been, since the beginning, the potential of instability. One might say that in their very elusiveness, their unknowability, resides equally the image of unreality. And we have since the beginning been fully aware of where the story is leading, though our willingness to forget is the product of Chaucer's art. As the poem approaches its climax – or anticlimax – the poet so manipulates us that while we continue our intense involvement with the characters, we begin to see them increasingly in the light of historical generalization. Halfway through the fifth book this manipulation appears most brilliantly. It is the ninth night after Criseide's departure, and we are taken to the Greek camp to see how she is faring with her plots to return to Troy, as she had promised, on the tenth day (Bk. V, 686 ff). Her pathetic soliloquy, so futile, so devoid of resource, so spiritless, leaves us infinitely saddened. The narrator, seemingly in hot pursuit of his story, turns quickly to Diomede, and for a moment we enter that blunt, aggressive, unillusioned mind. Diomede's interior monologue completed, the narrator, as if suddenly recalling his own failure to characterize Diomede earlier, gives us a one-stanza pen-portrait of him. And then, by a curious afterthought, he gives a three-stanza description of Criseide and a two-stanza description of Troilus (Bk. V, 806–40). The quality of these is, contextually, strange in the extreme: they are impersonal, trivial, oversimplified – as if a historian had collected all the information there was about several persons of no special significance and were listing it, not because of its inherent interest, but because the historian's duty is to assemble and preserve any sort of scraps turned up during his research. And indeed these scraps are in a very real sense the oldest historical material relating to the story of Troilus and Criseide, the sparse material from which the full-grown story eventually sprang. Chaucer's source for the portraits is not Boccaccio, but rather a sixth-century narrative of the fall of Troy ascribed to Dares the Phrygian. This book pads out its paltry [1142] fiction with brief descriptions of important people concerned with the Trojan war, among them Diomede, Troilus, and Criseide, described just as Chaucer describes them in Book V but still some centuries removed from the relationship later writers were to give them. When, nearing the end of his poem, Chaucer saw that it was time to turn from the guise of the passionately committed participant to the guise of the objective, remote, detached historian, he did so with a vengeance. Perhaps nowhere else in the poem are the two conflicting versions of reality more boldly juxtaposed. Certainly nowhere else is the shock so great as when the historian, having listed a miscellany of Criseide's attributes, some trivial but all agreeable enough, brings the portrait to the muted conclusion:

> Tendre-herted, sliding of corage –
> But trewely I can nat telle hir age.
>
> [V. 825–26]

Sliding of corage: the simple unemphatic statement of Criseide's instability of heart is not even the climax of the portrait. From the point of view of the realistic historian, human nature is capable only of anticlimax.

The sudden re-emergence of the detached historian at this point in Book V provides a kind of foretaste of the dominant mood in which the poem concludes; but the narrator's other guise continues to reappear whenever Criseide is mentioned. Indeed, Chaucer's manipulation of the two guises, and through them of the reader, is nowhere more adroit than in his handling of Criseide's betrayal. Time and again while the narrative inexorably demonstrates the progress of her infidelity the narrator leaps to her defense, and by the very inadequacy of the defense reinforces the reader's condemnation of her. The most striking instance of this technique occurs after Diomede has visited Criseide on the eleventh day, when she has already broken her promise to Troilus. The interview she has with Diomede is not described; instead the narrator rapidly summarizes all the later history of her amorous dealings with the Greek (Bk. V, 1030–50). And then, having given to the whole history of her treachery the emotional impact of a single action committed in a day or two, he indignantly asserts that while his books are silent on this subject, all this successful wooing by Diomede must have taken a long time! As if this were not enough, he carries us back to Troy to show us Troilus, standing on the walls, still scanning [1143] the outlying roads for his beloved. Months of action have rushed by in the Greek camp, but in Troy it is still only the tenth day, the day Criseide is to return.

Thus the poem moves with mounting emotional force to its conclusion. The actual ending of the poem (Bk. V, 1765 ff.) – generally though incorrectly called its epilogue – gathers up with extraordinary effectiveness the many moods and many attitudes which have alternated in the course of the narrative. There is both low and high comedy – and perhaps high truth, too – in the poet's prayer to "every lady bright of hue," that she not blame him for Criseide's faithlessness, and in his baldly illogical claim that he has told the story "not only" that men should beware of women but "mostly" that women should beware of men. There is comedy also in the poet's self-conscious fear that he has failed to make himself clear, that readers will mis-scan his lines and miss his meaning. The works of the great poets of the past with which he fears his "little book" (of more than eight thousand lines) might be compared make him nervous. His successive echoes of the first line of the *Aeneid* (1765–66) and of the first line of the *Iliad* (1800) suggest that he is afraid he ought to have written not a love poem but a martial epic – if only he were up to it. In any case, may God give him power to write a comedy.

These outbursts of nervousness – which are perhaps a kind of mocking image of man's inability to make sense of the materials his own history provides him – intrude upon the story before it is actually finished, and almost by an afterthought the poet returns to it in order to tell the end of Troilus. Inevitably enough, history does not permit Troilus to kill Diomede or to be killed by him: even that meager satisfaction is denied to our sense of the way things ought to be. Instead, Troilus is killed by Achilles. Only when he has been thus freed from his earthly misery is he rewarded for his earthly fidelity: he is admitted into heaven, a heaven that is physically pagan but theologically Christian. (It is not the first time in medieval literature that *trouthe* allows a non-Christian to enter into a Christian heaven, for according to both Langland and Dante the same quality had raised to heaven the Emperor Trajan.) From his remote sphere Troilus is granted that vision of the world he lately left which enables him to see in full perspective the pettiness and fragility to which he had committed his being: his *trouthe*, finally receiving its philosophic extension, is made whole. But Troilus' is not the ultimate vision [1144] in the poem. His could come only after his death, but to the Christian reader the vision is possible at all times during his life. In the last lines of the poem Chaucer gathers up all the flickering emotions, the flickering loves with which he has been dealing and unites them into the great harmony of the only true and perfect love. All the conflicting realities and illusions of the old story are subsumed under the one supreme reality.

Thus the conclusion asserts most solemnly the principle – toward which the poem has been steadily moving – that man's nature and his works are and must be unstable and unreal. Some readers are apt to feel, however, that the poet's final statement cancels all the human values which his own loving treatment has made real; that he is, in effect, saying either that he ought not to have written the poem or that the reader ought not to have read it. This feeling is natural enough in view of Chaucer's entirely specific condemnation of all things mortal except man's ability to love God. But it must be borne in mind that the ending is a part of the poem, and no matter how sincere a statement it is on the part of the poet, the ending combines with all the other parts of the poem to produce the poem's own ultimate meaning. As has been said before, nothing a poet writes is ever canceled out by anything else he writes, and both the haunting loveliness of the story of Troilus and Criseide and the necessity of rejecting it remain valid for the reader. And also, one may suppose, for Chaucer. For the lines in which he condemns the world –

> . . . and thinketh al nis but a faire,
> This world that passeth soone as flowres faire –
>
> [V. 1840–41]

poignantly enhance the very thing that he is repudiating. It is in the quality of these lines, taken as an epitome of the quality of the whole poem, that the ultimate meaning of *Troilus* lies. The simultaneous awareness of the real validity of human values – and hence our need to commit ourselves to them – and of their inevitable transitoriness – and hence our need to remain uncommitted – represents a complex, mature, truly tragic vision of mankind. The prayer of the poem's last stanza suggests the poet's faith that his vision is also subsumed under the vision of the Author of all things.

6

The Trojan scene in Chaucer's *Troilus*

JOHN P. McCALL

Originally published in *ELH* 29 (1962):263–75. Reprinted by permission of the Johns Hopkins University Press. The original pagination is recorded within square brackets. The endnotes originally appeared as footnotes.

For many years critics have accepted Kittredge's view on the role of the Trojan setting in Chaucer's *Troilus*, namely, that an atmosphere of doom pervades the Troy scene and is a fitting backdrop for the story of the doomed love of Troilus and Criseyde.[1] Still, two serious objections have been leveled against this interpretation. Patch has criticized it for being fatalistic and Mayo has contended that it is impressionistic.[2] My present aim is to re-examine the problem for the purpose of showing that Chaucer adapted the tragedy of Troy as a suitable background for the tragedy of Troilus, and that he made the characters, careers and fortunes of the two parallel and even analogous.

At the outset, a few things should be noted. First, according to classical and medieval traditions the fall of Troy was ascribed not simply to blind destiny, but to foolish pride and criminal lust.[3] The city freely and mistakenly had followed a course of action which not only brought it great prosperity, but ruin and [264] destruction as well. The history of Troy was accordingly looked upon as a civic or corporate tragedy, and in particular a tragedy of love or lust.[4] The rape of Helen and the subsequent determination of the city to defend the crime had provoked the subjection of Troy to a woman and to the caprice of Fortune. That Chaucer himself was acquainted with the tradition of the tragedy of Troy is clear.[5] It is also likely that he was aware of identifications between the city and his protagonist: by "medieval etymology" Troilus literally means "little Troy";[6] and Chaucer's principal source told him that Troilo was afflicted by the same love that doomed all Troy to destruction.[7]

But let us turn to the *Troilus* itself to see what Chaucer has done. In Book One, like Boccaccio, he begins by immediately setting the scene. A thousand Greek ships have come to Troy [265] to avenge the rape of Helen, and Calchas, learning that the city will be destroyed, flees and leaves behind his widowed daughter, Criseyde. Of the war between the Trojans and the

Greeks, Chaucer remarks only in passing what was commonplace – Fortune is in control.

> The thynges fellen, as they don of werre,
> Bitwixen hem of Troie and Grekes ofte;
> For som day boughten they of Troie it derre,
> And eft the Grekes founden nothing softe
> The folk of Troie; and thus Fortune on lofte,
> And under eft, gan hem to whielen bothe
> Aftir hir course, ay whil that thei were wrothe.
>
> (I 134–40)[8]

But with the "gestes" and how Troy fell, the poet will not concern himself. He will concentrate, instead, on the story of Troilus, and advises those who are interested in the long history of the city and its battles to read "In Omer, or in Dares, or in Dite." Although Chaucer's initial outline of the Trojan scene is brief, and drawn largely from the *Filostrato*, it is still significant. In a few stanzas he has given a threefold picture of the Troy story – the rape, the rule of Fortune in the ensuing war, and the destruction to come – a picture which is comparable to the initial three-part outline of Troilus' story in the Proem to Book One, "Fro wo to wele, and after out of joie."

From the twenty-first stanza of Book One until the beginning of Book Four, no mention is made of the destiny of Troy or of its fall.[9] With perhaps one exception,[10] everything that we read about Troy is favorable. At the feast of the Palladion we see the gaiety of Spring, and a crowd of Trojan knights and maidens at ease and well arrayed (I 155 ff). Later we hear two brief allusions to women of Troy, Helen and Polyxena (I 454–55, 676–79), [266] who are renowned for their beauty. In addition, Pandare quotes a portion of Oenone's letter to Paris (I 652–65), a good example for his argument, but also a reminder of the concern for love in Troy. Moreover, there are suggestions of victories by Troy and Troilus (I 470–83); we hear Pandare joke about the siege (I 558–60), and finally, we learn that Troilus is playing the lion amid the Greek host after Pandare has promised to help him in his cause (I 1072–75).

Before this relaxed and prosperous setting, we find that Troilus, like Troy, has become devoted to a woman and subject to the whims of Fortune. "Ful unavysed of his woo comynge," he determines with full assent, "Criseyde for to love, and nought repente." He is willing to offer full service to his love and even to deny his royal lineage; no longer will he fight for the city, or his family, or his own self-respect, but rather "To liken hire the bet for his renoun." Also, with this new devotion comes all the uncertainty of a love dependent upon Fortune (I 330–50). Even the bright future that Pandare sees is closely tied to the movement of the goddess' turning wheel; if you are now in sorrow, he tells Troilus, take comfort in the fact that Fortune changes.

> "Woost thow nat wel that Fortune is comune
> To everi manere wight in som degree?

> And yet thow hast this comfort, lo, parde,
> That, as hire joies moten overgon,
> So mote hire sorwes passen everechon."

(I 843–47)

Such comfort will be small when we hear it again under different circumstances (IV 384–99). But at this point there are no worries about the war, nor will Troilus need to worry about his love. All is well as Pandare leads the way: "Tho Troilus gan doun on knees to falle,/And Pandare in his armes hente faste,/And seyde, 'Now, fy on the Grekes alle!/Yet, pardee, God shal helpe us atte laste.'" (I 1044–47).

But if the pleasant Troy setting is significant at this early stage of the narrative, it becomes even more important in Books Two and Three. First we encounter the gay, mannered scene at Criseyde's house where the women listen to the romance of Thebes, and where Pandare urges Criseyde to forget her status as a widow and go out and enjoy the usual "Trojan" May games (II 78 ff). There is also the garden scene in which Anti[267]gone sings of love (II 813 ff), and there are the parties, first at Deiphebus' house and then later, in Book Three, at Pandare's. But the Trojans are not only happy at home; they continue to be fortunate in battle. We learn of Troilus' victories from Pandare (II 190–203), and also that he and Troilus spent half a day in the palace garden discussing a plan for defeating the Greeks (II 505–11). We hear of another victory when Criseyde watches Troilus return triumphant from putting the Greeks to flight (II 610–44); and later, in Book Three, part of the plan for deceiving everyone on Troilus' night of bliss is the fabricated story that he is waiting at the temple of Apollo for an omen, "To telle hym next whan Grekes sholde flee." (III 544)

But let us go back a moment to Chaucer's most colorful addition to the bright picture of Troy, the party at Deiphebus' house where we meet Helen. There is nothing of this in Chaucer's sources,[11] and its effect is to enhance the joy, beauty, and easy pleasures that we have already seen in the city. Helen is invited by Deiphebus to attend a dinner for those who want to "protect" Criseyde, but the reason for her being asked is independently interesting since it provides a background of male subservience at a particularly crucial time: "'What wiltow seyn if I for Eleyne sente/To speke of this? I trowe it be the beste,/For she may leden Paris as hire leste.'" (II 1447–49) At the gathering that takes place Helen holds the social center of attention and, along with Pandare, dominates the conversation. After Troilus' illness is mentioned, she complains so "that pite was to here," and when Pandare explains Criseyde's problem, Helen rises to the occasion with a speech that echoes with ironic associations between the two women:

> Eleyne, which that by the hond hire [Criseyde] held,
> Took first the tale, and seyde, "Go we blyve";
> And goodly on Criseyde she biheld,
> And seyde: "Joves lat hym nevere thryve,
> That doth yow harm, and brynge hym soone of lyve,

> And yeve me sorwe, but he shal it rewe,
> If that I may, and alle folk be trewe!"
>
> (II 1604–10)

Everyone at the dinner then determines to be Criseyde's friend in the suit brought against her by the traitorous straw-man, Poli[268]phete. But before the matter is dropped Helen and Deiphebus invade Troilus' sickroom to elicit his aid and to give us a glimpse of the gracious allurements of Menelaus' wife, whose actions are a prologue to Criseyde's.

> Eleyne, in al hire goodly softe wyse,
> Gan hym salue, and wommanly to pleye,
> And seyde, "Iwys, ye moste alweies arise!
> Now, faire brother, beth al hool, I preye!"
> And gan hire arm right over his shulder leye,
> And hym with al hire wit to reconforte;
> As she best koude, she gan hym to disporte.
>
> (II 1667–73; cf. III 168; 1128–34)

Without much prodding Troilus consents to help defend Criseyde, much to Helen's gratification. Troilus next deceives his brother and sister-in-law with a letter and a document which they take to the nearby garden. Finally, after the secret meeting of the lovers and the miracle of Criseyde's first kiss, they return, and "Eleyne hym kiste, and took hire leve blyve,/Deiphebus ek, and hom wente every wight."

As Mayo has already noted, the references to the Trojan scene through most of Book One, and all of Books Two and Three, show that Chaucer made no effort to direct attention to the final destruction of the city. And yet the picture of Troy is still important as a scene of prosperity. No mention is made of the fall of the city because Chaucer is describing Troy in good fortune, and this background suits the growing prosperity and good fortune of Troilus in love. With "wordes white" Pandare is hard at work undermining Criseyde's status, arranging for the exchange of letters, the meetings of the lovers, and the night of joy. And like Troy, Troilus is playing a game of chance for worldly bliss in which all depends on the roll of the dice (II 1347–49). Lucky occasions and the properly calculated time mean everything in this game for, as Pandare says, "worldly joie halt nought but by a wir . . . Forthi nede is to werken with it softe." (III 1636–38) Thus, as the exaggerated paradisiacal imagery accumulates in the last part of Book Three, we are often reminded of the inconstancy of earthly love.[12]

Then at the beginning of Book Four we learn that fickle Fortune is about to overturn Troilus and take away his joy.

> [269] But al to litel, weylaway the whyle,
> Lasteth swich joie, ythonked be Fortune,
> That semeth trewest whan she wol bygyle,
> And kan to fooles so hire song entune,
> That she hem hent and blent, traitour comune!

> And whan a wight is from hire whiel ythrowe,
> Than laugheth she, and maketh hym the mowe.

(IV 1–7)

Immediately after the proem, as a prelude and backdrop for Troilus' misfortune, we find that Troy, too, has come upon bad days. For the first time we hear of a serious set-back to the Trojan forces: "Ector and many a worthi wight" go out to battle and, after the long day's struggle,

> ... in the laste shour, soth for to telle,
> The folk of Troie hemselven so mysledden
> That with the worse at nyght homward they fledden.
>
> At which day was taken Antenore ...
> So that, for harm, that day the folk of Troie
> Dredden to lese a gret part of hire joie.

(IV 47–56)

In the Greek camp Calchas is soon pleading that Antenor be exchanged for Criseyde, and he reiterates at length the prophecy we heard at the outset: Troy shall be "ybrend, and beten down to grownde."

A parliament is then held in Troy to decide whether the Greek terms of exchange should be accepted. Here Chaucer alters and expands Boccaccio's account, and ironically describes the foolish self-betrayal of the people, who "sholden hire confusioun desire" by seeking the deliverance of Antenor, "that brought hem to meschaunce": "For he was after traitour to the town/ Of Troye; allas, they quytte him out to rathe!/O nyce world, lo, thy discrecioun!" (IV 204–6) With this mistake, on top of the defeat in battle, the atmosphere of Chaucer's Troy scene becomes dark and foreboding, and treachery lurks in the background.

Faced with the dilemma of disclosing his love for Criseyde or losing her, Troilus abandons all self-control. He batters himself about and roars useless complaints against Fortune and Cupid (IV 260–94). But even now, when all our attention seems fixed on the internal struggles of Troilus, we do not lose sight of the city. In his lament Troilus wonders why Fortune has not slain him, or his brothers, or his "fader, kyng of Troye" (IV 274–78) [270] – eventualities which will come soon enough. Moreover, after Troilus cries against the trick that Fortune has played on him, Pandare offers several cures. He suggests a different gift from Fortune, another woman; and failing that, he recalls the cause of Troy's predicament and advises that Troilus follow suit.

> "Go ravisshe here ne kanstow nat for shame!
> And other lat here out of towne fare,
> Or hold here stille, and leve thi nyce fare.
>
> "Artow in Troie, and hast non hardyment
> To take a womman which that loveth the,

> And wolde hireselven ben of thyn assent?
> Now is nat this a nyce vanitee?"
>
> (IV 530–36)

But for Troilus this will not do; another rape would be intolerable during the present misfortunes: "'First, syn thow woost this town hath al this werre/ For ravysshyng of wommen so by myght,/It sholde nought be suffred me to erre,/As it stant now, ne don so gret unright.'" (IV 547–50) Besides, Criseyde's "name" is at stake. Still Pandare goes right on, recalling how Paris solaced himself and asking why Troilus should not do the same. (V 608–9)

Later, when the lovers are together for the last time, Criseyde frenetically lists a number of ways by which they may be reunited. Among other things she mentions a current peace rumor: if Helen, the cause of the war, were restored to her rightful husband, then their situation – as well as Troy's – would improve.

> "Ye sen that every day ek, more and more,
> Men trete of pees; and it supposid is
> That men the queene Eleyne shal restore,
> And Grekis us restoren that is mys.
> So, though ther nere comfort non but this,
> That men purposen pees on every syde,
> Ye may the bettre at ese of herte abyde."
>
> (IV 1345–51)

Then toward the end of her exhortation Criseyde implies, as Troilus did before, that Troy has not been faring well of late; she urges Troilus to forget about fleeing the city with her, "'syn Troie hath now swich nede/Of help'." (IV 1558–59)

In Book Five Chaucer not only continues to paint the decline of Troy with an eye on his failing hero, but he comes close to identifying the two. The week-long feast at Sarpedoun's (V 428–[271]501), with its wine, women, and song, pathetically recalls the bright and gay parties in the Troy of Books Two and Three, and the letters which Troilus reads in seclusion recall the happier days when they were written. The vanity of past joys for Troy and Troilus is becoming ever more apparent. After his return home Troilus refers to the Trojan scene again when he links himself with the city: "'Now blisful lord [Cupide], so cruel thow ne be/Unto the blood of Troie, I preye the,/As Juno was unto the blood Thebane,/For which the folk of Thebes caughte hire bane.'" (V 599–602) Cupid, like Fortune, is cruel and blind,[13] and will – so to speak – destroy not only Troilus, but all the "blood of Troie."

But even more pointed are the comments of Diomede and Criseyde in the Greek camp. Diomede's persuasive love talk, for example, is shot through with an insistent dual purpose: Greeks are stronger than Trojans – he will be a better lover than any Trojan; the Greeks will destroy Troy and everyone in the city – including Criseyde's lover.[14] The high point of his argument is reached when he declares that those imprisoned in Troy will suffer unmercifully for the rape of Helen:

> "Swiche wreche on hem, for fecchynge of Eleyne.
> Ther shal ben take, er that we hennes wende,
> That Manes, which that goddes ben of peyne,
> Shal ben agast that Grekes wol hem shende.
> And men shul drede, unto the worldes ende,
> From hennesforth to ravysshen any queene,
> So cruel shal oure wreche on hem be seene." ...
> "What wol ye more, lufsom lady deere?
> Lat Troie and Troian fro youre herte pace!"
>
> (V 890–96, 911–12)

[272] Diomede has tied the failing fortunes of the city to those of Troilus with unerring insight into Criseyde's heart. For she herself, we may remember, had reminisced on the past joys of Troy and Troilus (V 729–35), and, in anticipation of Diomede's success, the narrator had commented that, "bothe Troilus and Troie town/Shal knottles throughout hire herte slide;/For she wol take a purpos for t'abyde." (V 768–70) For Diomede, Criseyde and the narrator, Troy and Troilus are one.

Meanwhile, waiting in vain for Criseyde's return, Troilus dreams that his love is taken by a boar. In the *Filostrato* Troilo understands that Diomede is the boar and that he has lost Criseyde, but Chaucer's Troilus knows nothing of the kind. Instead he asks the advice of his sister, Cassandra, who tells him that to understand the dream – and, by implication, his own tragic condition – he must learn its background: "'Thow most a fewe of olde stories heere,/To purpos, how that Fortune overthrowe/Hath lordes olde ...'" (V 1459–61) The sketch of Theban history that follows is primarily a list of tragedies, and the conclusion is that Diomede is the boar and Troilus' lady – whom Cassandra by a smile suggests she knows – is gone: "'This Diomede is inne, and thow art oute.'" The immediate effect of the introduction of Cassandra from the framework of the Trojan scene is to have her provide, in panoramic fashion, some concrete analogies to the condition of Troilus as a tragic victim of Fortune. Her speech is an historic or mythic counterpart of the Boethian philosophic discourse in Book Four. The latter deepens our insight into Troilus' psychic failure, but this extends the implications of his trust in Fortune beyond even the immediate Trojan setting and prepares for the ultimate vision of the closing stanzas of the poem.

We are now near the end, and in anticipation of Troilus' death Chaucer turns to the city which is on the verge of suffering its worst misfortune.

> Fortunee, which that permutacioun
> Of thynges hath, as it is hire comitted
> Thorugh purveyance and disposicioun
> Of heighe Jove, as regnes shal be flitted
> Fro folk in folk, or when they shal be smytted,

Gan pulle awey the fetheres brighte of Troie
Fro day to day, til they ben bare of joie.

(V 1541–47)

[273] The brightest feather of Troy is plucked when Hector is slain. Now the handwriting is clearly on the wall for Troy – and Troilus too, for soon after Hector's death Troilus sees the captured "cote-armure" of Diomede and on it finds the brooch he gave Criseyde. Fortune has played a game with him as well: "Gret was the sorwe and pleynte of Troilus;/But forth hire cours Fortune ay gan to holde./Criseyde loveth the sone of Tideüs,/And Troilus moot wepe in cares colde./Swich is this world, whoso it kan byholde." (V 1744–48) Again, foreground and background are closely knit: the imperial dominion will pass from Troy to Greece, as Criseyde passes from Troilus to Diomede; and as Fortune's tragic movement is completed for Troilus, Chaucer anticipates the fall of the city in the background.

Thus, in the last two Books of the *Troilus*, the initial analogies between the loves and fortunes of Troy and Troilus reach a classically symmetrical resolution. The change of the city's fortune, which comes with the capture and exchange of the traitorous Antenor, is simultaneously the occasion for the change of Troilus' fortune and an anticipation of Criseyde's betrayal.[15] In addition, the disenchantment regarding the war and the rape that caused it become minor motifs during the complaints of the lovers. In the thoughts of Criseyde and in the persuasive speeches of Diomede we find an insistent identification between Troy and Troilus. At the end there are the last explicit analogies between Fortune's shift from Troilus to Diomede, from Troy to Greece. Troy and Troilus, then, have become one in misfortune, just as they had been one in prosperity.

The similarities between the foreground and background of Fortune's activities in the *Troilus* lead to a conclusion, somewhat different from Kittredge's, that the tragedy of Troy is akin to the tragedy of Troilus in substance and contour. Moreover, these similarities disclose in Chaucer's poem an "intrahistorical" movement such as Auerbach has found generally lacking in antique literature. In the *Troilus* the fortunes of an individual are set against the background of a whole society enmeshed in similar fortunes, so that what happens to Troilus seems in no way [274] extraordinary, "especially arranged," or "outside the usual course of events." Thus the instability of Fortune in the case of Troilus "results from the inner processes of the real historical world" in which Chaucer portrays him as a real historical figure.[16] On one hand, then, Chaucer has portrayed a psychological tragedy in which the scene constantly enriches and enlightens his principal subject: it provides an additional dimension to the tragedy of Troilus. On the other hand, the tragedy of Troilus is a particular and concrete source of poignancy for the corporate tragedy of the city.

As Bloomfield has shown, despite all sorts of anachronisms, Chaucer displays a sense of history in the *Troilus*.[17] One aesthetic effect is that the narrative becomes more realistically and completely dramatic. The setting is an integral part of the main action, and not simply suited to it in a naive or rigidly rhetorical way; nor is Chaucer floundering about, as though only dimly aware of a basic tool of his art. But the fact that this background is first historical and dramatic in no way detracts from the fact that it is also symbolic. What we have in the Trojan scene is a social, civic, or what some medieval critics might call an allegorical level of meaning, founded in the realities of history and appearing from time to time as an analogue of the moral – or tropological – development of Troilus' particular tragedy. At one point in the *Troilus*, and perhaps only at this point, these three levels of significance – historical, moral, and social – converge with a transcendental or analogical vision of reality.[18]

[275] Finally, throughout the poem, wherever the Troy scene is mentioned, it is carefully under Chaucer's control. It is so unobtrusively shaded and colored by the hues of the foreground that it fails to call special attention to itself as something separate and distinct – as it might have if Chaucer had clumsily pointed out bold historical and moral parallels between Troy and Troilus. The analogies, then, are implicit and vital: felt or sensed, but not directly stated. Moreover, they are all real and historical, not arbitrary or manipulated. Thus we find something that critics are becoming more aware of: the subtle and skillful hand of Chaucer the artist.

Notes

1 G. L. Kittredge, *Chaucer and His Poetry* (Cambridge, Mass., 1915), pp. 117–21. [See Kittredge extract above – ed.] See also W. C. Curry, "Destiny in Chaucer's *Troilus*," *PMLA*, XLV (1930), 135; G. Dempster, *Dramatic Irony in Chaucer* (Stanford, 1932), pp. 12–13; J. L. Lowes, *Geoffrey Chaucer and the Development of His Genius* (Boston, 1934), p. 180; T. A. Stroud, "Boethius' Influence on Chaucer's *Troilus*," *MP*, XLIX (1951), 9; and D. Everett, *Essays on Middle English Literature* (Oxford, 1955), p. 133.

2 H. R. Patch, "Troilus on Determinism," *Speculum*, VI (1931), 225–43; R. D. Mayo, "The Trojan Background of the *Troilus*," *ELH*, IX (1942), 245–56.

3 In general, see Horace's *Epistle to Maximus Lollius* in the Loeb *Horace* (London, 1926), p. 263; and for Chaucer's knowledge of the pertinent passage, R. A. Pratt's, "A Note on Chaucer's Lollius," *MLN*, LXV (1950), 183–7. References to the pride of Troy ("superbum Ilium" from *Aeneid* III 2–3) are numerous: see Seneca, n. 4 below; *Troilus*, ed. T. Merzdorf (Lipsiae, 1875), pp. 37, 187; *Inferno* I 75, XXX 13–15; and Salutati's *De Laboribus Herculis*, ed. B. L. Ullman (Zurich, 1951), I 348. In *Adversus Jovinianum* (PL XXIII 280), Jerome blames the Trojan War on the rape of a single *respecteuse* ("muliercula"); and in the popular medieval *Pergama flere volo . . .* the blame is more bluntly ascribed to the "fatal whore": Carmina 101, ll. 43–45 in *Carmina Burana*, ed. W. Meyers, A. Hilka and O. Schumann (Heidelberg, 1930–1941), 2 vols. The criminal lust of Troy was simply an extension of Paris' crime to the whole city: see n. 4 below.

4 In *The Goddess Fortuna in Medieval Literature* (Cambridge, Mass., 1927), p. 114, Patch notes that Troy was a familiar civic example of Fortune's infidelity. For a classical example, see Seneca's *Troades* in the Loeb *Tragedies* (London, 1917), I 125. For the medieval encyclopedic tradition that Troy was an exemplar of tragic lust,

wantonness and foolish love, see A. Neckam's *De Naturis Rerum*, ed. T. Wright (London, 1863), p. 350; Brunetto Latini's *Li Livres dou Tresour*, ed. F. J. Carmody (Berkeley, 1948), p. 290; and Salutati's *De Laboribus Herculis*, I 252. In a poem by Godefroid de Reims, Achilles harangues the Trojans for being effeminate and sluggish devotees of Venus: A. Boutemy, "Trois oeuvres inédites de Godefroid de Reims," *Revue du Moyen Age Latin*, III (1947), 364. It would seem that the traditional interpretation of the judgment of Paris – and later the judgment of all Troy – has some bearing on the foolish love ascribed to the city. Paris was reputed to have preferred fleshly delight (Venus) to wealth (Juno) and wisdom (Pallas): Fulgentius, *Mitologia* II 1; Boccaccio, *Genealogie Deorum*, VI xxii; J. Seznec, *The Survival of the Pagan Gods* (New York, 1953), pp. 107 ff.

5 When Chaucer's Aeneas speaks of Troy's fall he echoes the commonplace medieval definition of tragedy: "'Allas, that I was born' quod Eneas;/Thourghout the world oure shame is kid so wyde,/Now it is peynted upon every syde./We, that weren in prosperite,/Been now desclandred, and in swich degre,/No lenger for to lyven I ne kepe.'" (*LGW* 1027–32). Compare the phraseology in the definitions of tragedy in Monk's Tale, 1973–77, and the translation of the *Consolations*, II, pr. 2. For these, and subsequent references I have used the edition of F. N. Robinson, *The Works of Geoffrey Chaucer* (Cambridge, Mass., 1957).

6 This would be not the Greek, but the Latin diminutive in -lus, -la, -lum: *Priciani Grammatici Caesariensis Libri Omnes* (Venice, 1527), pp. 28b–32a, and W. M. Lindsay, *The Latin Language* (Oxford, 1894), pp. 331–33. For suggesting the role of a character *by name*, see the comment on Boccaccio's use of *Pandaro*, "to signify one who 'gives all' for his friend" in N. E. Griffin and A. B. Myrick's translation of *The Filostrato* (Philadelphia, 1929), pp. 41–42; also, Chaucer's word-play on *Calchas* (I 71) and on the frequent epithet *queene Eleyne* (II 1556, 1687, 1703, 1714).

7 *Filostrato*, Bk. VII, st. 86. Casandra tells Troilo that he has "suffered from the accursed love by which we all must be undone, as we can see if we but wish" (my translation).

8 The reference to Fortune is Chaucer's own, although it was easily suggested by *Filostrato*, I, st. 16.

9 Mayo, *ELH*, IX, 250.

10 One passage (II 1111–13) may suggest that Sinon is within the walls of Troy. When Pandare meets Criseyde for the second time in his "paynted proces" of bringing her to love, he takes her aside to deliver Troilus' letter; as an excuse for speaking alone with her, he says he has just heard new tidings from the Greek spy who is a guest in the city: "'Ther is right now come into town a gest,/A Greek espie, and telleth newe thinges,/For which I come to telle yow tydynges.'" Although the activities of Sinon, or any spy, provide an analogy for the deceptions of Pandare (e.g., II 409–20; III 267–80, 1564–68), still the news is announced as another sign of Troy's good fortunes.

11 The incident may have been suggested by *Filostrato* VII, st. 84–85, but this is very different from Chaucer's scene.

12 *Troilus* III 813–36, 1527–47, 1618–38.

13 The close kinship between blind Cupid, or lust (*Troilus* I 202; III 1808; V 1824), and blind or blinding Fortune (IV 5) is clear throughout the poem – e.g., IV 260–94 – and Chaucer's knowledge of it doubtless dates back to his reading of the *Roman de la Rose* (*The Works of Geoffrey Chaucer*, pp. 605–6, lines 4353 ff.). See also Pierre Bersuire's *Metamorphosis Ovidiana Moraliter ...* (Paris, 1515), fo. viii^v–ix; in his *Studies in Iconology* (New York, 1939), p. 112, Panofsky notes the association between blind Cupid, Night, Synagogue, Infidelity, Death and Fortune, but makes a distinction, which is generally unnecessary, between Cupid in mytho-

graphical works and Cupid in literary works. For the kinship of Venus and Fortune, see Patch's *The Goddess Fortuna*, pp. 90–98, and M. W. Stearns, *Robert Henryson* (New York, 1949), p. 89 ff.

14 *Troilus* V 118–26, 141–43, 876–96, 904–24.

15 The connection between Fortune's change and treachery is proverbial, but see especially *Troilus* IV 1–5.

16 See E. Auerbach, *Mimesis*, trans. by W. Trask (Princeton, 1953), pp. 28–29. Perhaps Unamuno's treatment of the individual as an epitome of his society comes close to illustrating what Chaucer has done.

17 "Chaucer's Sense of History," *JEGP*, LI (1952), 301–13.

18 In the closing stanzas Chaucer directs our attention not only to Troilus, now departed, and to Troy, now in grief, but also to the relationship of both to the awesome facts of the after-life and the redemptive love of Christ.

> And down from thennes faste he gan avyse
> This litel spot of erthe, that with the se
> Embraced is, and fully gan despise
> This wrecched world, and held al vanite
> To respect of the pleyn felicite
> That is in hevene above; and at the laste,
> Ther he was slayn, his lokyng down he caste.
> And in hymself he lough right at the wo
> Of hem that wepten for his deth so faste;
> And dampned al oure work that foloweth so
> The blynde lust, the which that may nat laste . . .

(V 1814 ff)

7 Medieval doctrines of love

D. W. ROBERTSON, Jr

Originally published as the conclusion of the final chapter, "Medieval Doctrines of Love," in D. W. Robertson, Jr., *A Preface to Chaucer: Studies in Medieval Perspectives* (Princeton: Princeton University Press, 1962, pp. 472–501). Reprinted by permission of Princeton University Press. The original pagination is recorded within square brackets. Occasional references to illustrations in the original have been omitted as has one brief passage near the beginning. The endnotes originally appeared as footnotes and are here renumbered. The extract is a modified version of Robertson's "Chaucerian Tragedy," *ELH* 19 (1952):1–37.

Chaucer's most famous love story, the tragedy of *Troilus and Criseyde*, is neither a tale of true love, of what Jehan le Bel called love "par amours" [*Li ars d'amour*, ed. J. Petit (Brussels, 1867–69)], nor of courteous love. It is, rather, a tale of passionate love set against a background of Boethian philosophy. Those familiar with the *Consolation* [*of Philosophy*] and its major themes will realize at once that it is impossible to idealize passionate love for a gift of Fortune in Boethian terms. In the fourteenth century, Boethius was widely regarded as a saint. Iconographic devices inspired by his work, like the Wheel of Fortune, decorated churches and cathedrals throughout England, and the *Consolation* itself was widely read. Froissart tells us that Baudouin le Courageux, Count of Hainaut, could recite it by heart. The Boethian elements in *Troilus* and their implications were thus easily recognizable to the members of Chaucer's audience. And no one reminded of the doctrines of Fortune and Providence, fate and free will, the love of God and the love of worldly goods, or the Herculean nobility and heroism of virtue, could possibly regard passionate love for a fickle woman with anything but disfavor. This disfavor might appear either as amusement at the antics of the lover or as pity of the kind that one should, from a Boethian point of view, bestow on any sinner. If Chaucer had shown any inclination to doubt the wisdom of his philosophical master, we might have reason to approach his poem with something like a romantic point of view. But such doubt would have been strange indeed in fourteenth-century [473] English court circles, and the poem itself is one of the most moving exemplifications of Boethian ideas ever written.

It is, in the first place, a tragedy, a work, that is, as Radulphus de Longo Campo said, "altogether in contempt of Fortune." [Oxford, Balliol College MS 146b, fol. 101 verso]. In Chaucer's translation of Boethius, Lady Philosophy is made to say (2 pr. 2), "What other thyng bywaylen the cryinges of tragedyes but oonly the dedes of Fortune, that with unwar strook overtuneth the realmes of greet nobleye?"

Fortune is, as Boethius explains, no menace to the virtuous, but only to those who subject themselves to it by setting their hearts on a mutable rather than an immutable good. Such persons are those who abandon reason for the sake of false goals, in the pursuit of which they engage in criminal behavior. Hence Trivet in commenting on the above passage says that "a tragedy is a song of great iniquities beginning in prosperity and terminating in adversity."[1] In his commentary on Seneca's tragedies, he explains that Virgil in the *Aeneid*, Lucan, and Ovid in the *Metamorphoses* may be said to have written in the tragic manner, since they described the downfall of kings. A comedy, on the other hand, deals with private persons, and the plots of comedy are concerned with things like "the debauching of virgins and the love of prostitutes." Either mode may appear in three forms: in the form of narration, in which the poet speaks; in the form of drama (*dragmatico*), in which the poet does not speak, but only the persons introduced; and in a "mixed" form, in which the poet and the persons introduced all speak. The *Aeneid* is said to illustrate the last form.[2] In these terms, Chaucer's *Troilus* is a mixed tragedy which properly belongs, as he says it does, beside the works of "Virgile, Ovide, Omer, Lucan and Stace." This is not simply a conventional list of poets, but a list of what an educated man of Chaucer's time would have thought of as tragic poets. His own tragedy involves the fall of a prince who subjects himself to Fortune through an unworthy love. Medieval tragedy is, of course, very different from modern tragedy, in which the suffering protagonist becomes an emblem of humanity crushed by the mysterious iniquities of a strangely recalcitrant world. But to the medieval mind, that hostile world of fortuitous events was an illusion generated by misdirected love, and [474] this, indeed, is one of the great themes of the *Consolation*. Unless we realize that this conception is just as susceptible to profound elaboration and just as provocative of rich emotional implication as is the more modern conception, we shall have little opportunity to appreciate the force and coherence of Chaucer's poem. To attribute a modern conception of tragedy to Chaucer would be to deny his faith in the Providential order and to make him, in his cultural environment, a shallow fool. And to criticize him for not sharing our modern views on the subject would be a little like criticizing him for not making use of the latest photographs from Mount Palomar in his treatise on the astrolabe.

Chaucer begins his poem appropriately by invoking one of the furies, Thesiphone. Something of what this invocation implies may be gathered from the fact that in the *Anticlaudianus* (8.147 ff.) Alanus makes the furies leaders of all the vices that attack the New Man. Trivet tells us, in his commentary on Boethius, that the furies are three women with serpentine hair who are so named because of "three passions which produce many perturbations in the hearts of men, and at the same time make them transgress in such a way that they are not permitted to take any regard either for their fame or for any dangers that beset them. These are wrath, which desires vengeance, cupidity, which desires wealth, and libido, which desires pleasures. Hence they are called 'avengers of crimes' because crimes are always accompanied by mental pain. And they may be ordered according to their etymologies, for *Alecto* means 'incessant,' and signifies cupidity; *Thesiphone* means 'voice,' and signifies libido; *Megara* means 'great contention,' and signifies wrath."[3] [. . .]

[476] When we first meet Troilus, he is, so to speak, daring Thesiphone by spending his time at the festival of the goddess of wisdom "byholding ay the ladyes of the town," and proudly jesting about the blind foolishness of lovers.[4] The lovers are not the only blind ones, however, for as Chaucer observes, blind pride and presumption often precede a fall, and in the same way Troilus will have to descend from his height. It may be of some relevance to notice in this connection that pride is conventionally represented in Gothic iconography as a rider falling from his horse. Chaucer, perhaps taking a hint from the kind of equine imagery that appears in the preface to the *De amore* and in [pictorial] representations, compares Troilus with a horse. Just as a horse must obey "horses lawe," so Troilus will succumb to the "lawe of kynde" which dominates the fleshly or "horsy" aspect of man. [I. 223; 238] But this is an eventuality to be commended, Chaucer says, for love frequently makes worthy men worthier and causes them to dread vice and shame, so that it is best to submit to love, which, in any event, can hardly be resisted. This is very good advice, so long, that is, as the love acquired is properly channeled [477] so that the virtues it inspires are real virtues and not vices masquerading as virtues. But Troilus does not begin his amorous career very well. Among the ladies at the feast he sees Criseyde:

> And sodeynly he wax therwith astoned,
> And gan hir bet beholde in thrifty wise.
> "O mercy God!" thoughte he, "wher hastow woned
> That art so fair and goodly to devise?"
>
> [I. 274–77]

Instead of approaching her to discover what she is like, however, Troilus is overcome by the fact that Criseyde is "fair to the eyes and delightful to behold." He receives a "fixe and depe impressioun" [I. 298] and retires hastily to his chamber, where he begins to

> make a mirour of his mynde,
> In which he saugh al holly hire figure . . .
>
> [I. 365–66]

The pattern of these actions is familiar enough, and it is not one which Chaucer's contemporary audience would have been likely to miss. Troilus has fixed a phantasy of Criseyde in his memory and has begun to meditate on it; he has proceeded from "suggestion" to "delightful thought," or from "sight" to the beginnings of "immoderate thought." These are the initial steps which lead to an inner repetition of the Fall, to *passio*, or to mania and death. Cupid's arrow has struck Troilus with full force. The implications of these facts are not calculated to elevate Troilus in the minds of Chaucer's readers, nor to invite in them much vicarious sympathy for his predicament. On the other hand, the processes involved were a familiar part of everyday experience, for no one escapes from sin in one form or another, so that Troilus' behavior would have been familiar in a practical as well as in a theoretical sense. The underlying theory, in other words, did not make the situation purely academic.

The song Troilus sings in his chamber is a foreshadowing of the course of his love, typical of those who abandon reason for Fortune. His torments seem to him "savory," just as Bernard of Gordon says they are in such cases [*Lilium medicinae*]. The more he drinks the more he thirsts, for he has begun to experience something which we may call either the curse of Dipsas in classical terms or the unquenchable thirst generated by the water of the well of the Samaritan in Christian terms. Love seems to him a thing of clashing contraries – a "quike [478] deth," a "swete harm so queynte" [I. 411] – like the realm of Fortune itself, a suburb of which is that realm of illogical consonances which Matthew of Vendôme had long since ascribed to lovers. Troilus is "al steereles within a boot," [I. 416] an image which derives ultimately from Prov. 23. 33–34: "Thy eyes shall behold strange women, and thy heart shall utter perverse things. And thou shalt be as one sleeping in the midst of the sea, and as a pilot fast asleep when the stern [i.e., "rudder"] is lost." The perverse doctrines appear at once in the last two stanzas of the song. Troilus gives himself up to the God of Love and regards his lady as a "goddess". [I. 425] He is ready, therefore, to resign his "estat roial" to her, [I. 432] since love and majesty "non bene conveniunt nec in una sede morantur."

This is the neglect of duty which leads to the tragedy. Troilus is a "public figure," a prince whose obligations to his country are not inconsiderable, especially in time of war. But his external submission to Criseyde is based on an inner submission of the reason to the sensuality, for, in the words of Jehan le Bel, "einsi con li cors sur l'ame seignerist, ensi est-il quant la feme a sour l'omme signourie." [*Li ars d'amour*, I. 137] And when sensuality rules him, he can no longer fulfill the chivalric obligations of his station. To stress this fact, Chaucer tells us that Troilus fears nothing except the loss of Criseyde. He has submitted, in other words, to that fear which can lead to no real good which Andreas [Capellanus] describes at the beginning of the *De amore*. The "fire" which burns in the Book of Ecclesiasticus (9.9), in the description of Libido in the *Psychomachia* of Prudentius, in Lancelot's perilous bed, and in the torch of Venus in the *Roman de la rose* now burns him (lines 436, 445,

449, 490); and he finds himself in the "snare" or "cheyne" which had held Holofernes (Judith 10.5), Mars, [Andreas'] "Walter," and Guillaume's foolish lover. Although he seeks renown on the battlefield, he does so

> for non hate he to the Grekes hadde,
> Ne also for the rescous of the town,

> [I. 477–78]

but only to make an impression on Criseyde. His virtuous behavior should thus be regarded with what was called "caution." But it offers him little consolation, and he is soon complaining about "destine" and seeking death:

> [479]   "God wolde I were aryved in the port
>   Of deth, to which my sorwe wol me lede."

> [I. 526–27]

It does lead him there, but not without the aid of Pandarus. All of this woe, we should remember, arises from a mere phantasy in Troilus' mind. He has never talked to Criseyde, knows nothing of her character and manners, and has no idea whether she is a lovable person, a moral weakling, or a shrew. That is, there are very clearly no grounds for true love in Troilus' passion.

The character of Pandarus is a masterpiece of medieval irony. On the surface, he is an attractive little man, wise, witty, and generous. But his wisdom is not of the kind that Lady Philosophy would approve, and his generosity is of the type which supplies gold to the avaricious and dainties to the glutton. His prototype is Jonadab, a "very wise man," and the device he uses to bring the two lovers together is strikingly like that of his Biblical predecessor (2 Kings 13). Beneath his superficially attractive surface, this little grotesque has as his real function that of intermediary between a victim of foolish love and the object of his love. As an intermediary of this kind, he acquires something of the characteristics of a priest. Indeed, there is more than a suggestion in the poem that Pandarus is a blind leader of the blind, a priest of Satan (I. 625–630). It is true that he is not a Mephistophelian figure, for the Devil had not been romanticized when he was created; he is externally pleasant, somewhat commonplace, and a little unctuous. This "devel," as Troilus once jokingly calls him (I. 623),[5] is convincingly decked out in sheep's clothing. His "wit" is no better than his wisdom or his generosity. When we first meet him, his remarks reveal a witty contempt for "remors of conscience," "devocioun," and "holynesse" (I. 551–560). And when Troilus, with the blind unreasonableness of a typical tragic protagonist, complains against Fortune (I. 837), Pandarus can reply only that everyone is subject to Fortune and that she is by nature fickle (I. 844–854). Neither here nor elsewhere does he ever suggest that it is possible to rise above Fortune. He is so "friendly" and so full of pity for Troilus and natural generosity that he offers to get anyone for him if necessary, even his own [480] sister (I. 860–861). Much has been made of Pandarus as a "true friend," but friendship in Cicero, Boethius, St. Ailred, Andreas, Jean de Meun, Jehan le Bel, and, in fact, in almost any medieval account of the subject, is based on virtue and cannot lead to vice. Pandarus' offer of his sister is thus an unmistakable clue to his real nature and to the nature of his relationship with Troilus. He has no "psychological" motivation for what he does, and such motivation should not be sought; his actions depend upon the moral structure of his person.

When Pandarus discovers that Criseyde is the object of Troilus' desire, he gives him a little sermon, emphasizing Criseyde's "pitee":

> "And also thynk, and therwith glade the,
>   That sith thy lady vertuous is al,
>   So foloweth it that there is som pitee
>   Amonges al thise other in general;
>   And forthi se that thow in special
>   Requere nat that is ayeyns hyre name,
>   For vertu streccheth nat hym self to shame."
>
>   [I. 897–903]

Virtue may "stretch itself" to the kind of "pity" May shows for Damyan, and in Pandarus' view it will not reach the point of "shame" unless someone else finds out about it. Like Lancelot before him, Pandarus has great confidence in Bien Celer. Again, if Criseyde's other "virtues" are like this one, and, indeed, they turn out to be so, they are not very admirable. Pandarus closes his series of admonitions by urging Troilus to repent his earlier remarks about the foolishness of lovers. Like a good priest, he leads his sinner in confession:

> "Now beet thi brest, and sey to god of love:
>   'Thy grace, lord; for now I me repente
>   If I mysspak, for now my self I love';
>   Thus sey with al thyn herte in good entente."
>   Quod Troilus, "A, lord! I me consente,
>   And preye to the my japes thow foryive,
>   And I shal nevere more whil I live."
>
>   [I. 932–38]

Pandarus further admonishes perseverance and devotion, asserting that Criseyde will certainly not devote herself to celestial love:

> [481]   "Was nevere man nor womman yit bigete
>   That was unapt to suffren loves hete,
>   Celestial, or elles love of kynde.
>   Forthy som grace I hope in here to fynde.
>
> "And for to speken of hire in specyal,
>   Hire beaute to bithynken, and hire youthe,
>   It sit hir naught to ben celestial
>   As yit, though that hire liste bothe and kowthe;
>   But, trewely, it sate hire wel right nowthe

> A worthi knyght to loven and cherice,
> And but she do, I holde it for a vice."
>
> [I. 977–87]

The assertion that celestial love would be vicious in a woman so young and beautiful hardly enhances Pandarus' character; in fact, it again suggests its "diabolical" nature. He goes on to say, rather amusingly, that Troilus will serve the God of Love well, and, in fact, be "the beste post . . . of al his lay." [I. 1000–01] When Troilus protests that he means no "harm" or "vilenye," but only what will "sownen into goode," Pandarus laughs at his touch of courtesy, saying, "Am I thy borugh? Fy! No wight doth but so." [I. 1033–38] That is what they all say. Pandarus is perfectly aware that Troilus is not simply interested in what Jehan le Bel called love "par amours"; he knows what Troilus wants and is anxious to get it for him. As for Troilus, he falls on his knees, embraces Pandarus, and submits to him completely. "My lif, my deth, hool in thyn honde I ley," he says. [I. 1053] Pandarus, full of worldly wisdom, begins to plan his attack. Troilus plays the lion on the battlefield and, like Damyan, becomes very virtuous,

> For he bicome the frendlieste wight,
> The gentileste, and eek the moste fre,
> The thriftieste, and oon the beste knyght
> That in his tyme was, or myghte be.
>
> [I. 1079–82]

This is one way in which love can make a man who is "worthy" even "worthier."

At the close of Book I, Troilus has been struck by the phantasy of Criseyde's beauty, has lodged it firmly in his memory, and, encouraged by Pandarus to hope, has begun the immoderate thought necessary to passion. Wishing to make an impression on Criseyde, [482] he has begun to be "virtuous," without, however, manifesting any real interest either in Criseyde's virtues or in the condition of the city which he is supposed to be defending. Poetically speaking, he defends neither his own heritage nor the "reign" of his mind, which is now beginning to assume the "up-so-doun" condition symbolized in late medieval art by representations of Aristotle with the *pucele* on his back, or by grotesques carrying female companions to the tune of bagpipes. He has not yet begun to dance, but the dance is arranged for him in Book II, which is a study in false "curtesie," the Curtesie that leads the lover to the dance and finally overcomes the lady's scruples in the *Roman de la rose* or that accompanies Aray and Lust in *The Parliament of Fowls*. This courtesy has nothing to do either with the courtesy of Hector or with the courtesy recommended in the "Instructio regis ad filium Edwardum"; it is, rather, the activity of the unguided lower reason operating with its worldly wisdom in a sophisticated society. To speak of it as "courtly love" would be to take a very small-minded and cynical view indeed of the *mores* of our chivalric ancestors. The book furnishes us with a vivid picture of "manners," but they are the manners of the less noble of Chaucer's noble contemporaries, and are by no means intended as a model to be followed. The activities in the parlor, in the garden, and in the bedchamber combine, in fact, to form one of the first comedies of manners in English. The action opens on May 3, a significant day for lovers.[6] Pandarus, who is doomed to perpetual frustration, is especially downcast on that day. He can lead others down the road to *Amoenitas*, but he can never reach that happy land himself. With many an elegant flourish, he proceeds to guide Criseyde, although, as it turns out, she actually needs little assistance.

The meeting between Pandarus and Criseyde is characterized by a meticulous attention to the social graces. Pandarus finds her with two other ladies, listening to the Tale of Thebes. The story has reached the point where "Amphiorax fil thorugh the ground to helle," [II. 105] an event brought about by the fact that his wife coveted the brooch of Thebes, which, as we learn in "The Complaint of Mars" is a kind of emblem for that which attracts lovers. Pandarus hastily professes a full knowledge of these matters, since it is prob[483]able that he has no wish to dwell on their implications. "Lat us daunce," he says, and "don to May some observance." [II. 111–12] But Criseyde is perfectly aware of the obligations of her status, and knows that it is, or should be, inconsistent with the *amoenitas* of May and the dance of the garden of delight. "Is that a widewes lif?" she asks.

> "It satte me wel bet ay in a cave
> To bidde, and rede on holy seyntes lyves;
> Lat maydens gon to daunce, and yonge wyves."
>
> [II. 117–19]

The underlying principle in this assertion is from St. Paul, who said (1 Tim. 5. 5–6), "But she that is a widow indeed, and desolate, let her trust in God, and continue in supplications and prayers night and day. For she that liveth in pleasures, is dead while she is living." It was elaborated in St. Augustine's *De bono viduitatis* and became a recognized bit of standard doctrine. At the same time, however, in pastoral theology, a widow was thought to be not altogether responsible, having, presumably, lost the wise guidance of a husband.[7] What St. James describes as "religion clean and undefiled" (James 1. 27), that is "to visit the fatherless and widows in their tribulation: and to keep one's self unspotted from the world," became a feature of the late medieval chivalric ideal. On the other hand, widows are attractive to lovers whose interests are selfish rather than chivalric; and Criseyde, who is not only a widow but also beautiful, lonely, and fearful, is a peculiarly fetching possibility. With no chivalric motives whatsoever, Pandarus sets about the business of taking advantage of her vulnerable position and her fear, which at this point envisages the dangers of "Grekes." Her fear, it should be noticed, is always self-centered and never actually involves the fear of violating any higher principles, in spite of the fact that she is quick to allude to such principles, as she does in the above instance. Pandarus, playing on her fear of the Greeks, finds an opportunity to praise Troilus at some length, preparing the way for his message. Finally, he cleverly offers to leave without telling her the "good news" he has hinted at, and at the same time repeating his invitation to dance: "let us daunce, and cast youre widwes habit to mis-chaunce." [I. 221–22] Whatever May dances he may have [484] in mind at the moment, the dance he has in mind ultimately is the "old dance" at which he, although he does not practise it himself, is an expert.

Criseyde, overcome by feminine curiosity, will not let him leave. He plans very carefully his next Polonius-like bit of strategy (2. 267–273), opening this time with some remarks about good fortune. He who does not make the most of it when it comes, he says, is foolish, seeking to tempt Criseyde with rumors of prosperity. She remains fearful, so that he can reveal his message safely. When he does so, he repeats the familiar line that Troilus will die if he does not get her. Indeed, he will cut his own throat too. "With that, the teris burste out of his eyen." [II. 326] All of this is obviously a carefully prepared bit of acting. It is followed by a long sentimental lament, which has the desired effect of increasing Criseyde's fear. He is, he asserts, not a "baude," although it is perfectly obvious that that is exactly what he is. All he wants, he says, is "love of frendshipe," a "lyne" which Diomede uses with great success later on (5. 185). We may recall the same stratagem in the dialogues of the *De amore*. Friendship, as Raison explains in the *Roman de la rose*, has nothing to do with the pleasurable satisfactions of the flesh, but Criseyde is very much aware of what Pandarus and Troilus are actually after: "I shal felen what ye [he] mene, ywis." [II. 387] But after Pandarus has driven his point home with a little false philosophy from Wisdom 2, which is highly irrelevant to the subject of "friendship," Criseyde feigns shock and astonish-ment. At this, Pandarus pretends to be hurt by her suspicions and offers to go, but she catches his garment and agrees to "save" Troilus provided that she can also save her "honor." Like Fenice in Chrétien's *Cligés*, Criseyde has a great deal to say on this subject, but the "honor" she seeks to preserve is the honor of appearances, a middle-class virtue dear to the heart of the Franklin's hero Arveragus, but not altogether harmonious with the "aris-tocratic" qualities some modern critics have wished to see in her behavior. It is simply the hollow "reputation" cherished by the lovers in the *De amore* which Lancelot was so spectacularly successful at maintaining.

But to reassure Criseyde, Pandarus offers a little picture of Troilus as he expresses his love. In a "gardyn," which is thematic rather than scenic, Troilus is depicted "by a welle" confessing his sins to Cupid:

[485]   "Lord, have routhe upon my peyne.
           Al have I ben rebell in myn entente,
           Now *mea culpa*, Lord, I me repente . . ."

                                                    [II. 523–25]

Clearly, if Troilus has gone this far, he will not easily be disengaged, but if Criseyde had been a careful reader of the *Roman de la rose*, she might have recognized the little scene described for her as the beginning of a nightmare. Again, Troilus is depicted lamenting in bed. Pandarus assures Criseyde that his "entente is clene," and then, almost immediately, observes,

> "Ther were nevere two so wel ymet,
>   Whan ye ben his al hool, as he is youre.
>   Ther myghty god yit graunte us see that houre."
>
> [II. 586–88]

Criseyde understands what this implies, and pretends shock. But Pandarus is able to gloss over what he has said with little effort:

> "Nay! Thereof spak I nought, a ha!" quod she –
> "As helpe me god, ye shenden every deel."
> "A, mercy! dere nece," anon quod he,
> "What so I spak, I mente nat but wel,
>   By Mars, the god that helmed is of steel.
>   Now beth nat wroth, my blood, my nece dere."
> "Now wel," quod she, "foryeven be it here."
>
> [II. 589–95]

What Pandarus means by "meaning well" has long since been apparent. Criseyde's forgiveness is also interesting in view of the fact that she has never seen Troilus to know him. When she does see him, shortly thereafter, the serpent lifts its head again, this time in a somewhat more calculating way than it did when Troilus saw Criseyde. The lady's eyes betray her:

> Criseyda gan al his chere aspien,
> And leet it so softe in hire herte synke,
> That to hire self she seyde, "Who yaf me drynke?"
>
> [II. 649–51]

When Troilus saw Criseyde, he thought only of her "figure." In addition to his shape, however, she considers his prowess, estate, reputation, wit, and lineage. These things all contribute to a vast self-satisfaction:

> But moost hire favour was, for his distresse
> Was al for hire . . .
>
> [II. 663–64]

[486] Ultimately, her love is a self-love that seeks the favor of Fortune. The stars have something to do with it (2. 680–686). Criseyde will always be true to herself; she will always seek to escape from the fear of misfortune, no matter what effects her actions may have on others. If Troilus wishes to turn the order of things "up-so-doun" by submitting to her, she is equally determined that no husband will rule her:

> "Shal noon housbonde seyn to me 'chek mat';
>   For either they ben ful of jalousie,
>   Or maisterful, or loven novelrye."
>
> [II. 754–56]

The mastery of a man like Troilus, a man of prowess and renown, a prince, and a handsome prince at that, would be quite an achievement.

In the remainder of Book II we are given some lessons in "Messagerie," which accompanies "Foolhardinesse," "Flaterye," "Desyr," and "Meede" in the Temple of Venus (*PF*, 227–228). Pandarus instructs Troilus carefully in the art of writing an effective love-letter in which one says not necessarily what one thinks or feels, but what will have the desired effect on the recipient. Among effective objective correlatives, a few tears shed in the right places may help. Criseyde, having reluctantly, or coyly, permitted Pandarus to thrust Troilus' literary efforts into her bosom, knows well enough how to write an artfully ambiguous reply. When she sees Troilus again, she again reacts to externals:

> To telle in short, hire liked al in fere
> His person, his aray, his look, his chere.
>
> [II. 1266–67]

Meanwhile, the increased hope inspired by Criseyde's letter makes the "fir" of Troilus' desire hotter than ever. And Pandarus arranges his little plot to bring the young lovers together. The plot involves lying to Deiphebus, to Hector, to Helen, and to Paris, not to mention lying a little also to Criseyde, preying on her fear with a tale about "false Poliphete." Having made these very "honorable" arrangements, Pandarus informs Troilus about them, urging him to keep faith with an echo of Christ's words in the Gospels (Luke 8. 48, 18. 42): "Thou shalt be saved by thy feythe in trouthe." [II. 1503] Needless to say, no one in Chaucer's audience would have needed to be reminded of the Augustinian principle that "If [487] anyone engages his faith to commit a sin, it is not faith." There is little possibility that the Franklin of *The Canterbury Tales* was in his audience. In any event, Troilus, in whom desire has overcome rational perspective, is overjoyed – "so glad was he never in al his lyve." [II. 1538] He is quite willing to feign sickness like his illustrious predecessor Amnon so that he and Criseyde may come together, like Adam and Eve still earlier, "under cover of lies."[8] When the company is assembled with Deiphebus, and Troilus' "illness" is being discussed, Criseyde once more reveals the pride and self-love upon which her "love" for Troilus is based:

> For which with sobre chiere hire herte lough;
> For who is that nolde hire glorifie,
> To mowen swiche a knight don lyve or dye?
>
> [II. 1592–94]

She shows no real sympathy for the poor boy at all. This is the love for which Troilus meets his death, the lady for whom he sacrifices his wisdom, his honor, and his obligation to his country. As Pandarus leads Criseyde toward the chamber where Troilus lies, he preaches her a little sermon containing a *sententia* which might well serve as the motto of Book II, and, at the same time, as an emblem for Pandarus himself: "Whil folk is blent, lo! al the tyme is wonne." [II. 1743] Whose doctrine is this?

In Book III there is a great deal of religious imagery. Literary historians are apt to say that it is "conventional" and that it reflects the traditions of "courtly love." No one in the book, however, uses religion as an adjunct to courtesy. And Chaucer certainly does not "accept" the behavior of Troilus. The religious imagery serves exactly the same function it serves in Chrétien's *Chevalier de la charrete*: to suggest the values which the hero inverts and, at the same time, to furnish opportunity for ironic humor. Specifically, the religious imagery serves to show the corruption of the higher reason in Troilus as it submits completely to the wiles of the lower reason in pursuit of sensual satisfaction. When Troilus comes to regard the "grace" of Criseyde as a kind of divine Providence, his fall is complete. In the opening scene, both the religion and the humor are displayed. Troilus is busy concocting proper speeches to use when Criseyde approaches, but when Criseyde arrives, thinking [488] of the avowed purpose of her visit, she asks him for "continuance" of his "lordshipe." Troilus is no Hector, and "lordshipe" is the last thing he wants to hold over her; indeed, it is the last thing she wishes him to have, so that the request puts the poor man in some confusion. All he can do is finally to mumble, "mercy, mercy, swete herte!" [III. 98] When he regains a little composure, he asks her, in effect, for "ladyship," and concludes by saying that since he has spoken to her, he can do no more: "Now recche I never how soone that I deye." [III. 112] This "manly sorwe," of what might better be called an "unseemly woman in a seeming man," impresses Pandarus, who, shedding some well-timed tears, digs Criseyde persistently in the ribs:

> And Pandare wep as he to water wolde,
> And poked evere his nece newe and newe,
> And seyde: "Wo bigon ben hertes trewe!
> For love of god, make of this thing an ende,
> Or sle us bothe at ones, or ye wende."
>
> [III. 115–19]

Criseyde pretends prettily not to understand. But after some preliminaries in which Troilus promises to put himself, of all places, under her "yerde," and Criseyde stipulates that she will keep her "honour sauf," retaining, at the same time, in spite of her earlier request, the "sovereignete," she assures Troilus that he will for every woe "recovere a blisse." [III. 137–81] She then takes him in her arms and kisses him. This is a triumph for Pandarus, an event of truly liturgical significance for our little priest, the *elevatio* of his mass for which the bells all ring:

> Fil Pandarus on knees, and up his eyen
> To hevene threw, and held his hondes hye.
> "Immortal god," quod he, "that mayst nat dyen –
> Cupide, I mene – of this mayst glorifie.
> And Venus, thow mayst maken melodie.
> Withouten hond, me semeth that in towne,
> For this miracle, ich here ech belle sowne."
>
> [III. 183–89]

God, or at least Cupid, is rapidly drawing matters to what Alisoun of Bath would call a "fruitful" eventuality. This is the "miracle" Pandarus has hoped for; soon, perhaps, he can prepare the way for his communion, a "revel" accompanied by the old "melodie" of Venus:

[489]   "But I conjure the, Criseyde, and oon,
           And two, thow, Troilus, whan thow mayst goon,
           That at myn hous ye ben at my warnynge,
           For I ful wel shall shape youre comynge."

                                                    [III. 193–96]

Criseyde's "honour sauf" through the good offices of Bien Celer, the two young people will, of course, engage in a little light conversation:

           "And eseth there youre hertes right ynough.
           And lat se which of yow shal bere the belle
           To speke of love aright" – therwith he lough.

                                                    [III. 197–99]

Troilus is now quite ready to walk, perhaps even to dance, and very anxious to talk – "How longe shal I dwelle, or this be don?" [III. 201–2] Evidently the few words spoken earlier were not really enough before death takes him, after all. But Eleyne and Deiphebus approach, so that Troilus, to keep his "honour sauf," falls to groaning, "his brother and his suster for to blende." [III. 206–7] He is a king's son; his country is in danger of destruction by a foreign enemy. But he has a fiddle, or bagpipe, to play too.

When Pandarus and Troilus are alone again, Pandarus decides to confess openly what he has been doing all along. Troilus will not now object. He has become, he says, "bitwixen game and ernest" a "meene" between a man and a woman. [III. 254] This sentimental statement has won for Pandarus many adherents in addition to the one being addressed. But the "game," as Book II abundantly illustrates, was always simply a pleasant and clever device to ameliorate his real intention, to put a "witty" and hence "harmless" face on the matter; and the "ernest," involving such matters as his priestly services for Cupid, could have been directed toward no other end than the one now contemplated. He admonishes Troilus seriously and at length to keep counsel, to treasure Criseyde's reputation. A boasting lover is a liar, he explains, and we know that Pandarus detests lies and liars. Troilus returns a solemn promise. The surfaces must be kept clean. As for Pandarus' pandering, in Troilus' mind it was only "gentilesse," "compassioun," "felawship," and "trist." [III. 402–3] To show that he too has these noble virtues, which are typical of those fostered by Cupid and are best regarded "cautiously," Troilus says that he will be glad to do the same for Pandarus. His sisters, for example, or Helen, might please that gentleman:

[490]   "I have my faire suster, Polixene,
           Cassandre, Eleyne, or any of the frape.
           Be she nevere so faire or wel yshape,

Tel me which thow wilt of everychone
To han for thyn, and lat me thanne allone.

[III. 409–13]

Whether any of the "frape" are suitable or not – and their suitability seems to be a matter of shapeliness – Troilus is anxious to finish his business. He is thirstier than ever: "Parforme it out, for now is most nede." Those in Chaucer's audience who remembered Polixene's moving defense of her virginity as she was about to be sacrificed upon the grave of Achilles – "scilicet haud ulli servire Polixena vellet!" – might have detected perhaps a touch of discourtesy in Troilus' "courtly" offer. But the modern reader may be inclined to echo literally the wonderment of Andreas: "O what a wonderful thing is love, which makes a man shine with so many virtues and teaches everyone, no matter who he is, so many good traits of character!" Nobility, compassion, fellowship, and trust are certainly not to be sneezed at, especially when they are mentioned openly in the text so that their presence is incontrovertible.

After the first exchange of courtesies at Deiphebus' house, Pandarus keeps at his task, "evere ylike prest and diligent" to "quicke alwey the fir." [III. 484–85] He is no man to put the fire out, as should a true priest or a true friend, moved by a certain Boethian pity. In his "messagerie" he is very busy, arranging the proposed conversation at his house. Troilus devises an excuse to explain any absences from his usual haunts. He will be at the Temple of Apollo watching the "holy laurer." [III. 542] The chaste laurel, as Neckam tells us, is placed in the Temple of Apollo "to show that wisdom is imperishable."[9] But Troilus seems to have no real interest either in wisdom or in abstract truth, and Criseyde is no Laura. When Pandarus finally invites Criseyde to "supper," he swears that Troilus is not there, although he knows full well that Troilus is waiting in his little "stuwe." There is a very hard rain, encouraged by a sign of disaster in the heavens. Criseyde can make her way through it to Pandarus' house, but not back again. She "koude as muche good as half a world." [III. 638–39]

[491] Pandarus gets her safely bedded and goes after Troilus. Still unmindful of Pallas, and not actually very much concerned about the laurel of Apollo, Troilus says a little prayer to "Seint Venus," whose energies he will need in "hevene blisse." [III. 704–5] But before the lovers may be united, yet one more ruse is needed, another lie to get Troilus "honorably" into Criseyde's chamber. Never at a loss in such matters, Pandarus devises a little story of jealousy by means of which he finally, after a great deal of dissimulated hesitation on Criseyde's part, manages to arouse the lady's "pitee," so that she agrees to see her lover. But unfortunately the two find it necessary to engage in considerable talk, to "speke of love," as Pandarus had promised. They are impeded further by Troilus' confusion brought about by his own lies. He is so troubled that he falls "a-swowne." [III. 1092] Pandarus, ever ready with a sentimental remedy, tosses him in bed and disrobes him "al to his bare sherte," admonishing Criseyde to "pullen out the thorn." [III. 1099–

1105] But even after Troilus recovers, more talk ensues before Troilus, "sodeynly avysed," embraces his lady. Pandarus, at last satisfied that his services are no longer needed, since, after all, Faus Semblant may be abandoned when the goal is obvious to everyone concerned, offers a bit of parting counsel: "swouneth nat now." [III. 1190] When Troilus tells Criseyde that she must yield, she replies,

> "Ne hadde I or now, my swete herte deere,
> Ben yolde, I were now nat here."
>
> [III. 1210–11]

As Diomede later demonstrates, the very elaborate efforts of Pandarus were not really necessary. As the two enter their bliss, Chaucer warns the ladies in his audience,

> For love of god, take every woman heede
> To werken thus, when it comth to the neede.
>
> [III. 1224–25]

When the "need" arises will depend, of course, on which god one loves. Criseyde, perceiving what strikes her as his "trouthe and clene entente," makes Troilus a joyful "feste." [III. 1228–29] In the resulting "hevene," at a feast which is not exactly the Feast of the Lamb, Troilus appropriately sings a hymn. This hymn is in part a paraphrase of St. Bernard's prayer to the Virgin in the last canto of Dante's *Paradise*, in the original an aspect of the New Song of Jerusalem, but in Troilus' version a song to Cupid, ironically called [492] "Charite." [III. 1254–74] It is the grace of Cupid which Troilus praises, a grace to which at this time he can offer only "laude and reverence," but which will appear to him later in all of its bitterness. He has lost sight of Providence and turned instead to the "grace" of Fortune. He is no longer a free agent, no longer a man. He is a pawn to Fortune, a star-crossed lover, Fortune's fool. The priest of Satan has led him to his highest sacrament. But the "unequal weights" of the God of Love will soon make themselves apparent, and the follower of Venus will find himself naked in the sea.

The "hevene" in which Troilus finds himself is not without its qualms, the "doutances" which he foresaw before his eye fell upon Criseyde. The blessed are afraid in the midst of their bliss, as Andreas tells us they should be; they find

> That ech from other wende ben biraft,
> Or elles, lo! this was hir mooste feere,
> Lest al this thyng but nyce dremes were.
>
> [III. 1340–42]

Indeed, joys of this kind are dreams, revels soon ended and rounded with a sleep. The lovers are disturbed by the parting of the night, a necessary adjunct to the deed of darkness; and they curse the light of day, that "candel of jelosye," as the sun is called in "The Complaint of Mars," which follows Venus over the horizon and puts every degenerate Mars to shame. This love cannot withstand the light of truth and reason. Parting is torture for the lovers, especially for the fearful Troilus (3. 1472–1491). Although he treasures Criseyde's solaces more than "thise worldes tweyne," after he has left her he is far from being satisfied. If he was tormented by desire before, he is tormented more than ever now. As one old moralist put it, "And just as the fire does not diminish as long as the fuel is applied, but rather becomes hotter and more fervent when more fuel is cast upon it, so also the sin of lechery burns more fiercely the more it is exercised."[10] Pandarus brings the lovers together occasionally,

> And thus Fortune a tyme ledde in joie
> Criseyde and ek this kinges sone of Troie.
>
> [III. 1714–15]

This is the uncertain bliss, the fearful joy, for which Troilus has relinquished his "estat roial." To protect himself, he makes his [493] own feeling a cosmic force, this time paraphrasing Boethius on Divine Love, for which he substitutes a generalization of his own idolatrous lust (3. 1744–1771). The pleasure he finds in Criseyde's bed has become the center of his universe, a center that actually rests within himself.

"But al to litel," as Chaucer says at the beginning of Book IV, "lasteth swich joie, ythonked be Fortune." [IV. 1–2] Fortune can "to fooles so hire song entune" [IV. 4] that they become, as it were, asses to the harp of Philosophy's harmonies. Troilus is one of these fools. If he called for night and cursed the day, Night's daughters "that endeles compleynen evere in peyne" control him. As events progress, cupidity with its jealousy, and wrath with its desire for vengeance join libido. Specifically, the "unwar strook" which unsettles his proud realm appears when he learns that Criseyde is to join the Greek camp in exchange for Antenor. Thinking of her "honour," Troilus can do nothing to arrest the transaction. In despair he is like a bare tree (4. 225–231), for the false words of his idolatry no longer protect him. As he mourns alone in his chamber, he is like a "wylde bole," [IV. 239] whose wild acts "denote the unreasonable fury of a beast." He complains bitterly against Fortune, asking, "is there no grace?" [IV. 263] He has honored Fortune, he says, above all other gods always; his subjection is complete and self-confessed. He also blames "the verrey lord of love," Cupid, whose "grace" but a short time ago was all-pervasive. Actually, his difficulty is of his own making. "Nothyng is wrecchid but whan thou wenest it," said Boethius, but Troilus has made of himself a prisoner. Nothing destined him to subject himself to Fortune or to Cupid, but his reason has lost "the lordshipe that it sholde have over the sensualitee," and he is a hopeless thrall in the chains of Venus. Pandarus can offer no real comfort. No person, he says, can "fynden in Fortune ay proprietee." [IV. 391–92] He knows that Fortune is fickle and recommends expediency: he can find Troilus another. But Troilus is no mere sinner in the flesh, and Ovid's remedies will not help him. The only feasible solution seems to him to be suicide, the final act of despair and the ultimate sin against the true love for which he has substituted a false one. Criseyde's condition is almost as bad. With a touch of the comedy of manners developed in Book II, Chaucer shows her beset by her familiar companions, a group of chattering women, full of the gossip of her departure. She [494] thinks of herself "born in cursed constellacioun," [IV. 745] subject to the stars. She will do herself to death. Pandarus finds her with her "sonnysh heeris" falling untended about her ears, [IV. 816] like *Tristitia* in a picture, a condition which indicates in her a desire for martyrdom.

In the process of arranging another meeting between the two lovers, Pandarus discovers Troilus despairing in a temple. The frustrated prince laments that "al that comth, comth by necessite" and that to be lost is his "destinee." [IV. 958–59] This conclusion is followed by a long supporting discussion based on Boethius in which Troilus confuses "absolute" and "conditional" necessity in a way that would have taxed the patience of Lady Philosophy and astonished Bishop Bradwardine, who was not quite so unorthodox on this matter as a recent study seeks to make him. The purpose of the discussion is to show that Troilus has so far abandoned reason that he has practically no free will left. He has become a slave to his desire, a victim of Cupid, prepared for his position painted on the wall of Venus' Temple, along with Tristan, Achilles, Paris, and other worthies of his cause. When his love fails, "chaos is come again," a chaos in his own mind resulting from the universalization of a selfish passion. If he has so far abandoned reason that he can no longer choose, destiny, which controls the operation of Providence in particular instances among unreasoning creatures, will envelop him. Again, Pandarus is of little help. His "wise" philosophy is mere shallow Stoicism:[11]

> "Lat be, and thynk right thus in thi disese:
> That in the dees right as ther fallen chaunces,
> Right so in love ther come and gon plesaunces."
>
> [IV. 1097–99]

The old doctrine of "happes aventurous" can afford no real help to Troilus, just as it cannot help Boethius in the *Consolation*.

The lovers meet once more. Criseyde is so overcome that she swoons. Thinking her dead, Troilus offers to kill himself in Prome[495]thean defiance (4. 1192 ff.). He will conquer Fortune by committing suicide, a device attempted by Nero in the Monk's Tale, "Of which Fortune lough, and hadde a game." Since neither Jove nor Fortune is responsible for his plight, Troilus' defiance is a little hollow. It is especially hollow when we consider the character of the lady whose pleasant capabilities with reference to himself he finds more important than either his country or life itself. When she awakens, she finds a characteristic solution to their mutual problem. If reason fails, something else might help:

> "But hoo, for we han right ynough of this,
> And lat us rise and streight to bedde go,
> And there lat us speken of oure wo."
>
> [IV. 1242–44]

But there is no king in this bed of justice. When Troilus suggests that they "stele awey," Criseyde replies that if they did so, people would accuse them of "lust voluptuous and coward drede," [IV. 1573] weaknesses, naturally, of which Troilus would never be guilty. Moreover, she herself would lose her "honeste." She engages in a long and verbose promise of fidelity connected with that ancient symbol of fickle Fortune, the moon. Her doctrine is considerably better than that offered by Pandarus:

> "And forthi sle with resoun al this hete;
> Men seyn, 'the suffrant overcomth,' pardee;
> Ek, 'whoso wol han lief, he lief mot lete'.
> Thus maketh vertu of necessite
> By pacience, and thynk that lord is he
> Of Fortune ay, that naught wol of hire recche;
> And she ne daunteth no wight but a wrecche."
>
> [IV. 1583–89]

Criseyde can paraphrase Boethius and mean what she says, but since she has no notion of how to apply her words, they become, as Andreas' lady puts it, "more than empty." There is no stopping the heat of the fire lighted at the festival of Pallas now, and Criseyde's bed is no place to slay heat with reason. Neither Troilus nor Criseyde actually has any notion of how to become "lord of Fortune." She knows also that "love is a thyng ay ful of bisy drede," but this fact is adduced as a reason for Troilus to remain faithful, not as something to discourage him from being a [496] "wrecche." The book closes with one final touch of irony. Criseyde explains her love for Troilus:

> "For trusteth wel, that youre estat roial,
> Ne veyn delit, nor only worthinesse
> Of yow in werre or torney marcial,
> Ne pomp, array, nobleye, or ek richesse,
> Ne made me to rewe on youre distresse;
> But moral vertu, grounded upon trouthe,
> That was the cause I first hadde on yow routhe.
>
> "Ek gentil herte and manhood that ye hadde,
> And that ye hadde, as me thoughte, in despit
> Every thyng that souned into badde,
> As rudenesse and poeplissh appetit,
> And that youre resoun bridlede youre delit, –
> This made, aboven every creature,
> That I was youre, and shal, whil I may dure."
>
> [IV. 1667–80]

If this had been true, the lovers would not now be in difficulty – if Troilus had used his reason from the beginning and loved Criseyde for something more than her pleasing "figure" and surpassing competence in bed. This might have been true if Criseyde had actually been interested in "vertu" rather than in Troilus' "persone, his aray, his look, his chere," and in the further fact that the woe of this man of great estate was all for her. But as it stands, this little picture could not be more false, more distant from the furtive actions that Chaucer has described. Troilus' courtship was grounded on a tissue of lies rather than on "trouthe." Both he and Criseyde insisted on an "up-so-doun" relationship directly contrary to reason and honor. And Troilus very carefully renounced, under the direction of Pandarus, his denunciations of "poeplissh appetit." Criseyde can always think of some elevated doctrine to rationalize her situation, but she perverts it into so much idle talk. And idle talk cannot now save Troilus from pains "that passen every torment down in helle." [IV. 1698]

Book V is a picture of Hell on earth, the Hell which results from trying to make earth a heaven in its own right. In medieval terms, when the human heart is turned toward God and the reason is adjusted to discern the action of Providence beneath the apparently [497] fortuitous events of daily life, the result is the City of Jerusalem, radiant and harmonious within the spirit. But when the will desires its own satisfaction in the world alone, the reason can perceive only the deceptive mutability of Fortune. And the result, as one cloud-capp'd tower after another fades away, is the confusion and chaos of Babylon, the world without Christ so mercilessly described in Innocent's *De miseria humane conditionis*. Troilus has defied the gods and placed Criseyde above them. When adversity strikes, he becomes the "aimlessly drifting megalopolitan man" of the modern philosophers, the frustrated, neurotic, and maladjusted hero of modern fiction, an existentialist for whom Being itself, which he has concentrated in his own person, becomes dubious. He is hypersensitive, sentimental, a romantic hopelessly involved in a lost cause. These are, however, the results of a moral process, not the operations of a psychology. Cupidity not only isolates a man from God; it also isolates him from the free society of his fellows, who can no longer afford him any satisfactions when the idol of his lust has vanished away. In this last Book, as the Parcae dominate the unreasoning creature that Troilus has become,[12] Chaucer's ironic humor becomes bitter and the pathos of the tragedy profound.

It is Troilus who leads Criseyde out of town to meet the Greek convoy. All he can do, in spite of dreams of violence, is to mutter, "Now hold youre day, and do me nat to deye." [V. 84] Diomede recognizes the general features of the situation at once, being an old hand at love's stratagems. He takes Criseyde by the "reyne," and for a short time the little filly will be his, but she has no bridle that will hold her to "any certayn ende." Like Polonius or Iago, Diomede is a man true to himself: "He is a fool that wol foryete hym selve." [V. 98] Since he has nothing to lose but words, he begins the old game played by Pandarus in Book II, but without circuitous preliminaries. Just as Pandarus requested at first love of "frendshipe," Diomede asks to be treated as a "brother" and to have his friendship accepted. He will be hers, he says, "aboven every creature," a thing he has said to no woman before. This is the first time. This is different. And sure enough, by the time they reach the Greek [498] camp, Criseyde grants him her "frendshipe." She has nothing to lose either and can be thoroughly depended upon to be to her own self true. In the Greek camp, Diomede does not neglect his opportunity. "To fisshen hire, he leyde out hook and lyne." [V. 777] On her "day," when she was supposed to return to Troilus, she welcomes Diomede as a "frend," and is soon lying to save appearances again:

> "I hadde a lord, to whom I wedded was,
>   The whos myn herte al was til that he deyde;
>   And other love, as help me now Pallas,
>   Ther in myn herte nys, ne nevere was."
>
> [V. 975–78]

She allows Pallas to be of small assistance, for at the close of her conversation she gives Diomede her glove. Her fear helps Diomede, just as it had helped Pandarus. Moreover, Diomede is a man of "grete estat," a conquest to please her vanity. That night she goes to bed

> Retornyng in hire soule ay up and down
>   The wordes of this sodeyn Diomede,
>   His grete estat, the peril of the town,
>   And that she was allone and hadde nede
>   Of frendes help. And thus bygan to brede
>   The cause whi, the sothe for to telle
>   That she took fully purpos for to dwelle.
>
> [V. 1023–29]

"Wo hym that is allone." These are the same causes that led her to succumb to Troilus, for she was also fearful and alone in Troy, and Troilus was a man of "estat roial." Clearly, "moral vertu, grounded upon trouthe" has nothing to do with either affair. Criseyde has not changed at all. She is beautiful and socially graceful, but fearful, susceptible to sentimental pity, and "slydynge of corage." When the die is cast, and Diomede has what he wants, she says, "To Diomede algate I wol be trewe." [V. 1071] She meant to be true to Troilus too, but she is actually faithful only to her own selfish desires of the moment. Her beauty is the sensuous beauty of the world, and her fickleness is the fickleness of Fortune; but she is, at the same time, a sort of feminine Everyman. The world's poor sinners seldom go as far in idolatry as does Troilus or have the enterprise of "sodeyn Diomede." But the average man or woman can very sincerely say all the right things while pursuing selfish [499] ends. This is the reason that Chaucer warns his readers not to condemn Criseyde. She is no gay deceiver, no strumpet, and no mere graceless wench. But her conception of honor is pitifully inadequate, as is her understanding of virtue and truth. In the fourteenth century "sincerity" had not yet been elevated to its present eminence, so that it does not palliate her misdeeds; but it does make Criseyde a pitiable creature whom we can look upon with that compassion which Chaucer recommends to us at the beginning of his poem. Neither Criseyde nor Diomede, both of whom seek momentary footholds

on the slippery way of the world, is capable of the idolatry of which Troilus
is guilty, or of the depths to which he descends.

Left alone in Troy, Troilus curses all the gods together, including Cupid
and Venus. But he is still a slave to his cupidity, a "great natural," who has
no place to hide his bauble. In bed he wallows and turns like "Ixion in helle,"
[V. 212] for he has nothing but a pillow to embrace.[13] His "lode sterre,"
which has turned out to be no *Stella Maris*, has gone. In sleep, he is beset by
nightmares. He dreams that he is alone in a horrible place, that he has fallen
among his enemies, that he has fallen from a high place. These are symbolic
revelations of his actual situation, and Troilus receives small comfort from
the Pertelote-like scorn that Pandarus casts upon them. Pandarus gets him off
"to Sarpedoun," who provides singing and dancing, but there is no "melodie" left for Troilus without Criseyde. The celestial source of the world's
harmony, is, as it were, entertaining Diomede in the Greek camp. Troilus
spends his time, like a jilted schoolboy, moping over his beloved's old
letters. Hastening back to Troy, he hopes to find his lady there, but in vain.
The places where he has seen or enjoyed Criseyde have a perverse fascination
for him. First, having found an excuse to go into town, he visits her house.
When he sees it, he exclaims,

> "O paleys desolat,
> O hous of houses whilom best ihight,
> O paleys empty and disconsolat,
> O thow lanterne of which queynt is the light,
> O paleys, whilom day, that now art nyght!"
>
> [V. 540–44]

[500] The ironic pun on "queynt" is a bitter comment on what it is that
Troilus actually misses, and the change from day to night is, ironically again,
the fulfillment of his wish in Book III. The house is a shrine "of which the
seynt is oute," the empty inverted church of Troilus' love. Everywhere he
goes, he finds memories of Criseyde. He becomes intensely self-conscious,
aware of the eye of every passing stranger on the street. Everyone sees his
woe:

> Another tyme ymaginen he wolde,
> That every wight that wente by the weye
> Hadde of him routhe, and that they seyn sholde:
> "I am right sorry Troilus wol deye."
>
> [V. 624–27]

His spirit is the painful focus of creation, protected neither by the "harde
grace" of Cupid, nor by his empty hopes that Criseyde may return. Each
new rationalization leads only to more bitter frustration. On the walls of the
city the very wind itself blows from Criseyde straight to him, and as it blows
it sighs, "Allas, why twynned be we tweyne?" [V. 679] Criseyde lurks in the
form of every distant traveller, even in a "fare-cart." At last, jealousy adds to
Troilus' discomfort, and with it comes another nightmare. He tries an

exchange of letters, but the artfulness of Criseyde's epistolary style is now painfully apparent. One day he sees the brooch he gave her on parting on Diomede's armor. Now his worst fears are confirmed: "Of Diomede have ye al this feste?" [V. 1677] The jealousy of carnal love overcomes Troilus completely, and the furies dominate his heart. Pandarus' shallow reaction – "I hate, ywis, Criseyde!" [V. 1732] – is no comfort, and in the depths of despair Troilus goes out to seek Diomede in vengeance and his own death on the battlefield. His is no heroic defense of the city, no fulfillment of his political obligations, but a quest for Megara's vengeance and his own destruction. This is the ultimate loneliness, a loneliness he has brought upon himself. So far as vengeance is concerned, Troilus fails, fortunately for Criseyde, but "Ful pitously him slough the fierce Achille." [V. 1806]

If Fortune "lough" at the self-destruction of Nero in the Monk's Tale, Troilus can, in spirit, share that laughter as he rises through the spheres above Fortune's realm toward a destiny of which his own last acts are a sufficient indication. When the flesh with its cumbersome desires has been left behind, he sees the fool[501]ishness of his earthly plight. There, the "jugement is more cleere, the wil nat icorrumped":

> And in hym self he lough right at the wo
> Of hem that wepten for his deth so faste,
> And dampned al oure werk that folweth so
> The blynde lust, the which that may nat laste;
> And sholden al oure herte on heven caste.
>
> [V. 1821–27]

The laughter is the ironic laughter with which Chaucer depicts Troilus' "wo" from the beginning, a laughter which he, and Troilus from his celestial vantage point, would bestow on all those who take a sentimental attitude toward such love as that between Troilus and Criseyde. If, in the course of the poem, the plight of Troilus has moved us to compassion, we too can laugh, partly at ourselves.

Toward the end of *Troilus and Criseyde* Chaucer includes two stanzas in what St. Augustine would have called "high style":

> O yonge fresshe folkes, he or she,
> In which that love up groweth with youre age,
> Repeyreth hom fro worldly vanyte,
> And of youre herte up casteth the visage
> To thilke god that after his ymage
> Yow made, and thynketh al nys but a faire
> This world, that passeth soone as floures faire.

> And loveth hym which that right for love
> Upon a cros, oure soules for to beye,
> First starf, and roos, and sit in hevene above;
> For he nyl falsen no wight, dar I seye,
> That wol his herte al holly on hym leye.

> And syn he best to love is, and most meke,
> What nedeth feyned loves for to seke?
>
> [V. 1835–48]

This, in effect, is what Chaucer has to tell us about love, not only here but in *The Canterbury Tales* and in the major allegories as well. It is his "o sentence." It is, of course, also the message of the Bible, of the *Consolation of Philosophy*, of Andreas Capellanus, of Chrétien de Troyes, and of a great many other medieval writers. The idea, indeed, was a part of the normal expectation of [502] the medieval reader, and to say that an author intends it is simply to say that he is a Christian. The artist or poet, knowing that if left to itself in its abstract form it might become as empty as Criseyde's moral philosophy, sought to get at it indirectly, at the same time giving it a renewed vigor, incisiveness, and applicability in terms that a given audience could understand. To appreciate the value of Chaucer's artistry, we must seek to comprehend, insofar as our historical knowledge permits, the reasons why that artistry appealed strongly to his contemporaries. It does not stand alone, but depends for its effectiveness, like the artistry of any other period, on what the audience brings to it. No art reproduces nature or conveys ideas with absolute fullness; it simply affords hints which the observer rounds out in his own mind. The fact that our minds are conditioned to respond to the hints and stratagems of art in very different ways from those with which court audiences of the late fourteenth century responded to them makes the task of recovering Chaucer's art extremely difficult. If Troilus standing on the windy walls saw Criseyde in the form of a cart, we also, with the predispositions supplied to us by modern poetry, fiction, and music, may be likely to see Chaucer's poem as a celebration of the tragic potentialities in a relatively innocent romantic love affair. But it is improbable that Chaucer wrote either to titillate the young or to supply pap for the fancied appetites of the aged. He had instead a philosophical message of some profundity to impart, a message which, if properly elaborated, could be just as moving as any celebration of romantic love. It was not original with him; but the peculiar luminosity with which he presented it was his own achievement.

Notes

1 London, BM, MS Burney 131, fol. 20 verso.

2 Oxford, Bodl., MS Bodl. 292, fol. 1.

3 London, BM, MS Burney, 131, fol. 39 verso. The same explanation appears in the commentary on Seneca, fol. 3. A study of the classical imagery in *Troilus* is being prepared by John P. McCall. [*Chaucer among the Gods* (University Park: Pennsylvania State University Press, 1979)]

4 The following account of the *Troilus* is a modified version of the author's "Chaucerian Tragedy," *ELH*, XIX (1952), 1 ff.

5 Root's punctuation. [Robert K. Root, ed., *The Book of Troilus and Criseyde* (Princeton: Princeton University Press, 1926)] Pandarus is neither a devil nor a man, but an element in a poem; as a part of a poetic configuration, his actions sometimes suggest those of a devil.

6 See John P. McCall, "Chaucer's May 3," *MLN*, LXXVI (1961), 201–205.

7 See D. W. Robertson, Jr., and B. F. Huppé, *"Piers Plowman" and Scriptural Tradition* (Princeton, 1951), p. 111.

8 See "The Doctrine of Charity in Medieval Literary Gardens," *Speculum*, XXVI (1951), pp. 25–26.

9 *Super Marcianum*, Oxford, Bodl., MS Digby 221, fol. 61 verso. Holcot, *Super librum ecclesiastici* (Venice, 1509), pp. 9 recto and verso, explains in detail that the crown of Apollo is the crown of wisdom. Apollo was generally associated with wisdom or truth.

10 Gerard of Liège, ed. Wilmart, *Analecta reginensia* (Vatican, 1933), p. 201.

11 The Stoicism of Pandarus should be distinguished sharply from the philosophy of Boethius, whose lady complains (1 pr. 3) that the Stoics and Epicureans have torn shreds and patches from her garment. Pandarus is an Epicurean with respect to pleasure and a Stoic with respect to pain – a position that is hardly unusual. He seeks, in other words, to harden himself against what Boethius regarded as the lessons of both good and bad fortune. For further discussion, see Alan Gaylord, "Uncle Pandarus as Lady Philosophy," *Papers of the Michigan Academy*, XLVI (1961), 571–595.

12 The Parcae, invoked at the beginning of Book v, are said by Neckam, *Super Marcianum*, Oxford, Bodl., MS Digby 221, fol. 40 verso, to represent the "operations of Providence in worldly affairs."

13 Trivet, London, BM, MS Burney 131, fol. 49 verso, explains that Ixion sought the love of Juno. That is, he sought libidinous delight in the active life. He revolves on a wheel because a man dedicated to temporal affairs is "continually elevated by prosperity and cast down by adversity."

8 | Troilus and Criseyde: a reconsideration

ELIZABETH SALTER

Originally published in *Patterns of Love and Courtesy: Essays in Memory of C. S. Lewis*, ed. John Lawlor (London: Arnold, 1966, pp. 86–106). Reprinted by permission of Edward Arnold. The original pagination is recorded within square brackets. The endnotes originally appeared as footnotes and are here renumbered.

Although many academic critics have expressed 'second thoughts' about C. S. Lewis's overall view of *Troilus and Criseyde* – 'a great poem in praise of love'[1] – I suspect that most readers will continue to find him a precise and sensitive guide to Chaucer's meaning:

> It semed hire he wiste what she thoughte
> Withouten word, so that it was no nede
> To bidde hym ought to doon, or ought forbeede;
> For which she thought that love, al come it late,
> Of alle joie hadde opned hire the yate.[2]

It would be difficult, under the influence of *The Allegory of Love*, to miss the significance of those lines: original to Chaucer, they are offered as a tribute to the seriousness rather than to the fretting urgency of human love, which is poised at that moment in the poem between recognition and fulfilment. Criseyde surely refers back to 'such sober certainty' when she later tells Troilus

> Ne hadde I er now, my swete herte deere,
> Ben yold, ywis, I were now nought heere!
>
> (iii, 1210–11)

and it is an eccentric gloss which requires us to hear her words as an admission of connivance.[3]

In spite of the challenges thrown down by more recent criticism, the centrality, the 'passionate sanity'[4] of C. S. Lewis's writing on *Troilus* [87] has not been obscured or outdated: there are few important works which are not indebted in some way to the comparative methods of study he advocated in 'What Chaucer really did to *Il Filostrato*'[5] or to the wider interpretative modes of the *Allegory of Love*. If there is still a need to 'reconsider' *Troilus and Criseyde*, it is not because his directions were substantially wrong, but because many of these directions have not been fully explored. Intensive studies of *Troilus*[6] and its sources have not mined ore of the same quality as his short and exemplary article in *Essays and Studies*, and learning quite as impressive as his has been misapplied to the understanding of the poem, since it could not draw on the same kind of literary responsiveness which distinguished and stabilized *The Allegory of Love*.[7]

It is still possible to see the main area of *Troilus* criticism divided between writers whose effort is simply to demonstrate more precisely the 'grete worthynesse' of Chaucer's work, and those who are set to disturb traditional attitudes by exercising ingenuity at the expense of common sense and sensibility. But close attention to the form and texture of Chaucer's verse – an attention which marked all of C. S. Lewis's commentary – makes either extreme reverence or extreme inventiveness unnecessary. Much remains to be said about *Troilus and Criseyde*, but I doubt whether we shall improve on his way of encountering the poem.

No real confidence, for instance, could now be placed in judgements of the poem which are not prepared to take into account Chaucer's dealings with his sources. Minute or major changes, redispositions of material, are crucial to our understanding of 'the poet at work', and, ultimately to our understanding of the work itself. A simple and yet immensely important example of this occurs at the end of Book III. Chaucer's refusal to conclude this Book with Boccaccio's ominous lines –

> Ma poco tempo durò cotal bene,
> Mercé della fortuna invidiosa,
> [88]   . . . Crisëida gli tolse e'dolci frutti,
> e' lieti amor rivolse in tristi lutti[8]

is the climax of a series of actions designed to seal off that section of the narrative from its bleak hinterlands of violence and betrayal. So, too, the whole of Book II, with its perplexing heroine and its uncertain narrator, must first be seen as a struggle with materials only partially tractable to the poet's emerging purposes. The logical conclusion of an unbiased study of 'Chaucer at work' in *Troilus* may not yet have been fairly represented. The acceptability of such statements as 'he achieves a symmetry, a balance, in episode and detail', or 'he communicates to us a view of the whole in which tolerance and critical perception are harmoniously blended',[9] has still to be proved. For *Troilus and Criseyde* shows unmistakable signs of conflicting purposes, unresolved difficulties. And it is, above all, a striking example of a medieval poem which forbids the easy use of terms such as 'unity', 'consistency'. It would be possible to say that the very magnitude of what Chaucer attempted to do in *Troilus* was the guarantee of some measure of failure, and that, unless we allow for this, we minimize his imaginative strength, demonstrated with such special triumph in Book III of the poem.

The situation in *Troilus* is similar to that in other major poems of Chaucer's: given a narrative which cannot be *radically* altered, Chaucer proceeds to treat that narrative in ways which demand, for the sake of unity and consistency, just that radical action denied to him. And if the text is given close scrutiny, it is hard to resist the conclusion that Chaucer's dealings with his material were often arbitrary, and certainly not always the result of premeditated design. The greatest problem of *Troilus and Criseyde* is not the character of Criseyde, nor the adjustment of Boethian philosophy with courtly love, but the poet Chaucer – for his workings are, at times, most problematic.[10]

In brief outline, *Troilus* displays to us a poet whose gradually changing purposes involve him in greater and greater difficulty with his sources. Warnings, in Book I, of possible clashes of substance and interpretation are confirmed by Book II: this is perhaps the most con[89]fused and at the same time the most interesting of all five Books from the point of view of 'poet at work'. Out of its near-chaos comes the great resolution of Book III, which justifies, retrospectively, the uneven conflicts of Book II. And here I think Chaucer intended his readers to accept a break, a pause in the movement of the poem. Books IV and V can also be seen in terms of conflict: the poet's gradual – and at times extremely painful – accommodation to the dictates of his narrative. So the ending of *Troilus* has, indeed, been prepared for throughout the poem, but mainly in the sense that it is an urgent declaration of a predicament in which Chaucer began to find himself as early, perhaps, as Book I: a predicament born of the decision to free his imagination, and to write about the love of Troilus and Criseyde not simply as a gay, sensual episode, nor as an ennobling example of 'amour courtois', nor indeed as a proof of 'worldes brotelnesse', but as an embodiment of 'the holiness of the heart's affections'.[11] For the unique excellence of *Troilus and Criseyde* is not, surely, to be counted the creation of 'characters' such as Pandarus and Criseyde, nor the weaving of a rich and many-stranded poetic fabric, but, more basically, the growth and release of a poet's imagination.

In *Troilus*, triumphing momentarily over both his story and his age, Chaucer is in his element –

> . . . for his bounty,
> There was no winter in it: an autumn 'twas
> That grew the more by reaping . . .

But the operative word is 'momentarily'. It should not, nowadays, be anything but a commonplace to say that a medieval poet's conception of 'unity' in a work of art could differ sharply from that of later writers. The 'unity' of Malory's *Morte D'Arthur*, of *The Canterbury Tales*, of a cycle of Miracle Plays is loose-knit, and not easily categorized in terms acceptable to post-Renaissance criticism. In *Troilus* certain kinds of unity can be recognized immediately: the narrative completes the curve described by Chaucer in Book I –

[90]   In which ye may the double sorwes here
        Of Troilus in lovynge of Criseyde,
        And how that she forsook hym er she deyde;

                                                        (ll. 54–56)

there is a general unity of verisimilitude in the movement of the main characters in the context of the poem; and there is undoubted unity in the perfectly sustained quality of the verse over all five Books. But recognition of this need not make us anxious to press for a more comprehensive and thorough unity. Chaucer shows here and elsewhere that he is only too willing to work for local effectiveness at the expense of total consistency and continuity.[12] In a poem which still accepted oral recitation as a possible mode of delivery – 'And red wherso thow be, or elles songe' – discrepancies of tone, of attitude, of reference would not appear to be of paramount importance. We should not, however, fail to notice that they exist.

To take one isolated example: Chaucer's references at the close of the poem to 'payens corsed olde rites', 'what alle hire goddes may availle', 'Jove, Appollo ... Mars ... swich rascaille' (v, 1849, 1850, 1853) depend for their effectiveness on the reader's consent not to range back meticulously over the length of the poem, inquiring whether the poet's strictures are supported by the evidence of his work. They depend on an inaccurate recollection of the whole substance of Book III, and on the poet's right to establish a local forcefulness without regard to total congruity. However ingenious our arguments, the relationship between the ending of *Troilus* and Book III remains uncertain: the elevation of Boccaccio's terrestrial passion to 'love, that his hestes hath in hevenes hye ...', a process which occupies a good part of Books II and III, is not so much comprehended as misrepresented by the final judgements of Book V. The stanza in question is not only suspiciously vehement but careless,[13] and I doubt if we should spend much energy trying to justify what Chaucer himself preferred to ignore – or at most to notice cursorily.

Then also, we should allow for a considerable element of wilfulness in Chaucer's methods of procedure. The progress of his poem does not seem to have been controlled by steady consciousness of an overall plan. Book II, in particular, is a piece of writing in which sudden, happy [91] improvisation jostles with hesitation, and recklessness is followed by uncertainty. Here sometimes the poet's imagination is allowed to leap forward at a heedless pace, and the verse records the very uneasy commerce of creative invention with narrative discretion. But the vital point to make is that Chaucer assumes his right to take sudden decisions about the development of his work in mid-career. Book I gives only slight indication of what was soon to begin stirring his creative processes and setting his poem so decisively apart from Boccaccio.

Two factors must weigh in a fresh consideration of *Troilus and Criseyde*. There is a strong possibility that Chaucer's view of his poem allowed for discontinuity of attitude and mode of presentation as well as for the preservation of other kinds of continuity. There is the equally strong possibility that Chaucer's purposes were not entirely clear to him even when the poem was well under way: the graph of *Troilus* records sudden advances and recessions, as the poet realizes – and pauses to consider – where his independence is leading him. This is not to brush aside the significance of Chaucer's revisions of the poem, but simply to ask whether they do, in fact, argue his grasp of 'the parallels and the symmetry of the poem's structure'.[14] Such an approach need not seek to isolate *Troilus* from the rest of Chaucer's work. It is proper to recall *The House of Fame*, in which the tendency to sudden and arbitrary action is most freely – and perhaps disastrously – indulged: to recall also *The Canterbury Tales*, in which impromptu and disruptive episodes (the Canon's Yeoman episode is a brilliant example) are part of a complex pattern of continuities and discontinuities operated on narrative, dramatic and thematic levels.

Although Book I of the poem does not pose any very serious problems, it is clear, even as early as this, that Chaucer does not intend to allow his preordained narrative to keep him from ways of writing which may, ultimately, come into conflict with it. The narrator's advice to lovers is a case in point. The tone of the passage is not ironic: advice is plainly given, and it bases its argument on the power and the virtue of love:

> Now sith it may nat goodly ben withstonde,
> And is a thing so vertuous in kynde,
> Refuseth nat to Love for to ben bonde . . .

(i, 253–5)

[92] Boethian insights are already present:

> . . . Love is he that alle thing may bynde,
> For may no man fordon the lawe of kynde . . .

(i, 237–8)

Already Chaucer shows his inclination to write for the moment: the disastrous outcome of love – 'Swich fyn hath, lo, this Troilus for love!' – is not remotely in mind, as Chaucer invites his audience to honour the 'fall' of Troilus –

> Blissed be Love, that kan thus folk converte!

(i, 308)

and his dedication to a life of love, service and 'vertu':

> Dede were his japes and his cruelte,
> His heighe port, and his manere estraunge,
> And ecch of tho gan for a vertu chaunge.

(i, 1083–5)

This high valuation of human love, which the more prudent Boccaccio did not suggest, is confirmed by words given – incongruously, perhaps – to Pandarus. The Italian heroine's 'aptness' for love is turned by Chaucer from a cynical and slightly vulgar appraisal of woman's nature into a dignified statement about the proper sequential relationship of love 'Celestial, or elles love of kynde' (i, 979). This is the first time in the poem that earthly love is clearly set into some kind of cosmic pattern, and the significance of Chaucer's action cannot be over-emphasized. For not only is he anxious (we may think) to protect Criseyde from the casual lash of Boccaccio's remark: he seems also to be eager to establish high status for the quality and import of love between creatures. The dramatic unlikeliness of the words, coming from Pandarus, is a sure sign of their *thematic* relevance:

> It sit hire naught to ben celestial
> As yet, *though that hire liste bothe and kowthe* . . .

(i, 983–4)

The potentialities of Criseyde, and, through her, the potentialities of human kind, moving from terrestrial to heavenly love – these are the points at stake. If they have little to do either with the character of Pandarus or with the 'double sorwe' of Troilus, Chaucer is not greatly perturbed. It could be claimed that already there are signs of his [93] reluctance to feel himself wholly committed by accepting the story in its main essentials. As Book I closes, we cannot forecast exactly what he intends: Troilus 'dryeth forth his aventure', but the line gives no distinct foreboding of ill fortune, and could be hinting at happiness which 'vertu' will come to deserve. We can forecast, however, that the dignifying and deepening of the concept of human love will make for a more complex poem, and that the handling of betrayal and disillusion may be correspondingly difficult. It would be impossible to say how far Chaucer anticipates, or, indeed, cares to consider this.

The Proem to Book II, which he apparently added to his first draft of the poem, raises questions for the reader. If the value of its opening stanzas as high-styled apostrophe is undebatable, its main function is not so easily described. It seems to spring from a need to say something about artistic responsibility; it may be read, in part, as Chaucer's (retrospective) admission of the problems inherent in his treatment of the story. The desire to shed some responsibility for the nature and conduct of the poem is clearly pressing him, and when we remember how Book II develops, it is hardly surprising that he felt bound to make some kind of comment. Direct discussion of artistic motive and predicament is rare in Chaucer's period: there is no real precedent for him. But in these words which preface Book II a strong sense of Chaucer's uneasiness about the progress of his poem makes itself felt:

> Wherfore I nyl have neither thank ne blame
> Of al this werk, but prey yow mekely,
> Disblameth me, if any word be lame,
> For as myn auctour seyde, so sey I . . .

(ii, 15–18)

We need not deny that the stanzas are cast in the familiar rhetorical form of *dubitatio*, nor that their overt conclusion is 'In sondry londes, sondry ben usages'. What is crucial here is that Chaucer should return to enforce the point about 'myn auctour' (l. 49): anxiety to invoke his sources can be interpreted as a recognition, not a solution, of the 'cas' he finds himself in as Book II moves erratically to its precipice of suspense –

> – O myghty God, what shal he seye?

[II. 1757]

For it is, surely, in Book II that Chaucer begins to put his powers of independent action to the test: the angle of divergence from Boccaccio widens, and the passages which convey the poet's increasing – and not [94] always happy – awareness of the situation are more prominent. Although there have been intimations of change in Book I, Book II marks a quickening of the tempo of change: fresh energy is released to the business of adaptation, and the poetry swings dramatically between 'drede and sikernesse', showing doubt and confidence in the propriety of what is being done. This is particularly clear in the case of Criseyde: Chaucer's dealings with her in this Book are sometimes bold and imaginative, sometimes timorous in the extreme. She struggles to emerge from the poetry, but if she remains largely an enigma, this is less the result of subtle characterization than of an imperfect fusion of old and new material.

The nature of her reply to the first unmistakable suggestion that she should *love* Troilus is important here. The violence of her outburst is surprising in the immediate context; Pandarus has been calculating with her in terms of 'tendre wittes' (ii, 271): she has appeared demure, complaisant, a little playful and a little curious – 'I shal felen what he meneth, ywis ...' – and Chaucer has shown no great interest in developing the serious note he introduced in Book I. But the words she uses to Pandarus, in rebuke, are serious indeed – much too serious for the narrative as it has been forecast, and for the events which follow almost immediately. Her severe, intelligent complaint belongs to a narrative which might take a different course, to a woman who might either be steadfast in chastity, or prove worthy of a man's virtuous love, and faithful to him. At this point Chaucer does not resist the prompting of his imagination; the speech is magnificently inappropriate:

> What! is this al the joye and al the feste?
> Is this youre reed? Is this my blisful cas?
> Is this the verray mede of youre byheeste?
> Is al this paynted proces seyd, alas!
> Right for this fyn? . . .

> (ii, 421–5)

It is hardly relevant to debate whether Criseyde is genuinely outraged or not: the interesting fact is that Chaucer considered such language fitted to the occasion. The incisive quality of the verse is not so much a measure of his concern to save the reputation of Criseyde as a measure of his growing dissatisfaction with the nature of Boccaccio's narrative.

This dissatisfaction seems to centre more and more on the *status* of the love he is to celebrate in Book III. For it must be increasingly clear [95] to him that if he is to write solemnly, even responsibly, about this love, the Italian heroine, who makes most of her decisions on the basis of expediency and desire, will not do. He has already revealed something of the context in which he wishes to set this 'love of kynde'; it is a commitment which is both exciting and perturbing him by Book II. His efforts to manipulate

Criseyde, so that she may be a serious participant in his changing concept of the poem's theme, occupy a good part of Book II, but they are efforts often balked by the sheer weight of substance of the original. Chaucer may have felt free to deepen the reactions of this woman, to give her sharp protests of disillusioned wisdom: he did not feel free – nor, in all probability, did he feel obliged – to attempt a total recasting of her. The importance of the stanzas in question is thematic, rather than psychological: they belong as much to the poet and his readers as to Criseyde, and function as a warning that the gradient to love will be steep. By stating and then rejecting what his Italian source so patently deals in (a 'paynted proces'), Chaucer establishes his right to ask for a different valuation of the affair, even if he cannot re-order events.

So he proceeds, with a mixture of confidence and nervousness: his confident invention of the scene in which Criseyde sees Troilus riding back from battle 'so lik a man of armes and a knyght', and finds her fears about love assuaged by his sobriety as well as by his valour, is followed by a display of artistic misgivings. Suddenly he loses conviction about what is now superbly evident – that Criseyde is not approaching love easily, but with difficult self-adjustment. The comment by the narrator –

> Now myghte som envious jangle thus:
> This was a sodeyn love; how myght it be
> That she so lightly loved Troilus . . .
>
> (ii, 666 seq.)

is quite gratuitous from the dramatic point of view: it is highly significant, nevertheless, as a comment on Chaucer's creative battles, already partly over and won. That he feels it necessary is a gauge of the pressures constantly at work on him throughout this critical stage of the poem's development. For it is vital to his writing in the coming Book that some kind of transformation should be effected now: a transformation of values, since it cannot, in the medieval contract, be a total transformation of material.

[96] And in all these dealings, it is surely on Book III, no further, that his vision rests. The conquests being won so hardly are for near objectives, and will require fresh campaigning as the poem turns to its conclusion. There is no evidence that in the restless manoeuvring of Book II Chaucer had anything more than Book III in sight:

> For for o fyn is al that evere I telle . . .
>
> (ii, 1596)

The 'fyn' he refers to here is certainly not that of Book V: it is closer, more immediate. This emerges again in the elaborate Deiphebus episode. No one could deny that here, in the busy intriguing of Pandarus, Chaucer allowed himself splendid opportunities for dramatic verse – 'O verray God, so have I ronne!' He also, for very practical purposes, allowed the innocence of Criseyde to be enmeshed by Pandarus in his less endearing, slightly more sinister capacity – 'But Pandarus thought, "It shal nought be so . . ."' (ii, 1296).

But the episode has another special claim on our attention as a preparation for Book III. It marks a decisive severing of allegiance to the standards and expectations of the original Italian. It comes as a sudden burst of free composition after a period of uneven progress, and demonstrates the imaginative strength of the poet, who is now so confidently at variance with his original that he can allow himself a major addition to the narrative – and, in some respects, a redirection of the narrative. For the Deiphebus episode begins to intimate to the reader how love will grow uncorrupted out of the centre of intrigue:

> Lo, hold the at thi triste cloos, and I
> Shal wel the deer unto thi bowe dryve . . .

> (ii, 1534–5)

The transformation of values has been achieved, and Criseyde goes to Troilus freed of responsibility for events, and untouched, except by compassion for a man she has begun to trust:

> Al innocent of Pandarus entente,
> Quod tho Criseyde, 'Go we uncle deere.'

> (ii, 1723–4)

It is significant that Pandarus conjures Criseyde to behave with pity towards Troilus

[97]   On his half which that soule us alle sende,
> And in the vertu of corones tweyne . . .

> (ii, 1734–5)

Such language, with its particular Christian references and its nuptial imagery, is not only, of course, anachronistic, but uncharacteristic of the speaker: it is only appropriate to the developing theme of the poem. The general tone is right, if the dramatic context is not, and confirmation of this will not be long delayed. It says as clearly as it can that whatever *events* the narrative is destined to recount, the *theme* of the central part of the poem will be honourable and legitimate love. And if the breathless concluding line of the Book is not patently Christian in phrasing, it carries sufficient religious associations to act as a bridge to the Proem of Book III:

> . . . O myghty God, what shal he seye?

In this Proem, for the first time, religious language has an unambiguous part to play. Books I and II mingle pagan and Christian references in a way which is sometimes of obvious importance, and sometimes quite fortuitous. But now Chaucer takes the opportunity not only to reposition material from his Italian source, but to recast some of it in strongly Christian terms. The impulse towards change and the nature of the change are both notable. The first stanza of the Proem,

> O blisful light, of which the bemes clere
> Adorneth al the thridde heven faire . . .

could be dealing with the highest form of *amour courtois*: the second stanza could not. After translating Boccaccio's Boethian lines, 'Il ciel, la terra ed il mare e lo'nferno/ciascuno in sé la tua potenza sente ...' (*op. cit.*, p. 90), Chaucer gives us plain words:

> *God loveth, and to love wol nought werne,*
> And in this world no lyves creature
> Withouten love is worth, or may endure.

> (iii, 12–15)

The passage in Boccaccio is quite differently set:

> e gli uomini e gl'iddii; né creatura
> sanza di te nel mondo vale o dura.

> (*loc. cit.*)

[98] The substitution of 'God' for 'gods', and the assertion of heavenly benevolence in the matter of human love are both remarkable, and should not be passed over. In width of concept and precision of language the whole stanza bears comparison with many statements in orthodox religious treatises of Chaucer's own day:

> ... from out the great ring which represents the Eternal Godhead, there flow forth little rings, which may be taken to signify the high nobility of natural creatures ...[15]

> For this was showed: that our life is all grounded and rooted in love, and without love we may not live: and therefore ... the soul ... of his special grace seeth so far into the high marvellous goodness of God, and seeth that we are endlessly joined to him in love ...[16]

The effect of this stanza is felt throughout the Proem and beyond. It lends warmth and seriousness to the poet's invocation –

> How I mot telle anonright the gladnesse
> Of Troilus, to Venus heryinge?
> To which gladnesse, who nede hath, *God hym bringe*!

> (iii, 47–49)

But it is particularly interesting as a deliberate – and, in all likelihood, later – declaration of progress and intent. There can be no doubt now about Chaucer's desire to clarify and confirm his position. The tentative, exploratory move in Book I towards a definition of love which could touch simultaneously human and celestial boundaries[17] is here followed through with assurance – 'God loveth, and to love wol nought werne ...' With these words Chaucer crowns his efforts to achieve a 'reformation of feeling' in his poem. For they define the outer limits of the love that is to be the subject of the coming Book, and they announce a new mood of reconciliation – not simply the reconciliation of pagan and Christian elements in that cosmic dance described in this and surrounding stanzas, but the reconciliation of

Chaucer with his poetic materials and his inclinations. The words are a manifesto of intention about the conduct of the next stage of the story and, further, a manifesto [99] of Chaucer's status as a creative artist. They establish his right to present his narrative according to his imaginative convictions, and not according to the dictates of his original or the narrower doctrines of his age. He will not be subject to Boccaccio, nor to the homilists, and, indeed, throughout this Book he demands from his readers an unqualified sympathy with 'the high nobility of natural creatures'. He has won for himself freedom of action in a situation where freedom was scarcely to be expected, and he has won it by widening the perspectives of his poetry[18] to a degree uncalled for, and even unjustified, by his given material, with its evanescent delight and its sombre outcome. Book III is dedicated, in defiance of the known ending of the story, to what Spenser described in his *Epithalamium* as 'the safety of our joy', and the strength of the poetry is directly related to Chaucer's new-found security: 'God loveth, and to love wol nought werne.'

For Book III has, in a special sense, an independent existence, and Chaucer must have expected his readers to accept this. Not that, even now, there is total consistency of attitude and subject-matter: it is typical – and, in the long run, unimportant – that Chaucer should allow the odd jarring note to be heard. The careful and delicate phrasing of Criseyde's promises to Troilus –

> Bysechyng hym, for Goddes love, that he
> Wolde, in honour of trouthe and gentilesse,
> As I wele mene, eke menen wel to me . . .

(iii, 162–4)

and the equally fastidious account of her capitulation by Pandarus –

> For the have I my nece, of vices cleene,
> So fully maad thy gentilesse triste,
> That al shal ben right as thiselven liste . . .

(iii, 257–9)

are followed by that jaunty passage in which Troilus offers

> . . . my faire suster Polixene,
> Cassandre, Eleyne, or any of the frape . . .

(iii, 409–10)

[100] to Pandarus in return for his services. It is a careless adjustment of old and new.[19]

But much more noticeable is the confidence of the writing. It is confidence – based on persuasions of the goodness and legitimacy of this relationship – which allows Chaucer to take Book III at such a leisurely pace. The period between Criseyde's long-awaited words

> . . . I wol wel trewely
> . . . Receyven hym fully to my servyse . . .

(iii, 159, 161)

and their fulfilment is slowly and compassionately charted: their love is proved first in service and companionship. It is no accident that some of the most moving poetry about human love in this Book comes well before that 'blisful nyght, of hem so longe isought', and that an atmosphere of 'concorde and quiete' announces the central act of the story –

> That to ben in his goode governaunce,
> So wis he was, she was namore afered . . .
>
> (iii, 481–2)

It is also no accident that the bitter outcry of Criseyde against the 'brotel wele of mannes joie unstable . . .'[20] cannot really disturb the sense of safety which pervades the Book. The movement between momentary 'drede' and 'sikernesse' is simple, and Criseyde's sadness is easily transformed into a positive desire to solace Troilus:

> 'Hadde I hym nevere lief? by God, I weene
> Ye hadde nevere thyng so lief!' quod she.
>
> (iii, 869–70)

From that point to the end of the Book the poem's development is one of expanding certainty: the setbacks experienced by the lovers are [101] minimal, their humorous setting acceptable, because so many serious assumptions have already been made. And seriousness grows in exact proportion to the sensuousness of the poetry: every new move is endorsed by religious language.[21] When Troilus takes the final step towards happiness, it is with a benediction:

> This Troilus, with blisse of that supprised,
> *Putte al in Goddes hand,*[22] as he that mente
> Nothyng but wel; and sodeynly avysed,
> He hire in armes faste to hym hente . . .
>
> (iii, 1184–7)

After this, it cannot seem inappropriate that Criseyde's generosity in love should be praised in devout words:

> For love of God, take every womman heede
> To werken thus, if it comth to the neede,[23]
>
> (iii, 1224–5)

nor that the excited description of her beauty should be followed by a fresh affirmation of the cosmic power of love:

> Benigne love, thow holy bond of thynges . . .

The poet writes, and the characters act, out of a deep assurance of propriety; for all its delighted 'concreteness'[24] the dominant mood of the poetry is 'pees' and 'suffisaunce', and the dominant movement is *andante cantabile*:

> ... myn owen hertes list,
> My ground of ese, and al myn herte deere,
> Gramercy, for on that is al my trist!
>
> (iii, 1303–5)

Even at the very centre of misery, the moment of 'disseveraunce', [102] reconciliation is suggested: the immediate pressure of pain is reduced by wide-ranging allusions to Creation, Order, Purpose:

> O blake nyght, as folk in bokes rede,
> That shapen art by God this world to hide
> At certeyn tymes wyth thi derke wede ...
> Thow rakle nyght, ther God, maker of kynde ...
> Ther God thi light so quenche, for his grace ...
>
> (iii, 1429–31, 1437, 1456)

Criseyde comforts Troilus in an ascending series of passionate and religious statements, and it would be a perverse reading of the poetry at this stage which could find intended irony in her juxtaposition of

> by God and by my trouthe ...
>
> (iii, 1512)

It is not surprising that the warnings of Pandarus, next day, about 'discretion', 'moderation' are, in the circumstances, not so much portentous as inadequate. In the lighter Italian text they had a significant part to play, but in this changed context their concern with

> Be naught to rakel ...
> Bridle alwey wel thi speche and thi desir ...
>
> (iii, 1630, 1635)

seems peripheral. Even the additions to the Italian – 'For wordly joie halt nought but by a wir ...' (iii, 1636) are not strong enough to shake the belief that 'hire hertes wel assured were'. They witness more to Chaucer's sense that the original words fall short of touching the new situation than to an anxious sense of approaching doom. For they come between the lovers' dedication to each other, and Troilus's total dedication not simply to love but to love as the divine principle of the universe. Only one line gives a hint that all may not ultimately be well, and this is so firmly embedded in the celebration of 'suffisaunce ... blisse ... singynges ...' (iii, 1716) that Chaucer cannot have intended that it should halt his readers for long:

> And thus Fortune a tyme ledde in joie
> Criseyde, and ek this kynges sone of Troie.
>
> (iii, 1714–15)

The last stanzas of the Book, by their additions and omissions, ratify all that has gone before. Writing his own *finis* to this part of the story, [103] Chaucer invokes religious philosophy of the highest and most solemn kind. By setting Troilus to associate (not, it must be noted, to identify) his love with

> Love, that of erthe and se hath governaunce,
> Love, that his hestes hath in hevenes hye,
> Love, that with an holsom alliaunce
> Halt peples joyned ...

> (iii, 1744–7)

he makes his most moving case for 'the high nobility of natural creatures' and their 'holsom alliaunce'. No irony plays about his comprehensive statement of the interlocking of human and divine loves:

> So wolde God, that auctour is of kynde,
> That with his bond Love of his vertu liste
> To cerclen hertes alle, and faste bynde ...

> (iii, 1765–7)

The spirit of the words is hardly different from that of Julian's 'we are endlessly joined to him in love'. After this, Boccaccio's summary announcement of impending disaster would have been completely out of tune: its omission, and transference to the Proem of Book IV, is of greatest importance to our understanding of Chaucer's intentions. His admission that he has deliberately altered Boccaccio's ending is candid but unrepentant:

> My thridde bok now ende I in this wyse ...

> (iii, 1818)

And so it is in 'lust and in quiete' that the Book fulfils its promise. Giving religious sanction to a love which originally asked and needed none, Chaucer gave sanction to a freedom of imaginative movement hard to equal in any work of his age which dealt with 'love of kynde'. It is both a sad and a triumphant fact that the only medieval writings on love which rival the grace and intensity of Chaucer's language in Book III of *Troilus* are religious treatises, and Chaucer had to win the release of his full imaginative powers for this difficult subject by religious means. The word to stress is 'full': medieval literature abounds in descriptions of human love – sensual, casual, refined, ritualized, practical and brutal – but few artists found ways to take full imaginative grasp of this complex human condition, to admit its dignity as well as its [104] vulnerability, and to give serious status to bodily as well as spiritual compassion.

But the cost of this to Chaucer in *Troilus and Criseyde* should not be underestimated. If Book II records, by a series of surface disturbances, a deep turmoil of decisions, and if Book III records the confident outcome of decisions taken, the two remaining Books record a gradual, difficult readjustment to authority in the shape of the original narrative. By the end of Book III, Chaucer has worked certain transmutations: the rest of the poem must be a process of disenchantment. Expectations encouraged by Book III must be refused to the reader, and the divergence of narrative and presentation, by now wide and serious, must be reduced. With the beginning of Book IV, Chaucer tackles fresh problems: problems which he has, to a large extent, created for himself by energetic development of unsuspected potential in his sources. The admirable recklessness of his actions has to be paid for.

The unpalatable nature of what lies before him is the real subject of his Proem to Book IV, and we should see in it not only regret for the tarnishing of his bright image of Criseyde,

> Allas! that they sholde evere cause fynde
> To speke hire harm . . .
>
> (iv, 19–20)

but also his reluctance to begin the closing-down of the great imaginative vistas of Book III. From now on the story will lay strongest claims to his allegiance, and he will have only a small area for freedom of operation. The deepest 'drede' which fills him at this point is fear of imaginative restriction by the events henceforth to be 'matere of my book'.

The poem is, indeed, entering a new phase, and Chaucer warns his readers to look for decisive changes – not only in the way his characters must behave, but also in the attitudes he and they must begin to adopt towards such behaviour. Nothing he has so brilliantly evoked in Book III can be any help towards *understanding* what will happen: he has ensured that the rift between love and betrayal will now be unbridgeable except in terms of strictest narrative necessity. Consequently the poem must now be concerned with providing answers and consolations which may prove expedient in a situation otherwise unbearable and unacceptable. In Books IV and V, Chaucer ranges widely in search of philosophic and religious vantage-points from which to view his [105] 'matere' with some composure: his imaginative range, however, is strictly narrowed by what he has to do. The great passages on Fate, Necessity, Free Will function seriously as the poem moves to its bitter conclusion, but they give, in many respects, 'a comfort serves in a whirlwind'; we should not mistake philosophic and religious reconciliation for imaginative committal. The sad bewilderment with which Chaucer watches his poem shrink to a tale of treachery cannot be wholly remedied: like Troilus, seeing Criseyde's love fade from him, he can only state, in all truth, what *was*:

> . . . I ne kan nor may,
> For al this world, withinne myn herte fynde
> To unloven yow a quarter of a day!
>
> (v, 1696–8)

But answers to the extreme dilemma of the narrative have to be attempted.

The crux of the matter lies in the last answer Chaucer chose to give – his closing stanzas. E. T. Donaldson has shown conclusively that the poetry from line 1750 onwards reveals 'the narrator's quandary'.[25] Anxiety and evasiveness are strongly apparent: the only conclusion left is one which is not congenial. And when at length Chaucer comes to draw that conclusion, it is with a surprising and terrible forcefulness:

> Swych fyn hath, lo, this Troilus for love . . .
>
> (v, 1828)

Now he makes obeisance to the medieval theme of *vanitas vanitatum*, and the severity of his expression can be seen as a measure of the reluctance he has shown, in the central part of his poem, to give any weight to that theme. It is, in fact, in this severity, rather than in conciliatory references to 'floures faire',[26] that we can discern Chaucer's recollection of what he achieved in Book III. Having enriched and deepened the implications of the Italian narrative, he is now forced to erase the memory of his actions. The pounding of his rhetoric is meant to still questioning, but we may inquire more thoughtfully than Chaucer's readers could about the relevance of that stanza

> Lo here, of payens corsed olde rites,
> Lo here, what alle hire goddes may availle . . .
>
> (v, 1849–50)

[106] It is a revealing and, at the same time, a problematic stanza: revealing, because it shows quite clearly that Chaucer hopes we will not question this palpably unsatisfactory account of what we have just read or heard; problematic, because it is difficult to believe that any artist of integrity could turn his back on his work quite so decisively. 'Payens corsed olde rites', 'what alle hir goddes may availle', 'the fyn and guerdoun for travaille/Of Jove, Appollo, of Mars, of swiche rascaille', give poor coverage for the deliberate evocation of Christian belief and feeling in Books II and III. As an explanation of 'double sorwe' it is woefully inadequate, and we must not miss the fact that Chaucer offers it as an explanation:

> *Lo here*, what alle hir goddes may availle . . .
> *Lo here*, the fyn and guerdoun for travaille
> Of Jove, Appollo, of Mars . . .

The automatic listing of the gods (not all of them, as several critics have pointed out, properly operative in the poem) is in itself indicative of Chaucer's haste to be done with a troublesome matter. Automatic also is his dismissal of 'the high nobility of natural creatures' –

> Lo here, thise wrecched worldes appetites . . .

It was not this view which drew from him some of his finest poetry.

In short, Chaucer could never have intended his poem to be seen as a unified whole, except in the crudest narrative sense. It is a work of variable and fluctuating allegiances, of co-ordinate rather than complex construction, which relies on significant breaks and pauses between its separate parts. Beginning simply, it develops into a subtle and devout study of human 'worthynesse': ending simply, it fails to relate its findings meaningfully, and is even forced to revoke some of them – though not without some distress.

Like many of Chaucer's answers to complicated problems, the final answers given in *Troilus* do not match the intelligence and energy of the questions asked, the issues raised. For Chaucer, in the struggle between narrative authority and imaginative penetration, authority must win – 'all/ Life death does end, and each day dies with sleep'. But we should not be afraid to recognize the struggle, nor to admit that while authority could literally conclude his poems for him, it could never conclude the business his imagination loved to engage in.

Notes

1 *The Allegory of Love* (Oxford, 1936), p. 197.
2 *Troilus and Criseyde* iii, 465–9, ed. F. N. Robinson, *The Poetical Works of Chaucer* (Cambridge, Mass., 1961).
3 See D. W. Robertson, *A Preface to Chaucer* (Princeton, 1963), p. 491.
4 J. A. W. Bennett, 'The Humane Medievalist', An Inaugural Lecture (C.U.P., 1965), p. 27.
5 *Essays and Studies* XVII (1932), 56–75.
6 For example, the study by Sanford B. Meech, *Design in Chaucer's Troilus* (Syracuse University Press, 1959).
7 D. W. Robertson's treatment of the poem in his article 'Chaucerian Tragedy', *E.L.H.* XIX (1952), 1–37, and in *A Preface to Chaucer*, pp. 472–502, is often invalid for this reason.
8 *Il Filostrato*, ed. V. Pernicone (Bari, 1937), p. 94.
9 Meech, *op. cit.*, pp. 424, 427.
10 Two essential articles on Chaucer's methods of work are: D. S. Brewer, 'Love and Marriage in Chaucer's Poetry', *M.L.R.* XLIX (1954), 461–4, and E. T. Donaldson, 'The Ending of Chaucer's *Troilus*', *Early English and Norse Studies Presented to Hugh Smith*, ed. A. Brown and P. Foote (London, 1963), pp. 26–45.
11 This will not mean that the ending of the poem is 'not a part of the whole ... is detachable at will ... one need not of necessity consider it at all in an interpretation of the drama' (W. C. Curry, *Chaucer and the Mediæval Sciences*, 2nd ed., New York, 1960, p. 298). It remains an integral part of the poem, not least because it focuses our attention on the pressing and largely unresolved artistic problems which Chaucer faced throughout his work.
12 *The Canterbury Tales* seem to me to illustrate this point most aptly.
13 Curry, *op. cit.*, p. 295, noted some of its improprieties.
14 C. A. Owen, 'The Significance of Chaucer's Revisions of *Troilus and Criseyde*', *Modern Philology* LV (1957–8), 5.
15 Henry Suso, *Life*, tr. T. F. Knox (London, 1915), ch. lvi.
16 Julian of Norwich, *Revelations of Divine Love*, ed. G. Warrack (London, 1923), p. 103.
17 i. 977 ff.
18 T. P. Dunning, in 'God and Man in *Troilus and Criseyde*', *English and Mediæval Studies Presented to J. R. R. Tolkien* (London, 1962), holds that in Book III 'the narrator narrows the perspective ...' (p. 179).
19 Chaucer deliberately refined Boccaccio's cruder language for ll. 257–9:

'i' ho dal cuor di Criseida rimosso
ogni vergogna e ciaschedun pensiero

che contra t'era, ed hol tanto percosso
col ragionar del tuo amor sincero ...' (*op. cit.*, p. 71)
But he did not bother to refine Troilus's offer.

20 It is, of course, an outcry provoked by false representation, and the poet knows that his audience will take it less seriously than they otherwise might.

21 See ll. 1052–3, 1165–6.

22 The phrasing recalls that of Walter Hilton, in his *Scale of Perfection*, ed. E. Underhill (London, 1923), pp. 395–6: 'Other men that stand in the common way of charity, and are not yet so far forth in grace, but work under the bidding of reason ... have not put themselves all fully in God's hand.'

23 The point is even clearer in some MSS. of the poem which read 'whan it comth to the neede': see *The Book of Troilus and Criseyde*, ed. R. K. Root (Princeton, 1945), p. 201.

24 Lewis, *The Allegory of Love*, p. 196.

25 'The Ending of Chaucer's *Troilus*', p. 37.

26 ibid., p. 42.

9

Troilus, Books I–III: a Criseydan reading

MARK LAMBERT

Originally published in *Essays on Troilus and Criseyde*, ed. Mary Salu (Cambridge: Brewer, 1979, pp. 105–25). Reprinted by permission of Boydell and Brewer Ltd. The original pagination is recorded within square brackets. The endnotes originally appeared on pp. 139–40.

As its opening lines announce, Chaucer's poem is about the adventures of Prince Troilus. He is our representative in the work, the human being seeking happiness, just as you and I do, in sublunary things. And Criseyde, the charming, faithless heroine, is the good of this world, that which the hero seeks, finds, and must inevitably lose. In Chaucer's narrative statement, Troilus is the subject, Criseyde the object. Most readers of *Troilus and Criseyde* will, I think, agree on this much, and I say their opinion is good. But Chaucer's *Troilus* (and about this too I hope most of us will agree) is not only an extraordinarily rich, but a strangely shifting, shimmering work, and whatever things we say about it, we soon find ourselves adding 'yes, but . . .' The present essay is just such a 'yes, but' qualification. What I want to argue before parting from you is that in the first half of Chaucer's poem, that is from the opening through the end of Book III, the reader's experience is in fact more interestingly like Criseyde's than like Troilus's. It is not that I wish to justify the heroine's actions; what I want to present, rather, is a Criseydan reading of the sorrow of Troilus, a tracing of affinities between her sensibility and our sense of the work of which she's part.

Now of course there are few statements to be made about Criseyde's sensibility that will not themselves bring forth a throng of 'yes, but' qualifications: it is in good part because the reader must keep reinterpreting her that the entire poem shimmers as it does. What concerns me here is not any key to the whole character of Criseyde, but rather the thing about her which is most stressed as we experience [106] the early books: she is timid, she is cautious. In *The Allegory of Love*, C. S. Lewis took fear to be Criseyde's ruling passion;[1] not being quite easy with the idea of a ruling passion here, I'd rather say that fear is the dominant color in the initial portrait, or a clear tone sounded early, and never forgotten.

We start, then, with a markedly timid heroine. And one thing this easily frightened lady understands to be frequently true is something we, Chaucer's audience, know will be true in the present case: love brings suffering. We are reading a poem about the double sorrow of Troilus; the heroine believes love is 'the mooste stormy lyf,/Right of hymself, that evere was bigonne' (II, 778–9).[2] In moving through the first half of the narrative, both heroine and reader are soothed into hopefulness. Criseyde is made to overcome her timidity and worst suspicions, we to put aside our foreknowledge. The first hemisphere of the *Troilus* is a great poem of seduction.

The seduction of Criseyde is not, most significantly, an eroticizing but an heroicizing of her life. I have been referring to her as the poem's heroine, but this, after all, is not quite an appropriate term for Criseyde. That timidity has presumably led to, and in any case is usually accompanied by, a certain modesty of aspiration; like a Chaucerian narrator, she is someone who would rather not be carried about by eagles. Criseyde remains quietly within the bounds of the ordinary and expected, abiding, Chaucer tells us at the end of the brief episode in which she is introduced, 'with swich meyne / As til hire honour nede was to holde' (I, 127–8). Though herself a creature of superlative beauty, Criseyde has no taste for the extreme, little interest in any light beyond the light of common day. The *gods* of Love, endlessly invoked and referred to by others, are not named at all by Criseyde until fairly late in the fourth book.

For Criseyde the primary question is not, to what height of bliss? but, is this going to hurt? Thus, when she has her eagle dream, what is wonderful is the lack of pain:

> And as she slep, anonright tho hire mette
> How that an egle, fethered whit as bon,
> Undir hire brest his longe clawes sette,
> And out hire herte he rente, and that anon,
> And dide his herte into hire brest to gon,
> *Of which she nought agroos, ne nothyng smerte;*
> And forth he fleigh, with herte left for herte.

(II, 925–31)

[107] Not as snow or a lily, but white as *bon*: ivory, but the overtones are unpleasant. Criseyde needs to be reassured about terrible beauty, coaxed into joining the company of Gottfried's noble hearts and Yeats's tragic heroines.[3]

Finally, though, one can't quite be soothed into heroism; at best one can be convinced that although the price is high, it is worth paying. Criseyde, however, must be led to believe that the price is really no price at all: love isn't going to hurt one bit. The *Cantus Antigone*, that effective persuader, touches lightly on the truth of love as a heroic experience: 'No wele is worth, that may no sorwe dryen' (II, 866); love, scorned by wretches, is like the bright sun, which a man may not look at directly 'for feeblesse of his yen' (863). But Antigone's song is basically a case-history, and that history is of life led 'in alle joie and seurte' (833). It will seem to Chaucer's heroine that the important danger is on the other side, and frightful things may happen if she is unresponsive.

Now Criseyde as I have described her thus far should be recognizable to readers of Chaucer's poem and only too familiar to readers of Chaucer criticism: a low, trembling, unworthy thing, this Criseyde. True enough; but there is indeed a positive to this negative, and that positive, I shall say with heroic boldness, is the source of our main pleasure as we read through the early books of this narrative. In these books we have the poetry of just such a life as this Criseyde would find comfortable; the poetry of Chaucerian Trojanness, of the kindly, the endearing, the contained. To experience the first half of the *Troilus* is to be charmed by the unheroic.

This poetry of the unheroic (about which I shall be saying more in a moment) brings us close to Criseyde. What is still more interesting, though, is that way in which we, like Chaucer's timid widow, are seduced into forgetting the limitations of the quiet life – or, to put this more precisely, into overlooking the special demands of the heroic. Much as we know from the beginning of the work that Troy is doomed, and yet come to believe, while reading along from stanza to stanza, that somehow that Greek siege hasn't *really* changed things –

> But though that Grekes hem of Troie shetten,
> And hire cite biseged al aboute,
> Hire olde usage nolde they nat letten,
> As for to honoure hir goddes ful devoute . . .
>
> (I, 148–51)

– so we put aside our knowledge of what love is, and come to believe, [108] as Criseyde herself does, that there can be snugness amid hyperboles.

One may be easy in the presence of grand gestures. The heroic is manage-able, and, in fact, a hero's passion, rightly considered, may be quite a convenient thing. Of this Criseyde, with some help from Pandarus, con-vinces herself. More insidiously, Chaucer teaches a similar lesson to the reader by the manner in which he presents his hero. Consider Troilus, for a moment, not as either a psychological study or an Everyman, but as a representative of the Heroic. He is a fierce warrior, the second greatest in the city. He is very eager to strike tragic attitudes – those attitudes which will finally prove to be the appropriate ones. Troilus wants to understand clearly, and asks difficult questions: Boethian ones later, Petrarchan ones here. He laughs very little, and what humor he does have is of a markedly sardonic kind.[4] He deals in life and death: when he needs something to keep his brother and sister-in-law out of the room for a while, he luckily finds to hand a letter from Hector asking whether a certain man should be allowed to live or not.

Described in this way, Troilus seems fully qualified to represent the Other, Criseyde's opposite. Less schematically regarded, this Troilus sounds like just the kind of suitor to frighten Criseyde out of her wits. But of course

Chaucer's protagonist isn't *really* like that, doesn't seem a huge or forbidding presence, even though all the things I have mentioned are there in the text. Just so: it is the distance between our usual reaction to such characteristics and our response to Troilus in the early books of this poem which is the measure of Chaucer's artfulness, his domestication of heroic intensity.

Chaucer's Troilus is a sort of *trompe l'œil* performance; the heroism is rendered, but camouflaged by a peculiar background and the artist's cunning selection of an odd angle of vision. Troilus's warmaking is extramural, and not seen in detail. His behavior is impeccably heroic; but it is just here, when one is in love, that proper heroic behavior is largely a matter of going to bed and moaning with some frequency, and it is just this kind of heroic behavior that Chaucer puts in sharp focus. Troilus is a hyperbolist: whatsoever his hand finds to do, he does with his might. He is, as Pandarus sees, one of the great heretics who, when converted, become great champions of the faith. But, in the first half of the poem, Troilus seems the most comically ineffective of the characters we observe. Those large gestures of his are absurdly out of place. He has never noticed that this world he inhabits is manageable, providing more employment for good-natured engineers than for Titans. And if our heroine, Criseyde, [109] is not of Troilian intenseness, well, isn't that intenseness really a kind of silliness? Surely she is more than a match for this young man: the qualities she lacks and he possesses seem ridiculous encumbrances.

Chaucer's hero does some slightly foolish things, but the main reason he appears silly is that we see him within Chaucer's Troy. It is an extraordinary setting. This fourteenth-century Troy is, it seems to me, one of the great *città invisibili* of English literature, one of the wonderful places of our imaginations. What meanness there is here exists only to summon forth its opposite. Chaucerian Troy is the city of kindliness and friendship, and, at least for the post-Romantic reader – at least but perhaps inevitably for the post-Romantic reader – a town of childhood. Like Troilus's martial deeds, parents are absent or glimpsed in the distance; they are never directly quoted in this great poem of talk. (The exception here, the one substantial parent, is Calchas, and the narrative begins with his departure from the city.) In this Troy it is Pandarus who stands *in loco parentis*, and he is our remembered ideal uncle: all the competence of a father and none of the authority; half a peer, half an elder. (Thus the familiar question: how old are we to suppose Pandarus to be?) Nor is it only parents who are kept out of the way. No wives, husbands or lovers appear with their partners except for the hero and heroine themselves: Helen's Paris and Pandarus's lady are mere *data*. Sexual pairing, stern and venerable authority, the risking and taking of life, are things referred to, but not carefully observed. The clearly seen, directly audible world is populated, as we shall see, by people for whom friendliness is the principal emotion, people who seem to like simply being in one another's company.

Late in the work, Troilus speaks about things he fears may happen if Criseyde does leave the city of Troy and go to the enemy camp. Among the Greeks she'll find so many worthy knights doing their utmost to please her,

> '. . . That ye shul dullen of the rudenesse
> Of us sely Troians, but if routhe
> Remorde yow, or vertu of youre trouthe . . .'
>
> (IV, 1489–91)

'The rudeness of us sely Troians': it is in one sense a new idea about Troy, but when we come upon these lines they somehow seem right, the fear they express not unreasonable. Troilus's anxiety echoes something in our experience of the poem. Troy (and when considered as part of it, even the heroic Troilus) is not truly of the great world, [110] but remains innocent, sheltered, *sely*. The feared Greeks, to whom the heroine's father goes as the story begins, and who will be moved to pity by the plea of 'this olde greye' for the restoration of his daughter (IV, 64–133), are the grown-ups of *Troilus and Criseyde*.[5]

The *Troilus* is a poem about love, but it is set in Troy, which is supremely the city of friendship. The first books of the narrative do with the overwhelming experience of love what they do with the fierce warrior Troilus: not deny, nor even fail to mention, all that is high, and solitary and most stern (Chaucer's stanzas of commentary certainly tell of the uniqueness and power of Eros)[6] but emphasize what is comfortable. Here Chaucer plays to his own ends with the truisms, rhetorical habits, and philosophical interests of his age. What is friendship? What is love? How are they alike? How do they differ? As Gervase Mathew says of Anglo-Norman literature, 'it is notoriously difficult to distinguish between advice to friends and advice to lovers at a time when love between man and woman was expressed in terms of friendship, and friendship between man and man was expressed in terms of love'.[7] This is the kind of situation our poet loves, and one of the most delightfully vertiginous things in Chaucer's narrative is the way Pandarus and the author juggle and whisk around various ideas about love's relation to friendship. One may ask for the friendliness of a loved lady; one uses 'love of friendshipe' as a disguise for a love which is not friendship; but then, 'love of frendshipe' may be a stage in a progress toward a move not of friendship, etc. Pandarus plays more conspicuously with the categories, Chaucer with the textures of the two experiences.

The ecstasy of love is not to be described in words, no more than is the joy of heaven. But stanza by stanza, as I say, the narrative presence of love is something manageable, a special form of friendliness. Let's turn again to the scene in which Criseyde is introduced. There, we will remember, what she needs is the friendship Chaucerian Troy can so well supply. She is

> in gret penaunce,
> For of hir lif she was ful sore in drede,
> As she that nyste what was best to rede;
> For bothe a widewe was she and allone
> Of any frend to whom she dorste hir mone.
>
> (I, 94–8)

Initially she is observed as a disconsolate seeker of friendship; before long, Troilus is presented as a disconsolate seeker of love. We start [111] with the two needs as parallel, and Chaucer goes on to interweave the two emotions. The gestures of love are also the gestures of kindliness. On the night of the smoky rain, when Troilus, brought to his lady's bed and afraid that she is angry with him, kneels before her and pleads, 'God woot that of this game, / Whan al is wist, than am I nought to blame' (III, 1084–5), he is much like the friendless Criseyde who had knelt before Hector and excused herself. Though Troilus faints here and Criseyde did not in the earlier scene, the two emotions seem to be of like intensity: the lover of Book III 'felte he nas but deed' (III, 1081), the widow was well nigh out of her wit with sorrow and fear. In a work where a lovelorn character sounds much like a friendlorn character, the reader does not find it easy to keep the uniqueness of love steadily in view. Structure joins what doctrinal passages put asunder.

A more amusing example of the assimilation of love and friendship comes from the stanzas in which Pandarus is introduced. We have here, one need hardly say, a wonderful entrance scene. Pandarus is the narrative's great expediter, almost Human Resourcefulness itself. Appropriately, we first meet him as he bursts into a room where he is needed. Notice, though, that there has in fact been some interesting verbal preparation for his entrance. A few lines before Pandarus appears, we hear the last words quoted in direct discourse from Troilus's complaint to his absent lady: '... And with som *frendly* lok gladeth me, swete, / Though nevere more thing ye me byheete' (I, 538–9). Apparently one part of the hero's prayer is granted, the other carried off on the winds. Troilus is shown the friendliness he wants – but not by Criseyde:

> Bywayling in his chambre thus allone,
> A *frend* of his, that called was Pandare,
> Com oones in unwar, and herde hym groone,
> And say his *frend* in swich destresse and care.

(I, 547–50)

Some eighty lines earlier Troilus had wished for his lady's compassion:

> '... now wolde God, Criseyde,
> Ye wolden on me *rewe*, er that I deyde!
> My dere herte, allas! myn hele and hewe
> And lif is lost, but ye wol on me *rewe*'.

(I, 459–62)

[112] Now we hear:

> This Pandare, *that neigh malt for wo and routhe,*
> Ful ofte seyde, 'Allas! what may this be?
> Now frend', quod he, 'if evere *love* or trouthe
> Hath ben, or is, bitwixen the and me,

> Ne do thow nevere swich a crueltee
> To hiden fro thi *frend* so gret a care! ...'

(I, 582–7)

Thus Chaucer gives us Pandarus, the poem's supreme blurrer of love and friendship.

My friend's fortune in love is my fortune also: Pandarus's repeated *us* to refer to himself and Troilus as a pair whose happiness depends upon the kindness of his niece (a usage which has pushed up a fair number of eyebrows among our contemporaries) is much to the point here. That amiable *we* is perhaps most interesting when Pandarus assures Criseyde that Troilus's death for love will entail his own death for friendship. Consider the effects of this asseveration upon both the heroine and ourselves. Criseyde has heard about tragic, hyperbolic love:

> 'Unhappes fallen thikke
> Alday for love, and in swych manere cas
> As men ben cruel in hemself and wikke ...'

(II, 456–8)

She apparently goes on to accept the possibility of *Freundschaftestod* as well (II, 459–60). Seeing she must play 'ful sleighly', Criseyde immediately and successfully does so. Negotiations are conducted, and by the end of the scene there is no imminent danger of death for love, death for friendship, or scandal. What Criseyde has learned here, really, is that the universe of high emotions and death for grief has denizens as familiar as her uncle Pandarus – and she certainly knows how to deal with *him*. When people get up to leave, saying things like

> '... But sith it liketh yow that I be ded,
> By Neptunus, that god is of the see,
> Fro this forth shal I nevere eten bred
> Til I myn owen herte blood may see;
> For certeyn I wol deye as soone as he'

(II, 442–6)

[113] one can still control matters with the familiar gestures of a less operatic world. The stanza ends, charmingly, 'And up he sterte, and on his wey he raughte, / Til she agayn hym by the lappe kaughte'.[8]

Thus, by association, heroic love comes to seem familiar and manageable. In this case it is *perhaps* by Pandarian design that this impression is created, but elsewhere in the poem the domestication of the heroic for reader and heroine is of a sort beyond the powers of even the cleverest uncle. A nice instance here involves that dream of the eagle I spoke of a few pages ago. In itself, of course, that vision was reassuring – there was no pain in that exchange of hearts – but the reassurance was of a negative kind. Fortunate, then, that some two hundred lines later in the second book Pandarus unwittingly parodies and domesticates – Trojanizes – the eagle's gesture. Criseyde does not want to accept the letter her uncle has brought from Troilus, and so Pandarus, Chaucer tells us, 'hente hire faste, / And in hire bosom the lettre down he thraste ...' (II, 1154–5). (In Chaucer's English *bosom* can mean either the breast or the part of a robe covering the breast: a useful doubleness here.) The rapture of love now comes to seem rather like being seized by uncle Pandarus: familiar and out-maneuverable uncle Pandarus. He

> seyde hire, 'Now cast it awey anon,
> That folk may seen and gauren on us tweye'.
> Quod she, 'I kan abyde til they be gon';
> And gan to smyle ...
>
> (II, 1156–9)

And, reader, we smile with her. Thirty lines later, Criseyde finds that this man who thought he could trap her is himself quite trappable: returning from her reading of the letter, she takes Pandarus by the hood as he stands in a study. *She* is the one who can say, 'Ye were caught er that ye wiste' (II, 1182). This, in turn, is a statement we ought to recall when we hear her lover say to Criseyde, 'Now be ye kaught ... now yeldeth yow ...' (III, 1207–8).

Criseyde's uncle not only domesticates love but is himself love domesticated. Again: we are often unsure just where his manipulation ends and that of a larger, vaguer force begins, but if we wish to resist the poem's seductive blurring and try to sort things out, we may assume that Pandarus knows his niece will be affected by a reminder that he, her familiar *em*, is that strange creature, a lover. Out of such awareness, or 'by aventure, or sort, or cas', Pandarus does bring the running joke of his own unhappy love into the openings of both his [114] early embassies to Criseyde. But, whether he is being artful at these moments or not, it is clear that Pandarus's love service is real, a fact of the narrative and not merely a ploy. And *this* means, if one thinks about it, that the Pandarian version of love works upon the reader much as it does upon the heroine: quick death fades into that less horrific oxymoron, jolly woe. The sort of effect I have in mind here is perhaps most noticeable in the Pandarus-and-the-swallow stanzas which open the action of Book II. The friend and uncle is about to set off for the first of his visits to Criseyde. But it is May now, and so it happens

> That Pandarus, for al his wise speche,
> Felt ek his part of loves shotes keene,
> That, koude he nevere so wel of lovyng preche,
> It made his hewe a-day ful ofte greene.
> So shop it that hym fil that day a teene
> In love, for which in wo to bedde he wente,
> And made, er it was day, ful many a wente.
>
> The swalowe Proigne, with a sorowful lay,
> Whan morwen com, gan make hire waymentynge,
> Whi she forshapen was; and ever lay

> Pandare abedde, half in a slomberynge,
> Til she so neigh hym made hire cheterynge
> How Tereus gan forth hire suster take,
> That with the noyse of hire he gan awake,
>
> And gan to calle, and dresse hym up to ryse,
> Remembryng hym his erand was to doone
> From Troilus . . .

(57–73)

In Chaucer's Troy, the 'teene' of love seems contained and rapidly assimilated, as the Procne lines at the center of this little episode show us. Tragic 'waymentynge', appropriate to Ovidian passion and transformation, becomes the noise and 'cheterynge' (one of the Owl's favorite words for the Nightingale's sound) of the familiar morning, and Pandarus is ready to go about his business. In the lines bracketing those on the swallow, lovesickness changes from something which separates one from the world to an affliction that may cost you a day now and then: lie down for a while and you'll feel better.

Pandarus is not the only character to make grand passion seem a hearthside phenomenon. Particularly important in its effect upon the [115] reader is Chaucer's presentation of Helen and, along with her, of Deiphebus and the other charming Trojans of the second and third books. Here, in a part of the work owing comparatively little to Boccaccio, we feel love to be a snugly human thing, securely colleted with, but also blurred into, friendship. The situation is this. Pandarus, after his early exercises in persuasion, prying, and negotiating, has decided it is time for the lovers to have an interview. His first move in arranging this is to ask Troilus which of his brothers he loves best, 'as in thi verray hertes privetee' (II, 1397). Now that, it seems to me, is a rather curious phrase, suggesting something like a fraternal variety of *derne love*. Rather curious: no more than that. Given the general similarity of the language of love and the language of friendship in Chaucer's literary culture, it seems unlikely that any fourteenth-century reader was puzzled or startled by the phrase; doubtless few twentieth-century readers pause here. The phrase slips by, but quietly does its work. The whole inquiry is a bit odd in the way that phrase is just a bid odd. There is no practical reason why it must be his friend's *favorite* brother Pandarus uses to further Troilus's love. This is merely a managerial flourish, but a flourish suggesting the values of Chaucer's Troy: love of a brother, of a friend, of a lady, are things like one another and appropriate contexts for one another. In any case, the answer to Pandarus's question is Deiphebus; and Deiphebus, it transpires, is not only Troilus's favorite among his brothers, but Pandarus's second best friend. What is more, Pandarus himself is the man whom, after his brother Troilus, Deiphebus most loves. Pandarus sets to work and presents his cover story. He explains to Deiphebus that the favor he is asking is for Criseyde, a lady in this town who is his niece. But in Troy, and especially in this episode which brings the lovers together, all one's friends turn out to be each other's friends as well. Troilus's favorite brother is splendidly emphatic in his reaction:

'O, is nat this,
That thow spekest of to me thus straungely,
Criseÿda, my frend?' He seyde, 'Yis'.
'Than nedeth', quod Deiphebus, 'hardyly,
Namore to speke, for trusteth wel that I
Wol be hire champioun with spore and yerde;
I roughte nought though alle hire foos it herde . . .'

(II, 1422–8)

The scheme for the meeting of the two lovers involves a piling up of solicitude. Troilus may hope Criseyde will show some pity for the [116] suffering love causes him, and Troilus, because he is ill, arouses the compassion of the other kindly folk gathered in this house. Those other folk are, moreover, filled with sympathy for Criseyde in her difficulties with Poliphete. There are comic curlicues of compassion: Chaucer invites the reader to smile at the absurdity of anyone taking the trouble to urge Troilus to be a friend to Criseyde (II, 1553–4); Criseyde sees and, one assumes, savors the ridiculousness of other persons discussing cures for Troilus's malady when she, who would be his best physician, is in the room (II, 1581–2). The Trojans' kindliness is engagingly mixed up with small vanities and competitions (II, 1578–87). Thus we can feel slightly and comfortably superior to it and be just a bit patronizing: this is not a *caritas* of which we must stand in awe.

And here, in Deiphebus's house, we meet the extraordinary Helen of Chaucer's Troy. She is startling in one sense because of what she is not: the woman 'par cui li siegles est peior'.[9] Elsewhere in the *Troilus* we hear about the heroic queen: in the fifth book Diomede will emphasize both for us and for Criseyde the connection between the love of Paris and Helen and the great suffering there will be at Troy (V, 890–6); the narration also opens with the theme of destructive passion, Chaucer reminding us that the Greeks besieged the city to avenge the taking of Helen (I, 61–3). But now, in the second book, at the time when Criseyde is coming to take a prince of Troy as her lover, we actually see Queen Helen, and here Helen is altogether domesticated. She is, like Deiphebus, a great friend, the loving 'suster' of her two loving brothers. (Helen is fond of the words 'brother' and 'sister'.)[10] She is as warmly sympathetic toward Criseyde in her supposed troubles with Poliphete as she is with Troilus in his *accesse*:

Eleyne, which that by the hond hire held,
Took first the tale, and seyde, 'Go we blyve';
And goodly on Criseyde she biheld,
And seyde, 'Joves lat hym nevere thryve,
That doth yow harm, and brynge hym soone of lyve,
And yeve me sorwe, but he shal it rewe,
If that I may, and alle folk be trewe!'.

(II, 1604–10)

Chaucer doesn't tell us this, but she seems to have put on a few pounds. It occurs to Deiphebus that Helen would be a handy person to number among

Criseyde's friends, 'for she may leden Paris as hire leste' (II, 1449). Eros, the force behind those thousand ships and the siege, now drives a small, very convenient household appliance. Passion is [117] something that facilitates kindness. How cosy this is – and, for the fearfulest wight that might be, how seductive. Could even the smallest mouse's heart be afraid of heroic love when *this* comfortable creature is Helen of Troy? Who would find Pandarus's jolly woe unendurable? And so love blurs into the ordinary and the comforting. As we move toward the consummation of the passion of hero and heroine, Chaucer's language makes the Criseyde who in Book III takes Troilus into her bed an echo, a fulfilment of the maternal Helen who tried to cheer the bed-ridden hero in the second book:

> Eleyne, in al *hire goodly* softe wyse,
> Gan hym salue, and wommanly to pleye,
> And seyde, 'Iwys, ye moste alweies arise!
> Now, faire brother, beth al hool, I preye!'
> *And gan hire arm right over his shulder leye,*
> And hym with al hire wit to *reconforte*;
> As she best koude, *she gan hym to disporte.*

(II, 1667–73)

> *And therwithal hire arm over hym she leyde,*
> And al foryaf, and ofte tyme hym keste.
> He thonked hire, and to hire spak, and seyde
> As fil to purpos for his hertes reste;
> And she to that answerde hym as hire leste,
> And with *hire goodly* wordes *hym disporte*
> *She gan*, and ofte his sorwes *to comforte.*

(III, 1128–34)

I must confess to a great fondness for Chaucer's Helen, and would be glad to linger over this portrayal. But there are several other things of considerable interest I want to discuss here as well. Three aspects of Chaucer's poem I have not touched on as yet work subtly to make life – and especially love – in Troy seem more cushioned and less demanding than Criseyde finally discovers them to be. These three are the use of meals, the use of space, and an odd trick of narrative structure. The last of these is the most complex and, I think, the one to consider first.

As hero and heroine progress toward their first night together, two rather like scenes are presented in close succession: these are, of course, the one in which Troilus, put to bed in his brother's house, is visited by Criseyde, and that in which Criseyde, put to bed in her uncle's house, is visited by Troilus. Chaucer's arrangement here [118] lends itself to various sorts of explanations, but it seems to me particularly interesting when thought of as one of a group of doublings in this first half of the poem. One should consider especially: the way Troilus's second heroine-impressing ride past Criseyde's window follows pretty soon after his first; the two slowly, lovingly rendered embassies of Pandarus to his niece in Book II; the fact that here (as in Boccaccio) there are two accounts – the poet's and then Pandarus's – of how Troilus comes to tell his friend why he is suffering, and that the second, Pandarian account, being in part a fuller narrative, forces us to modify our understanding of what Pandarus knew when he entered Troilus's chamber. One might also pause here to consider one slightly odd thing about the way Chaucer's readers are made to experience Troilus's conversion to love. It is a single, sudden experience, that conversion, and in a moment it changes the hero's life forever. But because Troilus attempts to hide his feelings after seeing Criseyde in the temple, and Pandarus chooses to quote his friend's earlier statements, we hear some fifty lines of the jibes of Troilus, the mocker of love (I, 330–50, 908–28), after he has become Troilus, the woeful lover. Now cumulatively these doublings and overlappings I've cited are a bit confusing; we may not be perplexed while reading along, but we have a certain amount of trouble if we try to recall clearly just what happened when. Incidents meld with one another, and the experience of the reader attempting to keep things straight becomes somewhat like the heroine's experience in negotiating with her uncle. What with the strange suppleness of Pandarus's arguments, it is most difficult for Criseyde to be certain just where she stands in her dealings with him. (How well her sense of the Pandarian undertow is caught in that skittish exclamation: ' "Nay, therof spak I nought, ha, ha!" quod she; / "As helpe me God, ye shenden every deel!" ' (II, 589–90).) She would have to listen with uncommon attentiveness to know precisely what she had assented to at any given moment in her conversations with the charming Pandarus; readers of Chaucer (fox that he is) would have to be extraordinarily vigilant if they expected to remember just where a given change occurred, a certain stage in the lovers' relationship was reached. The first half of *Troilus and Criseyde* is a narrative of attractive, warm, subtly contrasting and then blending greys. Things take a while to happen; we come to a corner, but suspect we've turned it before, or, thinking back, find it hard to recall just when a certain corner *was* turned, or say to ourselves, ah, here at last is a corner! only to find we're wrong. Changes tend to blur in the reader's mind, just as [119] they surely ought to blur for someone like Criseyde, a timid widow who is to become a hero's lady.

The passage in which Criseyde does at last become the hero's lady – or, more exactly, the passage in which she confesses herself already yielded to him – is as lovely a comic exchange as Chaucer ever invented. At the deepest level, the reader's laughter here is celebratory laughter, but one ought to notice also how at this moment Chaucer plays with two things we have been discussing: the theme of the frightening heroic, and the blurring of important shifts. Troilus, as he enters his lady's bed for the first time, seems as absurdly unthreatening a figure as one could wish. He is of course not pretending to be weak here, had not planned to faint – but in the first half of the *Troilus* all things do conspire to bring the lovers together, and if one wanted to enter the bed of the fearfulest wight that might be, sorrow, fear, and a swoon would not be the worst of tactics: the lady is in command. Here, though, after the heroine receives the passive hero into her bed, hears his vows, grants him forgiveness, and before the sexual consummation, there is a reversal. For a moment, all Criseyde's persistent anxieties about the nature of love, about prince Troilus, about what I am calling the heroic, suddenly appear justified. Troilus takes Criseyde in his arms; she begins to quake like an aspen leaf; her newly revived lover, as insistent as that eagle was, is a sparrowhawk clutching its prey: '. . . Now be ye kaught, now is ther but we tweyne! / Now yeldeth yow, for other bote is non!' (III, 1207–8). But Criseyde's hovering fears are given this sudden justification only so that they may be climactically ridiculed and exorcized. And the speech destroying the threateningness of Troilus here is at once the speech in the poem we most like Criseyde for making, and the statement in the poem which forces us most directly to acknowledge that things *have* been blurry, that we don't know, or at least seem unable to recall, just when, just how, with just what understanding of the situation, a central decision *was* reached: 'Ne hadde I er now, my swete herte deere, / Ben yold, ywis, I were now nought heere!' (III, 1210–11).

Criseyde takes Troilus as her lover at her uncle's house, in the second of two nicely matched scenes. We are aware in both – in the scene at Deiphebus's house and in that at Pandarus's – of movement from larger to smaller rooms, and also of meals taken in common out there, in the great hall. Those meals, though they are not described in any detail, have their importance. One thing we know about grand, unhappy lovers is that they do not eat: in the first book, love has quite properly made Troilus's meat his foe (I, 485); in the fifth book, when [120] the hero is again out of joy, he will again cease to eat and drink (V, 1216). But Pandarus, one must never forget, is himself one of these lovers, and his modified hyperbole modifies our sense of the traditional phenomenon. Thus, these lines from the second of his visits to Criseyde's palace:

> Therwith she lough, and seyde, 'Go we dyne'.
> And he gan at hymself to jape faste,
> And seyde, 'Nece, I have so gret a pyne
> For love, that everich other day I faste –'
> And gan his beste japes forth to caste,
> And made hire so to laughe at his folye,
> That she for laughter wende for to dye.
>
> And whan that she was comen into halle,
> 'Now, em', quod she, 'we wol go dyne anon.' . . .
>
> (II, 1163–71)

Notice not only the deheroicizing jest, but its context: laughter, and 'go we dyne . . . we wol go dyne anon'. Communal meals mark the arrangements by which the Trojan lovers are brought together: Criseyde's dinner, the dinner at Deiphebus's house, and, finally, Pandarus's supper. Love itself, happy, consummated love, is a feast (III, 1228, 1312) and of course *feast* unobtrusively suggests both the religion of love and love as joyful friendliness. In the poem's rising action, Criseyde finds love to be not a *minnegrotte* in the wilderness where two noble hearts can be all in all to one another, and no food is, no food need be taken, but a small room near that hall where loving friends have dined together.

Architecturally, those small rooms, the little closet Criseyde occupies on the night of her visit to Pandarus, and the chamber where Troilus lies at his brother's house, would almost certainly have been located off to one side of the hall in which host and guests ate their meal.[11] But linguistically, each of them is the small area *within*: one moves *in* to and then *out* from the little chamber into the hall again. Criseydan love is contained, secure, unfrightening: the curtained bed in the little room in the walled city whose name rhymes endlessly with joy.[12]

The city, the friend's house, the chamber, the bed, sexual union. The movement of the first half of *Troilus and Criseyde* is centripetal, [121] that of the second centrifugal: Criseyde goes to the Greek camp, Troilus to the eighth sphere. (How fine that the hero looks back to 'this litel spot of erthe, that with the se / Embraced is' (V, 1815–16).) In the second part of the work those gestures which earlier seemed over-large are appropriate, and Troilus becomes the most dignified of the major characters. Now Criseyde tries to be more than she is. In Book IV she really does think, for a moment, that she would have used that sword to kill herself; she speaks the truth Gottfried's noble hearts know: 'hym byhoveth somtyme han a peyne, / That serveth Love, if that he wol have joye' (IV, 1305–6); for the first time, she names the god of Love (IV, 1216).

Now Criseyde takes a high tragic heroine's attitude toward the trivially comforting. She is visited, as in Boccaccio, by a group of Trojan women who have learned of the proposed exchange of prisoners. In Chaucer's poem, this social gathering, coming early in the falling action, recalls the dinner at Deiphebus's house not too long before the lovers' period of joy. Again there is the group of well-meaning, slightly self-important guests. One is glad that Criseyde will see her father again; another is sorry, 'For al to litel hath she with us be' (IV, 690); a third hopes Criseyde will bring peace – may God guide her when she goes (691–3). Chaucer's Helen might have enjoyed a visit from such women, but now Criseyde, the widow whom we first saw troubled and friendless, and who will later be vulnerably placed 'with wommen fewe, among the Grekis stronge' (V, 688), now Criseyde certainly does not like their company. At least as important as the heroine's desire to be free of her visitors is the narrator's scorn for these harmless comforters. They are 'fooles', these ladies (IV, 715). In fact, they are not called ladies at all; apparently 'wommen' is quite good enough for them, even if the word has to be used three times in one stanza (IV, 680–6).

It is both funny and moving, this new contempt for those who 'usen frendes to visite' (IV, 681). Grief at what is happening rechannels itself as satire. One wants to strike out at something, and these Trojan women are, alas, the available targets. But the women are more than this; they represent what has already been lost: the pleasures of the ordinary. A liking for that kind of thing ought to be behind us now, and since we readers find ourselves more sympathetic to those trivial comforters than is either Criseyde or the narrator, the change strikes us with especial force. *We* are the ones hopping along behind, not having yet made the adjustment, not quite willing to dismiss diverse folk speaking diversely as rash, intruding fools.

[122] Criseyde is ahead of us here. But she will not be able to bear heroic isolation for very long. In the last book she'll try to lessen her guilt, both in Troilus's eyes and her own, by treating friendliness as a fall-back position: certainly she will never hate Troilus, 'And frendes love, that shal ye han of me, / And my good work, al sholde I lyven evere . . .' (V, 1080–1); she asks him for his good word and his friendship always, 'For trewely, while that my life may dure, / As for a frend ye may in me assure . . .' (V, 1623–4). 'Frendes love': we will recall Pandarus's assurance that Troilus desired nothing but Criseyde's 'frendly cheere' (II, 332) and the granting of her 'love of frendshipe' (II, 962) as Criseyde began to move toward taking Troilus as a lover. In other words, she is now, perhaps without much conviction, trying to descend from love in the easy, ambiguously marked stages by which she ascended to it. This can't be done; the way up may seem a meandering path, but the way down is a cliff.

None of this excuses Criseyde: she forsakes Troilus who ought not to be forsaken. She is charming, and her mind is quick where his is slow and weighty; but finally it matters that Criseyde's is a smaller soul than Troilus's. He can bear pressures which she cannot; he thinks more important thoughts than she does. And again, it is Troilus whose experience in the work as a whole represents our experience in the world. What, then, is the reason for what I have been discussing in these pages, that deep Criseydan counter-current in the poem? Well, any question about the reason for a pattern in a complex narrative can be answered in a good number of ways: such a question is as bad as it is inevitable. Here one sort of answer is, I think, obvious enough: something which allows us to experience a complex situation in more than one way but does not cloud the central moral truth of that situation enriches the work of which it is a part. But having said this, I must confess another kind of answer – more speculative, if less pompous – appeals to me strongly.

If one should ask, for what sort of character Geoffrey Chaucer appears to have the greatest affinity, the reply would likely be (certainly mine would be), the Theseus sort of character. J. A. Burrow's discussion of Ricardian poetry is very useful here. Chaucer, Burrow suggests, can be thought of as, like his greatest contemporaries, a poet of middle age, his attitudes essentially those of the *Knight's Tale*:

> The Knight (like his Theseus . . .) is of an age when he no longer shares the preoccupations of Palamon or Arcite (or the [123] Squire) and does not yet share the preoccupations of the aged Egeus. From his middle

position among the three ages of man, the Knight can appreciate both the passionate Venerian vision of the young men and also the old man's Saturnine vision of earth as nothing but a 'thurghfare ful of wo'. But neither of these intensely serious visions is the poem's vision ...

[Such Chaucerian figures as Theseus, Pandarus and Harry Baily] with their characteristic 'jovial' wisdom, embody an image of man which is not heroic, not romantic, and not at all 'monkish'. It is an image of 'high eld' which stands at the centre of Ricardian poetry, an ideal of 'measure' which involves that sober acceptance of things as they are which Theseus advocates ...[13]

What does all of this have to do with Criseyde? Well, here some schematizing may prove helpful. If I present the sequence Palamon (and with Palamon, Troilus and Arcite) – Theseus – Egeus in the form A – B – A, the stages of heroic intensity on either side of the Thesean interheroic stage, then Criseyde might be placed at the very beginning of the sequence as the figure of a preheroic or subheroic life. My group would then be: Criseyde – Palamon (Troilus) – Theseus – Egeus, and this I might present in the form B – A – B – A – or more clearly:

> Criseyde
>> Palamon (Troilus)
> Theseus
>> Egeus.

Theseus and Criseyde are at different latitudes, let us say, but the same longitude: there are odd, almost comic, likenesses. 'The sober acceptance of things as they are': with the adjective deleted, Burrow's good, sounding formulation will serve for Criseyde. Consider for a moment two passages about not *grucching*. Why, Theseus asks, should we *grucchen* because good Arcite has left the foul prison of this life? Why do Palamon and Emily *grucchen* 'of his welfare'? It is wisdom, rather, 'to maken vertu of necessitee, / And take it weel that we may nat eschue' (*CT.* I, 3058–63, 3041–2). Pandarus asks Criseyde to stay at his house. It is raining fiercely. Criseyde's mind does not turn to the arrangements of Jupiter, prince and cause of all things; she thinks simply:

> [124]   'As good chep may I dwellen here,
>   And graunte it gladly with a frendes chere,
>   And have a thonk, as grucche and than abide;
>   For hom to gon, it may nought wel bitide'.
>
> (III, 641–4)

'As good chep'. There is acceptance in both passages, but not the same sobriety: sobriety is a function of latitude. Like Theseus, Criseyde quotes that proverb about making a virtue of necessity (IV, 1586), and we can listen for the Theseanism – debased, parody Theseanism, if you will – of

'. . . But syn I se ther is no bettre way,
And that to late is now for me to rewe,
To Diomede algate I wol be trewe'

(V, 1069–71)

Would it not be Thesean wisdom for Emily to have thoughts *something* like these?

Though I can't quite convince myself that Chaucer would have liked my character-chart, I do find it helpful to consider our poem's complex attitude toward its heroine in connexion with that odd similarity of the Thesean and the Criseydan. In themselves more limited goods, the sources of comfort in the earlier phase are like things nobly championed in the later one. Friendliness is related to sober pity; snug sociability as a reassuring setting resembles pubic ceremony as a validating setting. We consider the lovers again, and say, yes, it is better to be Troilus than Criseyde: he is the higher, the more fully human of the two. And yet the lower of these two is in certain ways the one closer to a type higher, more fully human than either – and a type one guesses to be, of all types, the one most congenial to Chaucer. If all of this sounds rather like a Romantic sequence of innocence – experience – higher innocence . . . well, one might brazen it out and say, simply, why shouldn't it? But I wonder whether this shadowy dialectic isn't more complex still. Theseus is in an obvious sense greater than Troilus, we have said – more richly human, more intelligent, more Chaucerian. Yet one may feel that Troilus's single-minded intensity is a more profound sort of response to the world than the humane irony of Theseus – or of his creator. Perhaps the man who sees both sides and makes the best of things always suspects, 'as in his verray hertes privetee' (II, 1397), that he's less in earnest than the fanatic. It is ultimately the hyperbolists and radicals who turn out to be right. Criseyde is oddly like Theseus; [125] Troilus less oddly like Egeus or the Parson. Chaucer is a poet of the unheroic, but a poet of the unheroic who knows (or suspects) the heroes are finally correct. Chaucer's two greatest works conclude with reversals. He is the poet of what is not the highest thing and must at the very end be given up. Much of the strength of the Criseydan strain in the *Troilus* comes from the peculiar affinity of Criseyde and what finally is not just Thesean man, but Chaucerian man. She and not the poem's hero may be the more profoundly autobiographical creation.

Notes

1 New York, 1969 (first published in London, 1936), p. 85.

2 The text quoted is *The Complete Works of Geoffrey Chaucer* edited by F. N. Robinson, 2nd edition (Boston, Massachusetts, 1957).

3 On Criseyde's much-explicated dream, see especially Joseph E. Gallagher, 'Criseyde's Dream of the Eagle: Love and War in *Troilus and Criseyde*', *MLQ* 36 (1975), 115–32.

4 When he first appears in the work, Troilus mocks the young knights love has made wretched. At the end, he laughs at the misery of those weeping for his

death. Between the two scenes, he laughs not at all. The one quip that does at least make him smile is Pandarus's 'God have thi soule, ibrought have I thi beere' (II, 1638).

5 See also the discussion of Troy in Stephen A. Barney, 'Troilus Bound', *Speculum*, 47 (1972), 445–58 (pp. 457–8).

6 Even in the doctrinal passages on the power of love there is often something comfortable, and our awe before the might of Cupid is somewhat lessened by the narrator's slight complacency, his touch of smugness, when pointing to that might. Troilus, when compared to 'proude Bayard' pricked by his corn and lashed by his master, seems a less than august character, and the force that controls him not a very strange one.

7 'Ideals of Friendship', in *Patterns of Love and Courtesy: Essays in Memory of C. S. Lewis*, edited by John Lawlor (Evanston, Illinois, 1966), pp. 45–53 (p. 46). For a far more moral view of Chaucer's play with love and friendship than is presented in my essay, the reader should turn to Alan T. Gaylord, 'Friendship in Chaucer's *Troilus*', *Chaucer Review*, 3 (1968), 239–64. [140]

8 Consider the only laps in Chaucer's beautifully constructed poem. In Deiphebus's house, it is 'by the lappe' that Pandarus brings Criseyde to Troilus (III, 59); later, in his own house, Pandarus guides Troilus 'by the lappe' to his niece (III, 742). Verbally, the heroine's sense of control in a frightening situation leads to her uncle's management of events.

9 Benoît de Sainte-Maure, *Roman de Troie*, 28429. Benoît's ringing denunciation of Helen is quoted by Singleton in his note to *Inferno*, V, 64 (Dante Alighieri, *The Divine Comedy, translated and with a commentary by Charles S. Singleton, Inferno* (2: Commentary) Princeton, New Jersey, 1970, pp. 79–80).

10 That in the Virgilian tradition Helen marries Deiphebus after the death of Paris is irrelevant here – or, better, relevant only as one more thing that makes the Chaucerian Helen a surprising figure, the scene at Deiphebus's house not what one might have expected. (For a discussion of the possibility that Chaucer wants us to think of Deiphebus and Helen as already lovers, see McKay Sundwall, 'Deiphebus and Helen: a Tantalizing Hint', *MP*, 73 (1975), 151–6. Sundwall's is a clear, sensible essay, but I find the interpretation he looks at unattractive as well as unnecessary.)

11 See H. M. Smyser, 'The Domestic Background of *Troilus and Criseyde*', *Speculum*, 31 (1956), 297–315.

12 See also Lewis, pp. 196–7: 'Outside is the torrential "smoky" rain which Chaucer does not allow us to forget; and who does not see what an innocent snugness, as of a children's hiding place, it draws over the whole scene?' Because Barney, in his exceptionally good article on the poem, connects images of containment in *Troilus* with the theme of bondage, it is perhaps important to emphasize containment need not be unpleasant. 'Troilus constantly finds himself in confined spaces: his bed ..., the temple ..., the closet ..., the walls of Troy itself' (p. 457). Yes; but the audience of *Troilus* is at least subliminally aware that the innermost and least spacious chamber here is what the Wife of Bath calls the chamber of Venus. At Pandarus's house Troilus enters the closet, enters the bed, enters Criseyde: this is the underlying rhythm of the joyously comic central episode.

13 *Ricardian Poetry: Chaucer, Gower, Langland and the Gawain Poet* (London, 1971), pp. 126, 129.

10 | Criseyde: woman in medieval society

DAVID AERS

Originally published in the *Chaucer Review* 13 (1979):177–200.
Reprinted by permission of the Pennsylvania State University
Press. The original pagination is recorded within square brackets.
The endnotes originally appeared on pp. 197–200.

Anyone attempting to contribute to the understanding of Chaucer's achievement and meaning in creating the figure of Criseyde will be well aware that, in a necessary reaction to much previous criticism, influential commentators in recent decades have eschewed all interpretation which might seem to treat medieval writing as though it was a nascent form of the kind of "naturalism" associated with some nineteenth century novels. Thus, in his important study of Chaucer, Robert O. Payne praised Charles Muscatine and Arthur Mizener for evolving approaches to "the patterns of characterization which remove it from the realistic and motivational-psychological categories in which earlier criticism had sought to define it." He himself wished to demonstrate that there is no ground in the poem for any "naturalistic reconstruction of 'personalities'," nothing approaching "individual psychologies."[1] In common with other leading critics, such as D. W. Robertson, Jr., Payne assumed that all late medieval poetry was governed by unambiguous "ultimate moral principles," that the past was viewed as an unambiguous "series of illustrations of intellectual abstractions," and that "the controlling ideas in the presentation of character" for many medieval poets, including Chaucer, were "fixity and fitness – character established and unchanging, given typical significance." So in *Troilus and Criseyde* the characters are discussed in terms of "their conventional fixity" which allegedly allowed them "to work out the logic of their positions without the chance inconsistencies and non sequiturs of actual existence": Criseyde, for example, "is a way of saying something about the lovely vanity of human wishes."[2] In such approaches, now widespread, all medieval art, including Chaucer's, tends to be seen as one aimed at transforming the multifarious forms of existence into a set of abstractions, at constructing a world of univocal signs and ideas where individuals have been eliminated. It seems to me, however, this more recent critical [178] model has blinded us to central currents in Chaucer's art, and I shall argue that in constructing Criseyde Chaucer was developing a social psychology which comprised a profound contribution to the understanding of interrelations between individual and society, between individual responsibility and given social circumstances and ideologies. Before developing this case it may be worth making some general observations about the enterprise.

All students of medieval literature will readily acknowledge how much has been learnt about medieval conventions and basic frameworks from scholars pursuing the kind of approach pointed to in the previous paragraph. Nevertheless, it is now becoming clear that in at least two vital areas a very different emphasis is needed for the further progress of medieval scholarship. The first concerns the much-debated issue of appropriate "historical criticism" in the study of medieval texts. Thanks to a growing and increasingly detailed body of work on the diverse developments and conflicts in the social and intellectual history of the fourteenth century, critics can readily free themselves from the mythologised version of a one-dimensional, coherent, static and harmoniously pious late Middle Ages handed on by Robertson and his followers as "historical" scholarship.[3] The expansion of this work by social and intellectual historians should help literary critics become more open to complexly diverse currents, contradictions, and new energies within their own field of medieval studies. Moving into closer contact with the actual practices, confusions, and aspirations of late medieval women and men, we will be less prone to impose a priori schemes on texts which were actually engaged with, and part of, a highly complex, dynamic, and shifting historical reality. The second area I have in mind is related and focuses on the "close reading" of medieval poetry. Theoretically, most critics are always in favour of this, but practice has not always taken the slogan seriously. Doing so demands scrupulous attention to the specific movements of language and feeling in texts, with the resolute refusal to substitute traditional ethical formulae, ideologies, or pieties for the particular literary product being examined.[4] In this area the critic needs to be open to the possibility that a text may involve important and unresolved divisions, that it may partly affirm but partly negate dominant ideas in the author's period and social group; he will bear in mind the possibility that such divisions or contradictions may be at the heart of the work's power and have their roots in the social and intellectual world with which the writer's imagination is engaged.[5] Ideally, the two general areas mentioned here should be drawn together, criticism moving from the closest attention to the particulars of the text, to the writer's social group, to the widest rele[179]vant cultural and social situation and back to the text with enriched and sharpened awareness of its historical and universal meaning.[6] Of course this is an *ideal* for transcending distortion and partiality, and one probably best achieved by collaborative work between scholars trained in different disciplines. Still, however short the present essay may fall of this ideal, it is worth clarifying and pursuing, and this I shall now do in relation to Chaucer's Criseyde.

With regard to *Troilus and Criseyde* the second area just referred to has recently received admirable attention. This is well illustrated by Alfred David's exceptionally sensitive book, *The Strumpet Muse*. As in Elizabeth

Salter's fine seminal essay on the poem, David pays careful attention to the specific movements of feeling in the text, and argues that "Chaucer was of Criseyde's party without knowing it." He sees *Troilus* manifesting a basic division between Chaucer's intellectual commitment to a Boethian-Christian moral and his emotional commitment to the human reality created by his own art, an art which attaches us more strongly than ever to the world that the intellectual scheme would detach us from. When he treats the breakdown of the central relationship, David sees Chaucer thinking in terms of Nature's cycles, claiming that Criseyde survives because she is "more like Nature herself – she is the stick that bends.... The weakness, the flexibility of her character paradoxically gives her the strength to survive."[7] While I believe that a reading such as David's is illuminating, I wish to show that it too still distorts and underestimates the nature of Chaucer's achievement in making Criseyde. For this actually involves a profound exploration of the ways in which individual action, consciousness, and sexuality, the most intimate areas of being, in fact, are fundamentally related to the specific social and ideological structures within which an individual becomes an identifiable human being. And far from thinking that Chaucer was either straightfor- wardly transporting his readers "away from contemporary reality to a distant and romantic Troy," or exemplifying preexistent and well-known ethical universals,[8] I believe he was *exploring* the position of woman in aristocratic society, ideology, and literary convention. Choosing Boccaccio's story placed in Troy certainly made it easier for him to write about love and sexuality without constant attention to the ready-made judgements of tradi- tional institutionalised Christianity.[9] This helped, at least partially, to free his imagination from the dominant religious codes of the period by encouraging detailed and loving explorations in spheres where the inquisitor's handbook held out no such encouragement. But it did not entail a flight from the world of his own audience. Quite the contrary, his handling of Criseyde shows concern with *women in* the [180] social group for which he wrote – the expectations they cherished, the manipulative pressures they had to accept and use, the contradictory self-images, ideologies, and realities with which they were presented, their own complex mixture of opposition and compli- city in a situation where women, at all social levels, were a subordinate group.

In the chief traditions of romance and court literature it seems true to say that love is quite removed from "contemporary reality," its confusions, compromises, and inescapable miseries. Conventional romances offered a welcome escape from its audience's world, not a painful and earnest ex- amination of it.[10] The formula of an outstanding knight committing his existence to the devoted service of a woman fulfilled a psychological need to create a more satisfying alternative to the real organisation of Eros and marriage in medieval society. For upper class woman was totally subordinate to man and to land, aristocratic marriages being primarily land transactions, and child marriages commonplace. Social practices and ideology (secular as well as ecclesiastical) demanded total obedience and submission of woman to man and land in marriage. It is in this context we should see the contradictory images and conventions of courtly literature in which the normal relations between women and men are inverted, the knight serving the woman, paying her homage and devotion.[11] The role of female patronesses in shaping this courtly literature is no coincidence, and the compensatory role of such conventions and fictions is not obscure. Certainly, as Eileen Power pointed out, such courtly conventions did little to elevate the actual position of woman, and the cost of their fictional development was to banish most human life and activity from the genre. In fact, Eileen Power's suggestion that such courtly conventions and genres served a psychological function for the upper class women not dissimilar to that served by modern romantic stories and magazines for working class women seems plausible, for the image of woman as goddess to be worshipped by aristocratic knight sorted very ill with the actual treatment and position of women in the period, dictated by a male aristocracy and a male church.[12] Now it seems to me that Chaucer was fascinated by these contradictions and was not prepared to leave them flaccidly co-existing. In *Troilus* he used the romance genre and the conventions of courtly literature to explore the anomalies between upper class literary conventions and realities, to explore the tensions between the place women occupied in society and the various self-images presented to them, and to imagine his way into the psychic cost for men and women in the relevant situation. He returns romance to society and locates Criseyde firmly within it.

[181] At the very opening of the poem Chaucer shows that he wants his audience to take Criseyde's social situation seriously in any assessment of her.[13] He emphasises her isolation in Troy, her danger as daughter of a traitor in a long war, and the aspects of her widowed state that meant she lacked a male protector. Having reported the general view that not only her father but all his kin "Ben worthi for to brennen" (I, 90–91), Chaucer writes of Criseyde that

> ... of hire lif she was ful sore in drede,
> As she that nyste what was best to rede;
> For bothe a widewe was she and allone
> Of any frend to whom she dorste hir mone.
>
> (I, 95–98)

Before critics venture any remarks about her "weakness" or her being "slyding of corage" they need to immerse their imaginations in this situation – as Chaucer did. Her fear is fully justified, her weakness is a genuine aspect of a social reality not of her own making, and her isolation is an essential part of her vulnerability. In these circumstances her only asset, her only leverage on the powerful, is her sexuality. She understands this well enough and, "Wel neigh out of hir wit for sorwe and fere," approaches Hector, one of the most powerful men in the city:

> On knees she fil biforn Ector adown
> With pitous vois, and tendrely wepynge,
> His mercy bad, hirselven excusynge.

(I, 110–12)

It is interesting to contrast this scene with conventional courtly images of the male prostrate before the female, images we later see enacted by Troilus and by the arch-manipulator Pandarus (III, 183–84, 953, 1079–80). Indeed, Chaucer already invites such contrasts by preceding her homage with a conventional description of her "aungelik" beauty and her appearance as "an hevenyssh perfit creature" (I, 102, 105). We immediately see the heavenly woman desperately on her knees in a totally subordinate role before the all-powerful male. (It is tempting to observe that if she is angelic, then Hector is deific – a fair social projection.) To survive in this society the isolated woman needs to make use of her sexuality and whatever courtly sexual conventions or fictions as may serve her.[14] She does so, and we should not miss the way Chaucer has begun his poem by placing the whole matrix of courtly forms of sexual relations and language in a setting which stresses the "aungelik" female's totally subordinate position and her urgent need for protection in order to [182] survive.[15] It is Hector, responding to her sorrow and beauty, who guarantees "hir estat" (I, 113–31). The esteem in which she is held by Hector and the royal family is of great importance to her, and it is not surprising that during her first discussion with Pandarus in Book Two she asks directly after Hector, the potentate whose goodwill and existence appear necessary for her well-being. Similarly when later it seems that there is a threat to her property we see the importance of the royal family as patrons to deliver Criseyde from trouble (II, 1414–91, 1611–36). And being reliant on this group, Criseyde is influenced by their opinions, whether about Troilus in Book Two, when her mixed feelings are soothed by hearing these powerful people sing his praises (1583–94), or in Book Four, when she considers Troilus' proposal that they elope.

The first interview between Pandarus and Criseyde confirms Chaucer's interest in the detailed process of interaction between individual consciousness and various social pressures, manipulations, and values, often bewilderingly conflicting (II, 87–597). Chaucer re-locates her fears and natural impulses in the particular situation he had drawn for us in his first book. It is May, and Pandarus invites her to cast aside her self-possession and dance (II, 110–12). At once Criseyde turns to one possible social role (in Chaucer's own society) to protect herself from risks that could be involved in her uncle's suggestion:

> "I? God forbede!" quod she, "be ye mad?
> Is that a widewes lif, so God yow save?
> By God, ye maken me ryght soore adrad!
> Ye ben so wylde, it semeth as ye rave.
> It sate me wel bet ay in a cave

> To bidde and rede on holy seyntes lyves;
> Lat maydens gon to daunce, and yonge wyves."
>
> (II, 113–19)

We saw before how well founded were her fears (both of her own people and, as she now says, the Greeks [II, 124]), and met one strategy for confronting them. But a widow's situation also allowed another – the posture of contemplative withdrawal from the life of the world and the overcoming of natural instincts.[16] Of course, Criseyde does not claim this is what she positively wants, only that it would be decorous and would fulfil certain, very different, social values. Later, we shall see, she can assess the situation of widowhood and its acknowledged values in yet another way.

As the conversation proceeds the war is the central topic until Chaucer tells us that Pandarus discussed "hire estat, and . . . hire governaunce" (II, 211–20). Here he focuses on his relationship to her [183] as uncle, elder male relative, and guide to subordinate female (II, 232–52, 295–98: the *authority* relations here should not be missed, for as the narrator notes, at III, 581, nieces should obey uncles). Having shifted the relationship into these roles, he uses his position to push Troilus' interest at her. Chaucer's handling of Criseyde's situation here is, as so often in this work, extraordinarily delicate. Its vulnerability has been stressed, and Pandarus' circumlocutions play on her fears (II, 278–315). When this has been done he introduces the core of his matter:

> Now, nece myn, the kynges deere sone, . . .
> The noble Troilus, so loveth the,
> That, but ye helpe, it wol his bane be.
>
> (II, 316, 319–20)

Pandarus emphasises the social status of the lover (the personal name follows three lines *after* the social identification), the king's son, using this as a bait but also as a threat. For what would become of Criseyde if she should be held responsible for his death (II, 320–50)? In a similar manner, Pandarus adds to the pressure by stating that if she does not acknowledge Troilus, then he, her uncle, will cut his own throat (II, 323–29). This added threat has a double force, for Criseyde is not only subordinate to him but also genuinely fond of his company. She plays for time and seeks clarification, using the social roles Pandarus has chosen – "'Now em,' quod she, 'what wolde ye devise? / What is youre reed . . . ?'" (388–89). Pandarus' reply is unequivocal and recommends total fulfilment of Troilus' sexual desires (390–406). Criseyde tries to forestall this demand by appealing to his identity as her quasi-father (408–28). This tactic fails badly, for Pandarus renews his previous threats, now getting up and setting off to carry them out (429–47). Criseyde's response is fully comprehensible and carefully traced in the next three stanzas (II, 449–69). Her great fear has again been given a thoroughly sufficient social basis, and there is no reason to treat it as a peculiar flaw.

Thinking of her uncle's suicide, she thinks of its social repercussions, trying to balance her own social survival with her uncle's personal survival – "my estat lith now in jupartie, / And ek myn emes lif is in balaunce ..." (II, 465–66). Her comment (to herself) that "It nedeth me ful sleighly for to pleie" (462), suggests how aware she is that her uncle is manipulating her, but it is not women who are final arbitrators of the games' rules, and she simply cannot dissolve the realities and constraints of her position and her past. What she can do is concede gracefully and so shift to the more favourable ground of [184] "Love." Here, as mentioned earlier, convention allowed woman a seemingly dominant role, and also legitimised expression, however discreet, of those natural sexual impulses so despised in official church teaching. This enables her to assert that she cannot love anyone against her own will, taking a certain initiative in the role of powerful beauty knowledgeable in the mysteries of love and able to bring even a king's son to woe (II, 477–79, 499–504). But by the time this occurs, Chaucer has taken us far into one of the major problems he was exploring – the contradiction between the aristocratic love conventions in which woman was an exalted and powerful figure, and the social reality in which she was a totally subordinate being to be used, manipulated, and taught obedience. Furthermore, and this cannot be given too much weight, he explores the problem concretely as it affected Criseyde's own consciousness and actions, showing subtle concern with the interactions between individual, conflicting ideologies and social situation. This concern is at the heart of Chaucer's imaginative, intellectual, and moral achievement in *Troilus and Criseyde*, and I intend to follow it through the poem.

When Pandarus, sure of his own success, leaves Criseyde, she withdraws "into hire closet" to examine her own feelings and the implications of Troilus' advances (II, 598–812). Her discussion takes into account her own erotic impulses, her social circumstances, and the psychological risk of loving. She does not choose to suppress her sexual feelings totally (II, 649–79), but Eros is always incarnate in time and place, so it is appropriate that Chaucer now reminds us how she is "allone" and shows her mind move to the implications of any involvement with Troilus for her own precarious social existence:

> Al were it nat to doone,
> To graunte hym love, ye, for his worthynesse,
> It were honour, with pley and with gladnesse,
> In honestee with swich a lord to deele,
> For myn estat, and also for his heele.
>
> Ek wel woot I my kynges sone is he;
> And sith he hath to se me swich delit,
> If I wolde outreliche his sighte flee,
> Peraunter he myghte have me in dispit,
> Thorugh whicch I myghte stonde in worse plit.

> (II, 703–12)

The opening two lines of this quotation imply some forces against giving Troilus her love, but for the moment they are left vague, and she immediately moves to positive grounds for involvement, within [185] legitimising social conventions ("honour," "honestee" – though these too remain equivocal as to precise content). We know how Chaucer has continually stressed her estate and its uncertain position, and so we should appreciate with sympathy this blend of self-preservation and care of another, for the poet, unlike some of his modern commentators, had a fine grasp of the complexity of human motivation. Indeed, in the quoted passage the complications increase as Criseyde sees that this very "estat" might not only be protected by "my kinges sone" but could be threatened from two directions. If she rejects him he could certainly undermine her position even further and she would be in a far "worse plit" than at the present. This is a thoroughly realistic assessment, as the court-poet well knew, and it shows the real power relations under the conventions of courtly and literary love. The second direction of the threat is quite contrary but also thoroughly social and realistic, showing Chaucer again considering his own world. Criseyde knows that despite her isolated position in Troy she is currently under Hector's protection and in possession of her estate. Furthermore a widow in medieval society, certainly a basic model for this fictional Trojan aristocracy, had a privileged place in relation to married women. As Eileen Power explained, "under English common law the unmarried woman or widow – the *femme sole* – was, as far as all private, as distinct from public, rights and duties are concerned, on a par with men. She could hold land, even by military tenure, and do homage for it; she could make a will or a contract, could sue or be sued. On the other hand when she married, her rights, for the duration of the marriage, slipped out of her hands. The lands of which she was tenant-in-fee at the time of her marriage, or which she might acquire later, forthwith became her husband's for the duration of the marriage."[17] These are the kinds of factors Criseyde bears in mind when she comments on the idea of remarriage:

> I am my owene womman, wel at ese,
> I thank it God, as after myn estat,
> Right yong, and stonde unteyd in lusty leese,
> Withouten jalousie or swich debat:
> Shal noon housbonde seyn to me "check mat!"
>
> (II, 750–54)

So the problem of having a male protector as husband was that whatever measure of independence she had, however risky, would be quite lost as soon as she married, since she would immediately come under the absolute rule of the husband.[18] Throughout the entire period before she explicitly commits herself to Troilus in bed, threatened as she is from many directions, she constantly expresses fears [186] about losing the relative independence she has and becoming totally dominated.

Finally she is aware that the relevant problems go beyond the issues of marriage and domination to embrace the way any full and serious love for another person necessarily involves risking oneself, jeopardising a self-possession often won with great difficulty. The whole process of lively commitment to another opens out the self and is experienced as both joy and painful constraint. She puts these fears well:

> Allas! syn I am free,
> Sholde I now love, and put in jupartie
> My sikernesse, and thrallen libertee?
> Allas! how dorst I thenken that folie?
> May I naught wel in other folk aspie
> Hire dredful joye, hire constreinte, and hire peyne?
> Ther loveth noon, that she nath why to pleyne.
>
> (II, 771–77)

This fear is quite distinguishable from the more material fears previously discussed, but in practice it overlaps, and Chaucer again reveals the inextricable links between objective social factors and the individual psyche.[19]

Chaucer's preoccupation with the issues under discussion is manifest in the dream about the eagle which Criseyde has after the delicate and many-layered scene in the garden. She dreams

> How that an egle, fethered whit as bon,
> Under hire brest his longe clawes sette,
> And out hire herte he rente, and that anon,
> And dide his herte into hire brest to gon,
> Of which she nought agroos, ne nothyng smerte;
> And forth he fleigh, with herte left for herte.
>
> (II, 926–31)

This dream highlights the violence and perils of loving concealed behind the traditional conceit of an exchange of hearts. Chaucer shows us that although the dreamer feels no pain she perceives herself as *passive* in the face of an aggressive, dominating, and savage male. Her feelings are described in negatives ("she *nought* agroos, *ne nothyng* smerte"), and there is a striking absence of any tenderness, mutuality, or pleasure. True, this is a dream focussing her fears, but the point is that these fears are well grounded in the social reality with which women had to cope, and the consequences this reality had for the most intimate areas of experience. It is, I believe, in such [187] terms that we can see how Chaucer is creating the "typical" and "universal," a "universal" which does not dissolve the individual consciousness and the particular social circumstances.

As Book Three progresses Troilus' behaviour gradually melts away Criseyde's fears as she comes to rely on him as one who, although her male social superior, is a loving protector willing to leave her identity and widow's status intact (III, 463–83). She remains subordinate to male initiatives and commands, but we also see her using this submission while conforming – for example, she dutifully *obeys* her uncle (III, 575–81), but the implications are that she may be doing so for her own advantage (the possibility of seeing Troilus) without having to accept any of the responsibility of being initiator or decision-maker. Still, in noticing the strategies open to women in this world, the possible uses of their subordination and passivity, we should not go to the extreme of claiming that woman is really the principal controller.[20] Even at this point, in a Book which contains one of the most powerful celebrations of fulfilled human love, of what Blake was to call "the lineaments of gratified desire" and what Chaucer called "the grete worthynesse" in love, we see that her final coming together with Troilus actually depends on Pandarus manipulating Criseyde's newly blossomed feelings in an exploitive and uncaring way.[21] Her confusion under the pressures of real distress at hearing how Troilus thinks her unfaithful, her sexual desires, her unaccustomed presence in her uncle's house at night, her social anxieties, all these bring her to her "wittes ende" and, hardly surprising, place her firmly in Pandarus' hands, "For I am here al in youre governaunce."[22]

However, once these manipulations, combined with Troilus' own sexual anxiety, have culminated in Pandarus' throwing Troilus into her bed ("O nece, pes, or we be lost!" – still playing on her fears as much as her erotic desire, III, 1065–1118), Criseyde takes the sexual initiative, kissing and reassuring Troilus (1116–34). Once she has done so, she delicately and trustingly hands over the initiative to him, in a transition Chaucer describes with marvellous tact and insight (III, 1177–83). Troilus, "with blisse of that suprised," responds joyfully, and the poet creates an atmosphere of mutual discovery and shared stimulation as a new serenity encompasses them, contrasting most strikingly with the tense, manipulative, and socially inescapable love-games played out previously.

Yet even in this admirable transition, we still have some images to remind us that the socially and ideologically subordinate position of woman leaves its imprint on this mutual satisfying and now intimate relationship. The timorous "mouses herte" Troilus, anxiously [188] swooning at Criseyde's bedside (III, 736, 1092) is transformed into the fulfilment of Criseyde's own violent dream –

> What myghte or may the sely larke seye,
> Whan that the sperhauk hath it in his foot?
>
> (III, 1191–92)

The power relations are again overt, the predatory nature of the "sperhauk" undisguised. Well may the narrator muse about what the lark may say from this position. Chaucer raises the question and immediately leaves it, only to show us the newly confident Troilus not thanking Criseyde for bringing him to erotic life and so generously giving him the sexual initiative, but turning his attention to "thanken tho the blisful goddes sevene" (1203). If this reading of Troilus here is too unsympathetic, there can be no doubt about this character's revealing use of conventional images which present the lover's relationship in terms of male hunter and female vanquished prey (1205–11). This, we saw, is mirrored in the narrator's sparrowhawk/lark image and in Criseyde quaking "as an aspes-leef" as Troilus takes her in his arms (1201–02). The elements of male domination in society are plainly reflected in the most personal acts.

While this needs pointing out, it would be wrong to leave the commentary emphasising these aspects of what is a characteristically multi-faceted, rich piece of writing. Despite the social and ideological forces Chaucer has focussed on with such imaginative integrity, and despite his refusal to make them vanish simply, he does indeed create a most powerful example of the way in which fulfilled Eros enables individuals to transcend social pressures, repressions, and fears. Mutual love, involving the total person, is achieved, and in this mutuality we celebrate not only the overcoming of adverse forces but the momentary and joyful abandonment of anxious selfhood as together they "Felten in love the grete worthynesse." The conflicts of power and the distortions of energy and of generous love are transcended in an oasis of "hevene blisse," of "perfit joie," and "grete worthynesse."[23]

The final point I wish to make about Book Three in the present study concerns the aubade (III, 1429–70). Here the coming of morning symbolises not some inquisitorial sun of righteousness and truth against which the evil worldlings are in damnable rebellion, but the re-intrusion of day-to-day society into their lives, the society in which practices and ideas concerning women have the deforming and elaborately contradictory effects we have followed in the poem so far, and which are about to become central once more. It is a society which subordinates human Eros and relations to extrinsic economic and power structures with disastrous results: as Troilus says, "For [189] many a lovere hastow slayn, and wilt ..." (1459). Nevertheless, although the lovers curse the day and promise an eternity of the kind of love they have just experienced, they do not yet question their own resumption of everyday aristocratic life, accepting that "it mot nedes be" (III, 1520), however antagonistic to their own love. It will not always be thus for Troilus, as we shall see in Book Four.

The Prologue to Book Four opens with the narrator castigating the abstraction "Fortune" for causing the misery we are about to witness. While this way of talking about events was traditional enough, it is far less relevant to what the poem actually shows us than many readers (and perhaps even the author himself) have been prepared to admit. For what Book Four carefully describes is the prime importance of social organisation and values in determining what happens to Troilus and Criseyde, making addresses to "Fortune" (and metaphysical speculations about destiny) seem an unnecessarily vague and mystifying concealment of human practices.

The Book itself opens by bringing the crucial social contexts to our attention (IV, 29–231). First of all Chaucer reminds the reader that Troy has immersed itself in a long war (29–56), and any reader might be expected to remember that its origins lay not in "Fortune" but in specific acts of male social aggression and greed leading to the present state of continuous legalised violence.[24] Chaucer reports a day-long battle in which men fight with all weapons, "And with hire axes out the braynes quelle" (IV, 46). The Trojans suffer severe losses and seek a truce and negotiations with the Greeks for exchange of prisoners. At this point the sudden intervention of Calkas underlines a key element in the social structure: woman is seen as a passive object to be disposed of by a male-dominated ruling group. Calkas decides that his daughter should join him to avoid the destruction of Troy, and however strange such paternal care may now seem from the father who abandoned his daughter to face hostility and possible persecution when he left the city, no one questions his right to reclaim her.[25] Indeed her alienation from her treacherous father is as total as her wish to remain in her homeland (IV, 659–871, 1128–69). But neither Calkas, nor anyone else, considers that a mere woman is a being with needs, desires, and choices to be honoured, even though she is close to court circles. Troilus sees this quite clearly when he reminds Criseyde that once she is with Calkas he can marry her off as he sees fit, persuading her verbally, "Or do yow don by force as he shal teche"....[26]

Highlighting these issues for us as ones we should continue to take very seriously, Chaucer moves us from Calkas and the Greek assembly to the Trojan "parlement" (IV, 141–217). The purpose of the [190] parliament is to discuss "Th'eschaunge of prisoners" (IV, 146). At once Criseyde is demanded in return for Antenor. The assumption here is extraordinarily revealing: that because Criseyde is a woman she has no different status than a prisoner. We now see from yet another perspective how much Hector's earlier promise to protect "so fair a creature" (I, 105–22) overlapped with courtly conventions of love in contradiction – as I pointed out – with many major elements in social organisation. Hector does speak out at the parliament:

> "Syres, she nys no prisonere," he seyde; ...
> "We usen here no wommen for to selle."
>
> (IV, 179, 182)

This gets to the nub of the matter. Criseyde is not officially a prisoner, and if this is taken seriously then what is being proposed is simply to sell her, to handle her as a commodity in a social market organised by and for male possessing groups. Parliament's decision to sell her is realistic enough in symbolising the social situation of women in Chaucer's world. The Trojan Antenor is "Daun Antenor," "so wys and ek so bold baroun," "ek oon the grettest of this town," whereas Criseyde is reduced to having no identity other than "This womman" (IV, 188–92). The fact that after Calkas' treachery and the immediate threats to her existence, Criseyde had become "both of yonge and olde / Ful wel biloved" (I, 130–31), and that she "nevere dide hem scathe" (IV, 207), and that her official status is not "prisonere," all this is irrelevant before her social status as "womman." The naming here signifies the exact power structure being invoked as once more the realities beneath the various courtly forms of love and respect for women are made plain at a key juncture in the poem. Hector is soon silent.

We should thus be quite clear that the ensuing disintegration of the love between Troilus and Criseyde, and their respective psychic disintegration, is precisely and unequivocally rooted in the current social structure and the treatment of women. Criseyde is being sold not because of her timidity or sinfulness, nor principally because of any mysterious "Fortune": she is being sold because she is a powerless commodity belonging to a male ruling group now prepared to cash her presently increased market value. At the heart of the tragedy, Chaucer emphasises, is a society in which people are turned into marketable objects and by various complex, often contradictory, conventions and controls taught to connive at this monstrous dehumanisation, and accept the appalling destruction of a great human achievement in a thoroughly corrupt social order.

[191] The long discussion between the lovers, once they have gone to bed after parliament's decision, is actually a process of such connivance with social forces the individuals are not equipped to withstand, despite their great love and commitment to each other.[27] Just as Criseyde took the sexual initiative on their first night together in Book Three, so she does now in offering comfort and reassurance that they will be re-united (1261 ff.). It seems like a brave attempt to make the best of a bad situation without capitulating to it, and it seems that she has taken the initiative in the face of tremendous pressures. But as we scrutinise the passage more closely we find that her admirable attempt at initiating action is actually the complex submission of a victim to the dominating groups that control her world, and is done without any adequate consciousness that this is in fact the case. Chaucer's own insight and art are especially subtle as he shows the ways in which her seemingly confident claims of being an initiating agent are gradually undermined within her own discourse by womanly accommodation and compliance to a specifically *social* fate. A fundamental social conservatism, the product of her whole life, traps her into total accommodation to an alien reality which sacrifices her to the self-interest of a male ruling group. In the present study there is just space to sketch the way Chaucer's art follows this complex path.

The overt claims of her role as agent are illustrated in sentences like the following:

> Now, that I shal wel bryngen it aboute,
> To come ayeyn, soone after that I go,
> Therof am I no manere thyng in doute.

> (IV, 1275–77)

This bodes well for Troilus. But having said that the urgency of the occasion means that she will have to pack "an heep of weyes" by which she will effect this "in wordes fewe," she expends the next twelve stanzas without specifying one way in which *she* will ensure the desired outcome, let alone a heap

(1279–1365). What does happen is significant, for she is not only completely vague: when she does envisage some ways by which she could be with Troilus again, the agents in these cases act quite independently of her:

> Men trete of pees; and it supposid is
> That men the queene Eleyne shal restore,
> And Grekis us restoren that is mys.
>
> (IV, 1346–48)

From being agent in a process she initiates ("I shal wel bryngen it [192] aboute") she has now become syntactically absolutely deleted, invisibly waiting upon events under the control of "men" and rumours about what "men purposen" (1350). This shift characterises these twelve stanzas. She may then sense that her promising opening has not been maintained, for she says, "Have here another wey, if it so be / That al this thyng ne may yow nat suffise" (1366–67). This involves persuading her father to send her back to Troy to collect, and intercede for, his property (1368–1414). Again the original initiatory role is dissolved as she substitutes accepted male authorities for herself in effecting her deliverance from misery. Her socialisation as woman has been so successful that she has internalised the values and norms of her male governors, leaving her unable even to imagine any coherent opposition to their utterly selfish and cruel decrees – "My goyng graunted is by parlement / So ferforth that it may nat be withstonde / For al this world ..." (1297–99). It is important to notice how in this she is quite unlike the male aristocrat Troilus, for despite his own deep vested interest in the *status quo*, his training and life have encouraged a far more active and independent role in the social world. He proposes that they defy the parliament's ruling and elope. He sees that their only way of surviving as fulfilled and happy lovers is to break out of this society so inimical to their relationship (1501–26). Nor is this an irresponsible flight of fancy, for he is a well-proven knight who has also taken thought of their need for material subsistence and survival (1513–26). It is Criseyde who refuses to pursue this rebellious course (though she later regrets it: V, 736–65), and the terms in which she does so again emphasise the manner in which the repressed and subordinate learn to internalise the values and assumptions of repressing and dominant groups – to their own detriment and destruction.[28] It is not mere idiosyncratic timidity that guides Criseyde, but official (male) ideology about women and values. She says:

> But that ye speke, awey thus for to go
> And leten alle youre frendes, God forbede,
> For any womman, that ye sholden so!
>
> (IV, 1555–57)

Here she, a woman, downgrades the full heterosexual love of a man for a woman in relation to inter-male friendship and the cohesion of the male aristocracy, and she downgrades woman. Next she places a male-instigated war above their love (1558–59) and uncritically accepts crude militaristic notions of "honour" (1561, 1575) rather than the claims of so fully humanising a love as we saw celebrated in Book Three. She moves on to consider what "the peple ek al aboute / [193] Wolde of it seye?" (1569–70). This is a fine representation of the uncritical nature of her ideology, for these are the very same "peple" we listened to in the parliament, in a scene already discussed (IV, 183 ff.). They showed a total contempt for Criseyde's identity as a mere woman, and no hesitation in selling her for their own (supposed) immediate advantage. Yet their obnoxious but conventional attitudes and behaviour are the norms their victim appeals to in a crisis where her own aristocratic lover advocates flight and rebellion. The power of training, habitual subordination, and convention could not be more powerfully demonstrated. So profoundly has she internalised anti-feminist norms, and the downgrading of Eros, that she defends a dominant ideology in which war, male self-interest, and the defence of the male ruling group are more important than human love and her own survival and happiness. Chaucer rounds off this brilliant exploration by having her appeal to stoical "reason" and "patience" to confirm her resignation in the face of a social fate against which cogent human action was, as Troilus asserted, possible (IV, 1583–89). There is not space to develop this observation here, and it will have to suffice for the present simply to note that this use of stoical and Boethian stances pervades Book Four. That is, the Book shows the narrator, Troilus, and Criseyde using Boethius to rationalise and sanctify resignation in the face of a social order willing to trade human beings and wage long and totally destructive war. As so often in the history of thought and religion, we see metaphysics being used to construct defences of contemporary social organisation. But the movements of the poetry subvert such strategies as they disclose human agency, ideology, and history at the core of metaphysical projections, however attractive and fascinating these projections were to Chaucer.[29]

By the opening of Book Five Troilus and Criseyde have accommodated themselves to the crippling social reality against which Troilus suggested they rebel. Chaucer shows them fully controlled as Criseyde is "muwet, milde, and mansuete" (V, 194), and Troilus completely involved in subduing his feelings and behaving in a supposedly manly fashion in public. To me it seems that criticism of the poem has again paid insufficient attention to Chaucer's continuing evolution of a rich social psychology in which the final disintegration of the mutual love is placed in a social situation imaginatively and aesthetically realised with precision and depth.

Chaucer stresses how Criseyde's weak and subordinate position, her social heritage as a woman (not as a morally weak or oddly timid individual), is made many times worse in the Greek camp (V, 687–765). She is a prisoner of the enemy army, much more isolated than [194] in Troy, even at the beginning of Book One, and completely lacking in that most vital of stays – warm human support. Whereas Troilus at least has Pandarus to talk with and is in his own customary milieu, a powerful figure with friends and public identity, Criseyde is frighteningly alone: "With wommen fewe, among the Grekis stronge ..." (688); "Ther was no wight to whom she dorste hire

pleyne" (728); "she was allone and hadde nede / Of frendes help ..."
(1026–27). The poet's emphasis is unmistakable, and the word "dorste" is
well chosen. When her father-ruler refuses to let her return she is frightened
of attempting a clandestine escape. Her soliloquy about these fears is very
moving and once more shows Chaucer imagining his way into individual
consciousness and history, in a manner quite untypical of medieval character-
ology represented by Lydgate, Gower, or saints legends. Away from any
idealising literary conventions, Criseyde voices her real and justifiable social
and sexual fears, fear of the Greek state, fear of rape.[30] Her movement away
from commitment to Troilus must always be discussed in these contexts
which Chaucer has created so understandingly. His approach is the absolute
antithesis to the abstract inquisitorial moralism favoured by certain groups in
many ages and countries.

Her total situation, with all its pressures working on an individual trained
by her society to *accommodate* to an antagonistic reality rather than rebel (as
Troilus recommended), now expands to include a new aristocratic lover,
Diomede (V, 771 ff.). In her painful isolation she is cruelly exposed to
Diomede, for whom she is a (doubtlessly goddess-like) fish to be netted
(775–77). So when we come to the now famous phrase describing aspects of
her being as "slydynge of corage" (825), we have been given ample grounds
for grasping this in the full light Chaucer has cast on the crippling social
reality and ideology which constitute her circumstances. He has created a
profound vision of a social individual whose bad faith was almost impossible
to avoid, encouraged and prepared for by the habits and practices of the very
society which would, of course, condemn such a betrayal with righteous
moral indignation. (The contradiction here is one endemic to western society
and ethics, and Chaucer grasps it finely.) The poet himself should be quoted
on this theme as Criseyde turns from Troilus:

> Retornyng in hire soule ay up and down
> The wordes of this sodeyn Diomede,
> His grete estat, and perel of the town,
> And that she was allone and hadde nede
> Of frendes help; and thus bygan to brede
> [195]   The cause whi, the sothe for to telle,
> That she took fully purpos for to dwelle.

(V, 1023–29)

Nothing could be more explicit in encouraging the reader to acknowledge
fully the role of social organisation and situation in breeding so many fundamental aspects of human moral and spiritual failure. It is a statement which
draws the reader's attention to the poem's social psychology and eschews the
simpler way of abstract moral accusation and judgement. There is also
wonderful comprehension in the way Chaucer reveals Criseyde's misery in
betraying Troilus during the very process of deciding to betray him, allied to
a pathetic, sad, but authentic wish to move from the extremely unsatisfying
life she is now immersed in to one more structured by freely chosen fidelity –

> Ther made nevere woman moore wo
> Than she, whan that she falsed Troilus....
> "But syn I se ther is no bettre way,
> And that to late is now for me to rewe,
> To Diomede algate I wol be trewe."
>
> (V, 1052–53, 1069–71: see 1051–85)

The power and universal relevance of this psychological realisation should never be lost in attempts to collapse Chaucer into the conventional platonising norms of medieval characterisation and abstract moralism.

Criseyde's final appearance in the poem shows her using her real fears and resignation to a most unhappy situation in a letter aimed at manipulating the sympathies of the lover she has betrayed, perhaps even to keep him hanging on to her a little longer:

> Come I wole; but yet in swich disjoynte
> I stonde as now, that what yer or what day
> That this shal be, that kan I naught apoynte.
>
> (V, 1618–20; see also 1627 and 1590–1631)

In Troilus' own compassionate response, free of all the earlier egotistical histrionics, Chaucer manifests the quality of love and commitment that has emerged from the relationship, for the male at any rate:

> Thorugh which I se that clene out of youre mynde
> Ye han me cast; and I ne kan nor may,
> For al this world, withinne myn herte fynde
> To unloven yow a quarter of a day!
>
> [196]   In corsed tyme I born was, weilaway,
> That yow, that doon me al this wo endure,
> Yet love I best of any creature!
>
> (V, 1695–1701)

This poignant and admirable commitment comes as a model of the real possibilities and achievements of human relationships, and of one in particular now foundering under the exploitations and practices of the contemporary society. It is Pandarus who represents this society's deepest conventional wisdom, for having treated Criseyde as an object to be poked about and manipulated for male gratification, he now turns on her in blind outrage:

> What sholde I seyen? I hate, ywys, Cryseyde;
> And, God woot, I wol hate hire evermore! ...
> And fro this world, almyghty God I preye
> Delivere hire soon! I kan namore seye.
>
> (V, 1732–33, 1742–43)

Chaucer's own work should have delivered us not only from such crude reactions, quite lacking in self-knowledge, but also from all abstract, one-dimensional moralisms which blithely ignore social realities and controls. In doing so, one of its most original and central achievements was, as we have seen, the poetic evocation of a social psychology which grasped the complex interactions between individual consciousness and action, conflicting ideologies, and social organisation.

There is not space in an article of this length to explore the relationship between the processes I have described and the Epilogue, with the bulky critical controversy surrounding it. For the present I will have to close with a few observations which must await full substantiation. Basically I accept the main outlines of the argument about the Epilogue put by Elizabeth Salter and Alfred David.[31] Chaucer's imaginative processes encourage us to leave the comfortably simple judgements of conventional and fixed moral schemes to approach the highly complex and fluid interactions between individual and circumstances pointed out in this essay. This approach, so open to real contexts and processes of human choice, makes it hard for a serious reader to go on repeating seemingly unshakeable formulae about unambiguous vices and virtues propagated in the mass of didactic guides and poems. This is inevitably disturbing to traditional and seemingly uncomplicated certainties as it works to subvert all absolutes and static finalities. Leszek Kolakowski's essay on the an[197]tagonism between what he calls "the priest and the jester" seems relevant: "The priest is the guardian of the absolute; he sustains the cult of the final and the obvious as acknowledged by and contained in tradition. The jester is he who moves in good society without belonging to it, and treats it with impertinence; he who doubts all that appears self-evident ... to unveil the nonobvious behind the obvious, the nonfinal behind the final."[32] Chaucer (unlike many of his exegetes) was, in the sense Kolakowski expounds, a jester rather than a priest or inquisitor. Nevertheless, as Kolakowski adds, "there are more priests than jesters at a king's court, just as there are more police-men than artists in his realm," and the poet was doubtlessly unsettled by the implications of his own profoundly social psychology and imaginative ethical thought, deeply disturbed by the implications of being a jester in a culture dominated by priests and intellectual policemen. It is quite understandable that given the social and ideological framework within which he himself lived he should at some stages feel the need to retreat into a more affirmative and conventional position with regard to the dominant norms of his culture. It is also intelligible that he would inevitably accept many of the priest's aspirations even while subverting them. His own poem has helped us to understand this kind of complexity, and its universal appeal and relevance are not dissociable from precisely this magnificent achievement. As for Criseyde, the woman in society, who disappears before the poet wrestles over the abyss he had uncovered: Chaucer was neither of her party without knowing it, nor one of the conventional moralists' party against her. Instead the jester developed a complex, profoundly dialectical grasp of the interactions between individual and society which is subversive of all priestly absolutes, medieval or modern.

Notes

This study would never have been written without the contribution, both written and spoken, of Yvonne McGregor, many of whose ideas have been incorporated in my own thoughts.

1 Robert O. Payne, *The Key of Remembrance* (New Haven: Yale Univ. Press, 1963), pp. 182–83, 222, 226. See Arthur Mizener, "Character and Action in the Case of Criseyde," *PMLA*, 54 (1939), 65–79, and, very similarly, Robert M. Jordan, *Chaucer and the Shape of Creation* (Cambridge, Mass.: Harvard Univ. Press, 1967), pp. 99–100.

2 *Key of Remembrance*, pp. 221, 81, 181–82, 223, 226.

3 A fruitful start on these lines has been made by Sheila Delany, *Chaucer's House of Fame: The Poetics of Skeptical Fideism* (Chicago: Univ. of Chicago Press, 1972) and Charles Muscatine, *Poetry and Crisis in the Age of Chaucer* (Notre Dame: Univ. of Notre Dame Press, 1972). I am currently completing a book on Langland, Chaucer, and creative imagination in just such contexts, to be published by Routledge and Kegan Paul. An earlier version of the first chap[198]ter appeared as "Imagination and Ideology in *Piers Plowman*" in *Literature and History*, 7 (1978), 2–19. The kind of work I have in mind as of great help to literary scholars may be exemplified by the following: R. Hilton, *Bond Men Made Free* (London: Temple Smith, 1973); R. W. Southern, *Western Society and the Church in the Middle Ages* (Harmondsworth: Penguin, 1970); G. Duby, *Rural Economy and Country Life in the Medieval West* (London: Edward Arnold, 1968); H. A. Miskimin, *The Economy of Early Renaissance Europe* (Englewood Cliffs: Prentice-Hall, 1969); Ruth Bird, *The Turbulent London of Richard II* (London: Longmans, Green, 1949); Silvia L. Thrupp, *The Merchant Class of Medieval London* (Chicago: Univ. of Chicago Press, 1948); H. J. Hewitt, *The Organisation of War under Edward III* (Manchester: Manchester Univ. Press, 1966). As examples of useful studies in intellectual and religious history I would cite C. Trinkaus and H. A. Oberman, eds., *The Pursuit of Holiness in Late Medieval and Renaissance Religion* (Leiden: E. J. Brill, 1974); R. E. Lerner, *The Heresy of the Free Spirit in the Later Middle Ages* (Berkeley and Los Angeles: Univ. of California Press, 1972); Gordon Leff, *William of Ockham* (Manchester: Univ. of Manchester Press, 1975) and *Heresy in the Later Middle Ages*, 2 vols. (Manchester: Manchester Univ. Press, 1967).

4 See, for example, E. T. Donaldson, "Patristic Exegesis in the Criticism of Medieval Literature: The Opposition," reprinted in *Speaking of Chaucer* (London: Athlone Press, 1970); A. C. Spearing, *Criticism and Medieval Poetry* (London: Edward Arnold, 1964), chapters one and two; D. Aers, *Piers Plowman and Christian Allegory* (London: Edward Arnold, 1975).

5 For some illuminating general comments on this dialectic of affirmation and negation, see H. Marcuse, "Art and Revolution," in *Counter-Revolution and Revolt* (Harmondsworth: Penguin, 1972).

6 See L. Goldmann's description and application of this method in *The Hidden God* (London: Routledge, 1964), esp. parts one to three.

7 Alfred David, *The Strumpet Muse* (Bloomington, Ind.: Indiana Univ. Press, 1976), chapter two, esp. pp. 29–36; Elizabeth Salter, "*Troilus and Criseyde*: A Reconsideration," in *Patterns of Love and Courtesy*, ed. John Lawlor (London: Edward Arnold, 1966), pp. 86–106.

8 Karl Young, "Chaucer's *Troilus and Criseyde* as Romance," *PMLA*, 53 (1938), 38–63; see also Morton W. Bloomfield, "Distance and Predestination in *Troilus and Criseyde*," *PMLA*, 72 (1957), 14–26.

9 In the current essay I have not the space to carry out the useful comparison with

Boccaccio's text in relation to the present argument, but it is worth noting how Chaucer deliberately turns Boccaccio's setting into a courtly, aristocratic one. Similarly it is significant that it is Chaucer who gives such careful attention to Criseyde's social situation and its ideological pressures, a central part of his transformation of Boccaccio's one-dimensional heroine. I intend to develop these comments in a future study.

10 See Eileen Power, *Medieval Women* (Cambridge, Engl.: Cambridge Univ. Press, 1975), pp. 16–28, 35–36; J. Stevens, *Medieval Romance* (London: Hutchinson, 1973), pp. 16–28, 35–36; Alfred David, *The Strumpet Muse*, pp. 17, 55–56.

11 See Eileen Power, *Medieval Woman*, chapters one and two. In these areas, H. P. Kelly's *Love and Marriage in the Age of Chaucer* (Ithaca: Cornell Univ. Press, 1975) is no help.

12 Eileen Power, pp. 23–28, 36. A useful anthology is *Not In God's Image*, ed. J. O'Faolain and L. Martines (London: Temple Smith, 1973), parts 5 to 8.

13 All quotations from Chaucer are from *The Works of Geoffrey Chaucer*, ed. F. N. Robinson, 2nd ed. (Boston: Houghton Mifflin, 1957); here, I, 85–135.

14 As Yvonne McGregor points out, the fact that Criseyde chooses not to [199] channel her request through her uncle (transformed by Chaucer into an older man and apparently the only male relative left to her in Troy), could argue a measure of strong-willed independence; but the fact is that she will get a better deal by prostrating her own sex and beauty before the top man.

15 This emphasis, here and throughout, is peculiarly Chaucer's and in my view comprises an ongoing critique of Boccaccio's superficial presentation of female being. Compare here *Il Filostrato*, Canto Two.

16 One recalls the commonplace exegesis of Matthew 13:8 as applying to marriage (thirtyfold fruit), widowhood (sixtyfold), and virginity (hundredfold).

17 Eileen Power, p. 38. Kelly's discussion of the poem in *Love and Marriage* seems oblivious to these vital issues, and this gravely distorts his approach.

18 Chaucer's own Wife of Bath in her *Prologue* and *Tale*, as well as the whole "marriage group" in the *Canterbury Tales*, shows his continuing preoccupation with these problems about love, power, control, and property in the domestic sphere: see David, *The Strumpet Muse*, chapter nine.

19 While there is not space to develop this, it is worth referring to further exemplification: in her letter to Troilus in Book II (1197–1225) she informs him that she will not "make hirselven bounde / In love," and in III, 169–72, she is still reminding him of this in a superbly equivocal passage.

20 Peter Elbow does just this in his interesting study, *Oppositions in Chaucer* (Middletown, Conn.: Wesleyan Univ. Press, 1973), pp. 55–58.

21 See III, 274–77, 785–98, 855–82. In a more detailed study here it would be worth commenting on Chaucer's crucial changes to Canto Three of *Il Filostrato*, for Boccaccio gave his woman total initiative in organising the lovemaking.

22 See III, 939–45. The passage preceding this, III, 918 ff., makes full use of broken syntax to reflect the confused movements of Criseyde's consciousness.

23 Here III, 1310–16, but the whole passage in III, 1226–1414 is relevant. I am of course aware of the difficulty many Christian ideologists have had in acknowledging what Chaucer has achieved here, the classic case being D. W. Robertson, Jr., "Chaucerian Tragedy," *ELH*, 19 (1952), 1–37. I have more to say on this issue in the study referred to in note 3, above.

24 One might also recall the condition of Europe in the Hundred Years War of Chaucer's time and the organisation and practice of war: H. J. Hewitt, *The Organisation of War* and J. Barnie, *War In Medieval Society* (London: Weidenfeld and Nicolson, 1974). Detailed work on Chaucer's attitudes to war and legitimised

violence, in comparison to the range of contemporary stances, might be particularly illuminating.

25 I am indebted to Yvonne McGregor for this point, as well as for the comparison of Antenor and Criseyde in the next paragraph.

26 IV, 1471–75: Chaucer again mediates medieval reality.

27 IV, 1242 ff. The poet makes Criseyde's commitments unequivocal: IV, 699–700, 708–14, 731–945, 1128–69. It is noticeable that whereas Troilus thinks only of himself and consoles himself with metaphysics, Criseyde actually thinks about her own grief *and* about how her lover will fare: IV, 794–95, 890–903, 942.

28 This major aspect is quite ignored in John Bayley's diagnosis that Criseyde's "trouble" is actually her "absence of passion" (*The Characters of Love* [London: Chatto, 1960], p. 107) despite comments that her love is too much part of the "present discreet regime" (pp. 116–17). The dialectic Chaucer develops here is a universal of the kind medieval critics have been largely closed to: compare D. Aers, "William Blake and the Dialectics of Sex," *ELH*, 44 (1977), 500–14.

29 On this both Alfred David and Elizabeth Salter have pertinent comments: see note 7 above. [200]

30 Here see V, 701–06, 712–14 especially.

31 I have summarised David's comments in the text, above: see note 7. The kind of detailed substantiation I hope to provide in my forthcoming book to be published by Routledge and Kegan Paul must be based on a close reading of the Epilogue which involves factors such as the following: the claim that Troilus' ghost ascends "ful blisfully" to enjoy "pleyn felicite" making our joys (and so those of Book Three) so despicable remains a hollow dogmatic assertion, devoid of any literary realisation. It simply offers no positive alternative to the splendid attempts of human love in the face of the antagonistic social world Chaucer examined so honestly. Similarly with the next stanza (V, 1821–25). Troilus laughs here *at* those who sorrow for his tragedy and damns *all* our work that follows our blind lust: again, there is the same shrill assertiveness and vapid generalisation which are the sign of simple-minded or desperate moralising, quite in contrast to the rich, complexly delicate moral and social imagination manifest throughout the poem. The same comments apply to the narrator's incantation at 1828–34: we do not even know what his "fyn" was, let alone its relation to Book Three and the difficult moral question about the relations between results and the quality of motive and intent. The contrast between the moralistic conventionality of "false worldes brotelnesse" and the poem's splendid focus on specific diversity, contradiction, and ambiguity in the human world, is as marked. And when Chaucer stands forth to preach to modern youth he appeals to the kind of clichéd generality which the poem's ethical and psychological exploration has quite superseded. The incantatory quality of the anathematizing of "payens corsed olde rites" and their gods may well be a veiled attack on the poem's preoccupation with erotic fulfilment and human love: if so, one could develop comments on its intellectual, moral, and imaginative insubstantiality in the face of the poem's own methods of exploration and illumination. But, as I said in the text, these points need expansion, and Chaucer's problems here must be understood in the way he understood Criseyde's.

32 L. Kolakowski, *Marxism and Beyond: On Historical Understanding and Individual Responsibility*, trans. J. Z. Peel (London: Pall Mall Press, 1969), esp. "The Priest and the Jester," pp. 29–57.

11 Troilus' swoon

JILL MANN

Originally published in the *Chaucer Review* 14 (1980):319–35.
Reprinted by permission of the Pennsylvania State University
Press. The original pagination is recorded within square brackets.
The endnotes originally appeared on pp. 333–5.

It is a pleasure to offer this article as a mark of gratitude for R. W. Frank's wide-ranging and important contributions to medieval scholarship. Since Professor Frank has recently taken on the courageous task of trying to develop our sympathy for the superficially uncongenial forms of medieval pathos, I have decided to follow this lead by examining Troilus' swoon in Book III of *Troilus and Criseyde*, and its cardinal role in Chaucer's narrative.

Troilus swoons only once in the course of *Troilus and Criseyde*. It is important to remind ourselves of this fact, because this isolated instance is sometimes casually multiplied and generalised, as if it were a frequent testimony to the emotional intensity of Troilus' love. The swoon is also largely responsible for the popular impression of Troilus as a passive and ineffectual lover. The swoon is absent from the *Filostrato* at this point, since Chaucer's whole account of the consummation scene is radically different from Boccaccio's. Boccaccio's Troilo does, however, swoon at a later point in the story – when he hears the request for the exchange of Criseida and Antenore in the Trojan parliament.[1] This swoon Chaucer removes, while preserving Boccaccio's prefatory description of Troilus repressing his anguish "with mannes herte" (IV, 154).[2] Why, then, does he introduce, at an earlier and apparently less disastrous point in the narrative, a swoon which provokes the questioning of Troilus' manhood ("Is this a mannes game?", III, 1126)?

The functional role of the swoon can only be understood by seeing it within the context of Troilus' courtship as a whole – and, in particular, of that area of it which represents Chaucer's elaboration of Boccaccio's account, stretching from the arrangement of the meeting at Deiphebus' house to Pandarus' fictitious story of Horaste. (In Boccaccio, when the lovers meet in the consummation scene, it is the first time they have come face to face apart from an encounter at Criseida's window.) It is generally acknowledged that by protracting the preliminaries to the consummation in this way, Chaucer removes any impression that Criseyde is an easy conquest, and strengthens our sense of the natural growth of the relationship between the lovers, and hence of its solidity. What I want to draw attention to is that the [320] developing relationship between Troilus and Criseyde is conceived and described in terms of power, and that the shifts and transformations in the way each of them either exerts or refuses to exert power over the other lead to the achievement of a mature and complex relationship on which the consummation can fittingly be based.

At the beginning of the poem, the power-relationships between Troilus and Criseyde are simply the result of their social situations. Troilus is the king's son; Criseyde is not only his inferior in rank, but is also in an extremely precarious social position as the daughter of a traitor, in need of the protection of Hector in order to maintain any position in Trojan society at all. When Troilus first sees Criseyde in the temple, she is ready to assert herself ("With ful assured lokyng and manere", I, 182) against any social opprobrium, but she prudently refrains from provoking it by standing humbly just inside the door, "ay under shames drede" (I, 180). Criseyde's position is also the weaker one just because she is a woman. When left alone to reflect on the news of Troilus' love for her, she is conscious of Troilus' power, as the king's son, to hurt or assist her (II, 708–14), but even more prominent in her mind is the fear of masculine dominance and possessiveness, in their particular manifestations of jealousy and boastfulness. These fears are at first introduced in negative form; Criseyde reassures herself that not only is Troilus no boaster, but that she will never give him any opportunity to "bynde" her "in swich a clause" (II, 728).[3] The idea that boasting is a linguistic "binding," an imprisonment of one partner within the linguistic freedom of the other, aligns it with jealousy, which is also conceived as a "binding." Criseyde congratulates herself on being without a jealous husband:

> "I am myn owene womman, wel at ese,
> I thank it God, as after myn estat,
> Right yong, and stonde *unteyd* in lusty leese,
> Withouten jalousie or swich debat:
> Shal noon housbonde seyn to me 'chek mat!'
> For either they ben ful of jalousie,
> Or maisterfull, or loven novelrie."

(II, 750–56)[4]

Reflections on her present freedom, however, lead Criseyde inevitably to tremble at the idea of its surrender, and her confidence gives way to fear:

> "Allas! syn I am free,
> Sholde I now love, and put in jupartie
> My sikernesse, and thrallen libertee?"

(II, 771–73)

[321] Like Troilus before he falls in love, she finds the most striking aspect of the lover's life to be its servitude:

> "May I naught wel in other folk aspie
> Hire dredfull joye, hire constreinte, and hire peyne?"
>
> (II, 775–76)

This fear of losing control of the self by submitting to love is countered, first, by Antigone's song – the joyous celebration of one "subgit" to love, which claims that love appears "thraldom" only to those who are outside its experience (II, 855–60)[5] – and, second, by Criseyde's dream of the eagle tearing her heart out without pain, which offers her (and us) a mysterious image of an aggression which is not felt as oppression.

Criseyde's fears of men are by no means unwarranted; ironically, she is eventually to give herself to a man whose behaviour is "maisterful," whose desire to win her is spiced with the delight of wresting a treasured possession from another man (V, 792–94), and who is also, it is suggested, a boaster ("som men seyn he was of tonge large", V, 804).[6] But Chaucer takes pains to show that in the case of Troilus, Criseyde's fears are unnecessary. So far from wishing to exert his control over Criseyde, Troilus has himself fallen "thral" to love (I, 439), and has acknowledged that in the realm of love the power which he has in the everyday social world is his no longer.

> And to the God of Love thus seyde he
> With pitous vois, "O lord, now youres is
> My spirit, which that oughte youres be.
> Yow thanke I, lord, that han me brought to this.
> But wheither goddesse or womman, iwis,
> She be, I not, which that ye do me serve;
> But as hire man I wol ay lyve and sterve.
>
> "Ye stonden in hir eighen myghtily,
> As in a place unto youre vertu digne;
> Wherfore, lord, if my service or I
> May liken yow, so beth to me benigne;
> For myn estat roial I here resigne
> Into hire bond, and with ful humble chere
> Bicome hir man, as to my lady dere."
>
> (I, 421–34)

In love, then, the ordinary power relationships are inverted; it is a sign of Love's supremacy that the weaker partner, the lady, wields power over the stronger. When Troilus and Criseyde first meet to talk [322] in Deiphebus' house, we are made conscious of both sets of relationships and their conflicting distributions of power. Externally, the situation casts them in their social roles – with Criseyde as suppliant and Troilus as her powerful protector. So far is this from the emotional truth, and from Troilus' mind, however, that merely to hear Criseyde's formal request for his "lordshipe" throws his carefully-rehearsed speech from his mind.

> This Troilus, that herde his lady preye
> Of lordshipe hym, wax neither quyk ne ded,

> Ne myghte o word for shame to it seye,
> Although men sholde smyten of his hed.
>
> (III, 78–81)

The embarrassment of the word-order in the relative clause demonstrates the unease with which Troilus entertains the idea that he might be Criseyde's "lord" rather than she his "lady." This humility works to his advantage; Criseyde, recognizing that his helplessness is a testimony to the genuineness of his feelings, loves him "nevere the lasse" for it (III, 85–89). In accepting him as her servant, however, she emphasizes that this relationship suspends and supersedes the external social one:

> "But natheles, this warne I yow," quod she,
> "A kynges sone although ye be, ywys,
> Ye shal namore han sovereignete
> Of me in love, than right in that cas is;
> N'y nyl forbere, if that ye don amys,
> To wratthe yow; and whil that ye me serve,
> Chericen yow right after ye disserve."
>
> (III, 169–75)

It is on this basis that the courtship of Troilus and Criseyde continues up to the point of their meeting by night in Pandarus' house in Book III.[7] But while it is clear that this situation is in itself a good one, since it balances and contains the social power structure which would otherwise threaten to make of love a real "thraldom" for the woman, it also brings a problem: how is it possible for this situation to lead into a consummation of love? For either the lady must convict herself of previous hypocrisy and merely pretended innocence by initiating the process of sexual consummation from her commanding position; or the man must convict himself of hypocrisy and merely pretended submission by urging it upon her. What is important in solving this problem is Chaucer's perception that human emotions and relationships are never static; [323] they are constantly subject to accidents from without and movements from within through which their nature is subtly and almost imperceptibly transformed. The word which Chaucer seems most frequently to associate with this imperceptible but ceaseless movement is "proces," which often serves to mark his reflections on the inevitable transmutations of human emotions and experiences in time. It is the key word, for instance, in the description of the gradual but inevitable slackening of Dorigen's first frenzy of grief at her husband's absence:

> By proces, as ye knowen everichoon,
> Men may so long graven in a stoon
> Til some figure therinne emprented be.
> So longe han they conforted hire, til she
> Receyved hath, by hope and by resoun,
> The emprentyng of hire consolacioun,

Thurgh which hir grete sorwe gan aswage;
She may nat alwey duren in swich rage.

(Franklin's Tale, F 829–36)

It is significant, therefore, that at the very beginning of the awakening of Criseyde's feelings for Troilus, Chaucer turns aside from his narrative to assure us that the growth of her feelings was not a sudden occurrence, but a "proces."

For I sey nought that she so sodeynly
Yaf hym hire love, but that she gan enclyne
To like hym first, and I have told yow whi;
And after that, his manhod and his pyne
Made love withinne hir herte for to myne,
For which, by proces and by good servyse,
He gat hire love, and in no sodeyn wyse.

(II, 673–79)

This passage has often been taken to be cynical or ambiguous; it seems to me to be neither,[8] but rather an acknowledgement and a warning of the difficulty of recreating the gradualness of an emotional "proces" within a narrative, where the selection of moments when the "proces" receives special stimulus or reaches recognisable stages may mislead us into thinking that these moments in themselves effect the whole movement from one point to another. The flowering of a plant may appear dramatic, but it depends on a long preceding period of slow and silent growth.

The aspect of the "proces" of love which is most important for this discussion is that its minute and constant movement means [324] that within the acknowledged structure of sovereignty and subjection there grows up another, alternative structure to the relationship, which will allow its consummation to take place, and allow it to mark a genuine transition, rather than an abandonment of hypocrisy, which would also constitute a confession of hypocrisy. The part of the poem where we can see this happening is the summarising description, near the beginning of Book III, of the tenor of the brief meetings between Troilus and Criseyde after the scene at Deiphebus' house, where Chaucer again refers to what is happening between them as a "proces" (470). In this passage, Chaucer emphasizes Criseyde's surprised delight at Troilus' ability to anticipate her every wish; so far from demonstrating any tendency to assert control over her, or to "bind her in the clause" of boasting, she finds in him that bending of the self to the contours of another's being which leads not to the issuing and execution of commands, the mimicking of one will by another, but the wordless and miraculous fusion of two wills into one, so that it is no longer possible to say whose will is dominant and whose is subjected. This view of the miraculous power of love to create "obeisaunce" to each other in lovers receives its fullest and, in some ways, most moving expression in the speech of the deserted falcon in the *Squire's Tale*, which I should like to quote in order to show how constant a part of Chaucer's view of love it is.

> And I so loved hym for his obeisaunce,
> And for the trouthe I demed in his herte,
> That if so were that any thyng hym smerte,
> Al were it never so lite, and I it wiste,
> Me thoughte I felte deeth myn herte twiste.
> And shortly, so ferforth this thyng is went,
> That my wyl was his willes instrument;
> This is to seyn, my wyl obeyed his wyl
> In alle thyng, as fer as reson fil,
> Kepynge the boundes of my worshipe evere.
> Ne nevere hadde I thyng so lief, ne levere,
> As hym, God woot! ne nevere shal namo.

(F 562–73)

(The last words of this speech echo Criseyde's protestation to Pandarus at III, 869–70.) The obedience here is not a matter of subservience to rules of behaviour, but the spontaneous moulding of oneself to another – and it is this that enables Chaucer to use the word "obeye" in the description of the consummation itself: "ech of hem gan otheres lust obeye" (III, 1690).[9] Troilus' subjection of himself ("So koude he hym governe in swich servyse," III, 475) thus mira[325]culously produces the subjection of Criseyde to his "governaunce."

> For whi she fond hym so discret in al,
> So secret, and of swich obeisaunce,
> That wel she felte he was to hire a wal
> Of stiel, and sheld from every displesaunce;
> That to ben in his goode governaunce,
> So wis he was, she was namore afered, –
> I mene, as fer as oughte ben requered.

(III, 477–83)

The repeated "so"s in this stanza seem to begin by being merely emphatic, but they then raise a sort of expectation of a result, a corresponding "that"; the onward movement of the syntax thus carries us on to the result, "she was namore afered," without this necessarily being envisaged at the beginning of the sentence. The movement of the syntax surely mimics the movement of Criseyde's mind; without any conscious decision to surrender the sovereignty she has reserved, Criseyde's emotions are led into enacting that surrender. The self-conscious correction of the stanza's last line – "I mene, as fer as oughte ben requered" – similarly imitates the mind's sudden realization of the point to which it has been led, and a return to the formally acknowledged version of the relationship. What these two lines reveal, in their forward movement and withdrawal, is the growth of an implicit trust, behind the formal structure of the relationship, which reverses that structure and prepares Criseyde to find herself in the power of another without feeling this as "thraldom." The importance of these lines is not only, however, in their demonstration of such a readiness for commitment; equally important is the fact that they show that this readiness is created by Troilus, not by Pandarus. It is not the response of weakness to insistent nagging or manufactured crisis, but a result of the trust which grows out of Troilus' "servyse."[10]

The commitment awaits, however, a formal summons, and the summons finally comes in the scene in Book III in Pandarus' house. But it comes in rather an unexpected form, and one that might well have worked to undo all the good effects of Troilus' "servyse." Pandarus enters Criseyde's chamber with an invented story about Troilus' supposed jealousy of one Horaste, and urges the need for her to see Troilus immediately to put his fears at rest. The dangerousness of this fiction has not, I think, been fully appreciated in discussions of the poem. In the light of all that has gone before, it is clear that Pandarus' story about Troilus' jealousy represents a serious miscalculation. In Criseyde's eyes, it might well seem that this is the [326] moment when the apparently "obeisaunt" lover throws off the mask of humility and asserts his "maistrye" over her.[11] We are alerted to this dangerous implication by Criseyde's long and passionate outburst against jealousy when she finally sees Troilus (III, 1009–43), and her vehement denial that jealousy is a mark of love – an outburst which shows that the "proces" of courtship has in no way made this manifestation of masculine possessiveness less repugnant to her. Pandarus is clearly relying on the traditional view that "jalousie is love" (III, 1024) in order to use this story as a stimulus towards the consummation. But he completely fails to understand, on the one hand, Criseyde's sensitivity to the threat of "thraldom," and, on the other, how remote from Troilus' nature is any tendency towards such possessiveness. So, far from being necessary to bring about the consummation, Pandarus' story very nearly destroys the whole love-affair.

What is it then that saves the situation? Firstly, it is that the implicit trust which Troilus has created by his "obeisaunce" has power to carry Criseyde through this crisis. Secondly, the story of Horaste does, of course, contribute to the consummation in that the very anguish which it causes Criseyde reveals to her (and allows her to acknowledge to her uncle) the extent of her feeling for Troilus:

> "Hadde I hym nevere lief? by God, I ween
> Ye hadde nevere thyng so lief!" quod she.

$$\text{(III, 869–70)}$$

But were this to be the only basis on which the consummation were achieved, it would mean that Criseyde accepted, along with the depth of her feeling for Troilus, the "thraldom" of becoming his claimed possession. It is the swoon, the third and most important means by which the situation is saved, which is crucial in ensuring that when the consummation does take place it does not represent the manoeuvring of one partner into an admission of "thraldom" but the mutual surrender of each partner to the other.

In order to see this, we must also look at the swoon, and the situation immediately preceding it, from Troilus' point of view. When he is confronted with Criseyde in tears, protesting her innocence, he is not pleasantly surprised at the extent of the obligation she acknowledges to him, but horrified at the pain she is suffering, and also at having provoked an anger which he assumes will destroy all her previous good-will.

[327]

> This Troilus, whan he hire wordes herde,
> Have ye no care, hym liste nought to slepe;
> For it thought hym no strokes of a yerde
> To heere or seen Criseyde, his lady, wepe;
> But wel he felt aboute his herte crepe,
> For everi tere which that Criseyde asterte,
> The crampe of deth, to streyne hym by the herte.
>
> (III, 1065–71)

There is, moreover, at least a strong suggestion – in Pandarus' admonition to Criseyde to broach the question of his jealousy to Troilus since his delicacy will prevent him from raising it – that the horror of Troilus' situation is increased by his having had no prior knowledge of the story Pandarus was going to tell, so that he is presented with a *fait accompli*.[12] We can thus see the intensity of the pressures on Troilus immediately before the swoon. He is in his lady's bedroom for the first time, having had his hopes raised to the highest pitch. But instead of showing him the grace and kindness he has earned from her before, she is upbraiding him for his mistrust of her. He cannot excuse himself by revealing the truth – that the story is Pandarus' invention – since this would reveal the extent of Pandarus' guile and raise suspicions about the whole previous course of the affair. Equally, he cannot go through with the story and dredge up some support for his accusations,[13] because this would be to belie his own nature, to cause further grief to Criseyde, and to connive at the shifting of their relationship to one in which he could claim mastery over her. Unable to discover an issue in speech or action, Troilus' mind is turned in on itself, trapped in deadlock, and this condition of his mind is so acute that it transfers itself to his body.

> Therwith the sorwe so his herte shette,
> That from his eyen fil ther nought a tere,
> And every spirit his vigour in knette,
> So they astoned or oppressed were.
> The felyng of his sorwe, or of his fere,
> Or of aught elles, fled was out of towne;
> And down he fel al sodeynly a-swowne.
>
> (III, 1086–92)

The swoon is an expression of Troilus' acceptance of – and indeed absolute identification with – the contradictory and destructive implications of the situation, to which, unlike Pandarus, he is fully alive. Although "nought to blame" (1085), he seems unwittingly to have created his own destruction; he can neither identify with, nor dissociate himself from, the fictional Troilus in Pandarus' story. He is unable to find his real self in the external situation, and this loss [328] of identity is mirrored in his loss of consciousness. The disorder in the outer world is transferred, by the completeness with which he perceives and accepts it, into his inner being, and the result is a dramatic and instantaneous loss of his own internal order. Troilus' swoon is comparable, in this respect, to the madness suffered by romance heroes – Yvain, Lancelot, Tristram; whatever the difference between the situations in which their madness occurs, those situations are all marked by an irresolvable disorder in the outside world to which the knight opens up his being, with a resulting dislocation of mental order.[14] It is, in all these cases, a mark of the hero's nobility of nature that he does not try to evade or diminish the horror of his external situation, even by such apparently acceptable means as an explanation or offered expiation of his own misdemeanours. He removes the horror from the external situation by the single expedient of taking it into himself.

Such a dislocation of rational consciousness is also a way of creating a "fresh start" in the narrative; it wipes out the first crisis by substituting a new one, and thus acts as a means of transition to the restoring of harmony and order in the external situation, even though that is not an end envisaged by the hero at the time. Troilus' swoon, similarly, although not designed to do so, offers Pandarus the opportunity to push the situation beyond the deadlock it has reached. But more important than this practical opportunity is the testimony it offers, of the most convincing and authentic kind, to the fact that Troilus has not in reality become the dominant possessive lover suggested by Pandarus' story. His swoon demonstrates, in the clearest possible way, his subjection to Criseyde and to his love of her, and his dissociation from the idea that she is not still her "owene womman." When he regains consciousness, under Criseyde's coaxing, he is still in this state of humble subjection (that is, their previous relationship has been restored), even though he finds himself in bed with his lady, and even his trumped-up substantiation of the Horaste story is due to the fact that "He most obeye" Criseyde's command to explain himself (III, 1157). As a humble suppliant, he begs forgiveness and puts himself in Criseyde's "grace"; she grants him forgiveness on condition he offends no more. Both are fulfilling their agreement that Criseyde should have the power to "wratthe" him for any misdemeanours.

At this point, therefore, the roles of the two lovers are still – or rather, have once more become, after the apparent threat of reversal – what they were at the beginning of the episode: Criseyde is lady and Troilus is servant. But now, at the end of a stanza, comes a sudden and entirely novel change:

[329]   "And now," quod she, "that I have don yow smerte,
         Foryeve it me, myn owene swete herte."

(III, 1182–83)

With these words, Criseyde for the first time yields power over herself to Troilus; in asking him for forgiveness, she submits herself to him. Troilus sees immediately the implication of her words, and takes up the offer she has made him:

> This Troilus, with blisse of that supprised,
> Putte al in Goddes hand, as he that mente
> Nothyng but wel; and sodeynly avysed,
> He hire in armes faste to hym hente.
>
> (III, 1184–87)

Troilus at last takes on the role of the sexual aggressor; Criseyde in his arms is compared to the lark in the grip of the sparrow-hawk, and trembles like an aspen leaf "Whan she hym felte hire in his armes folde" (1201). For the first time, the relationship between the two lovers conforms to the accepted pattern of sexual roles: the man aggressive and demanding, the woman submissive and yielding. But this is not a mere abandonment of the polite fictions of courtship in favour of the banal inevitability of a more "realistic" distribution of power. On the contrary, we can assent to and enjoy Troilus' insistence and Criseyde's submission precisely because this exercise of masculine power is based on, and still contains within itself, its opposite. Troilus exerts his dominance only *because* Criseyde has, of her own free will, made a submission, and her submission, read in context, does not imply a total surrender of power, once and for all, but a yielding on her part to match the yielding on his, and thus to make their relationship fully mutual. Moreover, even as Troilus takes up Criseyde's offer of power, of control, he is also making a submission; he "Putte al in Goddes hand, as he that mente / Nothyng but wel" – trusting to God and the goodness of his own intention, he takes a chance, puts himself at the mercy of fate and the possibility of a truly final rebuff. Troilus' action is a leap in the dark, an impulse to make himself vulnerable to chance, rather than a calculated seducer's decision that he is safe in going further. And, with a similar paradox, for Criseyde the submission to Troilus does not bring about the "thraldom" she feared, but a liberation; there is no sense of her being manoeuvred or coerced, but rather of her finding the opportunity for the fullest expression of her being, and even finding for the first time a full understanding of her own being.

>   And as the newe abaysed nyghtyngale,
> [330]   That stynteth first whan she bygynneth to synge,
>   Whan that she hereth any herde tale,
>   Or in the hegges any wyght stirynge,
>   And after siker doth hire vois out rynge,
>   Right so Criseyde, whan hire drede stente,
>   Opned hire herte, and tolde hym hire entente.
>
> (III, 1233–39)

It is in this light that we should read Criseyde's response to Troilus' claim of her surrender:

> "Now yeldeth yow, for other bote is non!"
> To that Criseyde answerde thus anon,

"Ne hadde I er now, my swete herte deere,
Ben yold, ywis, I were now nought heere!"

(III, 1208–11)

Criseyde's words, like Troilus', have been read as the dropping of a mask, a revelation of the truth behind an acted façade.[15] But if Criseyde uses the past tense here, it is surely because, like the earlier discovery that she was "namore afered," this is a discovery that can only be made retrospectively. She cannot decide, prospectively, to yield; she can only discover that she has yielded. The liberty that is left to her is the liberty to acknowledge, frankly and generously, that the undefined pressures that have brought her to this moment of definition have been inner as well as outer, and that she takes responsibility, fully and delightedly, for the situation to which they have led her and the self they have discovered for her.[16] What she does by using the past tense is not to indicate a hypocrisy, a split in herself, but to discover a wholeness; she can integrate her present with her past.

It is, to me, significant of the difference between Diomede's wooing and Troilus' that the phrase which seals her surrender to him is cast not in the past tense, but in the future: "To Diomede algate I wol be trewe" (V, 1071). This assurance of future amendment clearly undermines itself; if Criseyde had learned anything from her experience, it ought to have been that firm statements about the future are luxuries that human beings cannot indulge in – or, at least, cannot allow themselves to believe to be actual descriptions of what will happen. But in addition to this general problem about the use of the future tense at this stage, there is a more particular one. With Diomede, as with Troilus, we do not see Criseyde making a clear decision beforehand; we only see her retrospective recognition of the situation into which she has moved. But in her reaction to Diomede's conquest, Criseyde's acknowledgement of the situation to [331] which she has been led does not serve to integrate her past with her present, to enable her to look back at it and perceive a continuity between past actions, thoughts, wishes, fears, and the present situation in which they achieve full embodiment and meaning; in the case of Diomede, to look back at the past only emphasises the gulf between the self that she used to be and the self she has become. She must abandon the past, and can thus only gesture towards the future in order to have some sense of the continuity of her self, and of the integrity of the self which is denoted by the word "trouthe." It is the later speech which is hypocritical, if either is, despite its apparently frank acknowledgement of guilt, since it tries to pretend that the future can be used to wipe out the past, and thus the split between the past and the present.

The cruel irony is that it is Troilus' very sense of the necessity for Criseyde's love to be freely given if it is to be valuable that provides the opportunity for Diomede to urge it from her. Despite all counsels of wisdom, Troilus cannot in the last resort resist suggesting to Criseyde that they elope together before she is exchanged. If she cannot see the need for such drastic action, it is because she relies on the simple fact that she has no desire to do anything other than return to Troy and to Troilus as soon as she has left. Why, then, adopt a plan which seems to assume that, once in the Greek camp, she is bound to stay – and even worse, bound to want to stay? Troilus' further urging provokes a distraught response: if he insists on an elopement, it can only be because he mistrusts her. To this, Troilus can have no answer but to assent to her going.[17] An elopement might, to all practical purposes, have secured Criseyde's fidelity. But if she were only faithful because he had put it out of her power to be tempted, of what worth would be her fidelity? Troilus would then have taken on the role of the *fabliau*-husband, of such as the carpenter in the *Miller's Tale*: "Jalous he was, and heeld hire narwe in cage" (A 3224). Troilus is a different kind of lover; he takes only what Criseyde is willing to give, and her power to recall her gift must remain always with her, or it ceases to be a gift and becomes the tribute of a thrall.

Troilus' swoon is not, therefore, a piece of behaviour designed to show his ineffectuality, either as an individual or as a "courtly lover." It can only be properly interpreted within the whole context of Chaucer's examination of the complex evolution of the power relationships inevitably involved in the situation of any two people in love. In this context, we can see that it plays a crucial part in demonstrating that Troilus' "obeisaunce" to Criseyde is dictated by a deeply-felt emotion, rather than by the empty conventions of [332] courtship. Like the other major acts of surrender in medieval romance, its role is also creative; the disaster which is accepted, fully and completely, is miraculously dispelled by that acceptance.[18] In this case, the swoon, the demonstration of surrender, creates the opportunity for Troilus' exercise of dominance, his claim to Criseyde to yield; taken together with its causes and its consequences, it demonstrates the rich multiplicity of potential relationships in the love which here reaches its consummation, and the poise and responsiveness in both lovers which keep all the potentialities constantly in play.

When we understand the consummation scene in this way, we also find that there is no need to attack or defend the love-affair, and particularly Troilus' role in it, in historical terms. We not only can, but need to, respond directly to the emotions and instincts involved. If this discussion, then, has any implications for new directions in Chaucer studies, they are that we should, in a sense, go back to the old directions, and abandon some of our self-conscious historicism in order to examine Chaucer's representations of human relationships with no other preconceptions than our belief that a poet of profound humanity will have something complex and enriching to show us in them. We may then see his fine sensitivity to what is true and what is false, what is liberating and what is enslaving, in the coming together of men and women in the special "binding" of love; and we may see that Chaucer's conception of their roles is based, not on literary conventions or religious doctrine or social orthodoxy, but on the "lawe of kynde," which he must have trusted would work as powerfully on his twentieth-century readers as on his fourteenth-century ones.

> Love is a thyng as any spirit free.
> Wommen, *of kynde*, desiren libertee,

And nat to been constreyned as a thral;
And so doon men, if I sooth seyen shal.

(Franklin's Tale, F 767–70)[19]

These words seem to me in no way outdated or untrue; nor are they "unmedieval." But our admiration for Chaucer should not be based merely on this affirmation of the desire for liberty, which is perhaps easy enough to make, so much as on the way he fulfils the far more difficult task of developing the image of a complex and binding relationship in which that liberty is nevertheless preserved.

Notes

1 See *The Filostrato of Giovanni Boccaccio,* translated with a parallel text by Nathaniel Edward Griffin and Arthur Beckwith Myrick (Philadelphia and London: 1929; rpt. New York, Octagon, 1978), IV, st. 18–21. All quotations and translations of the *Filostrato* will be from this edition.

2 Cf. *Filostrato,* IV, st. 14, 7–8: "Ma con fatica pur dentro ritenne / L'amore e'l pianto come si convenne." ("But with difficulty he restrained the love and grief within, as was fitting.") All quotations from Chaucer are taken from the second edition of his *Works* by F. N. Robinson (Boston: Houghton Mifflin, 1957).

3 The possibly relevant senses of the word "clause" given in the *Middle English Dictionary* are: 1. "a sentence or clause, a brief statement"; 2a. "an individual statement, allegation, admonition, etc. (in a series of such statements)"; 2b (under which this line is cited) "a conclusion; ?an agreement; ?an inference". (The *Oxford English Dictionary* clearly errs in interpreting this line as the first example of the use of the word in its legal sense.) The difficulty in glossing the word is, I think, due to the originality of the idea that Chaucer is developing: that one can bind by language. Cf. the notion in the *Manciple's Tale* (H 357) that by speech, by telling one's secrets to another, a person can become another's "thral."

4 My italics. The images of binding in Chaucer's poetry have been fully dealt with by Stephen A. Barney, "Troilus Bound," *Speculum,* 47 (1972), 445–58, and John Leyerle, "The Heart and the Chain," *The Learned and the Lewed: Studies in Chaucer and Medieval Literature,* ed. Larry D. Benson (Cambridge, Mass.: Harvard Univ. Press, 1974), pp. 113–45.

5 Ida L. Gordon has observed that Antigone's song provides an answer to Criseyde's fears, but she makes this observation part of an argument that Criseyde "has no understanding of love," with which I do not agree (*The Double Sorrow of Troilus* [Oxford: Clarendon Press, 1970], pp. 98–102). See also Sister Mary Charlotte Borthwick, "Antigone's Song as 'Mirour' in Chaucer's *Troilus and Criseyde,*" *MLQ,* 22 (1961), 227–35, esp. 232–34.

6 John Leyerle shows perceptively how the images of binding denote a deep emotional commitment in Troilus, but with Diomede indicate merely the snares of the seducer ("The Heart and the Chain," p. 133).

7 The inversion of external social relationships is emphasized again at the very beginning of this episode, in Pandarus' comment on Troilus' falling to his knees beside Criseyde's bed: "se how this lord kan knele!" (III, 962).

8 For a different view, see E. Talbot Donaldson, "Criseide and her Narrator," *Speaking of Chaucer* (New York: Norton, 1970), p. 66.

9 The pathos of Chaucer's version of the Griselda story is increased if we see that Griselda is forced to reproduce by a deliberate and one-sided course of action that union of wills which in true love comes from a spontaneous and mutual

"obeisaunce" (compare *Clerk's Tale*, E 501–11, 645–67, with the lines from the *Squire's Tale* quoted above).

10 Cf. Charles Muscatine's comment on the consummation scene – that Criseyde's admission of surrender "is perhaps an ironic reflection on the labors of Pandarus. He ... has delivered the woman in the flesh, but she would not have been there if the woman in spirit had not yielded herself first. The spiritual woman yields to Troilus" (*Chaucer and the French Tradition* [Berkeley and Los Angeles: Univ. of California Press, 1964], p. 161).

11 For a medieval description of the lover's change from "serjant" to "mestre," see the speech of Amis, "Le Roman de la Rose," *Classiques Français du Moyen Âge*, 3 vols. (ed. Felix Lecoy [Paris: 1966–70], II, 9411–24).

12 For the view that Pandarus' story is invented, see J. Milton French, "A Defense of Troilus," *PMLA*, 44 (1929), 1246–51, at pp. 1246–47. It is, of course, [334] not unimportant that Chaucer refrains from telling us explicitly whether or not Troilus knew of Pandarus' scheme. The reason for this may be that he did not wish Troilus to be exonerated *simply* on the grounds of technical innocence of deception; on the contrary, he shows that Troilus cannot avoid some kind of deception, or what we may more accurately call "organised behaviour," from the moment he falls in love and has to disguise his feelings from those around him (I, 320–50). He also cooperates in the fiction of his illness in the visit to Deiphebus' house (see especially III, 206–07). But he makes the point, in that instance, that the fiction matches the truth (II, 1527–30); the problem with the Horaste story is that it does *not* match the emotional truth of the situation or the relationship Troilus envisages with Criseyde, and it is perhaps this, rather than Troilus' technical innocence, which Chaucer wishes us to feel as dissociating him from Pandarus' fiction.

13 It may be objected that he later does this, but this is after the swoon has acted to withdraw the accusation, as it were, and to make the substantiation of merely historic interest. See also n. 14 below.

14 Yvain's madness is provoked when he is accused of disloyalty in breaking his promise to return to his wife after a year (see Chrestien de Troyes, *Yvain*, ed. Wendelin Foerster and T. B. W. Reid [Manchester: Manchester Univ. Press, 1942], ll. 2704–2809). The damsel who makes the accusation holds up to him and the court of Arthur an image of "Yvain / Le desleal, le traïtor, / Le mançongier, le jeinglor" ("Yvain the faithless, the treacherous, the liar, the light talker"), which he can neither reject nor (given the earnestness of his love for his wife) accept. Lancelot's madness, as described in *Le Livre de Lancelot del Lac* (*The Vulgate Version of the Arthurian Romances*, ed. H. Oskar Sommer, Vol. V, Part II [Washington, D. C.: Carnegie Institution, 1912], pp. 379–81), is provoked by his realisation that he has for the second time been tricked into making love to Helaine in the belief that she is Guinevere. When Guinevere hears him talking in his sleep, she realises where he is and coughs to awake him; hearing her, Lancelot perceives that he has been deceived and is not with the real Guinevere. Like Yvain, he finds himself in a situation for which he must bear responsibility, but in which he cannot find an expression of his true self. Dismissed by the queen, Lancelot leaves without protest or explanation, and, taking to the woods, eventually becomes demented. Tristan's madness has a rather different context, which offers some interesting analogies with Troilus' situation; initially, the imputed guilt is not his but Iseut's. He discovers a letter she has written to another knight and accuses her of infidelity, then takes to the forest in grief. To a friend called Fergus, he expresses his regret at having accused Iseut, and says that he has been guilty of "folie" and "vilenie" in speaking ill of her; if she has done anything wrong, he ought not to have accused her but pardoned her willingly. It is only after this confession – in

which he dissociates himself from the self who accused Iseut and thus discovers that he has betrayed the true self who loves her without claiming rights over her – that Tristan's grief turns into madness (see the summary of the prose *Tristan*, based on Parisian manuscripts, by E. Löseth, *Le Roman en Prose de Tristan, Le Roman de Palamède et la Compilation de Rusticien de Pise* [Paris: Firmin Didot, 1891], pp. 64–68). A similar but slightly different case is that of Sir Orfeo, whose sojourn in the forest after the loss of his wife resembles those of the other romance heroes, but in whose case there is no question of guilt, either real or apparent; the dislocation originates entirely in the external order. On the other hand, this is the clearest example of a link between the hero's surrender to the disaster which overtakes him and the restoration of harmony and happiness (although the link does not imply a relationship of cause and effect, on either a logical or a moral plane). See *Sir Orfeo*, ed. A. J. Bliss (Oxford: Clarendon Press, 1954), 227–329. For the probability that Chaucer knew *Sir Orfeo*, see Laura Hibbard [335] Loomis, "Chaucer and the Breton Lays of the Auchinleck MS," *SP*, 38 (1941), 14–33.

15 The comments of Donald W. Rowe in a recent book (*O Love, O Charite! Contraries Harmonized in Chaucer's Troilus* [Carbondale: Southern Illinois Univ. Press, 1976], p. 101) lend themselves to quotation here, not because they are unusual, but because they are conveniently compact and illustrate not only this point but also the general critical failure to understand the dynamics of the consummation scene. "[Criseyde] herself admits, in a moment of candor, that if she had not earlier yielded she would not be there, though it baffles the reader to determine the precise point at which she did. This is not to say, of course, that she went to Pandarus's house intending to seduce or be seduced. . . . Troilus, for all his fainting and praying, is able to seize the prize, and he does so with vigor once Pandarus leaves the room, and immediately after the narrator asks, 'What myghte or may the sely larke seye, / Whan that the sperhauk hath it in his foot?' (III, 1191–92). Implications of ravishing are not far away." See also Rowe's earlier comments that Troilus "suddenly demands that she yield" (ignoring the reason for this demand), and the "questionable intention in that demand" (Ibid., p. 77). Cf. the account of the scene in Sanford B. Meech, *Design in Chaucer's Troilus* (Syracuse: Syracuse Univ. Press, 1959), pp. 70–71.

16 Likewise, Troilus cannot decide beforehand to fall in love at first sight, but there is room for the exercise of his will in the generous acceptance of the loss of his old self: "For with good hope he gan fully assente / Criseyde for to love, and nought repente" (I, 391–92).

17 See IV, 1506–1652. Criseyde's plea – "Mistrust me nought thus causeles, for routhe" (1609) – recalls her pleading against baseless suspicion in Book III.

18 An important example of the saving power of submission to threatened danger is Gawain's fulfillment of the beheading game promise in *Sir Gawain and the Green Knight*. The Green Knight himself formulates the operation of this saving power as follows: "Trwe mon trwe restore, / þenne þar mon drede no waþe" (ed. J. R. R. Tolkien and E. V. Gordon, revised by N. Davis [Oxford: Oxford Univ. Press, 1967], lines 2354–55). A parallel example in Chaucer's own works is Dorigen's resolve to fulfill her promise to Aurelius, which miraculously releases her from that promise.

19 My italics. As I have already suggested above, Chaucer's concern to develop images of relationships in which sovereignty and "obeisaunce" belong to both partners is not confined to *Troilus*. I hope to examine elsewhere, and more fully, the ways in which this is done in the *Canterbury Tales*.

12 | "Making strange": the narrator (?), the ending (?) and Chaucer's "Troilus"

MURRAY J. EVANS

Originally published in *Neuphilologische Mitteilungen* 87 (1986):218–
28. Reprinted by permission of the Modern Language Society of
Helsinki. The original pagination is recorded within square
brackets. The endnotes originally appeared as footnotes.

While the ending of Chaucer's *Troilus and Criseyde* continues to intrigue
Chaucer scholars, many of the extant studies see the narrator in *Troilus* as a
key element in the so-called epilogue.[1] A chief problem of the ending,
however, is one which many Chaucerians have created for themselves: the
narrator and the ending that we often look for in Chaucer's *Troilus* are in a
particular sense not there to begin with. Both historical-critical and (loosely
speaking) structuralist approaches, often regarded as utterly hostile critical
methodologies, can converge to provide a clearer view of the complexity of
this notorious crux of Chaucer studies.

Even a brief look at Chaucer's ending in comparison with that of his
source, Boccaccio's *Il Filostrato*, reveals Chaucer's originality. Part VIII of
Boccaccio's poem ends as follows: in stanza 27, Achilles kills Troilo in battle;
st. 28 contains a repeated "such end had Troilo" structure; stanzas 29 to 33
urge young men not to trust lightly in love, for Troilo found woman
inconstant; in part IX the poem concludes with the poet's suit for his lady's
favour. In contrast, Chaucer imports the topos of the heavenly ascent from
Boccaccio's *Teseida* and his apparent moral is that "yonge fresshe folkes"
should forsake worldly "feyned" loves for the steadfast love of Christ. The
ideological problem of the poem is how to reconcile the *contemptus mundi* of
the conclusion with the earlier sympathetic portrayal of the lover's pains and
joys, particularly the consummation scenes of Book III which Lewis calls
"some of the greatest erotic poetry of the world." Some critics point out that
the Christianized Boethian moral has been implicit in Chaucer's handling of
Boethian themes earlier in [219] the poem. On the other hand, there is
evidence that medieval audiences read the poem rather differently. C. David
Benson comments that the bulk of scribal readers' annotations in the *Troilus*
MSS. focus "on the love story itself, even on its physical aspects"; Lee W.
Patterson similarly indicates that a fifteenth-century treatise for women re-
ligious which discusses *Troilus* ultimately in terms of *amor* and *amicitia* does so

not by allegorizing the story but by facing the actions of the poem as real, dwelling on the psychological reality of the characters and quoting some of the poem's most beautiful passages.[2]

If the key to the ending of *Troilus* be the resolution of apparently conflicting ideals of love, this resolution is possible according to various models of *discordia concors* in the poem: the affirmation of a beautiful, flawed human love can stand, for example, with its later rejection in favour of a higher, perfect Love.[3] But a closer look at the rhetorical structure of the ending questions the aptness of a solely ideological approach. Medieval rhetorical treatises and practice suggest that the medieval poet has a wide range of choice of endings to his poem. Endings may include a proverb, an exemplum, or a summary epilogue; an apology for the author's lack, request for mercy, expression of hope for recognition, or flaunting of one's fame; there may be mention of a forestalled conclusion (due to death), an expression of thanks, prayer or a request for prayer; an admonition to sinners, an appeal to the indignation or pity of the audience, or perhaps mention of the poet's name and title of the work.[4] A comparison of this list with the ending of *Troilus* reveals that at least eight of the fourteen *topoi* are present. The narrator in effect apologizes for his story about Criseyde's guilt, saying that he would prefer to write about *good* women (st. 254). After the proverb to beware of men (l. 1785), the poet's desire for recognition is implicit in his placing his "litel bok" in the company of the "greats" (st. 256). Troilus's ascent to the eighth sphere serves as an exemplum, the "swich fyn" stanza (262) summarizes much of the action of the poem, and the following stanzas admonish the "yonge, fresshe folkes." The "Lo here ..." stanza is apparently meant [220] to arouse the indignation of the reader, and the poem closes with a double dedication and a prayer. In this light, it is not really accurate to speak of the "ending" of the *Troilus*; on the contrary, the multiple *endings* repeatedly draw attention to themselves in a way which exceeds what John M. Steadman refers to as the medieval and Renaissance concern with copiousness.[5]

The significance of these multiple endings is related to another of their features: Chaucer's narrator. In the body of Boccaccio's poem, the narrator makes only brief, obvious comments on the action and addresses Maria D'Aquino three times and the general audience only twice (Meech, 14). Chaucer's narrator, however, as has been well established, comments on his poem and addresses us very frequently; one of these passages is the ending. E. Talbot Donaldson's brilliant argument on Chaucer's "dramatization of his poetic ineptitude" sees the narrator falling deeply in love with Criseyde earlier in the poem, then unwilling to let his story "come to nothing" when she betrays Troilus:

> To avoid this – seemingly simple – conclusion he has done everything he could. He has tried the epic high road, he has tried the broad highway of trite moralization; he has tried to eschew responsibility; he has tried to turn it all into a joke; and all these devices have failed. Finally, with

every other means of egress closed, he has subscribed to Troilus's rejection of his own story. . . . Once having made the rejection, he has thrown himself into world-hating with enthusiasm. But now the counterbalance asserts its power [and so on].

Before our eyes Donaldson has the narrator emerge as a realistic, psychologically motivated character rather like ourselves: "Unable to get out of his hopeless predicament, he does what we all tend to do when we are similarly placed: he begins to wonder why he ever got himself into it." Murray F. Markland similarly comments on the narrator's having "done very well" up to a certain point; then he gets "boggled." He protects himself by an excess of endings; in his amusing fear, he chooses only the young folk as the target for his admonition; in fine, the "performer goes off stage awkwardly."[6]

Jonathan Culler in his *Structuralist Poetics: Structuralism, Linguistics, and the Study of Literature* criticizes this sort of approach as a reduction of the ambiguity and strangeness of a text

> by reading it as the utterance of a particular narrator so that models of plausible human attitudes and of coherent personalities can be made operative. Moreover, extrapolating from the postulated figure, we may tell ourselves empirical stories which make elements [221] in the text intelligible and justified. . . . He is arguing, or praising, or expostulating [etc.] . . . and the poem will find its coherence at the level of that action.

I believe that much recent Chaucer criticism and many of our readings of Chaucer suffer from this fault: often we are not reading the text at all but are plugging in our own reified sense of the "character" of Chaucer's narrator. H. Marshall Leicester Jr. asserts that this procedure arises from a "confusion of *voice* with *presence*," the demand "that the voice in a text be traceable to a person, a subject, *behind* the language, an individual controlling and limiting, and thereby guaranteeing, the meaning of what is expressed," "a self that existed prior to the text." Leicester's notion is an adaptation of Jacques Derrida's belief that writing should no longer be a poor cousin to speaking, "for ever acting as the 'dress' of a primary 'presence.'" Writing is an entity in its own right, its own distinctive system of signs rather than a servant to a "traditional word-meaning 'grid.'" This semiotic view of writing and "voice" is similar in its thrust to Vladimir Propp's emphasis in his *Morphology of the Folktale* on the function of character, not its identity.[7] These modern critical concepts are, moreover, strikingly similar to notions of persona and voice discussed in medieval rhetorical tradition.

In the *Poetria Nova*, for example, a thirteenth-century rhetorical treatise with which Chaucer was familiar, Geoffrey of Vinsauf advises the reciter of poetry acting the part of the angry man: "Veros imitare furores./Non tamen esto furens" (Faral, ll. 2048–49); the poet is to "imitate genuine fury" but avoid himself being furious; there is to be no complete identification of speaker and persona. The audience will accordingly be able to regard the persona, not literally as a "character", but as an impersonation, a kind of personification. Inasmuch as the narrator in Troilus represents such an oral poet in print, the notion of a less literal and autonomous persona clearly emerges. Medieval concepts of personification also support this line of argument. Morton W. Bloomfield, for example, asserts that "Of all the grammatical signs of personification . . . the use of animate verbs and predicates is the most characteristic and important. . . . The stress in most personification allegory is on the action. The personifier throws his creativeness into what he has figures do. The . . . aesthetic effect lies not in what nouns the writer chooses but in what predicates he attaches to his subjects." Bloomfields comments on *The Consolation of Philosophy* are particularly relevant in view of the importance of the *Consolation* for Chaucer's reworking of the Troy story. Concerning Lady Philosophy and the "Boethius *persona*," Bloomfield asserts that their "speeches are the predicates, so to speak." Medieval literary theory and current critical theory thus provide similar cues [222] for the critic to attend less to the inferred "character" of the narrator behind the text of the ending, and more to the narrator's speeches as "predicates."[8]

One thing these speeches are "doing," as we have already seen, is acting out various figures for endings, but I think even more specificity is possible. In the opening of his article on the narrator in *Troilus*, Donaldson suggestively reflects that "Chaucer discovered in the medieval modesty convention a way of poetic life" (p. 84). The comment is obviously linked to his notion of the character of the narrator, with its attendant problem of "presence" discussed above. Is there, though, a topos or figure which avoids this problem and which is predominant in the ending of the poem, some "predicate" more specific than topoi for endings?

The figure is *apostrophatio* (apostrophe), address to oneself or some-one/ thing else (Parr, 98). Geoffrey's *Documentum de Modo et Arte Dictandi et Versificandi*, a prose version of the *Poetria Nova*, relates *apostrophatio* to four subsidiary figures: *exclamatio* (emotional outcry), *conduplicatio* (word-repetition for emotional reasons or for emphasis), *subjectio* (self-question-and-answer, anticipating an adversary), and *dubitatio* (doubt or uncertainty about a matter, or "about a point that could be either affirmed or denied") [Parr, 50−51 & appendix].

Apostrophe is clearly prevalent in the ending itself. Address is made consecutively to women readers (sts. 254 & 255), the "litel bok" (sts. 256 & 257), the "yonge, fresshe folkes" (sts. 263–65), Gower and Strode (st. 266), and Jesus (st. 267). The single intervening passage (sts. 258−262) which narrates the ascent of Troilus, is effectively an apostrophe since it opens with an interjection, "as I bigan yow for to seye," and by st. 261, speaks of Troilus's cursing "al *oure* werk" that follows blind lust; we should "al *oure* herte on heven caste" (italics added). If apostrophe permeates the passage, so do its subsidiary figures. There are several examples of *exclamatio* (emotional outcry): the interjection concerning "false folk" who betray women – "God yeve hem sorwe, amen!" (l. 1781), the "Swich fyn" stanza, and the "Lo here" stanza; these last two stanzas also use *conduplicatio* (word-repetition for emotional emphasis). *Dubitatio* (hesitation over topic or stance) is an apt label for what Monica McAlpine sees as the tendency of multiple individual endings to "sputter out." St. 262 seems to lose its rhetorical steam after five lines beginning "Swich fyn," descending to thin plot summary: "And thus bigan his lovyng of Criseyde,/As I have told, and yn this wyse he deyde." The subsequent moving appeal to youth ends with a rhetorical question which some readers may still regard as a "genuine question": "And syn he best to love is, and most meke,/What nedeth feyned loves for to seke?" In the following rejection of pagan rites and "wrecched [223] worldes appetites," the stanza appears to end with an invitation to read the books containing the previously cursed matter: "Lo here the forme of olde clerkes speche/ In poetrie, if ye hire bokes seche" (McAlpine, 241–42). In short, the pervasive apostrophes in the ending emphatically address the reader while *exclamatio-conduplicatio* adds emotional emphasis and *dubitatio* cultivates the sense of inconclusiveness induced by the presence of so many figures for endings in the first place.

It is not unusual, of course, for the ending of a work of literature to address its readers. What is striking about *this* ending is the way apostrophe becomes so evidently part of, in Robert Payne's phrase, "the topography of its poetry" (p. 219). The predominance of apostrophe, moreover, is present beyond the ending of the poem. In *The Key of Remembrance*, Payne has shown that significant apostrophes throughout the poem are an important element in Chaucer's reshaping of his source, and occur at each major turn of events:

> The first *canticus Troili* comes at the beginning of the rising action, as Troilus chooses to love Criseyde. Antigone's song, in Book II, immediately precedes (and helps to precipitate) Criseyde's decision to accept his love. The three *aubades* mark the ends of the two completely happy meetings which are presented in detail. Troilus's hymn to Love concludes the joyful third book, and immediately precedes the announcement of Calchas's decision to recall his daughter. The predestination soliloquy follows Troilus's first interview with Criseyde after the announcement of the exchange. The two plaints of Troilus punctuate the waiting period following the separation. The second *canticus Troili* immediately precedes the exchange of letters which makes it evident that the separation is permanent. (p. 186)

Not only is apostrophe structurally significant in these ways, but there are grounds for saying that the larger shape or anatomy of the poem is that of apostrophe. Immediately in the proem of Book I, the narrator addresses "ye loveres," to pray for those in Troilus's situation, for the poet himself, those hopeless in love, or maligned, or successful. The poem is not only peppered with the addresses frequent in oral poetry, but many of these reinforce the readers' role as knowledgeable lovers: "ye [that] ben wise," "ye that han ben at the feste," "yow that felyng han in loves art," "thow, redere, [who] maist thiself ful wel devyne/That swich a wo my wit kan nat diffyne" (Payne, 228 f.). Evidently, the apostrophe so integral to the fabric of the whole

Troilus also pervades its conclusion. Structuralist Tzvetan Todorov calls this phenomenon "figuration," when the text of a poem may "enact the dominant 'shape' of a particular figure of speech, or pattern of syntax" (Hawkes, 105).

If from the beginning of the poem, we as readers are given the role of experienced lovers, by the consummation scene in Book III, that role is vastly expanded:

> But soth is, though I kan nat tellen al,
> As kan myn auctour of his excellence,
> Yet have I seyd, and God toforn, and shal
> In everythyng the grete of his sentence;
> And yf that ich, at Loves reverence,
> [224]   Have ony word in eched for the beste,
> Doth therewithal right as youreselven leste.
>
> For myne wordes, here and every part,
> I speke hem alle under correccioun
> Of yow that felyng han in loves art,
> And putte it al in youre discrecioun
> T'encresse or maken dyminucioun
> Of my langage, and that I yow byseche.
> But now to purpos of my rather speche.
>
> (III, 1324–1337)

Here we are invited to "T'encresse or maken dyminucioun" of the language of the poem, that is, to assume nothing short of the traditional role of the medieval poet to amplify or diminish his source material in order to weight its meaning, establish its significance (Payne, 77). No greater role could be assigned to the reader.

What, then, is the role of the audience, the reader, in the ending of the poem? There is a shift towards the end of Book V from the implied role already mentioned earlier. Now we are invited to judge the truth, and in particular the moral truth, of the action. In the deliciously ironic summary narrative of Criseyde's giving in to Diomede (1030 f.), "every man" is to check "his bokes" to confirm the narrator's statement that no source records how long it took Criseyde to forsake Troilus (1086–1090). The increasingly intrusive moralizing of the denouement, by including "us" invites us to line up with its moral judgement, to see the action from a world-denying vantagepoint:

> But Troylus, thow mayst now, est or west,
> Pype yn an ivy lef, yf that the lest.
> Thus goth the world, God shylde us fro myschaunce,
> And every wight that meneth trouthe avaunce!
>
> (1432–35)

> Swich is this world, whoso it kan biholde.
> In ech estat is litel hertes reste.
> God leve us for to take it for the beste!
>
> (1748–1750)

Then in the ending, as we have seen, there are a series of apostrophes, addressing women, the "litel boke," a general audience ("as I bigan yow for to seye," "shulden al oure herte on heven caste"), the "yonge, fresshe folkes," Gower, Strode, and Jesus. The general audience, the "lovers" repeatedly addressed throughout the poem, are now addressed during five stanzas only, however, when Troilus ascends to the eighth sphere and damns blind earthly works which ignore heaven. For three times as many stanzas, the audience is rather more particularized: women, the "litel bok," young people, a poet and a philosopher, and Christ. For most of the ending, in other words, the general audience cultivated throughout the poem is not being directly addressed; we are overhearing apostrophes and, I would suggest, judging their moral import as the immediately preceding apostrophes late in Book V have been preparing us to do.

[225] One factor that complicates our judgement, even if we avoid the notion of "presence" in our view of the narrator, is the "voice" of the narrator. Markland comments, for example, that the placing of the usually authorial *envoi* ("Go litel boke ...") in the middle of the final narrative, makes it appear that the narrator "might be speaking it"; our attention is thus turned "from the story ... which is not finished, to the person who is telling us the story" (148). It is probably the experience of most of us that we cannot read Chaucer for long aloud without assuming the expression of some narrative persona. The problem is, what tone of voice do we use? In a paper entitled "Flexibility and Ambiguity in the Performance of Chaucer's Works" at the 1979 MLA Conference in San Francisco, Betsy A. Bowden included a tape-recording of ten eminent Chaucerians all reading the same passage of the *Nun's Priest Tale*, the pleading speech of the fox after Chanticleer has escaped his clutches (VII, 3419–25); one reader's version dripped with guile, another sounded like a wounded father, another frightening, even menacing. And Bowden pointed out that this passage is not a particularly controversial one for interpretation of Chaucer. Medieval rhetorics include instructions on tone of recitation mainly under the heading of delivery (*pronuntiatio*), but short of an oral performance by the poet, *we* must recreate the voice of the narrator as we read, and we shall all recreate it more or less differently, as Bowden's paper substantiated.

By asserting that one of the things we as readers must judge in the ending is our own recreation of narratorial voice, I do not mean to imply that the poem therefore becomes a solipsistic playground. While there are other more publicly verifiable elements of the ending, which bear on voice, Chaucer himself is aware of relativity in the communication of his poem: in his long proem to Book II on changes over time in the language and customs of lovers, and in st. 257 in the ending, on the danger that diversity in written and spoken English might lead to misunderstanding of his poem. The relativity of poetic voice, in fact, forces us to judge all the more carefully other more definitive elements of the ending. Dorothy Bethurum reminds us that in French love poetry the narrator is both poet and lover, and is therefore trustworthy in what he tells us. From the beginning of the *Troilus*, we know that the poet is not a lover; he repeatedly implies that *we* are the lovers and, that by amplifying and curtailing his language, even the poets of the poem. As readers, we are like Boethius trying to reconcile free will and providence in Book V of the *Consolation*: "Everything which is known is known not according to its own power but rather according to the capacity of the knower." It is possibly not a coincidence in the to-some-extent Boethian ending of a rather Boethian poem that that ending should test our capacities as "knowers."[9]

[226] The manner of this testing is what formalist Viktor Shklovsky calls "making strange," the tendency of poetry "to disrupt 'stock responses,' and to generate a heightened awareness" (Hawkes, 62). "The process of 'defamiliarization' presupposes and requires the existence of a body of 'familiar' material, which *seems* to have content" (67). This idea is not new in literary criticism, least of all in Chaucer criticism, but the multiple operation of the process in the ending of the *Troilus* deserves special notice. James Kinneavy in his *Theory of Discourse* traces in the writings of literary theoreticians from Aristotle on, several elements in discourse of any kind, which Kinneavy rationalizes in his discourse triangle thus:

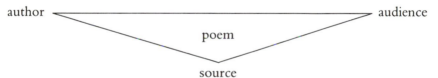

In a recent article, Payne argues that Chaucer was evolving from the twelfth-and thirteenth-century rhetoricians' model of poetic discourse – an informing idea which the poem embellishes (idea: poem), back to the classical model of discourse as a speaker using language to move an audience (speaker: language: audience). Sets of relationships similar to Kinneavy's and Payne's also appear in the writings of Roman Jakobson and C. S. Peirce as (respectively) "the theoretical foundation" of both Formalism and structuralism, and the "nature of the process of *semiosis*" (Hawkes, 83–87, 127). It is Chaucer's "making strange" of all four elements – author, ending, sources/tradition, and audience – that makes his ending problematic.[10]

The "body of 'familiar' material" which the ending of the poem "defamiliarizes" is the traditional relationships of the discourse triangle which Chaucer inherits from twelfth- and thirteenth-century rhetoricians such as Geoffrey of Vinsauf: the *author* reworks his *source* by rhetorical rearrangement and adornment in his *poem* in order to remind his *audience* of old truths to live by, truths which they do not have firsthand access to by experience (Payne, *Key*, *passim*):

> And yf that olde bokes were awey,
> Yloren were of remembraunce the key.
> Wel ought us thanne honouren and beleve
> These bokes, there we han noon other preve.
>
> (*Legend of Good Women*, 25–28)

[227] First, as we have seen, as readers we are not allowed to be passive recipients of some "truth" of the poem. The role we are invited to fill as knowledgeable lovers becomes that of poet by the middle of the poem, and by the end, judges of the moral significance of the action as, for the most part, we overhear apostrophes addressed to more fragmentary audiences. Where we might expect an ending to the poem to judge, there are, as we saw, eight or ten endings which, in drawing attention to themselves as *topoi* of endings, create a sense of chronic inconclusiveness, rather like pianist Dudley Moore on the "Beyond the Fringe" record who almost, but not quite, ends the piece twenty times: "This thing will never end," we say; then, "it isn't ending!" Yet the pervasive apostrophic structure of the ending, indeed of most of the poem, repeatedly puts the pressure on us to make our judgement as experts on love. For the author cannot ultimately help us; he, too, is "made strange." If we avoid the pitfall of "presence," of turning his voice into a character instead of regarding him as a "predicate," acted out in his speeches, his apostrophes – there is his voice which we cannot help hearing, even though we all reconstruct it a little, or a lot, differently. All of these factors put us to work judging that fourth element of the ending, its referentiality to its sources and some extra-literary moral on love. Has the narrator's attempted moral on the treachery of men (st. 255) a feathersweight of truth, flanked by Boccaccio's and Henryson's antifeminist morals, let alone much of Chaucer's poem? *Is* the poem really a "tragedye"? McAlpine points out that the rise and fall pattern of the *de casibus* tragedy exemplified in the *Monk's Tale* is too reductive for the *Troilus* whose "aventures fellen/Fro wo to wele, and after out of joye," not to mention *into* joy again for Troilus at the close (p. 144). *Has* scribal tampering or changes in English dialect (st. 257) distorted the poem for us? How reliable is Troilus's vision of earthly vanity and heavenly delight from the vantagepoint of the "eighte spere," the sphere of the moon, of mutability (Steadman, Ch. 1)? As the familiar is "made strange," the poem confronts us as a new, unfamiliar landscape. Ending becomes too many endings; apostrophe to the reader fragments into apostrophes to different groups of readers (we even feel a little left out); authoritative poet-lover becomes an elusive, mute student of erotic love (we must "voice" him) – and the moral to be submitted to our expert amatory judgements recedes in a cluster of qualifications.

"Everything which is known is known not according to its own power but rather according to the capacity of the knower." The interplay of these four "defamiliarized" elements of author, ending, sources, and audience combine to awaken in us a new capacity for knowing as readers. The multiple endings rob us of the expectation of closure, the "last word," compelling us into patience. Repeated apostrophes nonetheless exhort us to exercise our freedom to interpret, while our reconstruction of the narratorial voice reveals that *auctours* speak their words with our own voices, and multiple thematic ambiguities put to death the hope that certainty resides in moral epigrams. In other words, the ending manipulates us as readers into interpretation, even in face of no instant final answers, no absolutely reliable moral [228] one-liners, and the considerable subjectivity of our task. Such a role for the reader is miles away from the standard medieval role mentioned above: the passive reception of ancient moral truths which, stored in the memory, influence future moral action.

Does Chaucer by anticipation, then, fully subscribe to Derrida's rejection of "presence" and endorsement of infinite "free play" in interpretation; and does my combination of historical-critical and more current critical approaches mean to imply that medieval rhetoric and recent critical methodologies have identical premises? Roland Barthes' infinite peeling away of onion-layers of literary style to reveal no message, Derrida's debunking of authorial or narratorial "presence," and Stanley Fish's celebration of "the authority of interpretive communities" clearly part company with traditional critical notions of theme or message, authorial intention, and an objective literary text.[11] Medieval rhetorical theory is much closer to these three traditional critical tenets than to their antitheses in current theory, judging from the picture which emerges from the pages of medieval rhetorical treatises. There, an author is to begin with a mental preconception of his work as a literary whole – beginning, middle, and end, then write his work by amplifying and adorning his source so as to move and persuade his reader into discerning, and accepting, its sentence: identifiable text, authorial intention, and discernible message.[12] As we have seen, however, certain aspects of medieval rhetorical tradition discussed above, as well as much of Chaucer's poetic practice in *Troilus and Criseyde*, bear striking resemblance to current critical notions and strategies. The chief difference between Chaucer's "making strange" of the ending of the *Troilus* and current critical methodology is that while Chaucer "defamiliarizes," holds in tension without apparently rejecting, the traditional medieval rhetorical relationship of author, poem, audience and moral, Barthes, Derrida, and Fish have clearly rejected these concepts. Chaucer's poem arouses in the reader a new, more critical, open-ended awareness of the shortcomings of the traditional paradigm; Derrida and others deny the paradigm any real validity. While medieval rhetoric and historical criticism on the one hand, and current critical methodologies on the other, are therefore incompatible in their theoretical conclusions, similar concepts in each theory nevertheless illuminate the complexity of Chaucer's ending to his poem.

Notes

1 For a list of criticism on the ending, see for example Monica E. McAlpine, *The Genre of "Troilus and Criseyde"* (Ithaca & London: Cornell U.P., 1978), p. 237,

n. 19. Where convenient, references will be accumulated under one note at the ends of paragraphs, and second and subsequent references to the same author will appear in parentheses in my text.

2 Sanford B. Meech, *Design in Chaucer's "Troilus"* (Syracuse U.P., 1959), pp. 129 & 133; C. S. Lewis, *The Allegory of Love* (1936; paperback rpt. London: O.U.P., 1970), p. 196; on the Boethian moral throughout, see for example Ida L. Gordon, *The Double Sorrow of Troilus: A Study in Ambiguities in "Troilus and Criseyde"* (Oxford: Clarendon P., 1970); Benson, "Marginal Criticism: Scribal Responses to Chaucer's *Troilus,*" unpub. paper given at the first conference of the Society for Textual Scholarship, New York City, April 11, 1981; Patterson, "Ambiguity and Interpretation: A Fifteenth-Century Reading of *Troilus and Criseyde,*" *Speculum,* 54 (1979):297–330. References to Chaucer are from John H. Fisher, ed., *The Complete Poetry and Prose of Geoffrey Chaucer* (New York: Holt, Rinehart & Winston, 1977).

3 See for example on the Retraction of the *Canterbury Tales,* Paul G. Ruggiers, *The Art of the Canterbury Tales* (Madison & Milwaukee: U. of Wisconsin P., 1965), pp. 28–29 & n. 10.

4 On endings in the rhetorics, see Geoffrey of Vinsauf, *Documentum de Modo et Arte Dictandi et Versificandi,* tr. Roger P. Parr (Milwaukee: Marquette U.P., 1968), p. 98; Matthew of Vendôme, *Ars Versificatoria,* in Edmond Faral, ed., *Les Arts Poétiques du XIIe et du XIIIe Siècle* (Paris: Champion, 1962), IV, 50; Olive Sayce, "Chaucer's 'Retractions': The Conclusion of the *Canterbury Tales* and Its Place in Literary Tradition," *Medium Aevum,* 40 (1971), p. 233; Peter Dixon, *Rhetoric* (1971; rpt. London: Methuen, 1977), p. 30.

5 Steadman, *Disembodied Laughter: "Troilus" and the Apotheosis Tradition* (Berkeley & Los Angeles: U. of Cal. P., 1972), p. 149. See also McAlpine, p. 243; C. David Benson and David Rollman, "Wynkyn de Worde and the Ending of Chaucer's *Troilus and Criseyde,*" *Modern Philology,* 78 (1981):275–79.

6 Donaldson, "The Ending of *Troilus,*" in Donaldson, ed., *Speaking of Chaucer* (1970; paperback rpt. New York: Norton, 1972), p. 84; Donaldson, "Chaucer the Pilgrim," p. 9; "The Ending," pp. 99–100, 94; Markland, "*Troilus and Criseyde*: The Inviolability of the Ending," *Modern Language Quarterly,* 31 (1970), pp. 151–54.

7 Culler, *Structuralist Poetics* (London: Routledge & Kegan Paul, 1975), pp. 146–47; Leicester Jr., "The Art of Impersonation: A General Prologue to the *Canterbury Tales,*" *PMLA,* 95 (1980), pp. 216–17; on Derrida & Propp, see Terence Hawkes, *Structuralism and Semiotics* (Berkeley & Los Angeles: U. of Cal. P., 1977), pp. 146–47 & 68.

8 On Chaucer and the *Poetria Nova,* see Robert Payne, *The Key of Remembrance: A Study of Chaucer's Poetics* (New Haven & London: Yale U.P., 1963), pp. 16–19; Margaret F. Nims, tr., *Poetria Nova of Geoffrey of Vinsauf* (Toronto: Pontifical Institute of Medieval Studies, 1967), p. 90; on the oral poet and *Troilus,* see Derek Pearsall, "The *Troilus* Frontispiece and Chaucer's Audience," *Yearbook of English Studies,* 7 (1977):68–74; Bloomfield, "A Grammatical Approach to Personification Allegory," *Modern Philology,* 60 (1963), pp. 165 & 168.

9 Bethurum, in Richard J. Schoeck & Jerome Taylor, eds., *Chaucer Criticism II: "Troilus and Criseyde" and the Minor Poems* (1961; rpt. Notre Dame: U. of Notre Dame P., 1971), p. 211; Boethius, *The Consolation of Philosophy,* tr., Richard Green (Indianapolis & New York: Bobbs-Merrill, 1962), V, pr. 4, p. 110.

10 Kinneavy, *Theory of Discourse* (1971; paperback rpt. New York: Norton, 1980), pp. 18–20 – I alter Kinneavy's "code" terminology for the triangle; Payne, "Chaucer's Realization of Himself as Rhetor," in James J. Murphy, ed., *Medieval Eloquence* (Berkeley & Los Angeles: U. of Cal. P., 1978), pp. 72–73. For this

recurrent notion of a discourse triangle or triad, see also Alice S. Miskimin, *The Renaissance Chaucer* (New Haven & London: Yale U.P., 1975), p. 81 and Richard A. Lanham, *The Motives of Eloquence: Literary Rhetoric in the Renaissance* (New Haven & London: Yale U.P., 1976), p. 66.

11 Barthes cited in Culler, p. 259; Fish, "Interpreting the *Variorum*," *Critical Inquiry*, 2 (1976), p. 484, and Fish, *Is There a Text in This Class? The Authority of Interpretive Communities* (Cambridge, Mass: Harvard U.P., 1980).

12 See *Poetria Nova*, 11. 43–86, and Payne, *passim*.

13 | Introduction [to *Chaucer's Early Poetry*]

WOLFGANG CLEMEN

Originally published as the beginning of the Introduction in Wolfgang Clemen, *Chaucer's Early Poetry*, trans. C. A. M. Sym (London: Methuen, 1963, pp. 1–14). Reprinted by permission of Routledge. The original pagination is recorded within square brackets. The endnotes originally appeared as footnotes and have been renumbered.

Until a short while ago Chaucer's work was viewed and judged from the perspective of the *Canterbury Tales*. These have appealed most to the modern reader; with their humour and realism they seemed almost to be speaking 'our own language', and they could be understood and relished even by readers not versed in literary history. Indeed, the *Canterbury Tales* stand out from among the rest of English medieval literature as a remarkably modern work. A good deal of what is considered 'modern' in the *Canterbury Tales* is, to be sure, based upon faulty interpretation; yet the past three centuries have produced much evidence[1] that this quality of 'modernity' is precisely what has determined the value and the place which the *Canterbury Tales* hold in English literature. Furthermore, this same criterion has affected our judgment of Chaucer's early poetry;[2] for even up till quite recently his early poems have been thought of not so much as possessing a value and a discipline of their own, but rather as representing a transitional stage, a preliminary step towards the *Canterbury Tales*. Such a point of view, however, was bound to overlook much; for it involves succumbing to the bias of noticing and praising in the first place whatever seems to foreshadow the *Canterbury Tales*.

It led former critics to stress the humour and realism in Chaucer's early poetry.[3] Yet even qualities of this sort do not appear without foundation; and we shall only come to appreciate their uniqueness once we have grasped the characteristic changes in style and manner of composition which these early poems exemplify. We shall then realize that what is of importance are these structural alterations; the humour and the realism are [2] merely resultant phenomena, appearing at surface-level and denoting profounder fundamental changes.

Another prejudice which has hindered our approach to the early poems has been the idea that in writing his first poems in the French style and the idiom of allegory, Chaucer had as it were made a false start. It was thought that he only gradually discovered his true and individual manner after having tried out literary forms unsuited to his own temper and to the age he lived in. Any such opinion – surely untenable as so expressed – was bound to lead to an underestimation of the early poems; for it overlooked the task Chaucer had set himself from the beginning. This was to take the French mode of composition – which was then at a more advanced stage in regard to techniques and design – and by transposing it into English, to give the language of English poetry as it were the 'entrée' to the court.

Finally, overemphasis on French and Italian influences has adversely affected our assessment of Chaucer's early poetry. The now discredited division of Chaucer's work into a French, an Italian, and an English period, is based upon the delusion that he copied first French, then Italian, and finally English models. In reality he was always making use of sources in other languages, even in his 'English period'; even in his 'French period', too, he was continually altering and reshaping such sources until the expression and the manner became his very own. His 'English period' begins with his first poem – it is hoped in the chapters that follow to demonstrate the truth of this statement.

Chaucer's early poems can tell us much about the relation between outside influence and a poet's own manner of composition, between tradition and originality, between convention and its application in a new way; some of what we shall learn applies to medieval poetry in general, some in particular to Chaucer. The medieval poet was not primarily concerned with originality, with his own inventiveness, but with giving due consideration to prescribed forms and genres, rules of composition and stylistic conventions. These accepted forms and rules carried far more weight then than they did in later times. A precise knowledge of literary traditions, 'topoi', stylistic models and rhetorical devices, was among the most important conditions which the poet was obliged to satisfy if he was to do justice to his [3] task. For they outlined the well-defined framework within which the poet had to keep. His merit did not consist in stepping outside these transmitted forms, in contributing something completely 'new'; it lay in keeping – as tradition demanded – within this framework and yet at the same time moving freely within these given limits and displaying his individuality through his own particular use of the traditional formal and stylistic elements. The medieval reader or hearer, meeting with new poems or a new poet, had no wish to 'break new ground'. What he wanted was to be reminded of what he knew already, to meet once again with what was familiar, and at the same time to take pleasure in the variations and occasional differences in the shaping and treatment of these well-known phrases and expressions. This tension between adjustment to tradition and deviation from it should be kept in mind; for that is what must have determined both the poet's process of creation and his reader's attitude. In the case of each poem, we must not fail to recognize this mutual relationship between on the one hand the limitations diversely imposed by these models, poetic conventions and genres, and on the other, the poet's individual idiom revealed both despite and within these restraints.

Chaucer's case is a particularly strongly contrasted and unusual one. Not only was he conversant with the complex development of his own native literary tradition; he also knew the French and Italian writers – better, indeed, than his English contemporaries did – and he was widely read in medieval Latin literature. This enabled him to link up with the most diverse developments and to draw upon the most varied sources. Chaucer had an extensive knowledge of literary tradition together with a feeling for the formal and stylistic merits of what had been handed down; and both these faculties were united in a remarkable way with a superb ability to deal in a new and often quite revolutionary manner with all these differing elements rooted in tradition. He sets free much of what he borrows from the past by turning it to new uses. He disregards what had previously been the function of certain themes, and gives them a new connotation which often produces an ironic contrast between their former overtones and what they now imply and signify. With light-hearted dexterity he simply reverses the plus and minus signs in front of these [4] traditionally conditioned themes, and fits them into a context which is the very opposite of their previous one.

But Chaucer's early poetry displays the phenomenon of literary influence, too, in a new and unusual light. The very numerous instances in the early poems of either literal borrowing, similarity, or conscious imitation, at first seem to give colour to the view formerly held that French and Italian poetry must have 'very strongly influenced' Chaucer. But in this case we must carefully define and delimit what is meant by 'influence'. We shall have to consider what affinity or specific poetic aim may lie behind Chaucer's response to certain influences in a given case. We shall further have to distinguish between those elements in another writer which most strongly influenced Chaucer and other essential features in the same writer to which he was consistently resistant or unresponsive. We must recognize what fruitful impulses in Chaucer were released by these stylistic models, and what elements enriched his diction. By concentrating not merely on the authentication of parallels and similarities, but making a more general view which would include the function, connotation, context and aim of what he took over, we shall arrive at an appreciation of Chaucer's artistry in transforming what largely belonged to others until it became all his own. Often minute changes, inversion, trifling additions, or fresh arrangement suffice for Chaucer to bring the considerable material he borrows by almost imperceptible stages into line with the new basic aim and style of his own poems. Over and over again Chaucer takes two similar elements, and without necessarily altering much, makes them entirely different from one another. Even the poets of today who are particularly adept in the art of quoting, borrowing and alluding, can admire Chaucer's virtuosity in this field, a skill which he hides beneath a cloak of artlessness and improvisation.

As Chaucer's contemporaries read these early poems, it must have been an added delight to them to meet again with familiar turns of phrase in a new connotation, and they must have responded to Chaucer's skill in waking an 'echo' of other poets' work. But if we readers of today are also to appreciate this art we shall be obliged to undertake a comparison at different levels. The method used in former studies, that of comparing Chaucer's earlier poetry with its sources, models and literary [5] tradition, should be applied to a new purpose. For our aim will not be to establish Chaucer's 'debt' to this or that source or to detect isolated parallels in the texts, but to use comparison and contrast to recognize Chaucer's own achievement, the manner of composition which characterizes his writings even from an early stage. We shall also hope to assemble criteria for estimating his poetic intention and use the method of comparison in order to gain some insight into the development of literature during the later Middle Ages. Comparison and contrast can serve as 'heuristic principles' leading us to recognize what is characteristic and what is 'different'.

A study of Chaucer's early poems in particular brings out the truth now recognized that a historical method of analysis must be accompanied by intensive textual interpretation. If we merely ask what aspects of Chaucer's early poetry we feel to be 'alive' and aesthetically attractive today, we shall overlook much that is essential and the result will be a picture which is not only incomplete but even distorted. It would, however, be equally misguided to try to make Chaucer and medieval poetry in general fit into the modern conception of poetry whereby everything is "symbolic" and to be interpreted as an extended metaphor. This, too, would give a false picture. The 'historical approach' cannot of course claim to be the only gateway to an artistic appreciation of the individual poems. For what determines the artistic impact of a poem and of its individual themes is not their earlier development, provenance and historical limitations, but the entire verbal shaping and composition, the way in which each part is linked to the whole, how one item follows on from another and how certain images and impressions are awakened thereby. The aim of the three chapters devoted to the major poems (*The Book of the Duchess, The House of Fame,* and *The Parliament of Fowls*) will be to lay bare this essential structure, the cumulative effect of the poem and to show by what stages this is brought about. Every poem has, to be sure, two aspects; it does not exist purely in isolation as an individual work of art; it also represents a stage in its creator's development as an artist and in the course of literature. Every work of art is thus permeated with tendencies and trends that lead backwards and forwards beyond its own individual limits. The pursuit of literary history involves a [6] recognition of these overlapping processes of growth, these lines of development, and these relationships. Yet, we must also avoid misinterpreting or even disrupting the unity of the individual work of art which offers us once and for all its own imprint and shaping of the diverse material.

A consideration of the basic tendencies and lines of development in the course of late medieval literature will help us to recognize the foundations of Chaucer's early poetry. We must know something of this basis, too, if we are to appreciate Chaucer's own achievement in developing and recasting existing elements of form and style and in infusing them with new life. In the case of any poet we must know what he started with if we are to understand his subsequent artistic development. In Chaucer we have a striking example of how the earlier stages of artistic growth can throw special light on the establishment of certain characteristic features.

With Chaucer, however, 'artistic development' is by no means the same thing as the evolution of the poet's own personality. In his case, as in that of almost every medieval poet, it would be quite inappropriate to regard the development of the artist as reflecting certain individual experiences, to try to reach the person – even the 'inner life' of the poet, perhaps – by way of the poem. All we can do is to come to some idea of how he writes and of how at times he envisages the world about him. As a 'person', despite the many apparently personal touches in certain of his poems, Chaucer escapes us. More than other poets, he remains hidden behind a part he has assumed in his poems, in which he plays the dreamer, the narrator, the innocent and artless spectator. And even here there is a paradox; for while Chaucer himself more than once appears in his poems, with characteristic touches that portray both himself and his attitude, yet he always gives us a blend of what we can believe and what we can not; and we are never quite sure where we stand. Chaucer applies his own typical evasion and disguise, his quizzical manner, in his own case as well. He draws an ironical picture of himself; and what his poems offer is a composite and refracted image of the poet.

For this reason the present study makes no attempt to recapitulate the various theories concerning certain historical [7] personages or contemporary events which might fit in with the 'allegory' of the poems. None of these hypotheses can be proved to satisfaction; and even if it could be established, the fact that some event at court, in politics or within the country was alluded to in the poems, would after all do little to further our appreciation of their individual artistic quality.

But there is an important aspect of the connection between these early poems and a courtly audience. From the beginning it was Chaucer's intention to give the idiom of English poetry the entrée to the court,[4] to ennoble it after the French pattern. His contemporaries and successors held that by so doing Chaucer had done great service to English poetry; he was extolled as the master of refined eloquence, of rhetoric, as the man

> That made firste to distille and reyne
> The golde dewe droppis of speche and eloquence
> In-to oure tounge thourg his excellence
> And founde the flourys first of rethoryk
> Oure rude speche oonly to enlumyne.
>
> John Lydgate, *The Life of our Lady*[5]

– to quote the well-known passage from Lydgate. But Lydgate is not alone in his high opinion: Occleve, Shirley, Caxton, Dunbar, Hawes and many other fifteenth-century poets praise Chaucer in particular as the first to beautify and refine the English language, ridding it of 'roughness' and stiffness; like 'Tullius', he was a master of rhetoric. These views, then, all stress something less obvious to the reader of today who looks in the main for the more 'modern' elements in Chaucer's art.

The course of English literature since the Norman Conquest offers repeated instances of English poets seeking to transplant French poetry, with
its greater refinement and elaboration of stylistic forms, into their own
tongue. There were of course other tendencies besides, which aimed at
banning French elegance and fostering a style of poetry based on the tradition
of the country. Chaucer combines both tendencies. In fact he was [8] the first
to succeed in implanting within the English idiom the skilled discipline, the
polished speech, the elegance and the flexibility of Romance metres. He thus
realized an old ambition of English poetry;[6] and his example shows how
fruitful foreign influences can be to the literature of the country that receives
them. Yet despite this close familiarity with French and Italian thought and
expression, how very English Chaucer in essence remains![7] So English,
indeed, that many passages from his work can still be quoted today for their
typically English quality; and this quality is quite unmistakable even in the
poems of his youth. Chaucer combines two things in a most fortunate way;
he is exceedingly responsive to influences from other poets, and he possesses
the most vigorous poetic individuality imaginable.

The following chapters [in Clemen's book] will give concrete examples
from individual poems which illustrate Chaucer's attitude towards French
and Italian literature. His responsiveness to the qualities of Romance verse led
to a greater stressing of artistic considerations in the composition and structure of poems; more attention was now paid to achieving polished expression
and a clear, well-turned narrative style. Other examples of poetry of high
artistic standard in the fourteenth century, about the time of Chaucer and
Gower, *Sir Gawain and the Green Knight* and a few other alliterative works,
belong to quite a different literary tradition. It is not certain whether Chaucer
knew these poems; at least he did not draw upon them. The rhymed
romances, on the other hand, with few exceptions have no artistic preten-
sions and often try to give no more than an artless rendering of the story.
These works do occasionally contain a lively and forceful account, but there
is little sign of any subtlety in tone or mood, or of artistry in expression. If
we look at the works of doctrinal instruction, the political and religious
satires, the didactic allegories, then the general absence of artistic or aesthetic
principles is still more striking. It is true that the writers of these works had
other aims. [9] They intended to impart instruction and salutary doctrine in a
form which the laity could understand; their poetry served – in so far as it is
religious – to popularize the spread of doctrinal teaching during the thirteenth
and fourteenth centuries.

Chaucer's early poems contrast with most of these works; for they are the
creation of a conscious artist; in those works in particular, where he used
models and had before him formal patterns – largely lacking in artistic
principles – and applied them to the traditional forms he employs. We can
now do justice at more than one level to Chaucer's 'art' in these early
poems; we can, indeed, appreciate his skill in expression and portrayal, in
combination and transition, in veiled reference and subtle allusion. It is just
this subtlety, however, which often conceals Chaucer's art that may present
itself in an artless guise. Especially in the early poems he frequently expresses

something 'by implication', making the sense he intended reveal itself without the need of words, and keeping silent where others would have spoken out plainly. Today we see all this as an indication of a great degree of artistic skill; and it is by precisely these features (which are not found in this form in any of his contemporaries or immediate successors) that Chaucer anticipates developments not carried through in English poetry until very much later.

In general, new traits can only come to the fore when other and opposing tendencies recede. In Chaucer's case a strongly didactic basic tendency had to make way before any new qualities could emerge. Didacticism had been very largely dominant in the literature of the thirteenth and fourteenth centuries. Even those middle-English rhymed romances (now toned down to middle-class proportions) which seem at first glance to aim purely at 'entertainment', seek to edify and bring home some practical moral by means of a tale skilfully told. Their endeavour to make the story easier to follow and thereby to point the moral more clearly may be the reason for the lack of vivid description of milieu and for the very simplified action in these works.

Later generations praised Chaucer as a 'moral poet', and his work certainly contains didactic elements; but these are introduced in a subtle, unobtrusive fashion which exactly matches the form in which they are presented. He has achieved a new way of uniting entertainment with instruction. But the blending of the [10] two is not always the same; for at times the didactic element is entirely absorbed in the delight at telling a story, while at other times it may emerge more clearly. We may note this in the range of the *Canterbury Tales* from 'moral' tales to rollicking farces – although in the *moral tales*, delicate irony and skill in delineating characters and types not only balances the didactic element but often exposes it in a different light. What characterized didactic poetry at that time was that everything was expressly stated and made plain. The reader was very seldom indeed left in any doubt, he always knew what this or that 'meant' and he was always told what precisely was the point in question. This same endeavour to 'make things plain' is also present in allegorical poetry, for in spite of all the disguise allegory uses we find the significance of what is portrayed yet more strongly emphasized and expounded. Yet though he interposes as narrator, commenting and taking sides, we do not find Chaucer expressly stating the essential point in his early poems. Not that we get anything in Chaucer comparable to the obscurity of modern poetry. On the contrary, Chaucer almost invariably speaks clearly and plainly. But in regard to the significance of whole sections or poems, he developed a new art of silence, of reserve, of cautious suggestion, unique in his own age. His silence even amounts at times to what might be called mystifying the reader; and there are endless puzzles especially in the *House of Fame* and the *Parliament*. The individual themes and vivid scenes seem for the most part understandable, and yet it is a hard matter to discover what Chaucer means to convey by their sequence and by the essential relationship in which the individual parts of a poem are placed. Chaucer has clearly evolved a novel process to impart the significance of his poems – a process indeed that strikes us as almost modern. By putting different elements together without comment, simply by the sequence or juxtaposition of his episodes or symbols, he can convey a definite way of interpretation, a train of possibilities, a line of choice. The reader is always left to draw his own conclusions. The 'significance' however lies in the realm of imaginative, poetic logic, in the 'logic of imagination' rather than on the plane of mere logical deduction. And this makes things more difficult for any literary critic intent upon discovering some conclusive formula [11] and significance. Chaucer cannot be tied down like this; and in the early poems there are many juxtapositions and sequences which still leave scope for new interpretations in the future. We ought to admit these ambiguities and open questions and we should not feel limited to one meaning alone where Chaucer had so clearly avoided this. Chaucer did not want to present his reader with a complete answer and dismiss him, accurately primed, at the end of the poem; what he was seeking to do was rather to induce in him a state of questioning disquiet, of 'wonderment', to awaken his faculty of imagination and in this way to set him thinking. When we read Chaucer's early poems we feel the author's awareness of how complex and involved the events and circumstances of life are, of how they defy any single interpretation.

We have noted Chaucer's unobtrusive ease in dealing with didactic moralizing elements; and the same is obvious in his way of imparting knowledge and information in his poems. He is continuing the process of popularizing knowledge, a process particularly noticeable from the thirteenth century onwards; and his method is to lessen the gap between learning and entertainment. We find his 'Dame Pertelote' of the *Nun's Priest's Tale* in an entertaining and charming way discussing with 'Chaunteclere' the complex problem of the medieval doctrine of dreams; and in the course of her inimitable speeches on the burdens of the married state his 'Wife of Bath' considers certain doctrines held by the Fathers of the Church and by the ancient philosophers, as well as ideas from Dante and from Boethius. No other English poet of the Middle Ages has managed to incorporate so much philosophical and scientific material into his poems in so unobtrusive and natural a way, seeming indeed as he does so to increase rather than diminish the entertainment that his poems afford. The reader, however, is scarcely aware how much there is of book-learning and of things remembered behind these brisk, vigorous lines which often appear so spontaneously to reflect their author's own observation. The intimate connection between literary background and actual observation in Chaucer adds a particular charm to his poetry.

This remarkable ease in taking over and incorporating material reflects Chaucer's general receptiveness. Compared to his contemporaries, who usually followed only one direction, [12] Chaucer's response has a far more comprehensive range. He was helped here by the great improvement in the possibilities for exchange of ideas among the countries of Europe, which had taken place by the fourteenth century; the cultural links between England and the Continent had become closer and more varied. Chaucer's work is a particularly striking instance of this late medieval intercourse of cultures and literatures. In this case it was only made possible, however, by the intellectual mobility which distinguishes Chaucer from his contemporaries Gower and Langland.

This careless ease with which details of structure and of style, and themes from French, Italian and classical literature are mingled in Chaucer's poetry, as well as his technique of combining the most heterogeneous elements, are characteristic features of the style of any outgoing period, one already in process of breaking up. Chaucer's early poems in particular show that much of what he took over was of a light, decorative kind. It is typical of a transitional period that its writers make play with what had formerly been firmly-established and traditional forms. Often periods of fresh development make use of clear and simple forms, their style and essence can more easily be reduced to a common denominator, their characteristics are not so numerous but are more distinct and prevalent. It is harder for the literary historian to find some formula to cover the fourteenth-century variety of such diverse and often contradictory tendencies, the medley of genres and styles. Earlier forms are still utilized, but their underlying principles have undergone a change. Thus, inconsistency and the emergence of hybrid forms are favoured. Lack of harmony between expression and subject-matter, style and content, leads to exaggeration, to a purely decorative use of borrowed forms, to a trivial handling of themes and incidents. Chaucer's early poetry partakes to some degree of this development; it is therefore appropriate to ask to what extent he here made a virtue of necessity, displaying a new ease and confidence in this play with forms and themes to enrich his poetic and artistic resources.

For a poet of Chaucer's range this condition – typical of an outgoing literary period – offered an opportunity that was both tempting and beneficial. What proved fatal to other poets who [13] wrote on mechanically, confining their work within what had now become empty forms, seems to have acted as a most fruitful influence on Chaucer's art; particularly his early poems display a characteristic blending of greatly differing forms and genres. In a single work we find him combining not only material from contradictory sources but also the most varied literary forms. A new artistic unity serves to bridge the inevitable and irreconcilable contrasts.

Chaucer's poetry draws upon a century of development in forms, themes and ideas. It unites and combines much that had been typical of its various stages; Boethius, Martianus Capella, Alanus de Insulis, the *Roman de la Rose*, Virgil, Statius, Ovid, Seneca and Cicero (as seen through Macrobius) are but a few. But these authors' ideas and themes which Chaucer often recalls, touching on them in passing, had forfeited a good deal of their depth and authority in the course of the centuries. Their essence had become diluted as they were handed on from one writer to another. But the manner in which they are now brought in as passing references and simplified abridgements, reflects not merely the popularizing tendency already noted, but may perhaps also be taken as revealing a new desire for education on the part of Chaucer's audience. The audience was now a wider one, comprising courtiers, the

landed gentry, the upper middle-class. The standard of intellectual and literary education reached was far from negligible; Chaucer's readers must have
been able to recognize the many remote allusions in his works, and to follow
the explanations in the *Astrolabe* or the many references in *Troilus* to 'Free
Will'. Such readers will not have looked to Chaucer for any specific exhaus-
tive or systematic instruction. He does, however, meet a rather different need
felt by his readers; this was the unscholarly yet expert recognition and
enjoyment of the store of learning gleaned from past centuries. Confined
within a well-turned, attractive poem, this educational material was bound to
forfeit some of its gravity. The allegorical poem, too, no longer served as a
methodical analysis and a full exposition of whatever lesson was to be
imparted; it was now used in a new way, as we shall see, exploiting the
aesthetic possibilities of fanciful invention and imaginative description. In
interpreting Chaucer's early poems, we have to take into account this different [14] function of philosophical subject matter and doctrine. Alanus as he
appears in Chaucer's poems is not the Alanus of the twelfth century.

The fact that Chaucer is writing for a much larger circle of readers draws
our attention to the most significant sociological change that took place
during the fourteenth century – the rise of the middle classes. It is therefore
of importance to note how this development is mirrored in Chaucer's poetry.
Although he came of a middle-class family, Chaucer was living near the
court when he began writing; his literary models belonged to the sphere of
court and he wrote at first for a mainly courtly public. In what way, then, do
the 'middle-class' elements in him make themselves apparent within this
stylistic atmosphere with its artificiality and its exaggeration? What can be
described as 'middle-class' about Chaucer's poetry? Is it the sound common-
sense, the compelling vigour in his manner of portrayal, his way of making
'concrete' what had been 'abstract', the straightforward forcefulness of the
form in which certain basic truths are put before us, the preference for plain
and practical workaday wisdom? Asking and studying such questions, one
soon realizes how hard it is to single out individual essential traits in Chaucer
and to fit them into any supra-personal development. Even although one
finds numerous examples belonging to the above categories, no single feature
is present in isolation; its importance and artistic function depend upon how
it combines and works in with the other elements. Side by side we find
vigour matched with subtlety, the jargon of every day with an elaborate and
refined poetic diction, the ingenuous openness that 'blurts things out' with
an exceedingly cautious, suggestive 'disingenuous' mode of expression,
simplicity with complexity. This gives some indication of the wide range of
Chaucer's means of portrayal and the highly individual blend of diverse
characteristics within his own nature.

Notes

1 Cf. C. Spurgeon, *Five Hundred Years of Chaucer Criticism and Allusion*, 1925.
2 On this term, [see Clemen, *Chaucer's Early Poetry,*] p. 21 f.
3 Although, as Miss Spurgeon shows, it was not until during the nineteenth century

that Chaucer's humour came to be truly appreciated. Cf. the critical account in
H. R. Patch, *On Re-reading Chaucer*, 1948 Ch. 1.
4 This was the period, too, when English was ousting French as the language of the
courts and Parliament and then of instruction as well. In 1362 Parliament ordered
that court cases were to be tried in English; and in 1363 Parliament was opened for
the first time with an address in English, etc.
5 Spurgeon, *Five Hundred Years of Chaucer Criticism* I, p. 19.
6 Cf. W. P. Ker, *Essays on Medieval Literature*, 1905 p. 137.
7 This must be stressed in view of interpretations which see Chaucer as essentially a
French poet at heart. In Legouis and Cazamian we can still read: 'C'est son esprit
même qui est français comme son nom... Il descend en droite ligne de nos
trouvéres et il a tout d'eux sauf la langue' (*Hist. de la Littérature Anglaise*, 1925,
p. 131).

14 | Old forms and new content [*The Book of the Duchess*]

JOHN LIVINGSTON LOWES

Originally published in John Livingston Lowes, *Geoffrey Chaucer and the Development of His Genius* (Boston: Houghton Mifflin, 1934, pp. 116–28). Reprinted by permission of Houghton Mifflin. The original pagination is recorded within square brackets. A brief reference to a discussion later in the book has been omitted from p. 122.

The earliest of the four vision-poems, the *Book of the Duchess*, is one of the few works of Chaucer which we can certainly date. For we know from the poem itself that it is an elegy upon the death of the Duchess Blanche, the first wife of John of Gaunt, who died of the pestilence, September 12, 1369. And Chaucer had been with John of Gaunt in Picardy on the very day she died. [Jean] Froissart too, who longer than Chaucer had known her at court, writes of her with grace and feeling in *Le joli Buisson de Jeunesse*: 'She died young and *jolie*, about twenty-two years old, gay, gladsome, fresh, merry, sweet, simple, of modest bearing, the good lady whose name [117] was Blanche.' And Chaucer's exquisite and heartfelt tribute far more than bears him out. But before that eulogy – the heart and the *raison d'être* of his poem – could be reached, the conventions of courtly verse must be observed, and the elegy must assume the guise of a dream. And if for a moment Chaucer forgot that it was after all an elegy which he was writing, and let himself go at first for sheer delight in retelling the tale which had set him dreaming, I am sure that his contemporary readers did not feel his prelude to be irrelevant – nor need we.

But Chaucer, quite characteristically, was not content to accept the dream convention as an act of faith. Why *does* one dream? And what are the phenomena of dreaming which give verisimilitude to an invented vision? Chaucer pondered the first question at intervals throughout his life, and in the Proem to the *House of Fame* enumerates fifteen different causes of dreams, including among them – but not from experience! – too great feebleness of brain and abstinence. But the accepted conventional cause of such dreams as found vent in verse, was melancholy – the melancholy *par excellence* which arises from unrequited or otherwise unhappy love. The fact that one might not at the moment of composition be in love at all – wit[118]ness [Guillaume de] Machaut's love-melancholy, intermittent as a quartan ague and punctually synchronous with his stirrings toward a vision-poem – that fact had nothing to do with the case. And so, if Chaucer in this instance is to account for his dream (as he does) by the fact that he sat up in bed to read a book in order to beguile a sleepless night, he must, *de rigueur*, account for the sleeplessness. And he does so as they ordered such matters in France, but with a verisimilitude so disconcerting that his commentators ever since, with an industry that must have delighted Chaucer's ghost, have vainly ransacked records for the hypothetical lady of his love.

As for the second question – how give likelihood to an imagined dream? – Chaucer's keen observation of dream psychology is manifest from the very opening of the narrative. The book which he was reading when he fell asleep – he calls it a 'romaunce' – was, as his charming description makes clear, a collection of old tales, which included the *Metamorphoses*. And there he found the story of Ceyx and Alcione, which Ovid tells in his Eleventh Book. Ceyx had lost her husband Alcione by death. And the dream which in Chaucer follows, regarded as a dream, finds its suggestion, with irrefragable dream logic, in the narrative, fresh in his mind, of that [119] ancient loss. But Chaucer knew also later tellings of Ovid's story. For Machaut had told it too, in that dolorous lay of the Prince in *La Fonteinne Amoureuse* to which the poet had unscrupulously listened through the window. Froissart, no less conventionally sleepless, had likewise read in Machaut the same story before he in turn dreamt *Le Paradys d'Amour*. And Chaucer had omnivorously read all three – the eleventh Metamorphosis, *La Fonteinne Amoureuse*, and *Le Paradys d'Amour* – and as he retells the story, the three blend into a fresh and delightful *quartum quid* which is at once all of them, yet none of them but Chaucer. One has only to read the tale as Ovid, Machaut, Froissart, and Chaucer respectively tell it to see what all the books and lectures ever written can never show – the unmistakable, individual stamp which Chaucer, even at this early day, set upon everything he touched.

If one does read the four tellings of the tale together – and it is a rather fascinating enterprise – one will find Chaucer gleaning here and there among them with an eager relish and a keen eye for new or telling morsels. But we, with a wide field still to reap, may only glean among his gleanings. Juno in Ovid, at Ceyx's prayer, sends Iris to Morpheus to ask of him a [120] dream which shall bring to Ceyx tidings of her husband's fate. Froissart, for good measure, couples with Juno a baffling personage, Oleus, and names, among Morpheus's 'sleepy thousand sons,' one Eclympasteyr – a name otherwise unknown in rhyme or prose. Chaucer, as Professor Kittredge once remarked, shied at Oleus, cannily dismissing him as 'som wight elles, I ne roghte who.' Eclympasteyr, on the other hand, so charmed him – and no wonder! – that he not only kept him but raised him to the dignity of Morpheus's heir. And that eye of his like a falcon's, caught one of the only two mild essays at humour ('was never gentle lamb more mild') which have ever gladdened my eyes in Machaut's works – that delicious bit in *La Fonteinne Amoureuse* when Iris for the second time attempts to waken Morpheus, who has meantime gone to sleep again, and when the kindly but somnolent deity opens *un petiot* – just a tiny bit – *one* eye. That Chaucer could not resist, and he takes it. But it was he and not Machaut who was writing this poem. And so, instead of Iris's suave and urbane summons, Chaucer's messenger, unnamed but now unmistakably masculine, thus proceeds to waken Morpheus:

> This messenger com fleynge faste
> And cried, 'O, ho! awake anoon!'
> [121] Hit was for noght; there herde hym non.
> 'Awake!' quod he, 'whoo ys lyth there?'
> And blew his horn ryght in here eere,
> And cried 'Awaketh!' wonder hyë.
> This god of slep *with hys oon yë*
> *Cast up*, axed, 'Who clepeth ther?'
> 'Hyt am I,' quod this messager –
>
> [178–86]

who then delivers Juno's message. Few things, too, of the sort are more engaging than the contrasted gifts which in the three poems the would-be sleepers offer Morpheus, of which Chaucer has decorously omitted the night-cap, but retained the feather-bed. Then, the promise of gifts to Morpheus duly made, he falls at last asleep over his book, and dreams a dream so inly sweet, so wonderful, that not even Joseph who read Pharaoh's dream, nor Macrobius who wrote the dream of Scipio, would be competent to expound it. And instantly we are back in the May morning of the Garden of the Rose, save that Chaucer's birds, which in his dream awaked him, are on his chamber roof. The windows of his chamber are all of pictured glass, in which was wrought from the romances the story of Troy – of Hector and Priam, Achilles and Laomedon, Medea and Jason, and of Paris, Helen, and Lavinia; while on all the walls was somehow painted all the Romance of the Rose. And one wonders what were the pictures present [122] in Chaucer's mind as he wrote what to us is only a catalogue of names. For the *House of Fame* makes it clear ... that the classical romances did leave lively visual images upon his memory. And in the romances there were pictures in profusion: One recalls such details in the *Roman de Troie* as the scene which still indelibly imprints itself on the eye as one reads – the lines in which Medea, like Chaucer unable to sleep, gets up from her bed and opens a lattice, looks out at the just-risen moon, closes the window and turns sadly away, stops dead in the midst of the moonlit room and listens, and hears the sound of footsteps retreating down the stairs. And the Lavinia who is pictured in the windows of Chaucer's dream-chamber is not, I think, the shadowy Lavinia of the *Aeneid* at all, but she who through two thousand lines of the *Roman d'Eneas* fills the stage – that Lavinia, one scene from whose story, as told in the romance, Chaucer painted in the *Troilus* with such sweeping strokes that it stands out to the eye like a great canvas.

But what of the dream itself? The Dreamer hears a hunting horn, and promptly takes horse and joins the hunt – described as only a man who had hunted could do it – and asks a retainer leading a hound, 'Say, felowe, who shal [123] hunte here?' [366] And with the utter irrelevance of a dream the answer is, 'Syr, th'emperour Octovyen.' [368] But that startling *non sequitur* is flawless dream psychology. For Chaucer, as Dreamer, had fallen asleep over Guillaume de Machaut, and the tale of Medea and Jason was also fresh in his mind, and in both there is casual mention of Octavian. And no less casually he now appears, and with that fugitive appearance vanishes, as in a dream he should, completely from the poem. Chaucer had not pondered on the ways of dreams in vain.

Then at once another figure from the Dreamer's recent reading appears and vanishes. The lion in Machaut's *Dit dou Lyon*, after its office as watch-dog of the garden had been capably performed, and Machaut accepted by the Lady of the Land, came prettily and humbly to Machaut, as if it were a little whelp (*un petit chiennet*), and Machaut petted it, and it submitted, and did wonders with its tail (*De sa queue faisoit merveilles*), and joined its ears (*joint les oreilles*). And so, a dream changeling, the lion, no longer a lion but a puppy, comes up to Chaucer as the hunt rides off:

> I was go walked fro my tree,
> And as I wente, ther cam by mee
> A whelp, that fauned me as I stood,
> [124]   That hadde yfolowed, and koude no good.
> Hyt com and crepte to me as lowe
> Ryght as hyt hadde me yknowe,
> Helde doun hys hed and *joyned hys eres*,
> And leyde al smothe doun hys heres.
>
> [387–94]

Then Chaucer would have caught it, but it fled and, like Octavian, is never heard of more.

But Chaucer had started to follow it and in an instant he is in the identical dream landscape upon which Guillaume de Lorris entered as *his* dream began, and Chaucer has reached it by a leap of association over 9098 lines of the *Roman de la Rose* to a kindred description. And that leads him into Guillaume de Lorris's dream-forest, and then, with another leap of memory across thirteen thousand lines of the *Roman de la Rose*, he sees in the forest a Man in Black, sitting with his back turned to an oak, 'an huge tree' – a young man, some four and twenty years of age, and he, piteous and pale, is composing a Complaint, and the Dreamer, like Machaut in *La Fonteinne Amoureuse*, listens as he composes. And at last the knot for which the tale is knit is reached.

For the Man in Black has lost his wife, as Ceyx in the book read just before the dream had lost her husband, by *death*. But that we learn only later. For the Dreamer, with a touch of [125] art which is sheer genius, is represented as a little dull of understanding. And it is through the questions which, in his gentle bewilderment he keeps asking, that the Man in Black is led on to describe, with growing fulness and depth of feeling, in a Portrait of a Lady unmatched (I think) save by Dante in mediæval poetry, his lost love; until, at long last, with the final question: 'Sir ... where is she now?' [1298] and the answer, 'She ys ded!' [1309] the truth breaks in upon the Dreamer's mind. The artifice was meant to be transparent, for Chaucer's hearers would instantly have recognized, with the line: 'And good faire WHITE [i.e., Blanche] she het' [948] – the subject of the elegy. But the subtlety of the perception that one will tell to a *stranger* what reticence or convention will withhold from a *friend*, and the astuteness of the invention of an obtuse but sympathetic listener – those are Chaucer's own. Psychological insight and adroitness in its exercise go hand in hand through the poem.

But Chaucer's mind was full of his recent reading. For he possessed, among his gifts, a memory which flashed along links of association from what he was reading to what he had read; and as he wrote, the thing that he recalled came back, trailing with it recollections, still unfaded, [126] of this or that which elsewhere he had read. And his recollections coalesced, so that, like the tidings in his own House of Rumour, there was no longer 'one of two, but both at once.' And so now his memory, as he writes, darts back and forth like a swallow between eight of Machaut's poems. He catches the suggestion for his central situation from a love *débat* embodied in a pair of remarkable poems – *Le Jugement dou Roy de Behaingne* and *Le Jugement dou Roy de Navarre* – a *débat* which opens with a meeting in a wood between a knight whose lady has been false to him and a lady who has lost her lover by death. He takes over, with changed details and complete reversal of its application, the picturesque catalogue of lovers' exploits in *Le Dit dou Lyon* and substitutes for its preposterous climax a priceless transcript of reality – a dry sea and a name, the Carrenar or Black Lake, which had somehow travelled back along the silk-routes from the terrible deserts in the heart of Asia. And in the records of Sir Aurel Stein's most recent explorations the Khara-nor may now be seen, by the aid of photographs, within a stone's throw of Marco Polo's highway, while the ancient bed of a dried-up sea lies in the desert to the west. He recalls, too, bits from the *Remède de Fortune*, a poem on one of his [127] own pet themes, and weaves together close verbal reminiscences not only of these, but also of *La Fonteinne Amoureuse*, and the *Lay de Confort*, and a *Motet*, and a *Complainte* to boot. And the incredible result is a poem which is pure Chaucer – so potent already is that unanalyzable, individual Chaucerian idiom. One thinks – *mutatis valde mutandis* – of Coleridge's remark about certain lines of Wordsworth's, to the effect that if he had met them running wild in the deserts of Arabia he would instantly have screamed out 'Wordsworth.' Chaucer's image and superscription is on every line of the elegy. The *Book of the Duchess* is not a great poem. It is a fresh and lovely and (paradoxically, if you will) an original composition.

For such borrowing as we have been observing was no less a convention in Chaucer's century than the dreams and the recurring melancholy and the catalogues. There was no literary property at all, in the sense in which we employ the term. [Eustache] Deschamps could beg Chaucer to transplant him into his garden, as the highest compliment which he could ask. And

Chaucer was paying Machaut precisely the compliment which Machaut on his part had paid Guillaume de Lorris, and the *Ovide moralisé* and *Boethius*. No angel with a flaming sword kept the gate of [128] the garden of the Rose, or of the gardens of the Rose's subjects.

> Qu'il fu un temps qu'il n'estoit rien
> Qu'on peüst dire 'cecy est mien,'
> Car toute chose estoit commune
> Comme le soleil et la lune.

15 | Sleep, dreams and poetry in Chaucer's *Book of the Duchess*

LISA J. KISER

Originally published in *Papers on Language and Literature* 19 (1983):3–12. Reprinted by permission of the editor. The original pagination is recorded within square brackets. The square brackets used to cite line numbers after indented quotations in the original text have been changed to round brackets. The endnotes originally appeared as footnotes.

The *Book of the Duchess* is many things to Chaucerians – the poet's first attempt to work within the dream-vision form, an example of his youthful experimentation with the rhythms of his native tongue, and his first substantial work to clearly express his indebtedness to the French sources and conventions that would influence him throughout most of his life as a poet. Yet in spite of its early date of composition and its place as Chaucer's "first" in nearly every respect, *The Book of the Duchess* confronts the reader with many of the issues and techniques that characterize Chaucer's most mature works. Primary among these is this poem's complicated narrator, whose relationship to the characters and events in the story he tells forms as much a part of the poem's significance as the subject matter he relates. Indeed, *The Book of the Duchess* offers an early yet fully developed example of the complex Chaucerian persona, the shy, self-conscious man who seems to know so little about the truths he records so well. And the key to understanding this poem – like the key to many other Chaucerian works – resides in fully perceiving the attitudes this narrator has about himself and about the subjects in his poem.[1]

Although the narrator has been the focus of many critical studies of this poem, no one has yet satisfactorily explained why this Chaucerian persona is introduced in a belabored and self-conscious passage on his sleeplessness, a passage that appears to most readers to act as a [4] lengthy digression instead of a true prologue to the poem's issues and theme. Readers too often tend to ignore these lines about insomnia, or fail to relate them to the poem as a whole. Yet the narrator's sleeplessness is of great thematic importance to *The Book of the Duchess*, and what it reveals about the narrator helps to unify the poem's three major parts – the Ceyx and Alcione story, Octavian's hunt, and the poet's meeting with the Black Knight. These three sections are not as loosely related as they might appear, but are instead organized around the themes that the narrator introduces in the opening lines of his poem.

If, as many critics have suggested, dreams are metaphors for the activities and results of the poetic imagination in medieval courtly works, then Chaucer's sleeplessness in the first lines of this poem represents not only his failure to dream, but also his inability to write.[2] For a poet, whose business is to create well and to create often, sleeplessness results in a poetically barren state of mind, a period of disturbingly unproductive idleness:

> I have so many an ydel thoght,
> Purely for defaute of slep,
> That, by my trouthe, I take no kep
> Of nothing, how hyt cometh or gooth,
> Ne me nys nothyng leef nor looth.[3]

> (4–8)

In these lines (and the next thirty or so following them) lie the first glimmerings of a complicated Chaucerian irony. That idleness could be demonstrated by the waking state and not by the more obviously inactive state of sleep is an unusual and somewhat silly idea – at least to the non-poets among Chaucer's peers, who would naturally link sleep with sloth. But Chaucer's point here is one that the rest of the poem will attempt to prove – namely, that good poets work hard at what they do and that observers of a poet at work are not likely to regard closed eyes and idle hands as signs of frenzied poetic activity. Falling asleep, then, is actually the first step towards fulfilling a poet's role. It is "defaute of slep" that constitutes a threat to poetic "besyness."[4]

[5] The remaining introductory lines of the poem describe another bit of work by poets that seems to others like idle play-reading. If an artist is not actively composing, he might be working equally hard at finding "matere" for his fictions. Turning to Ovid, whose tales will provide the poet with, as he says, "beter play" than will chess or any other game, Chaucer finds the tale of Ceyx and Alcione, which makes several important statements about idleness, poetic labor, and the "resurrection" of the dead, a theme Chaucer finds useful for his own commemorative poem because the narrative involves the loss of a beloved spouse. In Ovid's simple story Chaucer also discovers an example of the process by which people can be "resurrected," a process which he will narrate in order to allow the reader to compare it to Chaucer's own poetic "resurrection" of Blanche. Because the narrator so luckily discovers this useful bit of "matere" from his reading, he is now free to sleep and to dream his own poem; the poet's successful search for subject matter is followed by his immediate "lust ... to slep" (273–74).

The Ovidian tale that Chaucer retells here (minus the metamorphosis of its original) is significant as a prologue to Chaucer's elegy for Blanche largely because of the character of Morpheus. Like Morpheus, Chaucer is asked to help someone recover from grief by creating a "vision" of a lost loved one. The bereaved mourners, both Alcione and John of Gaunt (the intended recipient of Chaucer's elegy), are given a chance to "see" their dead mates by means of a visionary experience. Alcione is provided with an actual "animation" of the dead Ceyx; John of Gaunt receives Chaucer's much less ambitious poetic remembrance of his dead wife. The difference between the ways in which Morpheus and Chaucer "raise the dead" constitutes the single most important reason for Chaucer's choice of this story (and not any other one) for his poem.

Morpheus, unlike Chaucer, is an example of true idleness. His sleeping is unproductive and unrelated to any subtle process of poetic labor. Chaucer emphatically writes that both Morpheus and his assistant Eclympasteyr "slep and dide noon other werk" (169). Moreover, the dark valley in which these deities live is as barren and as unregenerative as their lethargy:

> Ther never yet grew corn ne gras,
> Ne tre, ne [nothing] that ought was,
> Beste, ne man, ne noght elles,
> Save ther were a fewe welles
> Came rennynge fro the clyves adoun,
> That made a dedly slepynge soun. . . .

(157–62)

[6] Nothing grows in this infertile valley, and the "welles" that run here are part of the river Lethe (as Ovid makes clear), whose waters signify forgetfulness, not remembrance. Furthermore, the forms and shapes which these "goddes of slepynge" use to create dreams lie strewn about the floor of their cave instead of being stored and manipulated in their minds, as are the images the poets use.[5] In other words, while Morpheus sleeps he does nothing else, a point that directly contrasts with Chaucer's own dream-filled and thus highly creative sleeping.

The following interlude – the poor messenger's comic difficulty in waking up the sleeping deity – further reinforces Chaucer's desire to paint Morpheus as truly idle. It is next to impossible to arouse this god into action, and even when the task is finally done, Morpheus only begrudgingly fulfills the commission that Juno has given him – to resurrect the body of Ceyx, give it voice and animation, and make it appear before the grieving wife. The interlude parodies Chaucer's own situation: he is writing a commissioned poem to console a grieving spouse, and he will do it by a form of "resurrection." But his act, unlike Morpheus', will succeed. Morpheus' action is very mechanical: with his supernatural power, he recovers the body from the scene of death, places it before the grieving Alcione, and makes it speak as if it were his puppet. But the most damning feature of Morpheus' act lies not in its artificiality or in its obvious falseness (Ceyx will only appear to be alive), but rather in its effect. Juno's command to him is that he "shewe" Ceyx to his sorrowful wife (147). But after Ceyx has spoken his few moving words to her, Alcione looks up, presumably to lay eyes on the beloved man she hears, yet she sees nothing:

> With that hir eyen up she casteth
> And saw noght. "Allas!" quod she for sorwe,
> And deyede within the thridde morwe.
>
> (212–14)

This false "resurrection" has obviously been incapable of fulfilling its intended purpose. In fact, one could argue on the basis of Chaucer's lines that her death from sorrow was actually hastened by Morpheus' cheap trick, for it only strengthened in her mind the realization that her husband was gone. Thus, in their attempts to find an antidote to human grief, the gods have clearly failed. Chaucer leaves off the Ovidian metamorphosis (by which both husband and wife are turned into birds) precisely because he wishes the story to end unhappily, [7] thus allowing its tragedy to stand in marked contrast to his own handling of Blanche's death later.

The tale of Morpheus and his recovery of Ceyx is followed immediately by Chaucer's own carefully described attempt at resurrecting the dead, this time by means of his own method, writing poetry. For this reason the section takes place within a dream, one organized around the themes Chaucer has already announced: the hard work that goes into a poem's composition, the writing of poetry as an act of "besynesse" never to be confused with sloth, and the painstaking process by which memories of the deceased are transformed into living verse. The dream opens with the narrator "awakening" into a typical dream-vision May morning environment, whose silence is occasionally punctuated with the heavenly singing of birds. These birds, like minor poets of nature, do not feign their melodies, "for ech of hem hym peyned / To fynde out mery crafty notes. / They ne spared not her throtes" (318–20). More significantly, the poet's chamber is described: his windows, suffused with light, are glazed with images from classical poems, and his walls are painted with the "text and glose" of the *Romance of the Rose*. This complete environment, from the birds to the chamber decorations, suggests a particularly "poetic" atmosphere, for nature's poets (the birds) and former human poets (as represented on the windows and the walls) stand here as Chaucer's models, the artists to whom he turns to learn his craft. His natural and his literary heritage is appropriately evoked as part of a bedroom milieu because it is within that room of dreams that he works so diligently at "making."

By this stage in the poem Chaucer has presented his raw materials (Ovid) and his models (natural harmony and former literary artifacts). He now dramatizes the process of poetic creation itself, the beginning of which he describes as a hunt. This central episode of *The Book of the Duchess* has been variously interpreted as a lover's chase, a hunt for Christian truth, and a quest in search of the deceased Blanche. In Marcelle Thiebaux' *The Stag of Love*, however, the author points out a long tradition of the hunt as an image of the artist's pursuit of his subject matter and narrative line, citing as evidence this image in the works of Gottfried von Strassbourg, Wolfram von Eschenbach, Cervantes, and Chaucer himself, as he alludes to it in line 341 of

The Clerk's Tale.[6] This interpretation of the hunt is an attractive one, given its immediate context in the poem. Yet Chaucer is certainly acknowledging here another tradition associated with the hunt: the [8] ubiquitous truism that hunting successfully cures the onset of idleness. Hunting manuals routinely address this beneficial effect of the sport, usually in words that resemble these from *The Master of Game*:

> Now shal I preue þe how an huntere ne may by no re-
> son falle yn any of the seuene dedly synnes. ffor whanne
> a man is ydel & reccheles wiþ oute trauayle and men
> ben not occupyed to be doyng some þinges & abide
> oþer yn þeire bed oþer chambres, hit is a þing þe
> which draweþ men to ymagynacioun of fleshly lust and
> plaisere.... [By hunting] he is lasse ydel ... for
> he hath ynowe to do to ymagine, and to þenk on his office.[7]

For Chaucer, the hunt has a particular ironic relevance to this poem, for he can show with the hunt that poets can pursue the chase while they simultaneously lie in their "bed oþer chambres," a feat that the writer of *The Master of Game* may have found unbelievable. Furthermore, the hunt is relevant to this poem because it is another "game" or sport that is not merely a game alone, like the "beter play" of reading that Chaucer describes before his dream begins. This hunt, then, has all the ironic complexity of Chaucer's mature poetry; and, if viewed on one level, it gracefully redefines the poet's seemingly contemplative life as a truly active one.

Once the chase is under way, Chaucer is sidetracked by a little "whelp" to a fertile forest and garden landscape that contrasts with Morpheus' barren environment. Here, the poet's surroundings reflect the natural productivity of late springtime, with flowers, fully-leaved trees, and a variety of wild animals wandering about the forest. That this modest "paradise" is meant to describe a poetic environment, ornamented with the flowers of rhetoric, is suggested by its similarity to the rhetorically descriptive gardens that appear as exemplary bits of rhetoric in the *artes poetriae*, such as Geoffrey of Vinsauf's *Poetria nova* and Matthew of Vendôme's *Ars versificatoria*. Both treatise writers are fond of discussing poetry as if it were a natural landscape. Geoffrey uses images of floral cultivation to express his sense of a poem's figures of diction and thought. Matthew introduces his chapter on versification with a description of a dream-vision garden that contains, like Chaucer's, Flora and a variety of blooming flowers [9] which are admired by characters like Philosophy, Tragedy, Comedy, Satire, Elegy, and others, the major generic distinctions that the treatise covers.[8] Furthermore, the "litel used" path down which Chaucer proceeds (398–401) may directly reflect the concept of novelty as expressed by the *artes poetriae*: both Geoffrey and Matthew admonish poets never to travel a "well-worn path."[9] One may even wish to speculate that the whelp that leads the poet to his garden and ultimately to his encounter with the Black Knight is Chaucer's comic personal image of his poetic muse; the image at least affirms the modesty with which Chaucer typically views his own poetry. Youthful and unable to keep up with imperial chases, this domesticated little puppy stands as Chaucer's comic muse, who, however lacking in ferocity or natural competitiveness, is nevertheless suited to Chaucer's "queynt sweven."

Chaucer places his actual elegaic treatment of Blanche – the commissioned purpose of the entire poem – in the mouth of the Black Knight he encounters after his brief excursions in the flowery wood. That the Black Knight is himself a poet-figure (like the narrator) is made clear by several references in the text, the first occurring at the same moment the narrator first meets him. The Knight, with a "dedly sorwful soun," makes

> of rym ten vers or twelve
> Of a compleynte to hymselve,
> The moste pitee, the moste rowthe,
> That ever I herde. . . .
>
> (463–66)

Chaucer provides no more details about this particular bit of verse, but he does include a sample of the Knight's next lament, a "lay" without music, which Chaucer says begins like this:

> I have of sorwe so gret won
> That joye gete I never non,
> Now that I see my lady bryght,
> Which I have loved with all my myght,
> Is fro me ded and ys agoon.
>
> (475–79)

[10] I quote this excerpt here (and quote no more) largely as a reminder that the verse is not particularly inspired; as critics have pointed out, it is general, conventional, and empty of detail.[10] Despite the Black Knight's admirable productivity and the seriousness with which he attempts to commemorate his lady in art, he is sorely in need of a distinctive voice and a richer tradition than the one that the well-worn "path" of French convention offers him. His grief and love for "White" constantly seem to elude the forms in which he tries to capture them. Like the hunters who chase (but do not overtake) their prey, busy poets do not always succeed in fully recording the richness and sincerity of their emotions.

That the reader recognize the "besynesse" inherent in the Black Knight's attempts to remember White in his poetry is essential to Chaucer's purpose in *The Book of the Duchess*. To underscore the idea in the poem's introductory lines – that poets work hard at what they do – Chaucer lets his sincere Knight make the point himself in his long rehearsal of his youthful courtship:

> for to kepe me fro ydelnesse,
> Trewely I dide my besynesse
> To make songes, as I beste koude,
> And ofte tyme I song hem loude;

> And made songes thus a gret del
> Althogh I koude not make so wel
> Songes, ne knewe the art al. . . .

(1155–61)

Idleness and writing poetry are never compatible, even when a poet's hard work may not result in "good" verse. Poets do not "play" at their craft, for even when they are manipulating prefabricated units of formal courtly praise (as the Black Knight is doing), much can go wrong if they do not constantly attend to the difficult task of articulating their real experiences in acceptable, conventional forms. What goes wrong, in fact, is visible in the Knight's own unshaped reminiscing about his lady's beautiful physique: unassimilated bits of rhetorical flourish contrast wildly with scraps of realistic observation, show[11]ing that the raw materials of one's memory do not constitute "poetry" until they are made to conform smoothly to the available language of courtly commemoration. Poems are not merely random verbal memories thrown together in metrical lines; they are carefully wrought blends of reality and societal forms.[11] At the other extreme, however, lie the Black Knight's trivial lays, fashioned according to formulae alone, without the distinctiveness that all great poems show.

The correct balance between life and art is never achieved in *The Book of the Duchess.* Nor was it intended to be, because Chaucer wants to prove that even after a poet's sound education and hours of practice, perfection is not guaranteed; it is as difficult to attain for a poet as it is for any other hardworking craftsman. Yet the Black Knight's monologue fulfills Chaucer's commission – to praise and thus "resurrect" the dead Blanche – for readers are never in doubt about her existence as the prototype of "White," the woman whom the Knight so enthusiastically describes. This method of delivering an indirect (and somewhat clumsy) elegy succeeds because Chaucer handles the Knight so deftly and sympathetically. What the Knight says about "White" is believable because he is such a trustworthy character witness, even though he never delivers up a perfectly wrought elegy that succeeds in conveying his real grief for his real lady by means of socially acceptable art. Given his personal confessions of inexperience and of his deep and abiding love for this woman, it is impossible to make cynical judgments of him; he is enthusiastic and absolutely committed to the difficult task of sincere – yet artful – praise. And most of all, he knows what "feyning" is and he shuns it. He mentions Lady Fortune's "fals portrayture" (626) with disdain and disbelief, and he also spends several lines insisting that Blanche herself never "countrefeted" her mercy or her forgiveness (869–77). That the Knight tells truths (however ineffectively) is never once in question.

In addition to fulfilling a difficult commission, then, *The Book of the Duchess* leaves the reader with several important statements about the narrator's – and thus Chaucer's – office as a poet. The first and most significant is, of course, that creating a sincere yet artful elegy is extraordinarily difficult, especially when one wishes to avoid "feyning" yet to present a generally favorable portrait at the same time. This poem's labored attempt to "catch its quarry" – that is, to speak well of Blanche in art – may have failed on one level, like the hunt going on [12] in the background; but readers are certainly made to see the "besynesse" that informs it. For the poem continuously invites readers to contrast this attempt at literary resurrection with the failure of the idle Morpheus, whose success in literally raising the dead is finally inadequate fakery when compared to Chaucer's oblique, gentle, and pains-takingly constructed resurrection of Blanche.

Readers also come to realize that a poet's "games" are not really games at all. Reading and "hunting" (like playing chess with Fortune) are serious activities whose import may not be understood by uninformed observers. Even the narrator's sleeping is shown to be an act of diligent labor in the misunderstood world in which poets live. Finally, Chaucer wants readers to remember his narrator's bedchamber decorations, for they yield an unmistak-able clue to the poet's plans for his future "dreams." Readers are deliberately told that his classical models, represented by images on his windows, shim-mer with the sun's true light, because the windows are closed, and through "the glas the sonne shon" (335–36). The French courtly tradition, however, though equally colorful, is illuminated by means of reflected light alone, for the scenes from the "Romaunce of the Rose" (334) are painted on the wall. With this detail, Chaucer comments on his own poetic debts: though far from rejecting the French courtly traditions that the Black Knight has tried so hard to master, Chaucer seems to be saying that classical poetry, through whose windows one sees the world and the sun's heavenly light at once, has much more to offer a young poet in search of a voice.[12] After all, Ovid's tales (not those of Machaut, Froissart, or Deschamps) lie on the narrator's bedside table, ready to be carried with him into future dreams. *The Book of the Duchess*, then, although it is a Chaucerian "first," introduces a poet not only well aware of the challenges awaiting him in his life as an artist, but one also already committed to the quest for classical "matere."

Notes

1 On this poem's narrator, see Donald C. Baker, "The Dreamer Again in *The Book of the Duchess*," *PMLA* 70 (1955):279–82; Stephen Manning, "That Dreamer Once More," *PMLA* 71 (1956):540–41; J. Burke Severs, "Chaucer's Self-Portrait in the *Book of the Duchess*," *Philological Quarterly* 43 (1964):27–39; and R. M. Lumiansky, "The Bereaved Narrator in Chaucer's *The Book of the Duchess*," *Tulane Studies in English* 9 (1959):5–17.

2 See especially A. C. Spearing, *Medieval Dream-Poetry* (Cambridge, 1976), pp. 7–8, 187–218.

3 All references to Chaucer's poetry are to *The Works of Geoffrey Chaucer*, ed. F. N. Robinson, 2d ed. (Boston, 1957).

4 That readers are not to concern themselves with the reasons for the narrator's sleeplessness is stated in lines 40–44. There the poet summarily writes that the reasons for his inability to sleep are irrelevant to the poem; therefore, criticism that tries to discover a key to the poem in this passage is by Chaucer's own direction off the mark.

5 See *Metamorphoses* 11.603–18.

6 (Ithaca, 1974), p. 120.

7 Bodley MS. 546, fol 7 v°, as cited in *The Stag of Love*, p. 79. See also Gaston Phebus, *Livre de Chasse* (thought to be the source for the English *Master of Game*), ed. Gunnar Tilander (Karlsham, 1971), pp. 52–55; see also the other French hunting manuals described in James Fox, *A Literary History of France: The Middle Ages* (New York, 1974), pp. 334–36; and *The Stag of Love*, pp. 77–80.

8 For Geoffrey of Vinsauf's "garden," see *Poetria nova*, ed. Ernest Gallo (The Hague, 1971), ll. 1223–80; for Matthew's, see *The Art of Versification*, trans. Aubrey E. Gaylon (Ames, Ia., 1980), pp. 63–65.

9 *Poetria nova*, ll. 763–68; *The Art of Versification*, p. 26. This advice (in these words) comes originally from Lucan (*Pharsalia* 2.446).

10 On the Black Knight's use of courtly generalities, see John Lawlor, "The Pattern of Consolation in *The Book of the Duchess*," *Speculum* 31 (1956):626–48; Samuel Schoenbaum, "Chaucer's Black Knight," *MLN* 68 (1953):121–22; W. H. French, "The Man in Black's Lyric," *Journal of English and Germanic Philology* 56 (1957):231–41; Philip C. Boardman, "Courtly Language and the Strategy of Consolation in the *Book of the Duchess*," *ELH* 44 (1977):567–79; and Robert Burlin, *Chaucerian Fiction* (Princeton, 1977), p. 70.

11 See especially his awkward description of her neck (939–44) and his insertion of "non-courtly" details into the description of her arms, hips, and back (952–60).

12 Chaucer's rich and colorful bedroom is also described in order to strike a contrast with the house of the idle Morpheus, as Chaucer humorously furnishes it. It has gold wallpaper, but "of oo sute" (261).

16 | Dreams and truth [in *The House of Fame*]

SHEILA DELANY

Originally published as Chapter 4 in Sheila Delany, *Chaucer's House of Fame: The Poetics of Skeptical Fideism* (Chicago, University of Chicago Press, 1972, pp. 36–47). Reprinted by permission of the University of Chicago Press and the author. The original pagination is recorded within square brackets. A brief reference to a later chapter has been omitted from p. 46. The endnotes originally appeared as footnotes.

> God turne us every drem to goode!
> For hyt is wonder, be the roode,
> To my wyt, what causeth swevenes
> Eyther on morwes or on evenes....
>
> *The House of Fame*, 1–4

As a short compendium of medieval dream theory, the Proem to the *House of Fame* is a suitable induction to a dream-vision, even if its volume of information leaves us, with the Narrator, overwhelmed. The Narrator's presentation of the terminology, causes, and effects of dreams does more, though, than prepare us for the vision to follow. It represents the first stage in a process of expanding consciousness. The second is developed in Book 1, where the Narrator will retell at length the well-known story of Aeneas, and where he will confront the problem of conflicting heroic obligations. In Book 2 the Narrator will travel through the universe on his way to Fame's palace. In that section of the poem his interest will be the nature of the supraterrestrial environment: its landmarks, its laws, its effect on the cosmic traveller. The poem takes us, therefore, from psychology through history to cosmology, from microcosm to macrocosm, from the world of the mind through the world of men to the created world at large. This structural movement echoes one metaphysical structure by which men have linked themselves to the universe, [37] for according to the elemental theory of creation, man and the universe are composed of the same elements and governed by the same natural laws. The notion of correspondence between microcosm and macrocosm, derived from Platonic tradition and expressed in graphic and literary art throughout the Middle Ages, was well known to Chaucer from numerous sources.[1] In the *House of Fame*, the movement from inner to outer world supplies a changing, expanding backdrop for symbolic action. In each setting – psyche, history, cosmos – the Narrator confronts a set of alternatives, each of which is defined in terms of its literary tradition. Among these alternatives the Narrator is each time unable to choose, but he is able to transcend his indecision with a fideistic appeal to God or to Christ. Narrative material, then, changes in a pattern of progressive enlargement, very like the circles in water that form the basis of the Eagle's argument in Book 2. And, as with those same circles, the center remains constant, for the variation in narrative material causes no alteration in the overall structure of each episode.

It is appropriate, in the Proem to a dream-vision, for the author to introduce some remarks about the value of dreams. To do so amounts to an esthetic justification for the work to follow; for if the dream is acknowledged to be at least potentially a vehicle of truth, then the dream-vision frame may be considered to add authenticity. The dream-vision provides other advantages as well.[2] It permits the writer to treat questions which man cannot hope to answer by reason alone but which may require an epiphany or an [38] oracular answer. As a possibly supernatural phenomenon the device tends to absolve the writer from direct responsibility for statements that may be made in the work. It involves the reader more intimately than straightforward narrative, for the reader becomes both interpreter of the dream and judge of its truth. Moreover, since anyone is capable of dreaming, the reader can legitimately expect to participate in or benefit from the exemplary action portrayed in the vision – the dream-vision is anything but an elitist form. Finally, the dream-vision may serve as a device for disarming the literal-minded critic who might object to the presentation of improbable events in a context of waking life.

Since dreams were not accepted as uniformly valid, most dream-visions in medieval literature begin with an assertion of the truth of dreams in general, or at least of the particular dream about to be told. One of the best-known of these statements occurs at the beginning of the *Roman de la Rose*. I give it in Chaucer's translation:

> Many men sayn that in swevenynges
> Ther nys but fables and lesynges;
> But men may some swevenes sen
> Whiche hardely that false ne ben,
> But afterward ben apparaunt.
> This may I drawe to warraunt
> An author that hight Macrobes,
> That halt nat dremes false ne lees,
> But undoth us the avysioun
> That whilom mette kyng Cipioun.
> And whoso saith or weneth it be
> A jape, or elles nycete,
> To wene that dremes after falle,
> Let whoso lyste a fol me calle.

> For this trowe I, and say for me,
> That dremes signifiaunce be
> Of good and harm to many wightes,
> [39]   That dremen in her slepe a-nyghtes
> Ful many thynges covertly,
> That fallen after al openly.

(A, 1–20)

Such assertions of the validity of dreams form a branch of the extremely common "truth topos" found in many kinds of medieval literature.[3] The invention of historical or literary sources and the protestation of faithful reportage are other typical means of justifying the literary work.

That Chaucer knew the traditional uses of the truth apparatus is shown not only in his translation of the *Roman de la Rose* but in his use of that apparatus for his own original works. Two passages from the *Canterbury Tales* will illustrate Chaucer's familiarity with the tradition. In both of these passages, the justification rests on a mimetic theory of art. The first, from the General Prologue, absolves the poet from any suspicion of "vileynye" in adopting a low or uneducated style. Such, the Narrator claims, is the style in which his fellow-pilgrims spoke, and to use a more elevated style would be untrue to the event. Besides even Christ used a low style in the Scriptures.

> But first I pray yow, of youre courteisye,
> That ye n'arette it nat my vileynye,
> Thogh that I pleynly speke in this mateere,
> To telle yow hir wordes and hir cheere,
> Ne thogh I speke hir wordes proprely.
> For this ye knowen al so wel as I,
> Whoso shal telle a tale after a man,
> [40]   He moot reherce as ny as ever he kan
> Everich a word, if it be in his charge,
> Al speke he never so rudelich and large,
> Or ellis he moot telle his tale untrewe,
> Or feyne thyng, or fynde wordes newe.
> He may nat spare, althogh he were his brother;
> He moot as wel seye o word as another.
> Crist spak hymself ful brode in hooly write,
> And wel ye woot no vileynye is it.
> Eek Plato seith, whoso that kan hym rede,
> The wordes moote be cosyn to the dede.

(GP 725–42)

The second passage, from the Miller's Prologue, also uses the argument that the poet chronicles real events:

> What sholde I moore seyn, but this Millere
> He nolde his wordes for no man forbere,
> But tolde his cherles tale in his manere.

M'athynketh that I shal reherce it heere.
And therfore every gentil wight I preye,
For Goddes love, demeth nat that I seye
Of yvel entente, but for I moot reherce
Hir tales alle, be they bettre or werse,
Or elles falsen som of my mateere.

(3167–75)

Of course the irony in both apologies is that the reported event itself is a fiction (though one with analogues in real life), so that the low style is as artful and "feyned" as any other could be.

In both of Chaucer's other dream-visions, the dream is authenticated by means of a book which the Narrator reads just before falling asleep. The content of each dream is supposedly generated by the book: a "romaunce" of Ceyx and Halcyon in the *Book of the Duchess*, and "Tullyus of the Drem of Scipioun" in the *Parliament of Fowls*.

Despite his awareness of the conventional certification of literary truth, and his use of it elsewhere, in the *House* [41] *of Fame* Chaucer chooses to ignore it. Indeed he subverts it, undermining the reader's inclination to believe the dream that is about to be told.

The fifty-line sentence that opens and constitutes nearly all of the Proem is a plethora of contradictory information about dreams:

As yf folkys complexions
Make hem dreme of reflexions;
Or ellys thus, as other sayn,
For to gret feblenesse of her brayn,
By abstinence, or by seknesse,
Prison, stewe, or gret distresse,
Or ellys by dysordynaunce
Of naturel acustumaunce,
That sum man is to curious
In studye, or melancolyous,
Or thus, so inly ful of drede,
That no man may hym bote bede;
Or elles that devocion
Of somme, and contemplacion
Causeth such dremes ofte. . . .

(21–35)

One's first reaction to this extended *dubitatio* may be amusement, but the cumulative impression created by its piled-up clauses is of futility: it is hopeless to think of ascertaining the truth about dreams. The juxtaposition of so many opposed theories shows that too much information is as fatal to certainty as too little. Faced with this confusion, the reader can only repeat with the Narrator the wish that frames the Proem, "God turn us every dream to good!" (lines 1, 57–58). Since there is no rational way of choosing among theories, choice is abandoned; so is prediction, and the outcome of all dreams is left with God. The Narrator transcends given alternatives in a fideistic appeal to the highest authority – a suprarational authority. It is a structural pattern that remains constant throughout the work. And if the tone of the Proem is jocular or its [42] narrative material frivolous, the Narrator's attention will soon be directed toward weightier matters.

Besides eliminating any possibility of certainty about the truth of dreams in general, Chaucer further omits from both Proem and Invocation any reference to the validity of his particular vision. It is not said to be the result of any event in real life or of a special inspiration, nor is any claim made that this vision can in turn illuminate real life. Unlike most writers, Chaucer does not in the *House of Fame* encourage his audience to believe what it is about to hear. Nevertheless he does urge his audience to approach the work in good faith, calling down a curse on those who refuse to do so.

> And he that mover ys of al
> That is and was and ever shal,
> So yive hem joye that hit here ...
> And sende hem al that may hem plese,
> That take hit wel and skorne hyt noght,
> Ne hyt mysdemen in her thoght
> Thorgh malicious entencion.
> And whoso thorgh presumpcion,
> Or hate, or skorn, or thorgh envye,
> Dispit, or jape, or vilanye,
> Mysdeme hyt, pray I Jesus God
> That (dreme he barefot, drem he shod),
> That every harm that any man
> Hath had, syth the world began,
> Befalle hym therof. . . .

(81–101)

This is more than the conventional opening topos against envious detractors, though it does participate in that tradition.[4] It represents an important shift in emphasis, for the reader is invited to judge ("demen") rather than required [43] to believe. The question of truth is left aside entirely – an omission that can hardly be accidental when the point is so prominent a feature in medieval literature, especially in the dream-vision form which the *House of Fame* represents. Although the argument is made partly *ex silentio*, the Invocation clearly suggests a nascent awareness of the self-sufficiency of fiction. Chaucer does not, in this poem, present himself as the chronicler of real events, nor does he claim the reader's belief. Further, Chaucer is sufficiently skeptical about his traditional material to undercut it with irony, in the pointed juxtaposition of contradictory theories. He undercuts it again in altering the traditional May date of the courtly dream-vision to December 10 (line 63).

The Narrator's bitter curse on his hypothetical detractors eliminates still another traditional source of security for the audience: the poet's moral character and his elevated purpose. Another widely used device for opening a poem was the charity topos, in which the poet claimed his motive to be the edification of his audience through presentation of exemplary action.[5] The act of writing becomes itself a charitable act, through which the poet hopes to gain his heavenly reward. In the *House of Fame*, however, far from claiming any virtue to offset his vindictiveness, the Narrator reinforces the bitterness of his curse with this stubborn last remark:

> This prayer shal he have of me;
> I am no bet in charyte!

> (107–8)

With the work deliberately stripped of any external support from literary tradition or the Narrator's own character, [44] our trust will have to derive from the quality of the work itself.

The problem foreshadowed in the Proem and Invocation is that fame or tradition, being all-inclusive, provides too many answers; it encourages not certainty but doubt. Uncertainty about facts, whether historical or scientific, is disturbing to the scholar, but more disturbing to the poet must be uncertainty about his own position. In what ways can the poet use authorities whose authority he doubts? And if the poet's skepticism toward traditional material has subverted his old role as truth-teller, what amenities will govern the new and more difficult relation between poet and audience? These problems Chaucer does not fully resolve in the *House of Fame*, though he takes some tentative steps toward doing so. We must look ahead to *Troilus and Criseyde* for the integration of skeptical vision with literary practice.

The dream-vision frame is significant in relation to such questions. Chaucer's irony removes the traditional authenticating function of dream-lore so that it can no longer certify the validity of the work, and his silence about the real-life circumstances of the dream deprives us of a peg on which to suspend disbelief. Cut off from the usual supports of theoretical authority and historical fact, the composition, like the dream, becomes a free-floating quantum of creative or psychic energy, subject to good or evil influences and capable in turn of exercising a good or an evil influence on its audience. The Narrator requires protection as dreamer and as poet, for if neither dream-theory nor literary tradition offers certain truth, then neither dreaming nor writing offers any security of role. That the Narrator's position as dreamer and as poet is the same suggests that the dream is not only analogous to the composition but may be a metaphor for it – or, more accurately, for the poetic conception embodied in the work. The process of dreaming becomes nearly synonymous with the creative act.

[45] The classical invocations to the three books of the *House of Fame* suggest the symbolic relation of dream to composition. The first invocation asks Morpheus, god of sleep, for the power to tell the dream correctly:

> And to this god, that I of rede,
> Prey I that he wol me spede

> My sweven for to telle aryght,
> Yf every drem stonde in his myght.
>
> (77–80)

The connection seems straightforward and evident: because the poem relates a dream, the poem cannot be "true" unless the dream is accurately recounted. Yet when we recall the skeptical attitude toward dreams in the Proem, we realize that even to tell the dream "aryght" is no guarantee of its ultimate truth. In the second and third invocations the Narrator speaks more directly of his attempt to recreate a particular image:

> O Thought, that wrot al that I mette,
> And in the tresorye hit shette
> Of my brayn, now shal men se
> Yf any vertu in the be,
> To tellen al my drem aryght.
> Now kythe thyn engyn and myght!
>
> (II, 523–28)

> And yif, devyne vertu, thow
> Wilt help me to shewe now
> That in myn hed ymarked ys –
> Loo, that is for to menen this,
> The Hous of Fame for to descryve –
> Thou shalt se me go as blyve
> Unto the nexte laure y see,
> And kysse it, for hyt is thy tree.
>
> (III, 1101–8)

Here the poetic conception is described in terms that might apply either to a dream or to creative inspiration, inasmuch [46] as both are forms of intense mental activity, both are possibly the action of an external power ("vertu"), and both produce images that may require interpretation. Whatever its source, the poetic idea has to be translated into communicable form. Here the possibility of error can enter the creative process, for if the artistic form of the idea does not adequately represent the original conception, the work will be "false." The three classical invocations express the Narrator's desire to communicate what is in some sense accurate or true. Although "truth" is not clearly defined in the *House of Fame*, Chaucer's skepticism about dreams and his undercutting of traditional authority imply that this truth does not necessarily belong to the class of ascertainable facts. In his invocations Chaucer seems tentatively to define truth in fiction as fidelity to a poetic idea ("That in myn hed ymarked ys"). One might expect such a notion to dispel Chaucer's anxiety about truth in poetry. But a further difficulty remains, for even such a liberal notion of literary truth cannot guarantee the validity of inspiration itself – which, like the dream, may be delusive. Both imagination and the dream require special guidance, and this the Narrator invokes at the end of Book 1 in his prayer asking protection from "fantome and illusion".

We have seen how a superabundance of information about dreams led Chaucer to dispense with certain conventions of the dream-vision form: he cannot assert in good faith the absolute validity of this or any other dream. The traditional bond between poet and reader is at least partly severed, fair judgment replacing belief as the appropriate audience response. But a profusion of authorities existed in many other areas than dream-lore, and Chaucer's reading of contradictory literary texts was, as we shall see, an important source of his concern with poetic truth. His choice of one of the most famous stories in the medieval tradition – that of Aeneas and Dido – permitted him to explore that problem in terms of the different moral imperatives defined [47] by different literary authorities. His method in Book 1, where the story of Aeneas is told, is not substantially changed from his method in the Proem, though it is on a larger scale and its tone, no longer comical, is appropriate to the problem of heroic choice.

Notes

1 Among them the *De Mundi Universitate* of Bernard Silvestris, Prosa 13; Alanus de Insulis, *De Planctu Naturae*, Prosa 3; *Romane de la Rose*, 19021 ff. Other medieval sources of the microcosm theory are given in Jean Seznec, *The Survival of the Pagan Gods* (New York, 1953), p. 65; A. C. Crombie traces it to Plato's *Timaeus* and subsequent Stoic astrology, *Medieval Science*, 1:18. See also E. de Bruyne, *Études d'Esthétique Médiévale* (Bruges, 1945), 2:355–56.

2 For some of the following points about the dream-vision frame I am indebted to Francis X. Newman's dissertation, "Somnium: Medieval Theories of Dreaming and the Form of Vision Poetry" (Princeton, 1963), Chapter 5.

3 See, for example, Nicole Margival, *Le Dit de la Panthère d'Amours* (c. 1295), lines 41–43, ed. H. Todd, *SATF* 16 (1883); *Mum and the Sothsegger*, lines 873 and 1309–1333, ed. M. Day and Robert Steele, EETS 199 (1936); *Piers Plowman*, Passus 7, B-text, lines 151 ff. The classic biblical examples used to prove the validity of dreams were Joseph and Daniel. According to Robert Manning's manual *Handling Synne*, 390 ff., these illustrate two special types of revelation, caused respectively by God's warning and by too much study. On the tradition of the truth apparatus generally, see H. L. Levy, "As Myn Auctor Seyth," *Medium Aevum* 12 (1943).

4 The envious detractors topos has a particularly illustrious tradition, stretching from an inscription by Tiglath Pileser's scribe (see *The Gilgamesh Epic and Old Testament Parallels*, ed. Alexander Heidel, p. 139) to Rabelais' Prologue to *Gargantua*. It appears in the prologues to Einhard's *Life of Charlemagne*, Alanus's *Anticlaudianus*, Marie's lai *Guigemar*, and Chaucer's *Astrolabe*. F. Tupper traces the topos through the seventeenth century, "The Envy Theme in Prologues and Epilogues," *JEGP* 16 (1917). James A. Work suggests that the passage in the *House of Fame* echoes the great curse of excommunication, "Echoes of the Anathema in Chaucer," *PMLA* 47 (1932).

5 For the charity topos, see Chretien de Troyes, *Erec et Enide*, 1–18; Marie de France, Prologue to the *Lais*, 1–8; *La Venjance Alixandre*, Laisse 1; *Aymeri de Narbonne*, Laisses 1–3; and *Le Dit de l'Unicorne*.

17 | Chaucer's labyrinth: fourteenth-century literature and language

PIERO BOITANI

Originally published in the *Chaucer Review* 17 (1983):197–220.
Reprinted by permission of the Pennsylvania State University
Press. The original pagination is recorded within square brackets.
The endnotes originally appeared on pp. 216–20.

It has long been recognized that "the subject of the *House of Fame* is the art of poetry itself"[1] and that "in one sense the whole work is a vindication of poetry."[2] What I intend to show here is both more general and more specific. In the first place I shall illustrate the scene of fourteenth-century English literary culture as seen through Chaucer's eyes in the *House of Fame*. Chaucer gives us in this work his *idea* of that literature. Secondly, I wish to show how Chaucer asks himself some basic questions about literature, and, more deeply, about the relationship between literature, language, and reality. In this respect, Chaucer presents us here with his literary *problem*. Moreover, in the *House of Fame* Chaucer makes a series of decisive choices on the kind of literature, past and present, he prefers, and he points, however tentatively, to the kind of literature he will write in the future. He does this obliquely, allusively, and with a good deal of puzzled humor and irony, but he does it in earnest and with an astonishing thoroughness.

The *House of Fame* is dominated by five central images or *loci*, those of the Dream, the Temple, the Flight through Space, the Castle-Palace and the Whirling Wicker. I shall in the first instance follow Chaucer's own itinerary from the first to the last of these *loci* and will then move backwards from the poem's end to its beginning. Each of these images is, as we shall see, associated with a particular field of literary culture. All together, they indicate a deliberately secular choice (there is no Chapel, no Monastery, no Dark Wood, no Paradise in the *House of Fame*), one that moves from order towards disorder, from static iconography to swift movement, away from Love (the absence of a Garden in the *House of Fame* is an interesting departure from convention), away from tradition (in [198] the sense that the House of Rumor, in spite of its Ovidian features, is much less "traditional" than the Temple of Venus). All together, they constitute an exceptional achievement of poetic imagination.

The *House of Fame* itself is a dream – complex, full of colors and sounds, all the apparent disorder, the incongruity, the lack of conscious logical connections typical of dreams – a poem chaotic and ironical. Yet it is also clear that this December dream is a vision of the poet's literary universe, past, present, and future. No reader will fail to notice the presence in the *House of Fame* of the *Aeneid* and of the writers standing on the pillars, and Chaucer's many references to authors and quotations and adaptations from them. Nor is it by chance that the poem opens with a discussion on the causes of dreams. Considered as veils of a profound truth in the Middle Ages as well as today, in the course of the fourteenth century dreams became more and more metaphors for poetry, and they had come to constitute a separate literary genre.[3] Cicero's *Somnium Scipionis*, on which the poet of the *Parliament of Fowls* will muse before going to bed, is a vision of the inner meaning of the universe. The "Pleynt of Kynde" of Alanus, which Chaucer will also recall in the *Parliament*, is a dream. Visions are scattered throughout the Bible, from that of Ezekiel to that of John in the Apocalypse. The *Roman de la Rose*, the most widely read book of the fourteenth century after the Bible, is a dream poem: born as an "erotic" dream, it grows larger and more complex until it becomes an encyclopedia. Shorter French poems, such as some of those written by Machaut and Froissart in the fourteenth century, are dreams. And Boccaccio's *Amorosa Visione* and Petrarch's *Trionfi* are visions. Dream poems embrace the whole of reality, factual and imaginary.

Chaucer knew these dream poems: he mentioned, translated, and adapted them in his own works. He himself wrote dream poems – the *Book of the Duchess*, the *Parliament of Fowls*, the Prologue to the *Legend of Good Women*, the *House of Fame* itself. He may well have been acquainted with the extraordinary book of William Langland, who was at work endlessly on the many and multistratified dreams of *Piers Plowman* in those very last decades of the century and was resident in London itself.[4] He might have known – though they belonged to a tradition with which he seems to have had little acquaintance – that dream poems such as *Death and Life*, *Winner and Waster*, the *Parliament of the Three Ages* (if already in circulation) discussed themes far wider ranging than that of love – youth, middle and old age, life and death, the economic world. On the other hand, it is unlikely that he knew of a northern poet who was writing a short but ambitious dream poem, a heavenly vision and a [199] parable revolving around a jeweler-dreamer and a pearl-maiden set in the midst of fantastic landscapes. It is, however, certain that in the Proem to the *House of Fame* Chaucer mentions visions, revelations, dreams, *phantasmata*, *oracula*, dreams caused by "reflexions," sickness, meditation, melancholy, contemplation, love, foresight – all dreams, all literature, the literature of the past, of the present, of Chaucer's country, of all Europe. Medieval man falls asleep and dreams. In his dreams, he idealizes his world creating marvellous gardens, maidens, deities, temples, heavenly cities, and he discusses it, meditating on its philosophical, religious, economic, social, and literary problems. His dreams are voyages, ascents, debates, quests for truth, explorations of his mind and of all reality. Chaucer's dream in the *House of Fame* aims at precisely this comprehensiveness.

When, at the beginning of his dream, the protagonist finds himself in a "gothic" and strangely decorated Temple and contemplates on its walls an image of Venus, naked and floating on the sea, accompanied by Cupid and Vulcan, we realize that we are entering the ambiguous universe of Eros. Yet once more this coincides with the world of literature. Venus and her Temple, with which Chaucer authoritatively enters the mainstream of the icono-graphic and poetic tradition of Europe, are the inheritance of classical poetry, of Virgil, Ovid, Claudian, the descendants of the late Latin and medieval mythographers who transmitted their *ecphrases* – Fulgentius, Hyginus, the Mythographi Vaticani, Pierre Bersuire and his *Ovidius Moralizatus*. The goddess and her "chirche" are the sons of Guido delle Colonne, Andreas Capellanus, the *Roman de la Rose*, the products of the medieval "survival of the pagan gods" in the figurative arts and in literature.[5] It is in the four-teenth century that Venus Anadyomene reappears in Petrarch's *Africa* and in Boccaccio's *Genealogie*, while a Venus and a Temple identified with con-cupiscible appetite occupy a great deal of space in Boccaccio's *Teseida*, which Chaucer was to peruse throughout his career.[6]

The world of classical mythology penetrated not only the private studies of Italian poets, but also the severe theologically-minded rooms of Oxford University. The so-called "classicizing friars" wrote voluminous commen-taries on Scripture and the Fathers, inserting descriptions of pagan deities in their treatises. Waleys, Ridevall, Holcot, Lathbury used mythology to illus-trate points of ethics and theology but also enjoyed with undeniable pleasure its fascinating world.[7]

Attention to the classics was not, on the other hand, due simply to interest in mythology. Already in the twelfth century the English "humanist" John of Salisbury had read classical authors with great [200] fervor. Robert Grosse-teste and Roger Bacon had already recommended the study of Greek.[8] At the beginning of the fourteenth century John of Wales begins the exploration again, Nicholas Trevet comments on Seneca, Richard de Bury – the patron bishop of Durham, whom even Petrarch considered "[non] literarum inscius"[9] – searches monastic libraries for ancient texts.[10]

Mythology and "classicism" were not the exclusive concern of scholars. They permeated the literary production of vernacular poets and through them reached the Court and the households of aristocrats and merchants. Chaucer himself, stimulated by the Italians, exploits mythology in all his works. His great friend and colleague, Gower, uses Venus as the supreme narrative device of the *Confessio Amantis*, and his stories in that collection are very often drawn from mythology. A general yearning for classical Antiquity – that mythic Golden Age which had not been Christian but which appeared so rich, so wise, so orderly – seems to spread once again throughout Europe. Perhaps it had never really disappeared.

It is not strange, then, that Chaucer should find the story of Aeneas painted on the walls of his dream temple. This is indeed the shrine of literature and the temple of Virgil. Here, Chaucer contemplates the *Aeneid* as supreme model of art, Dante's "alta tragedìa," and faces the "altissimo poeta" who was also considered a *sapiens*, a magician and a prophet.[11] Virgil saved Dante from the Dark Wood (he had, according to Dante himself, showed the true light to Statius), he will be Chaucer's "lanterne" (*Legend of Good Women*, 926).[12]

Chaucer gives us an English translation of the first lines of the *Aeneid* and then a summary which replaces the *ordo artificialis* of the original with the *ordo naturalis* characteristic of medieval narrative,[13] for instance of the *Roman d'Eneas*, and which concentrates on Dido's episode (as did the "Epistle of Ovyde" the poet mentions to counterbalance "Virgile in Eneidos"). The moment is indeed solemn for English literature: to place at the beginning of a poem a "table of bras" inscribed with a translation of the words "Arma virumque cano," means pointing to an ideal and an ambition which will dominate the literary scene until the eighteenth century. Chaucer, however, operates within the existing tradition. He adapts a complex classical epic to the linear narrative of the Middle Ages[14] and to his audience's interest in the theme of love. The Middle Ages loved the labyrinthic, "interlaced" structure of the romances.[15] Chaucer's audience might have been able to understand the initial lines of the *Aeneid* in Latin. Langland inserts Latin quotations throughout *Piers Plowman*, and Gower writes an entire poem in Latin. But Chaucer makes a precise choice for the vernacular and a straightforward type [201] of narrative. He will be faithful to both throughout his career. Indeed the great arcades which the five Books of *Troilus* build as narrative units, the series of frescoed chambers "de claris mulieribus" which the *Legend* is meant to complete, the clearcut division "in partes" of some of the *Tales* – all these are witnesses of Chaucer's adoption of a "classical" model of narrative structure. His attempts in this direction are not very different from Boccaccio's in the *Filostrato* and the *Teseida* and in some of his late works in Latin. And the constancy with which Chaucer pursues exclusively the ends of his vernacular, discarding (unlike Gower) French and Latin, is even more extreme than Dante's passion for the "volgare," which does not stop him from writing two major works in Latin.

In the *House of Fame*, as in his *Boece*, his *Romaunt*, his adaptations and translations from French, Latin, and Italian, Chaucer shows us a fundamental aspect of his attitude as a man of letters. He is the "grand translateur" that Deschamps praised. Once more, he is not isolated in this activity, indeed he incarnates that tendency to translate and popularize which Georges Duby has seen as the culmination of the encounter between the Chivalric culture of the courts and the clerical culture of the schools which took place in fourteenth-century Europe.[16]

Significant examples of this tendency are to be found in England, and in all fields. Trevisa translates Bartholomaeus Anglicus's encyclopedia, the *De Proprietatibus Rerum*, and Higden's history, the *Polychronicon*. Mannyng translates Langtoft's *Chronicle* and adapts William of Wadington's *Manuel des Pechiez*. Others translate Jacobus de Voragine's *Legenda Aurea*, the *Travels* of a mysterious Sir John Mandeville. Still others adapt the *Seven Sages of Rome,* or French romances like Chrétien's *Yvain.* Some translate the *Mystica Theologia* of Dionysius the Areopagite (*Deonise Hid Divinite*), and offer summaries or adaptations of works by Richard of St. Victor and St. Bernard (*A Tretyse of þe Stodye of Wisdome* and *A Tretis of Discrescyon of Spirites*). Wyclif and his circle, finally, dare to begin to translate the Bible itself. And Wyclif, a famous Oxford master, is a protégé of John of Gaunt no less than is Chaucer.

The Temple, in other words, can be seen as the image of a flourishing literature, linked to the classical past, even ready, to a certain extent, for its "revival," its "renaissance," but also prepared to popularize, to translate, to mediate, to adapt itself to new needs. The desert which surrounds the Temple is the sandy waste around Carthage in the *Aeneid,* and also the desert of Mandeville. Nor is it surprising that the eagle the dreamer sees in the sky should be derived [202] from Dante, the greatest figure in what must have been for Chaucer the literary avant-garde of his century.

With the Flight through Space which the eagle imposes on the protagonist a new horizon opens up for the poet. This is of course a journey and it will follow the pattern of travel literature: not, however, the exotic literature of pilgrimages and travels to the East, but that of the voyage to the center of things, where man discovers the hidden order of the universe. It will be the literature of philosophical visions: the *Cosmographia* of Bernardus Silvestris, the *Anticlaudianus* of Alanus (which Chaucer mentions in the *House of Fame*), Dante's descent and ascent through the cosmos in the *Comedy* (of which the *Inferno* is explicitly recalled and *Purgatorio* and *Paradiso* imitated). It is again significant that Geoffrey should see the Galaxy draw near and the Earth fade to a point as the "ayerissh bestes" – clouds, rain, snow – are formed and generated.[17] His journey is suspended between the two worlds of natural philosophy and mysticism.

Once more, Chaucer appears to be an extraordinarily sensitive observer and interpreter of the general trends of English culture in the fourteenth century. After William of Ockham, who limits the field of action in theology, the two dominating tendencies in English (and not just English) philosophy and religion seem to center precisely on "science" on the one hand and mysticism on the other, as if philosophers felt they could no longer safely venture into the traditional realm of metaphysics.[18] It is natural philosophy that makes decisive progress in fourteenth-century England. The Merton "scientists," the "barbari Britanni" despised by Petrarch and the Italian humanists,[19] work on matter and space, mechanics and dynamics, and elaborate a mathematical physics.[20] Swineshead, Heytesbury, Burley, Bradwardine (the scientist, theologian and archbishop whom Chaucer recalls in the *Nun's Priest's Tale*), Strode (the "philosopher" to whom Chaucer dedicates *Troilus*) are but the best known names.[21] During the Flight the eagle significantly expounds a physics of sound, speaking by logical deduction and promising a "preve by experience." And "experience," which in Chaucer's works is constantly opposed to "authority," has played an important part in English medieval philosophy (setting the tone for future empiricism) ever since Grosseteste laid the foundations of experimental science and Bacon elaborated its theory: "nulla scientia sine experientia."[22]

Chaucer himself was interested in science (as all his works show, he had a good knowledge of astronomy, alchemy, and medicine at least) and in popularizing it, in making it available to those who, like "lyte Lowys" his son, cannot read Latin.[23] But in the *House of* [203] *Fame* Chaucer refuses to listen to the eagle when he offers to launch on a lecture in astronomy and astrology even though his guide explicitly links knowledge of "sterres names" and "hevenes sygnes" to "poetrie" (993–1010). He protests that he is too old, that he believes "hem that write of this matere," and finally that stars are too bright here to be looked at. Though this accumulation of excuses makes for an overall comic effect, it is clear that Chaucer, while acquainted with the literature on the subject,[24] sets a precise limit on the kind of scientific-didactic literature that the eagle would impose on him. He will not be a Dante.

On the other hand, Chaucer is tempted by mysticism. At one point in his Flight, he does not know whether he is there "in body or in gost," a phrase which echoes St. Paul's second Letter to the Corinthians (12:2–4) and shows that Chaucer seems to be thinking of himself as ready for a *raptus* similar to that of the Apostle. A few lines earlier, moreover, he had quoted Boethius's "Thought" which "may flee so hye, / Wyth fetheres of Philosophye, / To passen everych element" (*De Consolatione*, IV, m. 1). Chaucer is alluding to the two ways in which a man can try to attain a vision of God – the purely mystical one, experienced by St. Paul, and the philosophical one, which Boethius describes at the beginning of Book IV of the *Consolatio*. Nor can we exclude the possibility that Dante's beatific vision at the end of the *Paradiso*, the supreme example of how poetry can tackle such a theme, and one well known by Chaucer, is on the poet's mind at this point.[25]

Here again Chaucer is a man of his time and of his country. English poetry, too, attempts a description of the "gostly drem" with the splendid lunar landscape and the shining Heavenly Jerusalem of *Pearl*. English mysticism goes far beyond this in the fourteenth century. It shows the ways which interior spiritual discipline must follow so that the soul may gradually abandon itself to the union with God, and it does this with powerful images and a beautiful prose. Fire, song, and sweetness are the three characteristics of contemplative life for Richard Rolle, the famous mystic who had been a student at Oxford, became a hermit, and wrote commentaries on the Bible and religious lyrics. The image of the cloud dominates the writings of an anonymous author who follows the theology of Dionysius the Areopagite: for him, man is suspended between the cloud of unknowing and the cloud of forgetting, between the intellect's ignorance of God and the senses' oblivion of things created. For Walter Hilton, the scale of perfection, divided into the two stages of purification "in faith" and "in feeling," is characterized by the "dark night" in which the soul detaches itself from earthly things [204] and moves towards those of the spirit. And finally, in 1373 Julian of Norwich has sixteen "revelations," by bodily sight, by words, and by "ghostly" sight.[26]

The dreams, the visions of which Chaucer speaks in the Proem to the *House of Fame* (7–8 and 33–35) can be of this kind, too. Geoffrey, however, does not take up this opportunity. He avoids mysticism and makes once more a decidedly secular choice. The eagle invites him to "lat be" his "fantasye." Geoffrey does not altogether reject philosophy and philosophical poetry. He does indeed seem to choose for himself the kind of philosophical poetry represented by Alanus and Boethius (972 and 986). Yet just at this point (985) he also mentions Martianus Capella and thus significantly celebrates Philology – grammar and *literature* – with all the liberal arts.

What Chaucer has the eagle promise him at the beginning of the Flight are, on the other hand, "tydynges ... of love" and information about the real world, both "fro fer contree" and from his "verray neyghebores." Chaucer evokes here the primary muse of his inspiration, Love, which has made him compose "bookys, songes, dytees" and which is an endless source of literary material, of fictions and poetry (672–98). Love inspires the young Chaucer and his friend Gower, their colleagues on the Continent and the authors of countless "courtly" or "popular" lyrics. It is the love of Troilus and Criseyde, of Petrarch for Laura, of Usk's *Testament* – love, the literary universe *par excellence* of the Middle Ages.

At the same time Chaucer shows himself ready to look upon the world of reality. He points with self-irony to the life of bureaucrat and passionate reader that he lives and seems to pay a new attention to his neighbors and all human kind, moving away from books. We shall see where this readiness will lead him in the *House of Fame*. Meanwhile we arrive with Geoffrey and the eagle at the House itself. Significantly, this is called both "castel" (1161) and "paleys" (1398). And indeed the great fortresses of fourteenth–century European aristocrats were both castles closed to the outside world, strongholds built to defend barons and their retinues, and manifestations of their pride and prestige, of what Georges Duby has called "possession du monde."[27] Inside they are palaces, the places where courts meet and entertain themselves with feasts, games, erotic and chivalric fictions. It is this kind of Castle-Palace that appears to Geoffrey – as fantastic as the castle of Bercilak in *Sir Gawain* or as those which the Limbourg brothers were to illuminate for the Duke de Berry in his *Très Riches Heures*.

Around and inside his Castle-Palace Geoffrey finds heralds, coats of arms, the "chevalrie" of Africa, Europe, and Asia, the "armes" of [205] Alexander and Hercules, the "olde gestes" – in short, all "le donne e' cavalier, li affanni e li agi, / che ne 'nvogliava amore e cortesia" (*Purgatorio*, XIV, 109–10), all the tales onto which medieval man projects his wishes. The dreams of adventure and mystery which people these tales are full of forests, fortuitous encounters, duels, tournaments, castles, queens, enchanted swords, the Grail, the faeries. Is it by chance that Geoffrey sees here the harpers, Orion, Chiron, Orpheus, and "Bret Glascurion"? There is more than one connection between the harp, Orpheus, and the Celtic substrata of English medieval culture. One of the manuscripts of *Sir Orfeo*, the beautiful, enchanted fourteenth-century poem, maintains that the Bretons used to take their harps and sing stories of adventure and above all of love.[28] *Sir Orfeo* itself is a lay and, like *Sir Launfal*, it is dominated by the world of faeries, from which Orfeo, here a minstrel and a harper, frees Heurodis.

And it is the world of the minstrels and the "gestiours" that Geoffrey contemplates around the Castle. The "mynstralles" who "tellen tales / Both of wepinge and of game" are the creators (perhaps), the reciters (certainly) of ballads, interludes, fabliaux. They are the "jongleurs" who fill the halls of medieval lords and enliven their feasts, like Archambaut's in the Provençal *Flamenca*.[29] These are the ballads of Robin Hood, of Adam Bell, of Glasgerion (Chaucer's "Glascurion"),[30] comic tales of foxes and wolves, of clerks and procuresses, parodies of Paradise, of the "Land of Cockaygne." They are accompanied by music, dances, carols, "cornemuse" and "shalemyes," pipes, horns, trumpets. Geoffrey hears them now (1214–68); Richard II must have listened to them at Kennington, in 1377, when the Commons of London offered him a mumming show.[31] There are "love-daunces, sprynges, / Reyes" (1235–36), carols such as the famous "Blow, northerne wynd," roundels such as the one the birds sing at the end of Chaucer's *Parliament*: "Now welcome, somer, with thy sonne softe." There are jugglers, magicians, illusionists, sorceresses, witches (1259–81). In short, we have here all the pre-literary, paraliterary, peri-literary universe of the feast, of Carnival, Bakhtin's Carnival, Le Roy Ladurie's Winter Festival.[32]

The more specifically literary nature of Chaucer's dream, however, comes increasingly to the fore. Chaucer seems to accept with joy and without prejudice this world shared by aristocratic castle and popular market–place (interestingly, he omits any reference to mystery plays), and which is so distant from the Temple and its *Aeneid*. But he will soon return to literature proper. Together with the clarion players of Aragon and Catalonia, he introduces the trumpeters of the "great tradition": Virgil's Misenus, Statius's Thiodomas, [206] the biblical Joab. Inside the Castle, now significantly called Palace, Chaucer assembles novel and traditional elements, to create a completely new picture. A Virgilian and apocalyptic Fame dominates the scene. Chivalry, "olde gestes," precious decorations, gold, the *Lapidarium* surround her. The nine Muses, and in particular Calliope, the Muse of sublime poetry, sing her praises.

Chaucer is the first English poet to invoke the Muses, here in the *House of Fame*.[33] It is significant that he owes this to the example of Dante and Boccaccio, the two vernacular poets who thus act as intermediaries between him and classical tradition. And Dante and Boccaccio find their places in the poetic pantheon of the *House of Fame*, in the literary universe of fourteenth-century England. The Inferno, mentioned here by Chaucer (450), is on the same level as Virgil's Avernus and Claudian's Hades, and Dante himself will be recalled by Chaucer's friend, Gower.[34] Boccaccio, here called "Lollius," is celebrated with Homer and the other writers of Troy (1468). "Laureat" Petrarch is shortly to come to the attention of the poet and of his king.[35] England is the first country to become acquainted, and through her greatest poet, with the greatest writers of Italy.

By invoking Parnassus and Helicon, the Muses and Apollo, Chaucer implicitly indicates that he considers himself the heir of the Ancients and presents his candidacy for the place of "sesto tra cotanto senno" which Dante had been accorded by the great poets of Antiquity in his Castle of Limbo. Once more indirectly, but more explicitly than in the *House of Fame*, Chaucer will do this at the end of his greatest romance, *Troilus* (V, 1791–92). Here, Geoffrey contemplates in Fame's hall the great writers of the past and their "matters": Josephus Flavius and seven other Jewish authors, Statius and Thebes, the writers of Troy, Virgil and Aeneas, Ovid and Love, Lucan and Rome, Claudian and Hell. Myth and history, history and poetry, truth and "fable" are thus placed on the same level. Chaucer shows himself aware of this when, picking up a traditional medieval rumor, he humorously remarks:

> But yet I gan ful wel espie,
> Betwex hem was a litil envye.
> Oon seyde that Omer made *lyes*,
> *Feynynge in hys poetries*,
> And was to Grekes favorable;
> Therfor held he hyt but *fable*.
>
> (1475–80, italics mine)

For what interests Chaucer here is not a clearly demarcated distinction between historical truth and poetic fiction but the *imaginaire*, [207] as Georges Duby would call it, of the whole West. It is the image of himself that Western man has consecrated and transmitted in his entire literary tradition that Chaucer sees on the metal pillars of Fame's hall.[36] The case of Troy, whose fame is so heavy "That for to bere hyt was no game," is emblematic. Homer is the founding father, and he is followed by Dares and Dictys, by Guido delle Colonne and Boccaccio ("Lollius"), and finally by Geoffrey of Monmouth. "Englyssh Gaufride" has brought the Trojan cycle to Britain, where Brutus, grandson of Aeneas, "settez wyth wynne," as the *Gawain*-poet says, "siþen þe sege and þe assaut watz sesed at Troye." Troy (whose haunting presence is felt also in Statius's *Achilleid*, alluded to by Chaucer in lines 1462–63) survives, through Aeneas and Virgil's poem, in that Rome whose "grete werkes" Lucan and other "clerkes" have sung, that Rome which is New Troy, like London in the fourteenth-century English *St. Erkenwald* (line 25). The shadow of Troy dominates Western imagination, as Foscolo was to realize four centuries after Chaucer: "finché il Sole risplenderà su le sciagure umane" (*Dei Sepolcri*, 295). Chaucer himself will pay his great tribute to the Trojan cycle with his *Troilus*. In the same manner, and once more following Boccaccio, he will put in his Knight's mouth a tale which is also an episode of the Theban cycle.

Chaucer's stroke of genius in the *House of Fame* consists in having painted such a wide and interwoven picture of literature and culture in one panel. "Jewerye," the other great branch of Western tradition, is celebrated side by side with Troy and Rome. War, "olde mervayles," Love, and Hell are all parts of the *imaginaire*. Chaucer's choices, however (except for "Lollius") are not uncommon among English intellectuals of the fourteenth century, for example among people as diverse as Gower and Bishop Reed. Some illustrious names – for instance those of Theocritus, Pindar, Lucretius, and Sallust, who are mentioned by Richard de Bury in his *Philobiblon* (X, 35–40) – are even absent from Chaucer's list. De Bury, however, had been to Avignon, had met Petrarch there and had perhaps breathed the pre-humanistic atmosphere around him. In *his* "House of Fame," the *Triumphus Fame* inspired by Boccaccio's *Amorosa Visione*, Petrarch is much more thorough, more precise, and more historically conscious than Chaucer. We find in his garden all the heroes of Roman and Greek history and of ancient myth, all the great characters of the Old Testament, and then Arthur, Charlemagne, Godfrey of Bouillon, Saladin, even Henry of Lancaster, but above all philosophers, historians, orators, and poets of that world of Greece and Rome which Petrarch and his friends wanted to recover.

Chaucer is more limited, more insular, less extreme, yet probably [208] more representative of the average culture of his time. The *House of Fame* is the literary universe of a fourteenth-century Englishman with a rich cultural formation. These are his songs, his music, his tales; these, above all, his books. When, after a day of "labour," of "rekenynges," Geoffrey returns home, he sits, "also domb as any stoon," "at another *book*." It is this obsessive and slightly ridiculous bibliophily (not very different from that of Richard de Bury) that the eagle's mission purports to correct, offering instead "tydynges" of the real world and of love.

To find these, Geoffrey goes down a valley under the Castle and reaches the House of Rumor. Chaucer dissolves the Temple and the Palace into the twigs, the holes, the sounds of this gigantic Whirling Wicker. He himself declares that it is made more "wonderlych" and "queyntelych" than the House of Daedalus, the original Labyrinth. Here at last literature as such is not present. The *House of Fame* has its own way of de-composing a work of literature. This appears as a comprehensive, unitary "opus" in the *Aeneid* of the first Book. It becomes fragmented in the great "matters," the cycles and their individual authors of the second Book. In the third, it is atomized into the many "tydynges" which fill the House of Rumor and which are spoken or carried around by messengers, pardoners, shipmen, and pilgrims.

It will eventually be Geoffrey's task to put these very messengers, pardoners, shipmen, and pilgrims on the way from the Tabard Inn to Becket's tomb, to make them tell their tidings, their tales, in short to write a book of stories told orally, the *Canterbury Tales*. Thus the image, the intuition of a re-composed "opus" which will include oral and written, reality and fiction, "ernest" and "game," begins to take shape behind the Whirling Wicker of the *House of Fame*. This design which we can only see *a posteriori* will not, significantly, be fully realized. Like the *House of Fame*, the Canterbury Tales will remain incomplete.

II

For the moment, let us concentrate on the labyrinthine cage of Rumor into which Geoffrey and the eagle have led us. So far, I have illustrated only a part of my title, dealing with those aspects of fourteenth-century culture and literature which Chaucer takes into consideration in the *House* of *Fame*. Chaucer looks at them – classical literature, epic poem, mythology, scientific culture, mysticism, philosophical and didactic poetry, love literature, minstrelsy, music, the traditional "matters" – with great interest, but he nevertheless [209] discards them one by one. He accepts them as a whole, as the necessary components of his image of poetry, but he refuses to follow any of their single paths exclusively. His subsequent career, from the *Parliament* to *Troilus*, the *Legend*, and the *Tales*, will show that he held fast to the decision he made in the *House of Fame*.

In the House of Rumor Chaucer finally seems to abandon the world of literature and to tackle reality. The transition is not at all easy, and in describing it Chaucer reveals to us one of the fundamental problems he examines in Book III and through the whole *House of Fame*. From here, therefore, we begin a second exploration of the poem, going backwards from its end to its beginning.

Still outside the Whirling Wicker, Geoffrey hears all sorts of sounds: "rounynges," "jangles," "whisprynges," tidings. The list of their subjects occupies fifteen lines (1961–76). They comprise the whole world of man and of nature, from war, peace, and marriage, to life and death, winds and storms, "qwalm of folk, and eke of bestes," to fire and "dyvers accident."[37] Significantly enough, all transcendental and metaphysical subjects, such as God, hell, and paradise and being, matter, and the like, are excluded. Chaucer has indeed abandoned literature for reality. Yet what he contemplates here is not reality as such, as it *exists* in the sublunary world, or as it *is* in the hyperuranian universe of being, but as it is *told*. Geoffrey does not find war, but tidings of war. And these tidings, these rumors, are equally composed of "fals and soth": in passing from mouth to mouth they grow, "encresing ever moo," each becoming "more than hit ever was." Reality as told is different from reality as it existed before it was told.

The House of Rumor, which Chaucer himself compares to a labyrinth, is then an enormous warehouse of tidings, of "mythoi,"[38] a "mytho-theca" of Babel, the medieval, and oral, equivalent of Borges's "Biblio-theca," the "universe (which others call the Library)."[39] There is no reality here, but only its oral sign, or rather the oral signs of its single events as grouped in categories ("werres," not the Hundred Years War). It is a reality fragmented and transformed into its narrative sign. Moreover, it is inextricably (2103–37) composed of true and false, an anamorphosis beyond human control.

In this context, the image of the labyrinth which Chaucer uses for the House of Rumor becomes particularly interesting, not only because of its Borgesian reminiscences, but above all for its medieval implications. Chaucer's

Whirling Wicker encompasses the whole world, transformed into tidings. An inscription on an eleventh-century labyrinth in St. Savino at Piacenza declares that *"hunc mundum tipice* Laberinthus denotat iste,"[40] and a Christian's life is compared [210] to a labyrinth in an inscription at the Museum in Lyons.[41] Yet the labyrinth is also an image of the artist's activity, "Domus Dedaly," as Chaucer says, the house of that Daedalus who, as his Joycean descendant well knew, is the astute builder, the supreme artificer,[42] the ancestor of those medieval architects who at times celebrated themselves by inserting their portraits in the labyrinths on the floors of the cathedrals they had built.[43] The labyrinth is a *labor-intus* (and "Laboryntus" is Chaucer's spelling), the suffering and labor which accompany intellectual and artistic work (Chaucer's "what I drye or what I thynke"). In one case, that of Eberhard the German, *Laborintus* becomes the title of a formal "Ars Poetica."[44] Above all the labyrinth, "a tortuous edifice . . . where voices always resounded"[45] as in the House of Rumor, is for Ovid (the authority from whom Chaucer adapts his description of the Whirling Wicker) the "opus" where Daedalus "confused the usual passages [turbat *notas*] and deceived the eye by a conflicting maze of divers winding paths."[46] Virgil, the poet whose presence is felt throughout the *House of Fame*, says in the *Aeneid* that the labyrinth is the "ambiguous deception of a thousand ways" where the "inextricable and unrepeatable maze makes every trace [signa sequendi] false."[47] In short, the labyrinth is an all-encompassing image – life, the world, art – dominated by confusion and error; it is the place where *signs* (Virgil's *signa*, Ovid's *notae*) are lost, unrecognizable, undecipherable, where they become false like Chaucer's tidings.

Two strictly intertwined, fundamental themes emerge from Chaucer's description of the House of Rumor. The first concerns the origin of narrative, which is basically oral and has its roots in reports, rumors, chatter. These are the raw material of tales – events, sayings, facts, forecasts, hearsay (2047–54) – which immediately become true and false. The second is the relationship between reality, truth, and words. The elementary constituents of narrative, the tidings, are given by Chaucer's imagination a corporeal reality: they have wings and escape from the House of Rumor through its windows or crevices in the walls. They are concrete and they mirror the world of nature, of animals and men. But they are governed by Chance ("Aventure, / That is the moder of tydynges"), and they are distorted in their development from their primeval being, amplified until they are about to explode (2065–80). It is at this point that the tiding, until now true *or* false (2072), is joined to its contrary and leaves the House inextricably true *and* false (2087–2109). Reality, now concrete only inasmuch as it is spoken, is truth no more. Transformed into oral narrative, it is the daughter of Chance.[48] Such a [211] "modern" image of literature is not to be found elsewhere in the English and European fourteenth century.

Composed of true and false, the tidings fly from the House of Rumor to the House of Fame. Here Fame herself gives them "name" and "duracioun," and Aeolus blows them about, "Wynged wondres, . . . / Twenty thousand in a route" (2110–20). In other words, the primary elements of narrative, already removed from reality and truth, whipped around in the labyrinth of Rumor, dominated by Chance, are somehow ordered by Fame and spread all over the world by her ministers. Fame is Fortune's sister (1547), she is voluble, unjust (or beyond justice, 1820), unforeseeable; but she is not Chance, and above all her praises are sung by the Muses and her importance is celebrated by the writers who stand on the metal pillars in her hall. The Castle-Palace of Fame works like a clearing station. On the one side, the tidings enter it, are summarily ordered and blown out again. On the other, the "matters" of the great narrative poems are consecrated in the presence of the Muses, that is to say of inspiration. At the entrance, minstrels tell sad or happy tales; inside the coats of arms belonging to famous people from the entire world are exhibited (1197–1200 and 1336–40). In short, the great "matters" of poetry, the humble tales of storytellers, the emblems of famous men meet in the House of Fame. Poetry, narrative, and their materials are fused and melted there all the time.

More, however, is to be found in the House of Fame. Chaucer says that everything is amplified by the walls of beryl (1290–92). Once more, reality, its truth dissolved, is distorted into mere appearance. Moreover, it has two faces. On the one hand, the world of gold and "babewynnes" (as many as the flakes which fall "in grete snowes") mirrors the universe of dreams, of literary imagination – the idealized and sublimated reality which medieval "high" culture constantly projects around itself. On the other hand, "popular" art is represented by minstrels and musicians, while sorcerers and clerks who know "magik naturel" make "ymages" by which they transform reality with craft. High or low, bad or good, this is the world of the arti-ficial, of the arti-fact, of that "craft" which, following in the footsteps of old Daedalus, "countrefeteth kynde" (1213).[49]

In this context it is not surprising that the written signs of reality, the letters of the names inscribed on one side of the mountain, should be melted away, unreadable, while on the other side the shadow keeps writing fresh (1140–45 and 1151–64). This is the effect of Fame's action: it once more shows the two-faced nature of the linguistic sign – the sign employed by poetry.

If we take another step backwards, we shall see that this field of [212] language is carefully explored by Chaucer. During their flight, the eagle explains two things to Geoffrey: first, how words are generated; second, how they reach the House of Fame. Be it "lowd or pryvee, foul or fair," a word ("speche") is air "in his substaunce" (*substantialiter*), for a word is made of sound, and sound "ys noght but eyr ybroken." "Philosophi definiunt, vocem esse aerem tenuissimum ictum," Priscian and the other grammarians maintained.[50] The eagle, then, explains to Geoffrey the physical nature of words, gives him a short lecture on physiological linguistics. But a word is not only sound, *vox*; it is, as people knew from antiquity, something more. Dante had put it very clearly:

Hoc equiden signum [the linguistic sign, a word] est ipsum subiectum nobile de quo loquimur: nam sensuale quid est in quantum sonus est; rationale vero in quantum aliquid significare videtur ad placitum.[51]

A *dictio*, a word, says Michel de Marbais echoing Priscian, "includit in se vocem tamquam sibi materiam et rationem significandi tamquam sibi formam."[52] But what is meaning, *significatio*? As Petrus Hispanus had said and as the Modistae repeat with variations, it is the relationship between a sign (in language, a word) and what it signifies,[53] for instance between the word "man" and a man.[54] The problem lies in the way a real thing (a man) becomes a human verbal expression (the word "man"). It is a problem which involves gnoseology and logic, and which was hotly discussed in Antiquity and throughout the Middle Ages. England in particular contributed to the philosophy of language with men of the caliber of St. Anselm, John of Salisbury, Roger Bacon, and Robert Kilwardby. The last two anticipated several positions subsequently held by the Modistae. However, I shall not go through the history of the variations which the two fundamental theories on the subject (the idea of words as signs of intramental concepts and that of words as signs of extramental realities) underwent in the medieval period,[55] but shall instead briefly illustrate two ways of approaching the problem which can help us place Chaucer's quest in its appropriate context.[56]

The Modistae, the authors of the so-called "speculative grammars" of the thirteenth century, explain the passage from real things to human words in the following manner:

> Things possess various properties or modes of being (modi essendi). The mind apprehends these properties by means of the active modes of understanding (modi intelligendi activi) and they thus become the qualities of things as apprehended [213] by the mind (modi intelligendi passivi); the mind imposes on noises (voces) certain active modes of meaning (modi significandi activi) which become the qualities of things as signified by words (modi significandi passivi), thus completing the scale beginning with the thing and ending with its expression.[57]

Human intellect is at the center of the entire process by which a *vox* (sound), with the addition of meaning, becomes *dictio* (word) and then *pars orationis* (part of speech).

We have already seen how the eagle expounds the physical nature of words to Geoffrey. When, a little later, bird and man reach the place where they can actually see the House of Fame, Geoffrey asks his guide whether the noise he hears is produced by people on earth and comes here as the eagle has explained before, and whether any "body," that is, concrete physical person, lives in the Palace. The eagle replies that he has already revealed how words reach the House of Fame: by propagation. But as soon as a word ("speche") reaches the Palace, it becomes like the person who has pronounced that word on earth:

> And hath so verray hys lyknesse
> That spak the word, that thou wilt gesse
> That it the same body be. . . .

(1079–81)

Whether or not he knows the Modistae, it is evident that Chaucer is here exploring the field and problem of meaning, that is to say of the relationship between a sign and what it means. And he expresses this relationship by an ambiguous word, "lyknesse" – similarity, not identity.[58]

The Castle-Palace of Fame can, then, be seen as a sort of gigantic intellect, which apprehends the properties of things and gives them intellectual quality, imposes meaning on sounds and transforms them into words. Fame herself is indeed endowed with infinite eyes, *ears*, and *tongues* and reaches the earth on one side and heaven on the other. Yet this monstrous intellect distorts things, beryl makes them look bigger than they have ever been ("As kynde thyng of Fames is"). The words, spoken or written, of poetry are "similar" to reality, and yet different, more complex than reality itself.

The problem, however, does not involve literature – verbal art – alone. It regards all signs, all words, and human knowledge. The intrinsic characteristic of "lyknesse" lies in its being unquantifiable, its ambiguity. If words are not identical with reality, if post-babelic [24] *voces* are not *specula* of *res*,[59] – if, as Chaucer himself said (*Lak of Stedfastnesse*, 4–5), "word and deed . . . Ben nothing lyk" – what are they, how do they work, what are they worth? I think that these are some of the questions Chaucer asks himself in the *House of Fame*. And it is not strange that a fourteenth-century Englishman should do so.

England is the home of William of Ockham, the "Venerabilis Inceptor," the philosopher whom Boccaccio, in Italy, singled out as a paragon of logic.[60] And Ockham's whole *Summa Logicae* is devoted to a purely logical analysis of language as a self-contained system of signs. Though it cannot avoid facing gnoseological and epistemological problems,[61] the *Summa* is, thus, a work profoundly different from those of the Modistae. For Ockham, linguistic signs (*termini*) are of three kinds, written (*scriptus*), oral (*prolatus*), and mental (*conceptus*). The first two possess a certain physical substance; concepts, the third, are *intentiones* or *passiones* of the soul. *Termini scripti* and *prolati* acquire meaning by voluntary decision and can change it; the *conceptus* has a meaning *naturaliter*, and this cannot be changed. All, however, designate an object directly, although oral and written terms do so only because concepts have already signified the object "naturally."[62] Concepts are "natural" signs, born of a "spontaneous, psychosomatic reaction" of man. They are not "mental representations"; "they do not reproduce external reality on the intellectual level." As signs, they are "naked intellections."[63]

A sign, says Ockham, is that which makes something be known ("facit in cognitionem venire") and which is born to stand for it ("pro illo *supponere*") or to be added to it in a proposition.[64]

Propositions are the primary linguistic units, and the *suppositio* can only occur in a proposition. But there are various kinds of *suppositio*. In the sentence "every man is an animal," we have a *suppositio personalis*, because "man" directly signifies single real men. In the proposition "man is a species," we have a *suppositio simplex*: here, the term "man" does not stand for an existing reality, but for a conceptual linguistic sign ("species," which is an *intentio animae*). The *suppositio materialis* regards the arbitrary sign, the oral or written term ("quando terminus . . . supponit vel pro voce vel pro scripto"). For instance, in "man is a name," "man" stands for itself, that is, for the oral term "man." In "man is written," "man" stands for what is written.[65] "What we write are not the single existing things, but terms–graphemes."[66]

Truth and falsehood are properties of the proposition. Truth is not – as Thomas Aquinas would maintain – "adaequatio intellectus [215] et rei." What makes a proposition true is a coincidence of *suppositio* between subject and predicate. In the proposition "this is an angel,"

> non denotatur quod hic habeat angelitatem vel quod in isto sit angelitas vel aliquid huiusmodi, sed denotatur quod hic sit vere angelus; non quidem quod sit illud praedicatum, sed quod sit illud pro quo supponit praedicatum.[67]

Ockham's "metalinguistic" analysis – his view of words, signs, and concepts within the framework of the intramental *modus significandi* – operated on a highly technical level, and his friends and enemies[68] were also formal logicians and philosophers who used a very precise, sophisticated system of thought. Chaucer would find it difficult, if not, given his more traditional background, impossible, to follow them on their own ground. It is, however, significant that he should ask himself certain questions and that he should have doubts about the "suppositive" value of words. And we should not be surprised to see him find not things but tidings, that is reports, linguistic molecules. We should not wonder why what is true or false is the "sawe" (2089) – a saying, a speech (a *dictio*? a *propositio*?). Fame gives tidings their "duracioun" and above all their "name"; and if "name" means "reputation," there is no doubt that it also means what we all understand by "name" – *nomen*. Chaucer's Fame imposes names like Adam in Genesis. But whereas he gave name to things, she gives name to words and tidings. Chaucer's "Goddesse of Renoun" is a Fame-Language.

Earlier on, Geoffrey asks the eagle whether the noise he hears comes from people on earth and whether there is any "body" living in the House and making "al this loude fare." Is this a case of *suppositio personalis*? And are the letters inscribed on the sides of the Castle a case of *suppositio materialis*? If words, upon reaching the Palace, become "lyk the same wight / Which that the word in erthe spak" and have "so verray hys lyknesse / That spak the word, that thou wilt gesse / That it the same body be," what exactly are the minstrels, the magicians, the coats of arms, the Muses, Fame, the poets, Aeolus? Are they, as Prospero would say, "all spirits," or, as Ockham might put it, *termini concepti, intentiones animae*? Are "the gorgeous palaces" and the "solemn temples" which fill the *House of Fame* but a "baseless fabric" of Chaucer's vision?

What is certain is that in the Castle of Fame great poetic and historical cycles, minstrels' tales, written characters, news, rumors, reports, words, and sounds are simultaneously composed and de-composed. The story of Aeneas, the "Aeneid" narrated in the first part of the *House of Fame* is, then, the Book itself as Tale or narra[216]tive *in toto*. This Book contains all the tidings heard by Geoffrey in the House of Rumor and narrated in Virgil's *Aeneid* – wars, peace, journeys, love, storms, jealousy, famine, fire, life, and death – and Fame herself.[69]

The roots of Chaucer's inspiration in the *House of Fame* are indeed bookish and literary: Fame comes from the *Aeneid*, the eagle from Dante, Rumor from Ovid. The Book is at the beginning (the *Aeneid*) and at the center (the books of the great writers); it will be at the end, when pilgrims, pardoners, and shipmen will narrate the *Canterbury Tales*. The universe is indeed, as Borges would say, the Library – a *biblio-theca*, a *mytho-theca*, a *logo-theca* – dominated in turn by art (the Temple), Nature (the Flight), Fortune (the Castle), and Chance (the Whirling Wicker).

It is no wonder that in the Proem Chaucer should ironically ask what the causes of dreams are – physiology, environment, character, study, melancholy, fear, contemplation, love's labors, spirits, foresight. What gives a poet his inspiration? What makes him a poet? And what are words, reality, truth, the human mind? Chaucer seems to avoid answering these questions when he replies, "God turne us every drem to goode!" (1 and 58). But he does much more than this. As we have seen, he reviews his whole cultural and literary background, making decisive choices and speaking about art and language. He presents himself as a Daedalus figure. "Ignotas animum dimittit in artes":[70] like Daedalus, Chaucer builds a Temple, a Palace, and a Labyrinth. His Flight is compared to that of the Athenian architect (919), and Geoffrey "countrefeteth kynde" by writing a poem which is a maze where signs are lost and confused. The *House of Fame* is indeed A Portrait of Geoffrey as a Young Man. At the end we are back at our beginning, and Chaucer was perfectly right in telling us that never since he was born, and no one before him, had anyone had such a wonderful dream as he on that tenth day of December.

Notes

I am glad to acknowledge my debt to Patrick Boyde, Marcia L. Colish, Peter Dronke, Jill Mann, and Sergio Rufini for having made useful suggestions at various stages of my work on this essay.

1 L. K. Shook, "The House of Fame," in *Companion to Chaucer Studies*, ed. Beryl Rowland, rev. ed. (Oxford: Oxford Univ. Press, 1979), p. 417.
2 J. A. W. Bennett, *Chaucer's Book of Fame* (Oxford: Clarendon Press, 1968), p. xi.
3 See A. C. Spearing, *Medieval Dream-Poetry* (Cambridge, Engl.: Cambridge Univ. Press, 1976).

4 J. A. W. Bennett, "Chaucer's Contemporary," *The Humane Medievalist and Other Essays* (Rome: Edizioni di Storia e Letteratura, 1982), ed. Piero Boitani, pp. 13–29.

5 See Jean Seznec, *The Survival of the Pagan Gods* (Princeton: Princeton [217] Univ. Press, 1972). Myth survives in love poetry, both in Latin and the vernacular. See, for instance, Frederick Goldin, *The Mirror of Narcissus in the Courtly Love Lyric* (Ithaca: Cornell Univ. Press, 1967), and John Block Friedman, *Orpheus in the Middle Ages* (Cambridge, Mass.: Harvard Univ. Press, 1970).

6 See Piero Boitani, "Chaucer's Temples of Venus," *Studi Inglesi*, 2 (1975), 9–31, and references therein.

7 See Beryl Smalley, *English Friars and Antiquity in the Early Fourteenth Century* (Oxford: Blackwell, 1960).

8 See Hans Liebeschütz, *Medieval Humanism in the Life and Writings of John of Salisbury* (New York: Kraus Reprint, 1980), and D. A. Callus, "Robert Grosseteste as Scholar," in *Robert Grosseteste*, ed. D. A. Callus (Oxford: Clarendon, 1955), pp. 36–37 and notes.

9 *Familiares*, III, i, 4–6, in Francesco Petrarca, *Opere*, I, ed. M. Martelli (Florence: Sansoni, 1975).

10 *Philobiblon*, VIII, 20–48 (ed. A. Altamura [Naples: Fiorentino, 1954], pp. 99–100. J. A. W. Bennett also mentions Bishop William Reed as an important book collector and donor: *Chaucer at Oxford and at Cambridge* (Oxford: Oxford Univ. Press, 1974), pp. 65 ff.

11 For Virgil in the Middle Ages see Domenico Comparetti, *Vergil in the Middle Ages*, trans. E. F. M. Benecke (London: George Allen & Unwin, 1966).

12 All citations of Chaucer's text will be from F. N. Robinson, ed., *The Works of Geoffrey Chaucer*, 2nd ed. (Boston: Houghton Mifflin, 1957).

13 Bennett, *Chaucer's Book of Fame*, p. 29.

14 See William W. Rydyng, *Structure in Medieval Narrative* (The Hague: Mouton, 1971).

15 See Eugène Vinaver, *The Rise of Romance* (Oxford: Clarendon Press, 1971), pp. 68 ff.

16 Georges Duby, *Le Temps des Cathédrales* (Paris: Gallimard, 1976), pp. 241–45.

17 See Bennett, *Chaucer's Book of Fame*, pp. 52–99; and, for the presence of Alanus and Bernardus in Chaucer, Peter Dronke, "Chaucer and the Medieval Latin Poets (Part A)," in *Geoffrey Chaucer*, ed. Derek Brewer (London: G. Bell & Sons, 1974), pp. 154–72, esp. 161–64.

18 This, of course, does not mean that theology is altogether abandoned. See Gordon Leff, *Bradwardine and the Pelagians* (Cambridge, Engl.: University Press, 1957); J. A. Robson, *Wyclif and the Oxford Schools* (Cambridge, Engl.: University Press, 1961); Gordon Leff, *The Dissolution of the Medieval Outlook* (New York: Harper & Row, 1976).

19 E. Garin, "La cultura fiorentina nella seconda metà del '300 e i 'barbari britanni,'" *Rassegna della Letteratura Italiana*, 64 (1960), 181–95.

20 See A. C. Crombie, *Augustine to Galileo* (Harmondsworth: Penguin, 1969), ch. 5.

21 And see Bennett, *Chaucer at Oxford*, pp. 58–85.

22 See A. C. Crombie, *Robert Grosseteste and the Origins of Experimental Science* (Oxford: Clarendon Press, 1953), ch. 7.

23 *Astrolabe*, 1–40, 50–55, 61–64. These passages represent Chaucer's most explicit statement on his choice of the vernacular. It is significant that this should be expressed at the beginning of a "scientific" treatise, and with the admission, "I n'am but a lewd compilator of the labour of olde astrologiens, and have it translatid in myn Englissh oonly for thy [his son Lewis's] doctrine," where Chaucer once more confirms his interest in translation. The *Equatorie of the Planetis*, if his, would be another instance of his dedication to science.

24 It is interesting to note that Geoffrey, as if anticipating the eagle's "preve by experience" in astronomy as well as in the physics of sound, declares that he [218] will not look on the stars because they are too bright and that he is content to rely on "authorial" tradition. This is the other extreme of the "experience-authority" polarity on which I have remarked above – and a nice contrast to Galileo's future ideas and the personal, physical tribute of blindness he paid to them.

25 See Piero Boitani, "What Dante Meant to Chaucer," in *Chaucer and the Italian Trecento*, ed. Piero Boitani (Cambridge, Engl.: University Press, 1983), pp. 115–39.

26 On the mystics see Dom David Knowles, *The English Mystical Tradition* (London: Burns & Oates, 1961), and Wolfgang Riehle, *The Middle English Mystics* (London: Routledge & Kegan Paul, 1981).

27 Duby, *Temps*, pp. 296–327, esp. pp. 308–11.

28 MS. Brit. Lib. Harley 3810, lines 1–24. See A. J. Bliss, *Sir Orfeo* (Oxford: Oxford Univ. Press, 1954).

29 See Peter Dronke, *The Medieval Lyric*, 2nd ed. (New York: Harper & Row, 1977), pp. 25–26.

30 See Thomas Percy, *Reliques of Ancient English Poetry* (London and Edinburgh, 1879), p. xxx and pp. 206–07.

31 See Richard L. Greene, ed., *A Selection of English Carols* (Oxford: Clarendon Press, 1962), p. 19, and the reference there to E. K. Chambers, *The Mediaeval Stage* (London: Oxford Univ. Press, 1967), I, 394 and n. 4.

32 Mikhail Bakhtin, *Rabelais and his World* (Cambridge, Mass.: M.I.T. Press, 1968); E. Le Roy Ladurie, *Carnival in Romans* (New York: Braziller, 1979), ch. 12. But see also F. Bruni, "Modelli in contrasto e modelli settoriali nella cultura medievale," *Strumenti Critici*, 41 (1980), 1–59, esp. 40–49.

33 See J. A. W. Bennett, "Chaucer, Dante and Boccaccio," *Chaucer and the Italian Trecento*, p. 108.

34 *Confessio Amantis*, VII, 2329–37.

35 Through a letter of Philippe de Mézières to Richard II (1395), now published by G. W. Coopland, *War, Literature, and Politics in the Late Middle Ages* (Liverpool: Liverpool Univ. Press, 1976), p. xxix and n. 53.

36 Interestingly enough, there is no specific mention here of Germanic or Anglo-Saxon legends (the "tale of Wade" is mentioned in *Troilus*, III, 614), nor of the Charlemagne chansons and romances. They could, of course, be comprised within the "olde gestes" of line 1515.

37 I have analyzed this passage in *English Medieval Narrative* (Cambridge, Engl.: Cambridge Univ. Press, 1982), pp. 164–65.

38 "Mythos" is the Greek equivalent of "tidings": it includes news, reports, rumor, fame, announcement, (oral) tale, narrative. See Liddell and Scott, *A Greek-English Lexicon*, s.v. "mythos," I, 7 and II.

39 Jorge Luis Borges, *Labyrinths* (Harmondsworth: Penguin, 1970), p. 78 ("The Library of Babel"). In the Middle Ages, the Tower of Babel is the place where human languages become confused and where the direct relationship between *res* and *voces* (*speculum*) was lost – a theme which, as we shall see, emerges earlier in the *House of Fame*. See A. Borst, *Der Turmbau von Babel; Geschichte der Meinungen über Ursprung und Vielfalt der Sprachen und Völker*, 4 vols. (Stuttgart: A. Hiersemann, 1957–63).

40 W. H. Matthews, *Mazes and Labyrinths* (1922; reprint, New York: Dover Publications, 1970), p. 57. The best study of labyrinths is H. Kern, *Labirinti* (Milan: Feltrinelli, 1981). Stimulating pages by A. B. Oliva, P. Portoghesi, and U. Eco are included in the companion volume, *Luoghi del Silenzio Imparziale*, ed. A. B. Oliva (Milan: Feltrinelli, 1981). See also P. Rosentiehl, s.v. "labirinto," in *Enciclopedia Einaudi* (Turin: Einaudi, 1979), VIII, 3–30. For the [219] labyrinth as "world" in

Bersuire and *Piers Plowman*, see B. G. Koonce, *Chaucer and theTradition of Fame* (Princeton: Princeton Univ. Press, 1966), pp. 250–51 and notes 137, 138.

41 Matthews, *Mazes*, p. 68.

42 See F. Frontisi-Ducroux, *Dédale: Mythologie de l'artisan en Grèce ancienne* (Paris: Maspero, 1975). Daedalus is also the builder of temples, in particular of the platform of Venus's temple (then built by Aeneas, *Aen.*, V, 759) at Erice in Sicily, and of Apollo's temple at Cuma (*Aen.*, VI, 18–33, a passage which also describes the Labyrinth of Crete). Chaucer describes a temple of Venus in Book I and invokes Apollo in Book III of the *House of Fame*.

43 See H. Leclercq, s.v. "labyrinthe," in *Dictionnaire d'Archéologie Chrétienne et de Liturgie*, eds. F. Cabrol and H. Leclercq (Paris: Letouzey & Ané, 1928), VIII, 980. The labyrinth at Reims, now destroyed, and that of Amiens, now a reproduction of the original, were examples of this: Kern, *Labirinti*, pp. 213–14, 195–98, 247–48.

44 See Edmond Faral, *Les Arts Poétiques du XIIe et du XIIIe Siècle* (Paris: H. Champion, 1962), pp. 38–39, and text of *Laborintus*, pp. 336–77.

45 A gloss in MS. Vatican 3321, printed by G. Goetz in *Corpus Glossariorum 'Latinorum* (Leipzig, 1889), IV, 103, 26 *a post.*: "labirinthum aedificium tortuosum mechanica arte constructum a Daedalo, ubi sine adiutorio cuiuslibet semper voces resonabant. . . ."

46 *Met.*, VIII, 159–61: "Daedalus ingenio fabrae celeberrimus artis / Ponit opus turbatque notas et lumina flexum / Ducit in errorem variarum ambage viarum." Ovid's description of the house of Rumor occurs in *Met.*, XII, 39–63. For the image of the labyrinthic House of Daedalus in Chaucer, see *Boece*, III, pr. 12, 156; and for the labyrinth, *Legend of Good Women*, 2014 ("Ariadne").

47 *Aen.*, V, 588–91: "Ut quondam Creta fertur Labyrinthus in alta/Parietibus textum caecis iter ancipitemque/Mille viis habuisse dolum, qua signa sequendi/Frangeret indeprensus et inremeabilis error. . . ."

48 I have made some of these observations in *English Medieval Narrative*, pp. 138–92.

49 And compare Frontisi-Ducroux, *Dédale*, pp. 191–92: "Créateur de forme et de beauté, l'artisan est fabricant d'illusion. Ses oeuvres, qui émerveillent dans leur vérité saisissante, sont artifice et mensonge. L'imitation est piège, qu'il s'agisse de plaquer du métal sur du bois en un revêtement prestigieux, ou de recouvrir une femme vivante d'une vache de cuir et de bois. L'art, qui donne forme à la matière et l'embellit, falsifie. L'artiste est maître en contrefaçons et subterfuges."

50 Priscian, *Inst. Gramm.*, I, i, 1 (ed. M. Hertz [Leipzig, 1855], I, 5). And compare Donatus, *Ars Grammatica* (ed. H. Keil [Leipzig, 1864], p. 367): "Vox est aer ictus sensibilis auditu." Marcia L. Colish, to whom I am particularly indebted in this section, emphasizes in a letter that Priscian "stands at the end of the ancient tradition of describing *vox* in this fashion, essentially a watered-down version of that tradition, which goes back to Stoic linguistics. The earlier sources are Varro, Probus, Donatus, Marius Victorinus, Maximus Victorinus, Diomedes."

51 *De Vulgari Eloquentia*, I, iii, 3 (ed. P. V. Mengaldo in Dante, *Opere Minori* [Milan: R. Ricciardi, 1979], II, 40). Dante's relationship with some of the Modistae is discussed in M. Corti, *Dante a un nuovo crocevia*, Società Dantesca Italiana, Quaderno 1 (Florence: Libreria Commissionari Sansoni, 1981).

52 Cited in R. H. Robins, *A Short History of Linguistics*, 2nd ed. (London: Longmans, 1979), p. 77 and note 22. I have developed part of this argument in *English Medieval Narrative*, ch. 6, 1. [220]

53 For instance, Siger de Courtrai, quoted by G. L. Bursill-Hall, *Speculative Grammars of the Middle Ages* (The Hague: Mouton, 1971), p. 70, note 18.

54 Robins, p. 77.

55 For this see Marcia L. Colish, *The Mirror of Language: A Study in the Medieval*

Theory of Knowledge (New Haven: Yale Univ. Press, 1968); P. Rotta, *La filosofia del linguaggio nella Patristica e nella Scolastica* (Turin: Fratelli Bocca, 1909); J. Pinborg, *Die Entwicklung der Sprachtheorie im Mittelalter* (Münster-Copenhagen: Aschendorff-A. Frost-Hansen, 1967); J. Pinborg, *Logik und Semantik im Mittelalter* (Stuttgart: Frommann-Holzboog, 1972); H. Parret, ed., *History of Linguistic Thought and Contemporary Linguistics* (Berlin: de Gruyter, 1976), pp. 189–227 (O. Ducrot) and pp. 254–78 (J. Pinborg); E. J. Ashworth, *The Tradition of Medieval Logic and Speculative Grammar, from Anselm to the Seventeenth Century*, Subsidia Medievalia, 9 (Toronto, 1978); M. Dal Pra, *Logica e Realtà* (Bari: Laterza, 1974), in particular for Anselm and Holcot. Bacon is the author of a *Summa Gramatica* (ed. R. Steele, *Opera*, XV [Oxford: Clarendon Press, 1940]). Kilwardby composed *Sophismata grammaticalia* and *Quod fertur Commenti super Priscianum maiorem extracta*, published in *Cahiers de l'Institut du Moyen-Age Grec et Latin*, 15 (1975), 1–146. John of Salisbury discusses problems of language in the *Metalogicon* (Oxford: Clarendon Press, 1929).

56 I am not concerned to demonstrate that Chaucer knew and borrowed from specific philosophers of language (which I think impossible on present evidence), but only to show the background against which Chaucer's discussion in the *House of Fame* takes place.

57 G. L. Bursill-Hall, *Speculative Grammars*, p. 72. The whole of chapter 3 (pp. 66–113) is very valuable.

58 For other implications of this see Piero Boitani, *English Medieval Narrative*, pp. 138–92.

59 See note 39, above, and M. Corti, *Dante*, p. 49.

60 In the letter (addressed perhaps to Petrarch, whose years in Avignon, incidentally, coincided partially with Ockham's stay) "Mavortis miles extrenue": Giovanni Boccaccio, *Opere in Versi, Corbaccio, Trattatello, Prose Latine, Epistole*, ed. P. G. Ricci (Milan: R. Ricciardi, 1965), p. 1068.

61 For instance "cognitio" and "scientia" in Pars III, ii, "De Syllogismo Demonstrativo." The problem of universals is also treated: I, 14–25.

62 *Summa Logicae*, I, i (eds. P. Boehner, G. Gal, S. Brown [St. Bonaventure, N. Y., 1974]), pp. 7–10).

63 A. Ghisalberti, *Introduzione a Ockham* (Bari: Laterza, 1976), pp. 70–71.

64 *Summa Logicae*, I, i, 60–61 (p. 9).

65 *Summa Logicae*, I, lxiii–lxxvii (pp. 193–238; quotations from p. 196).

66 T. de Andrés, *El Nominalismo de Guillermo de Ockham como Filosofía del Lenguaje* (Madrid: Editorial Gredos, 1969), p. 250. See also Gordon Leff, *William of Ockham* (Manchester: Manchester Univ. Press, 1975), ch. 1, v, and ch. 2, i–iv.

67 *Summa Logicae*, II, ii, 17–20 (p. 250).

68 See J. A. Robson, *Wyclif*, pp. 9–31 and 97–111; Janet Coleman, *Piers Plowman and the "Moderni"* (Rome: Edizioni di Storia e Letteratura, 1981), pp. 11–16. Janet Coleman discusses fourteenth-century culture in *Medieval Readers and Writers: 1350–1400* (New York: Columbia Univ. Press, 1981).

69 *Aen.*, IV, 173–95, from which Chaucer borrows in the *House of Fame*, 1365 ff.

70 *Met.*, VIII, 18. It is also Joyce's epigraph for *A Portrait of the Artist as a Young Man*.

18 | In and out of dreams
[*The Parliament of Fowls*]

BERTRAND H. BRONSON

Originally published as part of Chapter 2, "In and Out of Dreams",
in Bertrand H. Bronson, *In Search of Chaucer* (Toronto: University
of Toronto Press, 1963, pp. 43–8). Reprinted by permission of the
University of Toronto Press and Mrs Bertrand Bronson. The
original pagination is recorded within square brackets.

The Parliament of Fowls, whether or not it was prompted by current events, is
a love-vision surprisingly unorthodox. The perplexities of love are the subject announced in the opening stanzas; love and its complexities are the
subject of the birds' debate. This debate is the patent reason for the poem's
existence: it is climax and end, and must in some form have been in Chaucer's mind from the start. Obviously, he wished to show love from various
points of view, masculine and feminine, high and low; to exhibit the refined
idealism of courtly love, and its unreality and egoism; the natural reactions of
simple creatures incapable of such exaltation, and their useful but also self-
centred motivation. To bring these all together was a practical difficulty.
Courtly love is secret as to its particular object. Moreover, mere vulgarity is
not necessarily amusing. There was also the realistic obstacle that the lower
orders may not freely criticize their betters to their faces. Allegory, therefore,
was essential. The inherent difficulties might be circumvented at one happy
stroke by personifying all these conflicting points of view as types of birds. A
vision would liberate from the inconveniences of verisimilitude and would
give the ironic imagination much freer, and probably safer, play. Vision,
moreover, would carry the question to levels of ultimate importance by
showing these human contrasts in a vaster perspective of universal powers,
the elemental forces of love and nature that influence heaven and earth. For
presiding deity of so diverse a scene, he might take his cue from Alain's
majestic conception of the goddess Nature, all-embracing and fructifying,
"vicar of the almighty Lord"; and from the same source a hint of that
arbitrary and self-willed divinity, the Venus whose confining temple walls
signified exclusive dedication to her sole worship, and whose service was a
consuming flame. The contrast between the large and life-[44]giving bounty
of the one and the anti-social inwardness of the other could be further
developed by drawing upon Boccaccio's convenient and engaging account of
the artifice of the Garden and Temple of Venus.

Obviously, the debate was pre-ordained to show love as a cause of dissension, not of accord. Granting a kind of idealism in the self-abnegation of courtly love, it was still a private and restrictive virtue, and "tid thereof as often harm as prow." There were other, and perhaps better, kinds of idealism that refined spirits all too easily forgot: in particular, the disinterested habit of, not the private, but the honest public, servant, who spent himself for the common weal. Such was the lofty ideal that Cicero of old had raised for emulation; and it was a gauge by which to measure the worth of that finely spun sentiment upon which courtly lovers set such a premium. Why not invoke the promise of Africanus in Scipio's Dream, where he declared:

> What man, lered other lewed
> That lovede commune profyt, wel ithewed,
> He shulde into a blysful place wende,
> There as joye is that last withouten ende. . . .

(46–49)

It would be interesting to note the response to such a shock of an audience expecting the conventional celebration of love in a courtly poem for St. Valentine's Day.

By some such train of thought, we may fancy, Chaucer might arrive at the rationale of his poem. He promises a love-vision, but even at the start there is a hint in his not referring to Love as a god but only as a feudal lord, and in his insistence on his personal detachment: he will say only, "God save swich a Lord!" [14] He knows nothing of him at first hand, but what he reads of his tyranny is almost dumb-founding. He is very fond of reading – it is his idiosyncracy – and recently he was hot in pursuit of some information in an antique volume and read on eagerly the whole day long. [45] What it was he was seeking, he quite deliberately refrains from saying. Obviously, had he wished us to know, he would have told us. Not telling, under the circumstances, is concealing. But our curiosity is whetted, and naturally everyone expects him to produce documentary evidence, from his reading, of Love's "myrakles and his crewel yre" [11] – something to bear out his speechless amazement. Instead, he proceeds to outline the Dream of Scipio, chapter by chapter: a work as far as possible from the track on which he had set our train of thought. Could any effect be more certainly calculated for surprise? For what do you think Africanus says, in Tully? He says that our present mode of existence is only a kind of death but, for the good, a dying into immortal bliss. And who are the good? They are those who find no delight in the life of the senses but exert their utmost efforts for the commonwealth. Lawbreakers and sensualists, on the contrary, when they die, shall age after age whirl painfully about the earth until they have atoned for their wickedness. Four times Africanus points his namesake the way into "that blysful place," "that hevene blisse," "that place deere" reserved for the "soules cleere" [49,72,76,77]; and when he appears in turn to the poet that night, to lead him into that blissful place, the paradisal garden of love, it would seem that the ironic point could hardly escape the most inattentive of Chaucer's listeners.

As the poet dropped his book and prepared for bed, he was troubled, both because he had what (he says) he didn't want, and did not have what he wanted. The phrase was caught from Boethius' *Consolatio*, and it occurs where Philosophy is instructing her pupil that however great the abundance of earthly goods, man's needs and desires are not sufficed. This has a very present bearing on African's down right injunction, "That he ne shulde him in the world delyte" [66]; and Chaucer, by his outline of Scipio's dream, has already set all earthly circumstance in a context that inevi[46]tably belittles the temporal in comparison with things eternal, both in quantity and quality. That this was his deliberate intention, who can doubt?

Indeed, in a variety of ways, Chaucer tacitly declares, over and over, that in so far as his poem is a vision of terrestrial love it is written against the grain. At its conclusion, he blandly apologizes, saying that another time, with luckier reading, he hopes to meet with a more auspicious dream. This parting testimony to the poet's implicit assumption of a connection between book and dream, the implied allusion here to the reading that had so wryly conditioned this particular vision, has been very oddly ignored as an evidence of the poem's intended unity and deliberate *ordonnance*.

The work, then, has moral depth and responsibility, a sound and coherent structure. But it has also unabashed lightness of heart; and in its own kind is a sort of Valentine's Day equivalent of a Midsummer Night's Dream. It is too nimble for criticism, which hops always behind. When we try to do justice to its serious implications, we lumber into travesty and all but extinguish its spirit of mocking gaiety. And when we try to appreciate its fun, we heavily explain or weakly paraphrase and quote, and fall short of its deeper meaning. Critical writing on this single poem is almost a paradigm of all the elucidatory inflections that have been tried on Chaucer's work through its whole extent. We have buried it under a mountain of commentary, both gravel and granite, only to find that, like Eulenspiegel, it was elsewhere during the obsequies.

A few further remarks about the parliament (im)proper will provide demonstration of what has just been asserted. Among the bird-folk who take part in the debate, the social distinction of the principals inevitably involves the others in a relative rating; and though their seating in Nature's "house" does not rank them, Chaucer's classification into seed-fowl, water-fowl, and worm-fowl more than invites us [47] to attach general labels to each from analogous human society. The simplest solution, in such a context, is surely the most acceptable. The purpose of Chaucer's allegory is not the propounding of riddles. The "fowles of ravyne," as all readers agree, correspond to the nobility great and lesser, whose proper business in feudal times was mainly to hunt, and to make love and war. The water-fowl are big and aggressive birds and they are the first of the commoners to come forward with a verdict. They have two spokesmen, the goose and the duck, one female and one almost certainly male, one chosen and one self-appointed, but both speaking to the same end. Their advice is strictly practical: to arrive at a working agreement, to get a return for the investment on both sides. It's as easy to fall in love "ther profyt sholde aryse" as to love where nothing can be gained. They would understand Tennyson's northern farmer: "Doän't thou marry for munny, but goä wheer munny is!" These clues, in a satirical reference, are consistent with the mercantile class, and there are no indications to the contrary. The seed-fowl are next to give their verdict, in the person of the turtle-dove. They are clearly gentlefolk, and their point of view, while not martial, is fairly close to that of the nobility. They are country-dwellers, and they have the country conservatism and some idealism. They can appreciate the idea of fidelity without thought of reward, and loyalty even unto death is an ideal to which they respond. They are contemptuous of the materialism of the water-birds. Though modest, they are happily a numerous company and cover the greensward. Their elected spokesman, the turtle-dove, declares modestly that love is an ever-fixèd mark, that bends not with the remover to remove.

Then comes the turn of the worm-fowl, folk of a nondescript way of life, pickers-up of scraps. Their idea of the "comune spede," it develops, is not even so lofty as the *quid pro quo* of the water-fowl: it is every bird for himself. [48] "Only give me *my* mate," says the cuckoo, speaking for them all, "and you're welcome to go on disputing forever. If those others can't agree, let each live solitary all his life long!" [605–07] The merlin, with heavy irony, bestows the fitting comment on this position. "Of course: – when the glutton has stuffed *his* paunch, how can anyone else be discontented?" [610–11] It is evident that the worm-fowl are a miscellaneous lot, with neither a definable mode of living nor a code based on principle. In a pre-industrial society, the Masses lack a proper name.

When we look back from the dream–debate to the book, we can discern a sufficient latent motivation for the political colouring. As a Valentine's Day poet, Chaucer had apparently – but deliberately – started off on the wrong foot. Cicero's political theory was no very orthodox springboard for a love-vision. But Chaucer, as royal ambassador in marriage negotiations, had seen love being made the specious pretext and nominal goal of the most cold-blooded bargaining for material and diplomatic advantage: "Though his fair daughter's self, as I avowed/At starting, is my object!" So that, in an unexpected and ironic way, politics was an entirely appropriate leading-note for a love-vision. The poet had not ostensibly found what he had been looking for, but perhaps he had achieved something even more valuable – a surer basis for sound counsel. "For out of olde feeldes ... Cometh al this newe corn from yer to yere." With continued study, he might on some lucky day attain his ideal: the felicity of a perfect coincidence between the wisdom acquired and the occasion to use it. On that day, the double sense of the word *rede*, a word upon which in his last stanza he lays such purposive stress by fourfold repetition, will be fused in perfect accord. Reading and counselling will be united in the harmonious function of the scholar-diplomat. Tully, in fact, had pointed the way, and in his own person had realized the wished-for fusion.

19 | The discordant concord of *The Parliament of Fowls*

JOHN M. FYLER

Originally published as the conclusion of Chapter 3, "Love and the Law of Nature," in John M. Fyler, *Chaucer and Ovid* (New Haven, Conn.: Yale University Press, 1979, pp. 81–95). Reprinted by permission of Yale University Press. The original pagination is recorded within square brackets. The square brackets used to cite line numbers after foreign quotations in the original text have been changed to round brackets. The endnotes originally appeared on pp. 184–7 and have been renumbered.

The *Parliament of Fowls* is Chaucer's most sophisticated comment on the world ruled by Nature; indeed, it is in many respects [82] the thematic epitome of his poetry. This dream vision re-explores the Ovidian themes of the earlier poems, but with a new clarity and economy. It sets out to unravel the paradox of love, which is the favorite subject of Chaucer's major poems, early and late. Chaucer's narrator tries to disentangle the paradox in a series of juxtapositions; but he succeeds in creating only a spurious clarity, and the conflicts he exposes are left unresolved. The narrator's failures of understanding are given depth by his enforced separation from the natural world around him. As fallen, conscious man faces instinctive Nature, the systems that the mind discovers in the world, or imposes on it, verge on collapse.

The first few stanzas of the poem recall the *Book of the Duchess* and the *House of Fame*, and open up a similar range of thematic issues. Once again the narrator is a dreamer, and once again his dream is provoked by his reading. Moreover, this dream too, like the one in the *House of Fame*, begins in a rather literary manner: Cicero's *Somnium Scipionis* gives Chaucer his dream-guide, and Dante is the source for the gate to Love's garden.[1] Just as the lover dreams of love and the knight of battle (99–105), so by implication the reader dreams of books. To dream of books is not a matter for reproach. It does, however, imply a certain distance from the complexities of experience, a distance even greater than the normal gap between reality and a dreamed wish-fulfillment: "The lovere met he hath his lady wonne" (105). Chaucer's narrator may read in order to understand; but his reading leads to more dreams about life, not to life itself:

> I wok, and othere bokes tok me to,
> To reede upon, and yit I rede alwey.

> I hope, ywis, to rede so som day
> That I shal mete som thyng for to fare
> The bet, and thus to rede I nyl nat spare.
>
> (695–99)

Yet the narrator's distance from experience – to *mete* ("dream") something is, unfortunately, not the same as to live it – is not entirely [83] self-imposed. His dream, like the one in the *House of Fame*, is a payment for his poetic service to Love; and the payment, as before, is not a love affair, but additional material for his love poetry.

The *Parliament* is in this respect, like the *Book of the Duchess*, reminiscent of a good many medieval lyrics, in which a loveless narrator yearningly sees the amatory excitement and promised fruition of Nature quickening in spring. But the device, conventional as it is, also has deeper resonances. In most of his major works Chaucer explores the paradox of the non-lover writing about love. The *Parliament* explicitly raises the question of what it means to be a reader instead of a lover. When the promises of heaven and hell on the gate to Love's garden have left Chaucer paralyzed, Africanus pushes him through:

> "For this writyng nys nothyng ment bi the,
> Ne by non, but he Loves servaunt be:
> For thow of love hast lost thy tast, I gesse,
> As sek man hath of swete and bytternesse.
>
> "But natheles, although that thow be dul,
> Yit that thow canst not do, yit mayst thow se.
> For many a man that may nat stonde a pul,
> It liketh hym at the wrastlyng for to be,
> And demeth yit wher he do bet or he."
>
> (158–66)

The image is apt, for it raises the issue that is central in most of Chaucer's works: how do we know things, and how do we know if what we know is the truth? Books can lie, or at least disagree, as Vergil and Ovid differed about Dido, and the Troy-poets about Troy. Or, as proves to be true of Macrobius in the *Parliament*, they may simply answer the wrong question: "For bothe I hadde thyng which that I nolde,/And ek I nadde that thyng that I wolde" (90–91). Experience, as the wrestling image suggests, raises its own problems; it is by no means a fulfilling substitute for written authority. The wrestler knows a lot about wrestling, but loses detachment and objectivity by his involvement in process. The [84] spectator can judge who is the better wrestler, but how can he tell the full meaning of the experience he observes? Chaucer's dreams are themselves in the realm of experience; yet, as the Proem of the *House of Fame* stresses, dreams are notoriously difficult to define or interpret. In the *Parliament*, the result of the dream is much the same as the result of the narrator's reading – not surprisingly, since the dream springs from the reading and in some sense mirrors it. Although we are not called upon to decide that either is a lie, they are both inconclusive, and do not satisfy the narrator's unstated needs (695–99).

The unsatisfying, loose-ended quality of the dream depends on, though it is not fully explained by, the inconclusiveness of the debate at Nature's parliament. Chaucer's use here of juxtaposition and unresolved dramatic contrast directly forecasts the debates in the *Canterbury Tales*. Specifically, the dispute about love among the birds, who are divided pretty much along class lines, has a great deal in common with Miller versus Knight. In each instance no resolution of the conflict seems possible, at least on the issue of truth. There are other issues at stake, to be sure; but Chaucer's comments as a spokesman for genteel behavior and social rank are too self-consciously witty to be considered entirely serious. In the *Canterbury Tales*, his disingenuous apology for the Miller's "harlotrie" (I. 3167–86) is so intrusive that it breaks the illusion of verisimilitude: we remember that Chaucer himself of course wrote this "cherles tale." What the apology primarily accomplishes is to show him as a character rushing to join the "gentils" who so much liked the *Knight's Tale* (I. 3113). His remarks in the *Parliament* on the "large golee" (556) of the "lewednesse behynde" (520) run awry for a different reason. For the birds' comments about the folly of *fin amour* are in fact cogent: however human their characters seem to be, they are after all simply birds, who are driven to mate by natural impulse, not by love as humans define it. As in the *Nun's Priest's Tale*, where a rooster's notion of beauty sometimes jars rather sharply with our own (VII. 3161), there is a comic wavering between human attitudes and avian realities. Indeed, the debate becomes in[85]creasingly hilarious once we realize that the birds are feeling an avian version of estrus and can barely restrain the pressing urgency of their drive to copulate and reproduce, an urge that Nature, as the vice-regent of God, has given them. Nature herself is well aware of the need for haste: "'And for youre ese, in fortheryng of youre nede,/As faste as I may speke, I wol me speede'" (384–85); even one of the three tercel eagles promises, on such grounds, to be brief (464–68). The impatience of the lower birds is predictable, indeed welcome, once it becomes disconcertingly apparent that the three courtly lovers have debated all day long (489–90). They resent, quite rightly, being trapped in the wrong genre; and their just resentment prevents any confident arbitration of the debate on the nature of love.

There is also, of course, unresolved dramatic conflict in the courtly debate of the three eagle suitors, each with a different claim to the formel. Their unfinished courtship, set against the union of the other birds and the joy of the concluding roundel to spring, contributes crucially to the tentative mood of the poem's ending. Although the formel will, in a year's time, have to choose one eagle or another as her mate, she is at least given that much delay for her present inclination not to love at all. Except that she has freely chosen her detached position, the formel mirrors the narrator's state of mind: half in paralysis before the alternatives of a choice, half tentative about even choosing whether or not to choose.[2]

Nature responds to the formel's quandary with a rational solution:

> "But as for conseyl for to chese a make,
> If I were Resoun, certes, thanne wolde I
> Conseyle yow the royal tercel take."
>
> (631–33)

Nonetheless, it is important that we leave up in the air, as the formel does, what her choice will eventually be.[3] Love is not rational; and Nature after all is not Reason,[4] even if, as sometimes happens in the *Roman de la Rose*, their advice occasionally coincides. The response [86] of the other birds is absolutely correct, and sums up a problem that can be resolved only by the formel's decision: "'How sholde a juge eyther parti leve/For ye or nay, withouten any preve?'" (496–97). There is no compelling argument, in the love logic of this *demande d'amour*, for favoring one suitor over the others: the first has the highest social rank; the second is of a lower degree but has loved the formel longer; the third has loved not long but deeply. Judicial combat – the solution of the *Knight's Tale* – is averted, though the three eagles voice their willingness to fight it out (540). And Nature's futile appeal to Reason complements the indecisive love debate between the higher and lower birds. If this were a poem in which Reason, Love, and Nature always coincided, the narrator presumably would be content simply to expound Scipio's dream. Instead, he explores a "lower" form of love; and in Love's earthly garden, the appeals of social hierarchy give a genteel answer, not one that can be considered an absolute truth.

These inconclusive debates present in miniature the structure of the whole poem. The *Parliament* opens with an awed recital of the confusing, paradoxical qualities of love: *ars longa, vita brevis*; and "the dredful joye, alwey that slit so yerne" (1–3). At first sight the task of the poem will be to unravel the confusion and resolve the paradox of love's nature. Appropriately, its structure is built by repeated division and subdivision: Macrobius versus the garden; the two inscriptions on the garden gate; Venus versus Nature; the three competing eagles; courtly views of love versus more down-to-earth ones. But what happens at the end of the poem happens each time before, as Chaucer works out an Ovidian paradigm. The clarity gained by division produces no resolution; we are left with opposing but unreconciled viewpoints, thesis and antithesis with no synthesis. Moreover, at the very moments when division lends clarity to an issue, we discover that the clarity is artificial, an unstable separating out of elements that are all too ready to blur together again into the paradoxes that begin the poem and continue to be love's reality.

The first such division, between Macrobius and the garden, creates not so much a false clarity as a distinction so encompassing [87] as to be not very useful for the narrator's concerns. Scipio's dream is about love as the cosmic bond of the universe, next to whose immensity and sweeping order "the lytel erthe that here is" (57) merits the wise man's contempt, since "oure present worldes lyves space/Nis but a maner deth, what wey we trace" (53–54). Love, in this rarefied scheme of things, is defined as "commune profyt" (47); its adherents will be rewarded, Scipio is told, by eternal life in "a blysful place" (48). As this summary suggests, there are some striking analogies between Cicero's picture of universal order and the Christian one: the promise of an afterlife, with reward or punishment; the comparable positions of "comune profyt" and of charity as man's way to find truth by love. Yet even though Chaucer does delete some of Cicero's specifically pagan ideas,[5] he is careful to preserve the pagan atmosphere of the dream, chiefly by reporting the heterodox notion that even "brekers of the lawe" and "likerous folk" will eventually be "foryeven al hir wikked dede" and be allowed to "come into this blysful place" (78–83). The reason for doing so is clearly its distancing effect: if Chaucer had chosen St. Paul for his bedtime reading, the *Parliament of Fowls* would be a very different poem. As it stands, Chaucer is able to express some dissatisfaction (90–91) when he has completed his reading of Macrobius. He is also able subtly to bring into question the truth value of what he has read, when he says: "And therupon, a certeyn thing to lerne,/The longe day ful faste I redde and yerne" (20–21). For "a certeyn thing" has two possible meanings: both "a particular thing" and "something that is certain."[6] Cicero is not gospel truth, "something certain," nor does he answer the "certeyn thing" that Chaucer is interested in. As the narrator's own dream shows, that certain thing is how love works in a less rarefied sense, how it operates in the world. Cicero presented a picture of universal order, ruled by Love, in which the mire and complexity of earthly concerns are dissipated and resolved. The rest of the *Parliament* returns us to the quandaries of its opening paradoxes, to the "myrakles" and "crewel yre" of love as it manifests itself on earth.

The inscriptions on the garden gate sum up the antithetical [88] possibilities of earthly love and appropriately – given their source in Dante – describe them with hellish and heavenly connotations. The clarity of opposition between the two inscriptions has misled a good many readers of the *Parliament*, in precisely the way that the "two Venuses" have distorted interpretations of the *House of Fame*. The temptation has been to make the poem into an analogue of Boccaccio's *Amorosa Visione* or of a ballade by Oton de Grandson, where there are two gates to the garden of love.[7] According to this reading, one has only to choose the correct side of the gate in order to achieve love's heaven and avoid its hell.[8] But Chaucer's point, quite unmistakably, is that the same gate leads to both extremes, just as a single Venus, in the *House of Fame*, both aids Aeneas and brings about Dido's tragedy. There is no way of knowing beforehand whether one will find heaven or hell, or both, in love's garden;[9] hence, the narrator's paralysis in front of the gate:

> These vers of gold and blak iwriten were,
> Of whiche I gan astoned to beholde,
> For with that oon encresede ay my fere,
> And with that other gan myn herte bolde;
> That oon me hette, that other dide me colde:

> No wit hadde I, for errour, for to chese,
> To entre or flen, or me to save or lese.
>
> (141–47)

He is, as he says, like "a pece of yren set" "betwixen adamauntes two/Of evene myght" (148–49); and his indecision here echoes his dazed reflection on love at the beginning of the poem: "Nat wot I wel wher that I flete or synke" (7).

Africanus's solution is to shove Chaucer through the gate, and inform him that "'this writyng nys nothyng ment bi the,/Ne by non, but he Loves servaunt be'" (158–59). The narrator's leap into experience can remain a rather tentative one, confined to a dream and without extreme consequences of either sort. He gets past the necessity of choice by being told that he does not have to choose. Indeed, he will not be permitted to do so; and the limits on his [89] freedom of will create some degree of pathos. For the price of detachment is muted response, an inability to taste the sweet as well as feel the bitter: "'For thow of love hast lost thy tast, I gesse,/As sek man hath of swete and bytternesse'" (160–61). The most one could hope is that the narrator's detachment, whatever the cost to himself, might allow him to tell the rest of us how to find love's joy and escape its torment.

Nothing of the sort happens, of course. The antithesis of the two inscriptions on the gate repeats itself in the garden; but we are shown no narrow path to heaven, no wide one to hell. Critics have often been tempted to find exact equivalences: "This gate seems to symbolize two distinct kinds of love to be found in the garden; love according to Nature, which promises ever-green joy, and love of a more courtly kind which leads to barren sorrow and despair."[10] The trouble is that the pairs of opposing terms are in analogous but not exactly identical relationships. As many critics have said, Venus in her temple does manifest the disagreeable side of love. Indeed, Chaucer darkens the already maleficent tone of his source, a description in Boccaccio's *Teseida*, by adding to it a list of doomed lovers from the *Inferno*. Nonetheless, the more one looks at this antithesis of Venus and Nature, the less sharply defined it seems.

The reason for the blurring is implicit in the Chartrian myth of the goddess Nature, which Chaucer adopts directly from the *De Planctu Naturae* of Alanus de Insulis, and as it comes filtered through Jean de Meun's *Roman de la Rose*. Venus in this system stands for the human notions and trappings of love, which lead to unrequited longings as well as to courtly elegance; and she so stands in contrast to Nature's simple demand for fecundity and regeneration, uncluttered by the distortions and malaises of consciousness.[11] Yet, as distinct as their attributes are, the two goddesses merge: Venus is part of Nature's realm, and serves her larger purposes of regeneration and the fight of the plenum against the ravages of time. As Alanus's Nature explains, "Venerem in fabrili scientia peritam, meaeque operationis subvicariam, in mundiali suburbio collocavi, ut ipsa sub meae praeceptionis arbitrio ...

humani generis seriem in[90]defessa continuatione contexeret" [in the out-skirt world I stationed Venus, who is skilled in the knowledge of making, as under-deputy of my work, in order that she, under my judgment and guidance ... might weave together the line of the human race in unwearied continuation].[12] Proprietary rights are, accordingly, left rather vague in Chaucer's dream: there are not two gardens, any more than there are two gates. As Clemen has pointed out, the fact that Chaucer sees Cupid "under a tre" (211) "reminds us that the poet has not passed into some new region; he is still in the same park whose individual trees had been enumerated at the outset of the description."[13] Venus's temple likewise is an enclosed, hothouse space within the airy *locus amoenus* of Nature's domain – just as, in the *Book of the Duchess*, the self-conscious, sorrowing Man in Black punctures the natural innocence of his Golden Age setting. Chaucer implies a link between what he sees of the garden before he enters the temple and what he sees after he comes out. The catalogue of trees (176–82) presages the catalogue of birds (330–64): each is a conventional part of the usual description of the plenum of life, filling every niche of Nature's domain, falling under her tutelage and beneficent rule.

The catalogues also force on us an increasing awareness of ambiguity and the blurring of what were at first clearly defined oppositions. This blurring occurs even within Venus's temple: if the emphasis there is on the evils of human sexuality, it must be admitted that some of its good, or at least morally neutral, qualities are presented as well. One can hardly find fault with Curteysie and Gentilesse; and Plesaunce, Lust, and Delyt are open to contradictory interpretations.[14] Furthermore, if Venus's temple contains some good attributes among the predominantly bad, Nature's realm has bad among the good. To say this is to oversimplify matters considerably, from a theological viewpoint.[15] But it is fair to say that the catalogues of trees and birds, describing individual species by their function in Nature's plan, contain a great deal that is disagreeable and – from a limited human perspective – morally questionable. The fullness of Nature contains "the cofre unto carayne," "the [91] cipresse, deth to playne," and "the dronke vyne" as well as "the byldere ok" and "saylynge fyr" (176–80); "the drake, stroyere of his owene kynde" and "the cukkow ever unkynde" as well as "the wedded turtil, with hire herte trewe" and "the raven wys" (355–63). Indeed, in the catalogue of birds especially there is a preponderance of unpleasant attributes. Nature's realm, even in its purified, eternal setting as a *locus amoenus*, is not all roses and sunshine. Yet the birds which seem most disagreeable – to the extent, unfortunately, that they echo the immoral qualities of human beings – fulfill their mysterious functions in Nature's scheme, and are included in her constant injunction: be fruitful and multiply.

Nature's unfailing purpose does directly oppose the inscription that de-scribes love's hell as a wasteland of sterility and of unrequited, unfulfilled longing (134–40). Elsewhere in fourteenth-century poetry such an antithesis is conventionally used to set off a conscious, loveless narrator from the

unconscious, fulfilled creatures of the world in spring. In several instances
man is contrasted specifically with the birds. Gower so begins his *Confessio
Amantis*:

> And that was in the Monthe of Maii,
> Whan every brid hath chose his make
> And thenkth his merthes forto make
> Of love that he hath achieved;
> Bot so was I nothing relieved,
> For I was further fro my love
> Than Erthe is fro the hevene above,
> As forto speke of eny sped.

(I. 100–07)

The comparison in fact frames the poem; Gower repeats it toward the end of
Book Eight:

> Ferst to Nature if that I me compleigne,
> Ther finde I hou that every creature
> Som time ayer hath love in his demeine,
> So that the litel wrenne in his mesure
> Hath yit of kinde a love under his cure;
> And I bot on desire, of which I misse:
> [92]   And thus, bot I, hath every kinde his blisse.

(VIII. 2224–30)

This *topos* has a special appropriateness for St. Valentine's Day poems,
because the separation of man from nature is at its sharpest on the day when
all the birds choose their mates for the coming year. The contrast between
mating birds and an unrequited human lover appears in Chaucer's own
"Complaynt D'Amours" (*Works*, p. 541). It also shows up in one of Gower's
ballades, in terms that recall quite pointedly the *Parliament of Fowls*:

> Chascun Tarcel gentil ad sa falcoun,
> Mais j'ai faili de ceo q'avoir voldroie:
> Ma dame, c'est le fin de mon chançoun,
> Qui soul remaint ne poet avoir grant joie.[16]

(Every gentle tercel has his falcon, but I have lacked what I would wish
to have; my lady, this is the end of my song; he who remains alone
cannot have great joy.)

Yet Chaucer's purposes in the *Parliament* are more complicated. The closest
analogue to his blurring of Venus and Nature, of the human and the animal,
is Oton de Grandson's *Songe Saint Valentin*, which also gives human attributes to the birds assembled on St. Valentine's Day.[17] The narrator takes
"grant soulas" (78) from the joy of the mating birds, paired off "deux et
deux" (75). He himself, it appears, is an unrequited lover; and he learns that a
peregrine falcon, alone among the birds, shares his plight. The falcon is far
away from his loved one, in status as well as distance: he is afraid to ask for

her as his "par" (242) ("companion" or "mate," but also "equal"), because her social rank and inherent worth are so much higher than his. When the dreamer awakes, he meditates at length on the differences between birds and human beings, and is unable to suppress a certain amount of envy at the easy, unreflective success of birds in love (315 ff.). Among people things are more difficult:

> Les oyseaulx a leur gré choisissent,
> Et lez gens pour aimer eslisent
> [93] La ou leur plaisance s'acorde.
> Dont bien souvent y a discorde,
> Car a l'un plaist, a l'autre non.
>
> (328–32)

(The birds choose at will, and people elect to love where their pleasure decides – from which there is very often discord, for it is pleasing to one, to another not.)

Yet, although "Amour est chouse naturelle" (340) (love is something natural), Grandson asks for no easy retreat from consciousness into the blissful oblivion of

> ... les oyseaulx et les bestez
> Qui n'ont point de sens en leurz testez,
> Et ne doubtent paour ne honte,
> Et de dongier ne tiennent compte,
> Mais vivent sans entendement.
>
> (344–48)

(the birds and the beasts who don't have any sense at all in their heads, and do not care about fear or shame, and do not take reckoning of refusal, but live without conscious judgment.)

Though man's consciousness opens the possibility of misery, it also allows a happiness in love beyond the powers of animate nature to achieve (334–39, 349–56).

Grandson's rather complex response to the contrasts between man and other earthly creatures leads us to Chaucer's meaning in the *Parliament of Fowls*. As in *Le Songe Saint Valentin*, complications arise from the fact that there are unrequited lovers among the birds as well as among men. In fact, the blurring of human and animal is somewhat stronger in Chaucer. Grandson's solitary falcon is, after all, little more than a stand-in for the lovelorn narrator. The three tercel eagles of the *Parliament*, on the other hand, are like the narrator only in being unfulfilled. Through them Venus invades Nature's realm, and partially frustrates the "evene acord" (668) by [94] which all the other birds are happily paired off. Diana shares the blame, it is important to remember: the formel is not yet willing to choose a mate. By their intrusion upon the instinctive world of Nature, the two goddesses exacerbate our human awareness of the problems of consciousness.

Chaucer, as always, responds to this issue with an Ovidian paradox, by treating man's distance from natural harmony with a mixture of deeply felt regret and comic ruefulness. The *Parliament* no doubt does show "the disruptive force of individual personality":[18] the happiest creatures in the poem are the ones least aware of learning, conscious motive, and genteel behavior. Yet whatever envy we may feel for the unreflective happiness of creatures must be a temporary one. Ignorance is not really bliss. Chaucer's point is certainly not that courtly love and consciousness are simply bad, or that uninhibited sexual activity, on behalf of the instinctive drive to reproduce, is the answer to the eagles' problems, let alone the narrator's.

After all, man is stuck with his consciousness, for better as well as for worse.[19] In the *Parliament of Fowls* human consciousness does lead to a paralysis of choice about issues which have no apparent solution. But it is well – as Theseus reminds us at the end of a similar *demande d'amour* – "to maken vertu of necessitee" (I. 3042). The opening lines of the *General Prologue* offer a guide to recognizing the positive side of our predicament. There, too, the tonal effect of contrasting man and nature is double-edged; and, as in the *Parliament*, humanized birds mark the point of transition between Nature's realm and our special province within it (I. 9–11). The magnificent simplicity of Nature, renewing the world, following the archetypal pattern of God's plan, gives way within the first eighteen lines to the many-motived chaos of scurrying human beings. But if the shift from Nature in its pure form necessitates a loss of simplicity and uncluttered harmony, the entrance of man also makes possible the bursting vitality and energy of the Canterbury pilgrims and their tales. The *Parliament of Fowls*, with its uneasy balance of [95] stasis and energy, and its discordant range of perspectives on the meaning of love, thus foreshadows the exuberant variety of the Canterbury stories, with all their unresolved conflicts of viewpoint, social class, and moral scope.

Notes

1   D. S. Brewer lists this and other allusions to the *Commedia* in his edition of *The Parlement of Foulys* (London: Nelson, 1960), pp. 45–46.

2   The subtlety of the narrator's position is most evident in the second stanza of the poem, especially in the variety of readings editors have made of the phrase "his strokes been so sore" (13). Should the line read "I dar nat seyn 'His strokes been so sore,'" as Brewer prints it? That is to say: "I dare not utter these words because I am not a lover." Or is its meaning, as Robinson and Donaldson imply, and as seems to me more likely: "I dare not say, because his strokes are so sore, anything but 'God save swich a lord!'"? That is, that love, as the paradoxes of the first stanza made apparent, is as terrifying as it is attractive; and that Cupid delights in punishing his detractors (e.g., Troilus). [185]

3   Critics have too readily made her choice for her. For a more restrained statement than some, see Brewer, ed., *Parlement of Foulys*, pp. 11–12: "But the first suitor is obviously preferable. He is the most noble, eloquent, dignified. Granted the premises of the whole concept of love in the *demandes d'amour*, he is obviously and

eminently preferable. In contrast with the usual *demande d'amour* ... no-one could be puzzled whom to choose."

4 Robert W. Frank, Jr., makes this point: "Structure and Meaning in the *Parlement of Foules,*" *PMLA* 71 (1956), 538.

5 He changes Cicero's "Know, therefore, that you are a god" (trans. Brewer, p. 137) to "Know thyself first immortal" (73); and he de-emphasizes "commune profyt" as a political virtue.

6 Clemen, p. 136 n.

7 Arthur Piaget, *Oton de Grandson: Sa Vie et Ses Poésies*, Société d'Histoire de la Suisse Romande: Mémoires et Documents, ser. 3, 1 (Lausanne: Librairie Payot, 1941), p. 197:

> Le dieu d'Amours a fait une maison
> Comme un chastel auprés de son manoir,
> Et si a fait deux huis en son dongon,
> Dont l'un a nom Joye et l'autre Douloir.
> Et si vous di, se la l'alez veoir,
> Par Joye fault que dedens vous entrez
> Et par Douloir fault que vous en partez.

[The god of love has made a building like a castle, next to his manor, and also has built two doors in its donjon, of which one has the name Joy and the other Dolor. And thus I tell you, if you go to see it there, by Joy you will have to enter within and by Dolor you will have to depart.]

8 The usual form of this mistake is a too close identification of Venus's temple with love's hell and of Nature's garden with its heaven. See Brewer, ed., *Parlement of Foulys*, p. 41. Also S. S. Hussey, "The Minor Poems and the Prose," in *The Middle Ages*, ed. W. F. Bolton (Sphere History of Literature in the English Language, 1; London: Sphere Books, 1970), pp. 245–46: "The first gate leads the way to 'all good fortune,' 'the heart's delight' and 'green and pleasant May,' a love which is not specifically [186] 'courtly.' The inscription above the second gate seems to show an extreme courtly love ... as an unattractive, indeed arid occupation."

9 Bertrand H. Bronson, *In Appreciation of Chaucer's* Parlement of Foules (University of California Publications in English, 3, No. 5; Berkeley, 1935), p. 203: "Heaven and Hell are now one; and the gates invite and threaten at the same time." Also Clemen, *Chaucer's Early Poetry*, p. 140: "For he is not concerned with two gates or paths of which one has to be selected, but with *one* entrance bearing *two* inscriptions. No 'choice' then is possible; whoever goes through the gateway accepts both possibilities."

10 Charles O. McDonald, "An Interpretation of Chaucer's *Parlement of Foules,*" rpt. in *Chaucer: Modern Essays in Criticism*, ed. Edward Wagenknecht (New York: Oxford University Press, 1959), pp. 312–13. Also Brewer, ed., *Parlement of Foulys*, p. 41. Such an interpretation is analogous to the frequent effort to find Scipio's "commune profyt" at work in Nature's parliament.

11 This Chartrian myth is another version of the Ovidian theme that Chaucer develops in the *Book of the Duchess*: Nature and Venus define more emphatically, by their timeless relationship, the tonal difference between an artless, innocent past and the self-conscious, deceitful present.

12 *De Planctu Naturae*, ed. Thomas Wright, in *Anglo-Latin Satirical Poets and Epigrammatists of the Twelfth Century*, Rolls Series (London, 1872), 2:470. Translated by Douglas M. Moffat, Yale Studies in English, 36 (New Haven, 1908), 45. See also *Roman de la Rose* 19305–11.

13 Clemen, *Chaucer's Early Poetry*, p. 146. J. A. W. Bennett also makes this point: "Yet between Chaucer's park and his temple precincts there is ... no clear division. Nature's glade is not precisely located, Cupid's well seems to be under one of the sempiternal trees...." *The Parlement of Foules: An Interpretation* (Oxford: Clarendon Press, 1957), p. 115.

14 Clemen, *Chaucer's Early Poetry*, p. 147. Also Dorothy Bethurum Loomis, "The Venus of Alanus de Insulis and the Venus of Chaucer," in *Philological Essays: Studies in Old and Middle English Language and Literature in Honour of Herbert Dean Meritt*, ed. James L. Rosier (The Hague: Mouton, 1970), p. 192: [187] "I think she is still the handmaiden of Nature, who presides as beneficently over this poem as she did over Alanus' *De Planctu*, and I do not find quite the contrast between the Temple of Venus and the Garden that Professor Bennett finds. To be sure, Venus is here sexual desire in a rather pure form, but I do not see it as necessarily evil or corrupt. Intense it is, and it is its intensity that Chaucer emphasizes, and its singlemindedness." She adds, on p. 193: "The principal reason why I cannot see the love of the Garden outside the Temple as good and that within as evil is simply that there are too many dubious characters in the Garden. Rape, for example, is not in the Temple but outside in the open air, and no distance at all from 'Curteysie,' 'Delyt,' and 'Gentilesse.'"

15 For example, the *City of God* XII. 4, trans. Henry Bettenson (Harmondsworth: Penguin, 1972), p. 475: "As for those defects, in things of this earth, which are neither voluntary nor punishable; if we observe them closely we shall find that ... they attest the goodness of the natures themselves, every one of which has God as its sole author and creator."

16 "Balade XXV," 22–25, in *The French Works*, ed. Macaulay, p. 366. Also see John Lydgate's St. Valentine's Day poem. "The Flour of Curtesye," in *Chaucerian and Other Pieces*, ed. W. W. Skeat (Oxford: Clarendon Press, 1897), pp. 266 ff.

17 Ed. Piaget, *Oton de Grandson*, pp. 309–23. For a full summary of the poem, see Brewer, ed., *Parlement of Foulys*, p. 131.

18 H. M. Leicester, Jr., "The Harmony of Chaucer's *Parlement*: A Dissonant Voice," *Chaucer Review* 9 (1974), 25. The phrase is his, but not the argument carried to its extreme.

19 *City of God* XII. 1 (p. 472): "Yet the other things in the created universe are not in a better condition because they are incapable of misery; for the other members of our body are not to be called better than our eyes, just because they cannot be blind. A sentient nature, when suffering, is better than a stone which is quite incapable of suffering; and in the same way the rational nature, even in wretchedness, is superior to the nature which is bereft both of reason and sense and therefore cannot be the victim of misery."